CW00345292

BRITISH
RAILWAY
JOURNEYS

BRITISH RAILWAY JOURNEYS

Caroline Dakers

**Fourth Estate · London
in association with the
English Tourist Board**

© Caroline Dakers 1986

First published 1986
Fourth Estate Limited
Classic House, 113 Westbourne Grove, London W2 4UP

Design and maps by Richard Kelly
Text illustrations by Robert Shadbolt
Cover illustration by Michael O'Brien

British Library Cataloguing in Publication Data

Dakers, Caroline
British railway journeys.
Compendium vol.
1: Great Britain—Description and travel—1971–
Guide-books
I. Title
914.1'04858   DA650

ISBN 0–947795–45–6
ISBN 0–947795–31–6 Pbk

The publishers have made every effort to ensure that the
information contained in this book is correct. They cannot,
however, accept responsibility for any errors or inaccuracies
contained herein.

All rights reserved. No part of this publication may be
reproduced, transmitted or stored in a retrieval system, in any
form or by any means, without permission in writing from
Fourth Estate Ltd.

Typeset in Gill by
M.C. Typeset Limited, Chatham, Kent.
Printed and bound by
Richard Clay (The Chaucer Press) Ltd,
Bungay, Suffolk.

Contents

GENERAL MAP

How to use this guide

Rather than adopt a continuous narrative which would only be of benefit to passengers travelling out of London, I have adopted a gazetteer approach. Landmarks appear in **bold type** for quick reference. All journeys have been compiled travelling from London – facing the engine – to the InterCity destination. A capital *R* signifies the landmark's position to the *right* of the track travelling away from London. A small *l* signifies the landmark's position to the *left* of the track travelling towards London. Thus: (*L:r*) **Wormwood Scrubs** (p. 37) signifies that Wormwood Scrubs is to the left of the track travelling away from London (Paddington) and to the right travelling towards London. If travelling with your back to the engine then the letters must be reversed: Wormwood Scrubs is to the right of the track leaving London and to the left approaching London.

Each major landmark is numbered and may be referred to on a map prefacing the journey or section of the journey.

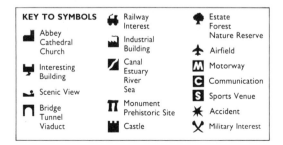

KEY TO SYMBOLS	Railway Interest	Estate Forest Nature Reserve
Abbey Cathedral Church	Industrial Building	Airfield
Interesting Building	Canal Estuary River Sea	Motorway
Scenic View		Communication
Bridge Tunnel Viaduct	Monument Prehistoric Site	Sports Venue
	Castle	Accident
		Military Interest

Acknowledgements

I owe particular thanks to Robert Thorne, who first suggested the idea and gave me much help and advice, and to the following members of the Victorian Society: Alan Crawford, John Minnie and Ian Wells. Other members of the Victorian Society gave me many useful snippets of information. I want to thank W.A. Porter, the Regional Public Affairs Manager, BRER York; and also J. Dennis, Hugh Douglas, John Dawson, David Lawrence and G.J. Smith of British Rail and the many helpful station masters and ticket collectors; A.H. Hogden of the Environmental Services Swindon; Colin Woodley of Thorn EMI; R.A. Shaw, local history librarian at Battersea District Library; F.W. Manders at the Central Library Newcastle; Peter de Figueiredo, Chief Planning Officer of Macclesfield Borough Council; John Storrs of the Berol Company; Bernard Joy; Ian McCaig; Sir Peter Allen; Ron Cohen of the London Brick Company; Mr Tungay of DRG Envelopes; press officers at British Steel, the CEGB, Wander Foods (Ovaltine), Ford at Halewood, ICI; the Milton Keynes Development Corporation; the GLC Press Office; librarians at Winchester and Basingstoke Public Libraries; the Information Department of BR Southern Region; and Maggie Hallett of East Surrey Health Authority. Friends and relatives who have helped me include Lawrence Burton, Neil Burton, Barry and Audrey Cross, John Cross, Hazel Dakers, John, Elizabeth, Mark and Paul Dakers, John Falding, Kerry Kennedy, Michael Mason, Sarah Morcom, Michael Oakley and Pam Worskett. For updating the journeys I would like to thank John Thompson and Elizabeth Rosser.

Introduction

When Francis Coghlan compiled one of the first railway guides, *The Iron Road Book and Railway Companion from London to Birmingham*, in 1838, he encountered difficulties in carrying out his research and deciding what to include in his travelogue:

> The author of the Iron Road Book having *walked* the entire line of Railroad now open, between London and Birmingham, at great personal fatigue ... considers it necessary to state that a great number of places described *cannot be seen from the line*; the barrenness of the immediate neighbourhood of the railway has, however, been supplied by giving descriptions of the most interesting towns and villages on either side, though not distinguishable from the carriages.

As the author of *British Railway Journeys* I did not *walk* the InterCity lines: it is an offence to walk on British Rail tracks, punishable with a fine of £100. The main problem for the writer of a railway guide in the 1980s, catering for travellers inside carriages hurtling across the landscape at anything up to 125mph, is the complete opposite of Francis Coghlan's dilemma. There is far too much to be seen and not enough time to see it in.

As the sleek High Speed Train crosses over the River Tyne, momentarily slowing down to enter Newcastle Station, only the briefest impression can be gained of the docks below, of ships on the Tyne, of the six bridges which now cross the river, the unusual ornate spire of St Nicholas Cathedral rising above the combination of classically proportioned Victorian streets and twentieth-century buildings. Only a volume length description could do justice to this panorama.

Speed was hardly a problem for Francis Coghlan.

In 1825, the year the Stockton and Darlington Railway was opened, the *Quarterly Review* expressed the hope 'that Parliament will in all Railways it may sanction limit the speed to eight miles an hour, which is as great as can be ventured on with safety.' By 1836 a canal proprietor, worried by the effect of the railway on his canal trade, wrote to his local newspaper about the speed of the trains:

> Twenty miles an hour! Why, you will not be able to keep an apprentice boy at work; every Saturday evening he must take a trip to spend the Sabbath with his sweetheart. Grave plodding citizens will be flying about like comets. All local attractions will be at an end. It will encourage flightiness of intellect. Veracious people will turn into the most immeasurable liars; all their conceptions will be exaggerated by their magnificent notions of distance. And then, there will be barrels of pork, and cargoes of flour, and chaldrons of coals, and even lead and whiskey, and such like sober things, that have always been used to sober travelling, whisking along like a set of sky rockets! It will upset the gravity of the nation!

To cope with the problem of 1980s speeds I have attempted to offer a guide which can be used both on the train and in the armchair – before or after the journey. It can also be used by the regular InterCity traveller because I have attempted to include as many items of interest as possible: it might take half a dozen journeys between Paddington and Bristol to become familiar with the main features on the line. Though modern train travel is usually fast, every passenger will have encountered some delay, some unscheduled stop or even a breakdown. With this in mind I hope I have included enough information to fill some of the time during a frustrating and inexplicable stop in the middle of rural England or an industrial landscape, or inside an impressive but black Victorian railway tunnel. The unscheduled stop can be rewarding. Edward Thomas wrote his popular anthologised poem *Adlestrop* after his express train pulled up at the tiny Cotswold station (which is now a jungle of brambles and fireweed):

Yes. I remember Adlestrop –
The name, because one afternoon
Of heat the express-train drew up there
Unwontedly. It was late June.

The steam hissed. Someone cleared his throat.
No one left and no one came
On the bare platform.

I have not included the times at which trains pass through stations as the variations are too great. Also it is impossible to calculate around the delays and unscheduled stops caused by points freezing in cold weather, rails buckling in hot weather, embankments slipping, tunnels flooding, industrial action or 'incidents on the line'. The most dramatic variations to a journey by train occur on Sundays when repairs to the tracks often lead to elaborate re-routing. I found it particularly frustrating to embark on a journey along the former Trent Valley Railway between Stafford and Rugby, equipped with maps and camera, only to find myself being taken on a special Sunday outing over the suburban system north of Birmingham at a speed so slow it would have been perfect for researching a railway guide – but not the guide I was trying to write. This problem of speed led me to plan my journeys on the slowest trains possible, much to the amazement of British Rail booking clerks, who would try to persuade me to take the fastest possible train to the destination stamped on my ticket.

If readers are surprised by the number of

churches mentioned on some routes, the answer is simple. From the window of a fast train it is often easier to distinguish the tower or spire of a church and then identify the town or village. There are long stretches on the line from Kings Cross to Edinburgh, for example, with little to pinpoint the train's position in the landscape except the occcasional church or power station. The traveller can of course take these opportunities to visit the bar, buffet or lavatory, luxuries for which obvious reasons I could not enjoy.

One of the problems I encountered with my bundle of Ordnance Survey Maps, notebook and camera was their effect on my fellow passengers. I have never had so many conversations with strangers. There was the charming American tourist who, on discovering the purpose of my research, plied me with questions all the way from Euston to Liverpool about what could be seen from the window. As I was myself trying to find out what could be seen his curiosity stretched my politeness to its limits. An enthusiastic team of trainspotters accompanied me from Westbury to Penzance explaining where all the disued railway lines went to, pointing out the abandoned bridges and engaging me in a heated discussion about British Rail policy − all this while I was desperately trying to look out of the window.

Inevitably there will be omissions. Though British Rail fares are considerably cheaper than train fares in the early decades of the railways, they have prevented me from repeating journeys as often as I would have wished. The view from the window is very different in summer and winter: foliage obscures houses in the height of summer and different crops are grown according to the season and rotation system. The view is also dependent on the type of carriage, older compartments offering the most restricted view of the landscape. And of course the view is changing all the time: forestry plantations cover once bare hillsides, warehouses spring up next to cornfields, older buildings are knocked down, motorways are built over and under the line.

The train now provides one of the safest forms of transport in the world. This was not always the case and the Victorians, though eager to try out the new invention, were aware of the dangers to be encountered. Third Class passengers were herded into cattle trucks with no seats and no roofs and the *Railway Monitor* advised:

> Make up your mind for unmitigated hail, rain, sleet, snow, thunder and lightening. Look for a double allowance of smoke, dust, dirt, and everything disagreeable. Be content to run a twofold risk of loss of life and limbs. Do not expect the luxury of a seat. As an individual and a traveller, you are one of the lower classes; a poor, beggarly, contemptible person, and your comfort and convenience are not to be attended to.

Punch 'reported' an accident in the 1840s: 'the body of the unfortunate man who received such hard treatment from the tender has not been found. An inquest is to be held upon his legs, which were happily so jammed against the wall, as to be preserved, entire; and they furnish sufficient "remains" for the purpose of the coroner. The unhappy legs have left a widow and a young family.' Dickens was quick to exploit the dramatic potential of the railways and dispatched the villain of Dombey and Son with the aid of an express train: 'He ... felt the earth tremble – knew in a moment that the rush was come – uttered a shriek – looked round – saw the red eyes, bleared and dim in the daylight, close upon him – was beatened down, caught up, and whirled away upon a jagged mill, that spun him round and round, and struck him limb from limb, and licked his stream of life up with its fiery heat, and cast his mutilated fragments in the air.' In 1865 Dickens was himself involved in a serious accident on the South Eastern Railway between Staplehurst and Headcorn. He was returning from a holiday in France with his mistress Ellen Ternan when their train was derailed because a ganger on the line, mistaking the day, authorised the removal of a rail: 'I worked for hours among the dying and dead. I was in the carriage that did not go over, but went off the line, and hung over the bridge in an inexplicable manner.'

Trains not only caused injury to life and limb: they also provided the perfect setting for robbery, indecent assault and murder. Corridor trains only began to be introduced at the turn of the century. Before then adulterous couples, eloping young lovers or murderer and victim might be placed alone together in a carriage, unable or unwilling to escape until the next station. Women were frequent victims, particularly on lines which passed through tunnels. Samuel Harry, a respectable innkeeper, was unable to restrain himself from assaulting Miss Mary Kennedy as their unlit carriage plunged into a mile long tunnel on the Furness Railway. He was fined £9.14s. In 1876 Colonel Valentine Baker was foolish enough to put his arm around a Miss Dickinson's waist without even the excuse of a dark tunnel. Miss Dickinson pulled the communication cord – only recently introduced by Act of Parliament (1868) after a brutal murder on a train – but it was broken. Undaunted she climbed on to the footboard outside the carriage and screamed for help. Colonel Baker gallantly held on to her to stop her falling off the train. The alarm was raised and the train stopped after a man working on the line saw Miss Dickinson hanging from the carriage. Sentencing the Colonel, the

Judge recalled the 'thrill of horror' which 'rang through the country at learning that a young and innocent girl, travelling by a public conveyance, had been compelled to risk her life in order to protect herself from gross outrage.'

The result of such assaults was that many Victorian ladies carried hat pins to place in their mouths as their train entered a tunnel. But tunnels are still risky places. In 1983 a girl was assaulted on a train as it passed through the Severn Tunnel. And the surviving corridor-less trains can still be the scene of robbery and murder.

It would be wrong to suppose tht catering facilities on trains and in railway stations have only recently become the subject of criticism. Early travellers had either to carry their own supplies or wait until their train stopped at a main station. The stop would only be for ten minutes, never sufficient time to queue up and then consume hot soup or coffee. Dickens was disgusted by the 'glutinous lumps of gristle and grease, called pork pie ... sponge cakes that turn to sand in the mouth ... brown patties, composed of unknown animals within.' However, when the luncheon basket was introduced on the Midland Railway in 1875 the better-off traveller could enjoy a reasonable standard of provender. For 3 shillings, the passenger received a basket at Derby Station containing 'Half-a-Chicken, with Ham or Tongue Salad, Bread, Cheese, Butter &c., and a Half-Bottle of Claret or Burgundy.' Once emptied the basket was either left in the carriage or handed over to a porter to be returned to the Midland Hotel in Derby. Particular railways stations were famous for their refreshment rooms. 'Bright silver urns, silver pots, silver tea pots, cups, saucers, cakes, sugar, milk' awaited the thristy traveller at Wolverton, while Basingstoke Station offered 'mock turtle soup or cold fowl', 'iced lemonade or aristocratic champagne (George Measom, 1861). The dreadful uniformity of the instant snack has since taken over. First Class commuters have praised British Rail's breakfast for many years but it does cost £7.50. Some travellers have gone to extraordinary lengths to get a decent cup of tea. The poet Siegfried Sassoon recorded in his *Memoris of a Foxhunting Man* his youthful embarrassment when accompanying his Aunt Evelyn on a train from Waterloo to Paddock Wood in Kent. On this rare occasion they were travelling first class:

> Now among the numerous light articles which she had brought into the carriage there was a certain plebeian-looking basket which contained every facility for making tea. Most essential among the facilities was a patent spirit-lamp for boiling the water; and this lamp was apt to misbehave itself and produce an unpleasing smell . . . I disassociated myself from her preparations, while she muddled about with the lamp, which for some time refused to function and then flared up with sudden explosive ardour . . . I was conscious that our fellow-travellers were exchanging scandalised glances, and their haughtiness intensified itself with every phase of the capricious conduct of the lamp . . . when her persistance had been rewarded by a cloud of steam and she held out a cup of moderately hot China tea, I felt so annoyed that I could almost have chucked it out of the window.

Uniformity has also cast its shadow over railway stations. The Victorian designers delighted in using every conceivable style for their railway architecture: fanciful Gothic, gracious Italianate and stately classical. Ironwork, awnings and bargeboards on the smallest wayside stations would be individually designed and imaginatively decorated. The *Building News* of 1875 went so far as to claim that 'railway termini and hotels are to the nineteenth century what monasteries and cathedrals were to the thirteenth century. They are truly the representative buildings we possess ... our metropolitan termini have been leaders of the art spirit of our time'. Not everyone agreed. John Ruskin, for example, hated the 'strange and evil' tendency to decorate stations:

> It is the very temple of discomfort, and the only charity that the builder can extend to us is to show us, plainly as may be, how soonest to escape from it ... Better bury gold in embankments, than put it in ornaments on the stations. Will a single traveller be willing to pay an increased fare on the South Western, because the columns of the terminus are covered with patterns from Nineveh? ... or on the North Western, because there are old English looking spandrels to the roof of the station at Crewe?

Now, in an age of dull cheap uniformity, the ebullient railway architecture of the Victorians is a surviving but unfortunately diminishing pleasure. And the individual details of the stations are lost, behind British Rail plastic livery and the inevitable advertisement hoardings. Late 20th century needs continue to threaten 19th century achievement. The demolition of the Doric Triumphal Arch at Euston Station in 1961 could have been avoided. Plans to save Broad Street Station have been defeated. Liverpool Street and Victoria Stations are undergoing dramatic modernisation which involves much demolition work. The *Architects Journal* described the plan for Liverpool Street as 'one of the most boring, soul-less and repetitive developments in London'. The Gothic-style listed office block will be demolished and British Rail promises that the new concourse roof 'will undulate to echo the form of the Western Train shed'. Marylebone

Station is the latest to be threatened with closure.

The novelist E.M. Forster was openly emotional about London's termini. Margaret Schlegel, the heroine of *Howards End*, confessed her attachment:

> Like many others who have lived long in a great capital, she had strong feelings about the various railway termini. They are our gates to the glorious and the unknown. Through them we pass out into adventure and sunshine, to them, alas! we return. In Paddington all Cornwall is latent and the remote west; down the inclines of Liverpool Street lie fenlands and the illimitable Broads; Scotland is through the pylons of Euston; Wessex behind the poised chaos of Waterloo ... he is a chilly Londoner who does not endow his stations with some personality, and extend to them, however slyly, the emotions of fear and love.

Forster was writing in 1910. Today we have coolly efficient and sterile Euston. Individuality and sometimes welcome frivolity are condemned in an age of speed and efficiency.

Up and down the country small rural stations stand beside the railways lines, abandoned, boarded up and a prey to vandals. If only some of these small stations could be reopened to provide some public transport in a countryside increasingly deprived of bus services, where elderly people are stranded or forced to become reckless drivers. If only government would support the railway system. No national railway network in the world makes money, and just as we are quick to defend our costly National Health Service, so should we rise to the defence of our railways, which also provide a vital public service. John Bright's observation in the 19th century is still true today: 'railways have rendered more service, and have received less gratitude than any other institution in the land.'

Caroline Dakers – 1986

PADDINGTON TO THE WEST

(Bristol · Cardiff · Penzance)

Contents

PADDINGTON TO THE WEST

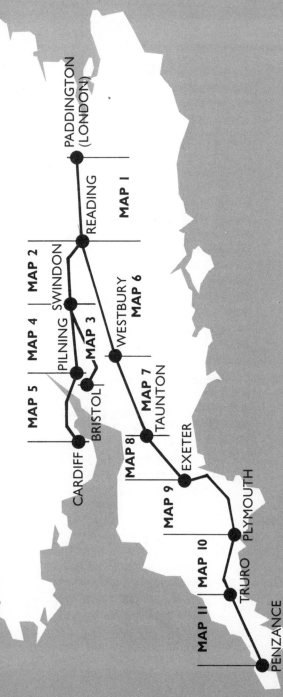

PADDINGTON (LONDON)

READING

MAP 1

SWINDON

MAP 2

PILNING

MAP 4

MAP 3

BRISTOL

MAP 5

CARDIFF

WESTBURY

MAP 6

MAP 7

TAUNTON

MAP 8

EXETER

MAP 9

PLYMOUTH

MAP 10

TRURO

MAP 11

PENZANCE

Introduction

When Edward Churton wrote *The Railroad Book of England* (1851) for Victorian train-travellers, he was overwhelmed by the splendour of Brunel's achievement in building the Great Western Railway. He marvelled at 'the wonders of nature and art' revealed along the route to the West Country and 'above all, those stupendous works which the hand of science, undaunted by the aspect of those solid rocks, which even the Egyptians and Romans would have regarded as impenetrable barriers, has achieved by the union of genius and labour, by penetrating into the very bowels of the earth, and overcoming the stubborn obstructions opposed to man's project by nature's original structure'. As the sleek High Speed Trains travel effortlessly towards the west, reaching Bristol in a mere 92 minutes and Penzance in only five hours, it is still possible to appreciate the engineering feats of Brunel and his workforce: bridges, viaducts, tunnels, cuttings and embankments all constructed without the benefit of modern equipment.

The first proposal for a railway from London to Bristol was made in 1824 by a group of Bristol merchants, but came to nothing. Eight years later the idea was resurrected and a committee formed for its implementation. In 1833 the twenty-seven-year-old Isambard Kingdom Brunel, who had recently won the contract for the Clifton Suspension Bridge, was appointed engineer. Royal Assent was given to the proposed route on 31 August 1835, work began immediately, and six years later, on 30 June 1841, the first train travelled from London to Bristol in four hours. The entire line, including the track, engines, rolling stock and the building of locomotive works at Swindon and coke ovens at Bristol, cost just over £6 million.

One of the unusual features of Brunel's Great Western Railway (GWR) was his adoption of the broad-gauge track of 7' $0\frac{1}{4}$". The narrow gauge of 4' $8\frac{1}{2}$' was the recognised gauge for British railways by the time Brunel made his survey, but he argued that a broader gauge would enable trains to travel faster: 'looking to the speeds which I contemplated would be adopted on railways and the masses to be moved, it seemed to me that the whole machine was too small for the work to be done, and that it required that the parts should be on a scale more commensurate with the mass and the velocity to be attained.' The broad gauge was only finally abandoned in 1892, the last broad-gauge express train leaving Paddington on 20 May.

Neither gauge offered passengers particularly comfortable travelling conditions in the early years of the railways. George Henry Gibbs, a Director of the GWR, travelled on the narrow-gauge Birmingham Railway to assess the competition: 'the carriages and engines are much lighter than ours. The engines make less noise and the general noise is less, but the wheels on the rails make more. The bumps and jolts at the joints are very frequent indeed, and are in some places very uncomfortable, and the joints show plainly the effect of the heavy blows they receive. The serpentine or lateral motion, of which we have none on our railway, is very striking; but, on the other hand, they have no pitching or see-saw motion whatever, produced with us by the yielding of the timber between the piles.'

Undeterred by bumps and jolts, Queen Victoria made her first journey by train on the GWR, travelling from Slough to Paddington on 13 June 1842. The platform at Paddington was covered with a crimson carpet and 'precisely at 25 minutes past twelve o'clock the Royal Special train entered the Paddington terminus having performed the distance in 25 minutes and on Her Majesty's alighting she was received by the most deafening demonstration of loyalty and affection we have ever experienced'. A special station was later designed for the Queen at Windsor and a branch line connected Windsor to the main line at Slough. When the Prince of Wales was married in St George's Chapel, Windsor, many of his aristocratic guests travelled to Windsor by train. The return journey was far from sedate, however: 'a mob had disrupted everything, the station was closed, and the aristocracy were forbidden the platform. They had to climb through windows to get into the station and when the train came in there was a mad rush for compartments. Lady Westminster found herself, loaded with diamonds, among a rough crowd, and "the great ones of the land were too thankful to find themselves safe in a 3rd class" carriage to worry about the proprieties of being there.'

After reaching Bristol, Brunel was employed by the Bristol and Exeter Railway to continue the line to Exeter. On the opening day, 1 May 1844, Daniel Gooch drove 'Orion', hauling the

Directors' Special from London to Exeter. He recalled: 'We had a special train with a large party from London to go down to the opening. A great dinner was given in the Goods Shed at Exeter Station. I worked the train with the Actaeon engine, one of our 7' class, with six carriages... it was a very hard day's work for me... next day my back ached so that I could hardly walk.'

The South Devon Railway constructed the next section of the line, from Exeter to Plymouth, reaching Plymouth on 2 April 1849. As engineer, Brunel chose to experiment with an alternative form of propulsion for this part of the line: the atmospheric system. The train was propelled by compressed air. Stationary engines pumped out air from a continuous pipe laid between the rails. A piston in the leading vehicle of the train entered this pipe through a specially designed valve and was held in place by the brakes. When the brakes were released the train was drawn swiftly and smoothly up an incline – the return journey being made by gravity. Brunel designed pumping stations along the line and on 10 January 1848 atmospheric trains were reaching Newton Abbot. However, the remarkable system created too many problems and the pipes laid between Newton Abbot and Totnes were never used. Now, little remains of the system; only part of the pumping stations at Starcross and Totnes. L. T. C. Rolt praised the system, which he saw as more than a 'fantastic mechanical joke'. 'If our experience of land travel had been limited to the stage coach or the first steam locomotive we, too, might have hailed the atmospheric railway as the transport system of the future. To be borne along by the powers of the air so smoothly, swiftly and silently, to accelerate so rapidly and with such a complete absence of any apparent effort must have been a breathtaking experience' *(Isambard Kingdom Brunel)*.

Plymouth to Truro, which included Brunel's magnificent Royal Albert Bridge over the Tamar between Plymouth and Saltash, was completed by the Cornwall Railway on 4 May 1859 and the West Cornwall Railway reached Penzance on 11 March 1852. All these railways – the Bristol and Exeter, South Devon, Cornwall and West Cornwall – were eventually absorbed by the GWR.

The direct route between Paddington and Penzance was not completed until 1906 and involved a series of cut-offs and the use of other lines. Competition with the London and South West Railway (LSWR) spurred the GWR to create the direct route. The LSWR reached Exeter from Waterloo in 1860, a distance of 172 miles. The GWR route from Paddington to Exeter via Bristol was 194 miles. The GWR's Berkshire and Hampshire line was opened between Reading and Hungerford in 1847 and extended to Devizes in 1862. A cut-off opened Patney to Westbury in 1900 and another, in 1906, opened Castle Cary on the Weymouth line to Langport and Taunton. The GWR thus cut their route between Paddington and Exeter to 174 miles, only 2 miles more than their LSWR rivals.

A particular feature of Brunel's line through Devon and Cornwall is the series of magnificent viaducts he designed to cross the numerous steep-sided river valleys. The viaducts were built of yellow pine from Memel in the Baltic. The pine was 'kyanised' — a process which impregnated the wood with a solution of corrosive sublimate as a preservative against decay. The average life of the viaducts was 30 years but some lasted 60 years. They were examined 4 times a year by highly skilled bridge gangs and parts could easily be renewed without disrupting train services. By 1908, when the line was doubled, good timber was too expensive and the viaducts were rebuilt in steel and masonry. St Pinnock Viaduct was altered by heightening the original stone piers and laying a steel girder frame across them. The original stone piers of the Cornwood and Ivybridge Viaducts can be seen alongside the new masonry bridges. The longest viaduct was at Truro — 443 yards; the highest at St Pinnock — 151'; the last to be replaced at Penrhyn — in 1934.

While Brunel was taking the railway ever further into the south-west of England, South Wales was experiencing the arrival of the railway. The South Wales Railway between Gloucester and Swansea was authorised in August 1845 and the section between Chepstow and Swansea opened in June 1850. The GWR extended their empire by acquiring the line in 1863.

The railway had a dramatic effect on the economy and social life of South Wales, helping to create a boom with the expansion of the iron and steel industries. Special trains were designed by Churchward and Collett to carry the heavy loads of coal through the valleys, and a new coal dock was constructed at Barry on the Bristol Channel with a railway line directly to Cardiff. With the opening of the Severn Tunnel in 1886, the possibilities for a fast line between Paddington and South Wales were raised and in 1900 the direct line via Wootton Bassett and Patchway was opened. High Speed Trains now travel from Paddington to Cardiff, with a stop in Newport, in 108 minutes, at an average speed of over 80 mph.

The GWR concentrated on excursion and holiday trains to the west as soon as their line to Penzance was open. A typical example was the Redruth and Camborne Temperance Societies' outing to Hayle in 1852. Three locomotives pulled 76 mineral trucks full of singing teetotallers:

> Happy Camborne, happy Camborne,
> Where the railway is so near;
> And the engine shows how water
> Can accomplish more than beer.

A newspaper reported that when the locomotive ran out of steam on the return journey and the train stopped beside an orchard, 'it may have been their extreme anxiety to take measures against such an intoxicating beverage as cider, but at all events that army of teetotallers swarmed down from the trucks and up the apple trees until the orchard resembled the famous cupboards of Mother Hubbard'.

The first 'Cornish Riviera' express left Paddington on 1 July 1904 and marked the beginning of an elaborate campaign to attract holiday-makers to the West Country. The

GWR publicity department produced *Holiday Haunts* and a series of books: *Castles*, by Sir Charles Oman, *Abbeys*, by M.R. James, and *The Cornish Riviera*, by S. P. B. Mais. Bands would welcome the holiday trains at Dawlish and Teignmouth, 'flags floated from every tower and eminence', and 'joy and hilarity' reigned throughout the West Country...

PADDINGTON
TO
BRISTOL

MAP I

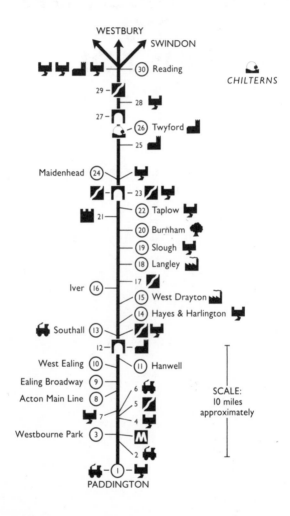

WESTBURY

SWINDON

(30) Reading

CHILTERNS

29 –

28

27 –

(26) Twyford

25

Maidenhead (24)

– 23

(22) Taplow

21

(20) Burnham

(19) Slough

(18) Langley

17

Iver (16)

(15) West Drayton

(14) Hayes & Harlington

Southall (13)

12 –

West Ealing (10)

(11) Hanwell

Ealing Broadway (9)

6

Acton Main Line (8)

5

7

4

Westbourne Park (3)

W

2

(1)

PADDINGTON

SCALE:
10 miles
approximately

1 PADDINGTON STATION The GWR was completed from London to Bristol in June 1841, but the permanent terminus at Paddington was not opened until 1854. Then, Paddington was little more than a village, for Marble Arch was on the western edge of London. Brunel, chief engineer of the GWR, designed the station with the assistance of Matthew Digby Wyatt and Owen Jones. Brunel was strongly influenced by the Crystal Palace, designed by Joseph Paxton for the Great Exhibition of 1851. His station consisted of ten tracks and four platforms filling three parallel train sheds each spanned by a roof of Paxton glass and iron reaching up to 55 feet above the platforms. The fourth shed, which covers platforms 9–11, was added in the twentieth century and has a roof of steel and glass with a span of 109′.

To reach the platforms, passengers cross an area called 'the Lawn', which was built over the location of the old turntables used in Brunel's time for shunting locomotives. The Lawn, now a jumble of newspaper and magazine stalls, vending machines, telephone kiosks and billboards, is dominated by the arrivals and departures boards which, though essential, obscure the otherwise magnificent view along the length of the train sheds. The diminutive statue of Brunel by John Doubleday (unveiled on 26 May 1982) goes largely unnoticed, as waiting passengers gather around it only to look up at the departures information.

Wyatt was Secretary of the Executive Committee of the Great Exhibition and his decorations of Paddington Station were influenced by the Moorish pavilion at the exhibition. There are vaguely Moorish decorations on the cast-iron columns supporting the roof and also around the oriel windows on the first floor of the offices along Platform 1. From these ornate windows, the station-master enjoyed a clear view of the whole station. The Queen's Apartment was immediately below and was frequently used by Queen Victoria. A war memorial by T. S. Tait, unveiled by Winston Churchill, stands between the doors which originally led to the royal apartment.

Paddington Station Hotel Travellers who arrive at Paddington by Underground will not see the ponderous Station Hotel in Praed Street, built at the same time as the terminus itself. The architect, Philip Hardwick (the younger), designed a hotel with proportions to match the monumental impact of the railway age. In its day, it was the largest hotel in London, with 150 rooms, the largest apartment comprising 'Drawing Room and Two Bed Rooms (with Water Closet enclosed) en suite, per day, 22s 6d.' The massive mansard roof, borrowed from the reign of Louis XIV, was considered a 'startling novelty' at the time. John Thomas sculpted four giant caryatids to support the balcony above the entrance. Above the pediment an allegorical sculpture, also by Thomas, depicted 'Peace, Plenty, Industry and Science', a tribute to the optimism of the age. Sadly, the 1930s were less optimistic; in the cleaning and modernisation of the hotel, much of the flamboyant decoration, including the caryatids, was removed.

2 ROYAL OAK (Metropolitan line, 1866, island *R:1* platform, pale green buildings). The Metropolitan line was not only London's first underground railway but the first underground railway in the world. When opened in 1863, it extended from Bishop's Bridge Road (Paddington) to Farringdon; by 1889 it had reached Chesham in Buckinghamshire: 'Metroland/Beckoned us out to lanes in beechy Bucks', John Betjeman wrote.

Westbourne Green once covered the site of the station; the great tragic actress Sarah Siddons (1755–1831) lived at Westbourne Farm in 1805.

3 WESTBOURNE PARK (Metropolitan line, 1866; BR, 1871; yellow- and red-brick Victorian ticket office above tracks). Railway and motorway (the **M40**) begin their journey together. *R:1* The 30 minutes have three distinct phases. First, the vast reaches of West London suburbs that grew in the late nineteenth century: Greenford, Ealing and Acton. Then a great scrubby stretch of waste land, scrapyards and light industry, extending as far as Slough. Industries such as mechanical engineering, foodstuffs, clothing and light electrical goods sprawled over the Middlesex fields in the first half of this century and long uniform rows of houses surrounded and engulfed the county's villages. Then, at the edge of the industrial belt, over the Thames in Berkshire, is the beginning of a leisure-ground for retired and wealthier Londoners: dormitory villages, pleasure-cruising, rural retreats.

4 KENSAL HOUSE (block of flats, dull pale *R:l* green wash, next to railway line, immediately west Ladbroke Grove Bridge). The two tall slab-shaped blocks of flats of reinforced concrete with a low steel-framed block (for a nursery school) in between may appear to be little different from many housing developments of recent years. However, when Kensal House was built in 1936 it was of radical design. The architects were Maxwell Fry, R. Atkinson, C. H. James and Grey Wornum. Fry had been a partner of Walter Gropius — the designer of the Bauhaus in Dessau — from 1934 to 1936, and Kensal House was influenced by pre-war German designs for housing schemes for working people. It was built on the site of an abandoned gasometer between the railway and the Grand Union Canal.

Kensal House

5 GRAND UNION CANAL The Paddington *R:l* branch of the Grand Union Canal flows close to the railway line from Ladbroke Grove, where it passes behind Kensal House and the gasometers, into Old Oak Common Sidings. The canal is obscured from the railway by a high, very dirty brick wall but it is occasionally possible to see the tops of narrow boats just above the wall. The canal was authorised by Parliament in 1795 and originally terminated at Paddington Basin. It was later extended as the Regent's Canal to enter the River Thames at Limehouse. Praed Street — in which Hardwick's Paddington Station Hotel is situated — was named after William Praed, the first chairman of the Grand Junction (later Union) Canal Company.

6 OLD OAK COMMON The Grand Union *R:I* Canal disappears into the extensive network of sidings and sheds which now covers Old Oak Common. The sidings were opened in March 1906 after the sheds were moved from their earlier site at Westbourne Park. In the days of steam, 'Old Oak' had the largest coal stage and water tower on the Western Region. The depot now houses High Speed Train stock and a training school for engine drivers.

7 WORMWOOD SCRUBS Wormwood Scrubs *L:r* is clearly visible across the playing fields. Convicts built the prison, completing the boundary wall in 1883. The prison was designed by Sir Edmund Du Cane, who supervised the work for a fee of a guinea a day. He had already organised convict labour in Western Australia and his British workforce built cells for 1381 convicts, a cookhouse, bakery, laundry, workshops, chapel and baths. Du Cane was influenced by the great prison reformer, John Howard, and created a well-planned complex of parallel cell blocks joined by covered ways, each cell supplied with heating and ventilation. Du Cane is also known for encouraging the use of finger-prints in the detection of crime.

8 **ACTON MAIN LINE** (BR, 1868)

9 **EALING BROADWAY** (BR, Central and District lines) The original nineteenth-century buildings have been replaced by an unprepossessing modern office block which rears up above the line.

10 **WEST EALING** (BR, 1899) In the 50 years after the opening of the station, the borough of Ealing's population grew five times.

11 **HANWELL** (BR, 1839; rebuilt, 1877) Hanwell is an example of the many mass-designed red-brick stations erected in the 1870s on the GWR. The woodwork is at present painted a pleasant white and creamy yellow; the roof is hipped with shallow eaves; the awnings are distinctive with deep cut-outs in the shape of pointed arches.

Hanwell Parish Church

12 **WHARNCLIFFE VIADUCT** (1838; 8 spans
of 70'; 65' above ground level; 900 ' long). Hanwell Station is at the Paddington end of the
Wharncliffe viaduct, built by Brunel to carry the
GWR high over the surrounding countryside,
and named after Lord Wharncliffe, Chairman of
the Parliamentary Committee when the GWR
Company Bill was being considered by the
House of Lords. Suburban London now
stretches to the north and south and it is
difficult to appreciate the height and length of
the viaduct from the train. Queen Victoria was
so impressed by the view, however, that she
used to ask the train driver to slow down. She
would have seen the spire of **Hanwell Parish** *R:1*
Church (George Gilbert Scott, 1841) which
still emerges from the horse chestnut trees.
The viaduct cost £55,000 – 12 shillings (60p)
per cubic yard. It is of yellow London stock
brick with stone for the capitals of the piers.
When seen from the Uxbridge Road immediately to the south, its Egyptian style is apparent
– Brunel also used the Egyptian style on the
Clifton Suspension Bridge at Bristol.

13 **SOUTHALL** (BR, 1 May 1839; yellow- and
red-brick station buildings 1876; booking office
above line with two French chateau-style
towers). The arrival of the GWR radically
altered the 'hitherto retired neighbourhood of
Southall', according to its parson, the Rev.
Armstrong: 'Moss-grown cottages retired
before new ones with bright red tiles, picturesque hedgerows were succeeded by prim
iron railings, and the village inn, once a pretty
cottage with a swinging sign, is transmogrified

to the "Railway Tavern" with an intimation gaudily set forth that "London porter" and other luxuries hitherto unknown to the aborigines were to be procured within.'

The red-brick **goods shed** opposite the station *L:r* contains steam locomotives and carriages being restored by the GWR Preservation Society; it is sometimes possible to see steam trains through the arcaded side of the shed.

The **Victorian water tower** to the west of the *R:l* station with turrets and a battlemented parapet has recently been restored. The **Grand Union Canal** flows through the waste ground to the west of the tower and then under the railway line.

Victorian Water Tower

14 **HAYES AND HARLINGTON** (BR) The station is dominated by the buildings belonging to **Thorn EMI Electronics**. The Electrical and *R:l*

Musical Industries Ltd (EMI) was formed in 1931 with the merger of the Gramophone Company and Columbia, creating what is still the biggest and longest established international recording organisation in the world. The first factory at Hayes was built for the Gramophone Company and the foundation stone was laid by Dame Nellie Melba in 1907. When the present factory was built by EMI, an Egyptian statue was discovered as the foundations were being excavated. A quarter of a million records can be produced here every day.

15 **WEST DRAYTON** (BR, 1838; Italianate yellow- and red-brick station buildings). West Drayton (for Uxbridge) was the first station to be opened out of London. In November 1837, two broad-gauge locomotives, 'Vulcan' and 'Premier', were delivered by sea and canal barge from Liverpool to West Drayton, where they were slung ashore with the aid of an adjacent elm tree. The canal, which was so useful in the building of the GWR, was eventually to lose its trade to the cheaper railway. Coal, for example, once transported by barge, quickly became one of the most lucrative products carried by the railways: the presence of the sprawling **Coal Board Depot** beside West *R:l* Drayton Station shows the continuing role of the railways in the coal industry.

16 **IVER** (BR, 1924)

17 **GRAND UNION CANAL** The canal flows to *R:l* the north of the line between Iver and Langley but the landscape through which it passes is

hardly picturesque. Its banks are distinguished by pale blue and white cranes, an untidy jumble of caravans and a car dump. William Jessop was the principal engineer of the canal; James Barnes was the resident engineer. The network of artificial waterways constructed across Britain in the second half of the eighteenth century dramatically changed the lives of those living nearby. Imported goods were no longer confined to the rich or the inhabitants of British ports, but were transported cheaply all over the country. Sir Frederick Eden, writing in 1797, commented on even poor families in Middlesex cottages drinking tea brought to London by the East India Company: 'tea is not only the usual beverage in the morning and evening, but is generally drunk in large quantities at dinner'. The tea was sweetened with sugar which came from the British West Indies: both products came into Middlesex by canal.

18 **LANGLEY** (BR, 1845; French chateau-style *R:l* station building with flat-topped pavilion roof adorned with intricate trellis-work by Lancaster Owen, 1878). The **oil terminal** adds to *R:l* the industrial waste land through which the train passes. A railway guide of 1924 was able to declare 'such a village as Langley is definitely rural, and grazing cattle gives the landscape a touch of active life'.

19 **SLOUGH** (BR; red-brick buildings by J. E. Danks, 1886; curved mansard roofs covered in fish-scale tiles and with bulls-eye windows). Sir John Betjeman was less than complimentary about Slough when he wrote in 1937:

Come, friendly bombs, and fall on Slough
It isn't fit for humans now,
There isn't grass to graze a cow
Swarm over, Death!

The station is particularly attractive, however, and to the north of the line, immediately west of the station, is the equally imaginative **Hor-** *R:I* **licks Factory**, built in 1908, of red brick, with a castellated tower at one end.

The overall impression of Slough is of one vast industrial estate. The first trading estate was created in 1920 using buildings on a 600-acre site which had been erected by the War Office during the First World War. This had become a 'white elephant' at the end of the war – a vast car dump for the repair and reconditioning of thousands of vehicles incapacitated during active service. Over 100 years before, Slough had been a place of scientific pilgrimage, the home of the great astronomer Sir William Herschel, a pioneer in nearly every branch of modern physical astronomy, who discovered Uranus in 1781. He lived in Slough from 1786 until his death in 1822 and was buried in St Laurence's Church.

20 **BURNHAM** (BR, 1899; red-brick platform buildings, wide awnings). **Burnham Beeches** is *R:I* about two miles to the north. Beech trees grow most luxuriously in chalk districts, forming extensive forests of great beauty. The citizens of London have owned Burnham Beeches since 1879 and the forest is a popular weekend retreat. John Evelyn, the seventeenth-century

diarist, described the use of beech leaves as mattresses 'to lay under our quilts instead of straw; because, besides their tenderness and loose lying together, they continue sweet for seven or eight years, long before which time straw becomes musty and hard'.

21 **WINDSOR CASTLE** On a clear day it is poss- *L:r* ible to see Windsor Castle over the tops of the houses and trees at intervals between Burnham Station and the Sounding Arch Bridge over the Thames. The oldest part of the castle is the Round Tower, built by William of Wykeham for Edward III. The castle was extensively altered in the early nineteenth century by Sir Jeffry Wyatville, who made it fashionably romantic with mock defensive loop-holes and battlements, refacing the old walls with white stone and black cement, and turning the once military stronghold into a castle from toytown.

22 **TAPLOW** (BR, 1872; red- and yellow-brick buildings by J. E. Danks, 1883–4; wooden footbridge with GWR initials picked out on side).

The Tudor-Gothic red-brick mansion **Taplow** *R:l* **Court** can be seen on the hillside to the north of the station. The house was built for Charles Pascoe Grenfell (in 1855, architect William Burn), who made a fortune from his Cornish copper mines. His grandson Julian Grenfell wrote the war poem 'Into Battle' before being killed in France in 1915.

23 Crossing the **RIVER THAMES** on Brunel's **Sounding Arch Bridge** (1838, widened 1891).

This is one of Brunel's finest bridges. It cost £37,000 and consists of two of the largest, flattest arches ever built in brick, each with a span of 128′ and a rise of only 24′ 3″. In 'Rain, Steam and Speed' J. M. W. Turner painted one of Daniel Gooch's 'Firefly' steam engines crossing the bridge in stormy weather.

The **road bridge** (1777; 5 stone arches, stone *R:l* balustrade), designed by Sir Robert Taylor, cost nearly £19,000. Immediately below, on the west bank, is the Edwardian hotel **Skindles**, the setting for the first murder in Robert Hamer's film *Kind Hearts and Coronets*.

24 **MAIDENHEAD** (BR, 1838; red- and yellow-brick platform buildings). The fanciful **clock** *R:l* **tower** was built in 1897 by E. J. Shrewsbury.

Maidenhead grew up around the GWR and became a popular boating centre in the Edwardian period. Before the arrival of the railway, travellers to the west had to negotiate Maidenhead Thicket, just to the south-west of the town and a well-known haunt of highwaymen. Maidenhead was the birthplace of Hugh Lofting, the creator of Dr Dolittle.

25 **RUSCOMBE** The cluster of cottages and farm *R:l* buildings just above the line and around the red-brick **church** of Ruscombe marks the beginning of real countryside for travellers to the West Country. The nave and tower of the church are seventeenth-century (1638–9). William Penn, the Quaker founder of Pennsylvania, died at Ruscombe in 1718.

26 TWYFORD (BR, red- and black-brick platform buildings, 1892–3). The village began to expand after the arrival of the GWR and a new **parish** *R:I* **church** was built in 1846.

Twyford Gravel Pits are a feature of the land- *R&L* scape to the west of Twyford. The London Basin covers the whole of the Kennet–Thames Valley, part of Thanet, most of Essex and the eastern parts of Suffolk and Norfolk, and consists mainly of clays, sands and gravels. To the north and south of the Basin (between Reading and London) are chalk hills, the Chilterns and the North Downs. Windsor Castle was built on an outcrop of chalk. The London Basin provided the materials for some of the earliest brick-making in England although, until the eighteenth century, bricks were used only on buildings of importance. A kiln constructed at Slough in the mid-fifteenth century provided $2\frac{1}{2}$ million bricks for Eton College.

27 SONNING CUTTING The 'Firefly' was the first train to steam through Sonning Cutting on 17 March 1840, carrying the Directors of the GWR and their friends. The cutting through Sonning Hill is nearly two miles long and 60′ deep, and is particularly wide because it was designed to accommodate Brunel's broad-gauge track (see p. 24). The cutting may not look particularly remarkable from the window of a High Speed Train, but it was an enormous project to undertake without the benefit of modern machinery. At one point Brunel had 1220 navvies and 196 horses working in the cutting, struggling in a morass of mud caused by severe gales and rainstorms.

The train emerges from the western end of the cutting and enters the valley of the River Thames. The Thames flows roughly parallel to the line all the way to Cholsey and Moulsford: Brunel deliberately chose to follow the river through the Goring Gap.

28 CAVERSHAM PARK On the far side of the *R:l* Thames is the large cream-coloured mansion which is Caversham Park. The 1st Earl of Cadogan built the original house early in the eighteenth century and Capability Brown land- scaped the gardens. Now, however, the gar- dens are engulfed by housing estates. The present house is a nineteenth-century struc- ture, built in the Palladian style after the first house was burnt down and used as a BBC monitoring station.

29 RIVER KENNET Immediately east of Reading the line crosses over the River Kennet. This part of the Kennet forms the first link in the route by water from the Port of London on the Thames to the Port of Bristol on the Avon.

30 READING The town of Reading sprawls to the south of the railway line. It expanded dramati- cally in the early nineteenth century with the arrival of the canal and, more especially, the GWR. Trains left for London once an hour and took 75 minutes (the fastest time now is 29 minutes). In the last few years Reading has undergone further expansion because of its favourable position on the 'M4 corridor'.

Reading Gaol (George Gilbert Scott and W. B. *L:r*
Moffat, 1844) is one of the first buildings of
interest to be seen to the east of the station. It
is of red brick, with a massive ventilating tower
rising from the centre. One of its most famous
prisoners was Oscar Wilde, who wrote 'The
Ballad of Reading Gaol' after serving two years'
hard labour:

> Each narrow cell in which we dwell
> It is a foul and dark latrine,
> And the fetid breath of living Death
> Chokes up each grated screen,
> And all, but Lust, is turned to dust
> In Humanity's machine.

Reading Gaol

Reading Abbey is almost totally obscured by *L:r*
offices and trees. Founded in 1121 by Henry I,
it was one of the six great abbeys of England.
Hugh of Faringdon, the last Abbot of Reading,
was executed by Thomas Cromwell outside the
Abbey Gate. The platform was 'decked with
the gallows for partially hanging, the knife for

disgustingly mutilating the still living body, and the cauldron of boiling pitch into which to fling the limbs when the quartering was accomplished' (*Victoria County History*). Little now remains of the Abbey but some of the massive flint walls. The gateway, of flint and stone, was mostly rebuilt by George Gilbert Scott in 1861.

Reading Station The station was one of the last survivors of Brunel's one-sided stations, a design he created for towns lying mostly on one side of the railway line. The Up and Down platforms were side by side, a short distance apart on the south side of the main line. All that now remains of the original station is the mid-nineteenth-century building on the southern-most platform (**platforms 1–4**; of sienna and *L:r* light-ochre brick). Above the awning rises a pantiled clock turret painted white with a ball and spiked finial on top, which is an imitation of the type used in semaphore signalling.

Reading is an important railway junction. Lines leave for Ascot and Staines; Guildford; Basingstoke; Westbury, Taunton and Penzance; Didcot, Swindon and Bristol. One of the first railway accidents on the GWR occurred at Reading while the station was being built. Henry West, carpenter, was blown from the roof by a 'whirlwind'. A piece of rail marked his grave.

Immediately west of the station, and below the line on the south side, a jumble of sheds and stalls comprises **Reading Abattoir**. This is just *L:r* before the line divides; travellers to the West

MAP 2

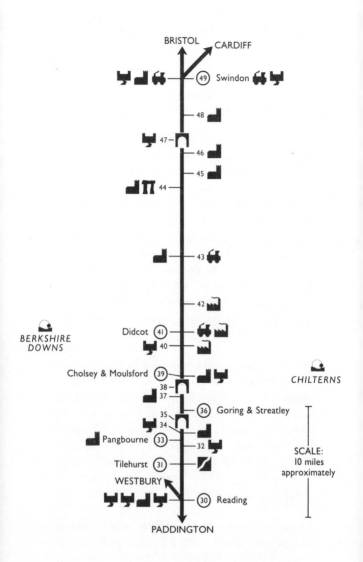

Country continue west towards Swindon or turn south-west towards Westbury (see p. 98).

The line from Reading to Swindon is flat and historically very fast – never faster than today. One of the pleasures of the journey is the sense of speeding gracefully through an open land-scape.

31 **TILEHURST** (BR, 1882) The railway line fol-lows the River Thames as far as Cholsey and Moulsford and it is possible to see some of the villas and boathouses built along the river banks. A group of seven Edwardian villas near Pangbourne, popular for illicit country week-ends, is known as the 'Seven Deadly Sins'.

32 **MAPLEDURHAM HOUSE** can be seen *R:l* across the valley just as the river meanders away from the line. The house (open to the public) was built between 1581 and 1612 of softly-patterned red brick by Sir Michael Blount, the Lieutenant of the Tower of Lon-don. It has remained the property of the Blount family ever since. Teresa and Martha Blount, residents of the house in the eighteenth cen-tury, were particular favourites of the poet Alexander Pope, who was a frequent visitor to the house, and gave the family advice on their gardens. When Pope died he left most of his possessions to Martha; some of his books are still at Mapledurham. Another literary connec-tion: Galsworthy borrowed the name of the house for a villa by the Thames in which part of the Forsyte Saga was set.

33 **PANGBOURNE** (BR; red brick by J. W. Armstrong, 1890s). Pangbourne is a popular rural retreat, particularly for Londoners tired of city life and fond of 'messing about in boats'. Kenneth Grahame, the author of *The Wind in the Willows*, spent the last eight years of his life at Church Cottage, Pangbourne, close to the river which had inspired his masterpiece and was the home of Ratty, Mole and Mr Toad. **Pangbourne Church** has an eighteenth-cen- *L:r* tury brick tower.

34 **BASILDON PARK** The east front of Basildon *L:r* Park, with its wide bay and central Venetian window, overlooks the Thames valley and can just be seen from the south side of the train. The octagonal lodges either side of the main entrance, built by J. B. Papworth in 1842, are more visible.

The house was built between 1776 and 1783 for Sir Francis Sykes, who made a fortune working for the East India Company. Sykes employed John Carr of York to build him a Palladian villa (Disraeli called it a 'Palladian palace') in Bath stone. Papworth continued work on the house after the Liberal MP James Morrison bought the estate in 1838 for £97,000. Morrison made his fortune in the haberdashery business. One of his coups was the cornering of the market in black crepe at the time of Queen Caroline's death in 1821.

The close proximity of the railway line made Basildon particularly attractive to Morrison, who wrote: 'we shall soon not want a Town House. In three years all the best Physicians will recommend a ride in a steam carriage an hour before dinner as much better than a ride in the Park, and my cards will run thus: Train off at 6; dinner on table 7 precisely; return steam up at $\frac{1}{2}$ past 10; carriages to Paddington at $\frac{1}{4}$ past 11; Brunel and 50 miles an hour.'

Basildon Park was empty from 1910 until the Second World War, when its park was used for practising tank warfare. After the war it was used as a billet for prisoners of war. The house was restored by Lord and Lady Iliffe and is now the property of the National Trust.

On the opposite side of the line to Basildon Park is a group of trees, including a fine cedar, surrounding an attractive pink-washed farm house, some old barns and **Basildon Church**. *R:l* Jethro Tull, the 'father of British agriculture'. author of *Horse-Hoeing Husbandry* (1731) and inventor of the drill, was born and buried at Basildon.

35 **BASILDON BRIDGE** (1839; extended 1890s; four 63′ arches of red brick with Bath stone facings). The railway line crosses the Thames over Basildon Bridge from **Berkshire** on the east side to **Oxfordshire** on the west. The white house on the river bank is called **'The** *L:r* **Grotto'** (c.1810), backed by steep slopes planted with yew and beech.

36 **GORING AND STREATLEY** (BR; red brick by J. W. Armstrong, 1890s). Goring and Streatley are typical of the dormitory villages that cluster around London within an hour or so's train journey of the city: the commuters' houses extend into the farmland that once surrounded the old villages.

37 SOUTH STOKE, ST ANDREW'S CHURCH *L:r*
(thirteenth and fourteenth centuries; Perpendicular tower; restored 1857) is close to the line
in the little huddle of the old village. Close by is
an attractive seventeenth-century dovecot of red
brick, a large square building with four gables.

38 MOULSFORD BRIDGE The line crosses over
Moulsford Bridge to pass from **Oxfordshire** on
the east bank of the Thames to **Berkshire** on
the west. The railway, like the river, follows the
path of least resistance along the valley floor
and, as the Thames marks the division between
Berkshire and Oxfordshire, for 30 miles from
Reading to Didcot, it runs along the boundary
line. The chalk escarpments which rise so beau-
tifully and often unexpectedly on either side are
the **Chilterns** to the east and the **Berkshire** *R:l*
Downs to the west. *L:r*

39 CHOLSEY AND MOULSFORD (BR; red
brick by J. W. Armstrong, 1890s). There is a
fine view of **Cholsey Parish Church** (Norman *R:l*
tower of flint and stone) to the west of the village. The flint and stone **barn** nearby is on the
site of the ancient monastery of Cholsey. The
barn is some 300′ long and was built in 1815
using stones from the much older Cowper's
Barn which had been demolished. The original
Cowper's barn, built in the late twelfth century,
was the largest barn in the country, 303′ long
and 51′ high. As the outer walls were only 8′
high, the expanse of roof was enormous.

40 SOUTH MORETON This is an attractive *L:r*
Berkshire village of half-timbered and brick cot-

tages and old brick walls surrounding larger houses. On the other side of the line, standing alone in the middle distance, is the large white melt kiln of the **Associated Brewers &** *R:l* **Melters**.

41 **DIDCOT** (BR, 1844; rebuilt after fire in 1885; white awnings, wooden station buildings painted cream and chocolate brown). Passengers alight here to change trains for Oxford.

The medieval village of **Old Didcot** is lost in *L:r* the sprawl of nineteenth- and twentieth-century housing developments. **Didcot Power** *R:l* **Station**, proclaiming 'Energy for the People', dominates the view to the north. Built around 1972, with four 500-megawatt generators, it is the southernmost point of a little-known rail network: the 'merry go round', which provides non-stop supplies of coal from the collieries to power stations throughout the country. Day and night (except during miners' strikes and at Christmas), the power station is supplied with coal from wagons which pass through the station at 1 mph, dropping their contents as they pass. During the summer of 1984 Didcot was completely overhauled and now can burn oil as well as coal. A nature reserve in its grounds provides a natural haven for wild life and flora.

It is sometimes possible to see old steam trains at Didcot. From 1932 to 1967 there was an important central locomotive depot immediately north of the railway station which was used as a storage and maintenance yard. This is now the home of the **Great Western Society,** which *R:l* was founded in 1961. Didcot Railway Centre covers 16 acres and includes the original 1932 engine shed of the GWR, a workshop, coaling stage, turntable, carriage restoration and storage shed and even a length of Brunel's original broad-gauge track. A complete small station is under construction, there are 23 steam locomotives and many coaches and goods wagons, all on display to the public, and enthusiasts can take a ride on one of the many 'Didcot Steamdays' throughout the year.

42 **MILTON TRADING ESTATE** The expan- *R:l*
sion of Didcot was partly helped by the establishment of the Ordnance Depot at Milton
during the First World War. The Milton Trading
Estate has since grown up in and around the
original depot to the north of the line.

43 **STEVENTON** The railway line passes through
the centre of this picturesque village — no
doubt much to the annoyance of the residents.
All that remains of **Steventon Station**, *R:l*
originally called Oxford Road, are the two
Tudor-style houses built of Bath stone at the
eastern end of the village. They were once used
by the GWR Company for board meetings, as
Steventon is halfway between London and
Bristol.

At the western end of the village the line
crosses '**The Causeway**'. This is a raised flood-
path nearly a mile long, lined with trees and fine
medieval, sixteenth- and seventeenth-century
houses and cottages of timber, brick and plas-
ter. The old lead roof of **St Michael's Church** *L:r*

(fourteenth-century limestone) can just be seen through the trees.

The railway line has now left behind the comfortable villages set on the banks of the Thames and entered a wide, uncluttered landscape: giant arable fields stretch to the north as far as the eye can see. To the south, rising in the middle distance from the rich alluvial soil, is the chalk scarp of the **Berkshire Downs**. *L:r*

44 UFFINGTON and the **VALE OF THE WHITE** *L:r*
HORSE St Mary's, Uffington is at the foot of **White Horse Hill**, the point at which the Downs to the south come closest to the railway line east of Swindon. St Mary's is known locally as the 'cathedral of the vale'. It is a very fine Early English church with an octagonal tower. The tower originally had a spire, but this fell off in 1740, 'beat down by a tempas, wind, thunder and liten'. Thomas Hughes, the author of *Tom Brown's Schooldays* (1857) was born and lived at Uffington as a boy, when his grandfather was vicar of St Mary's.

There are several white horses cut out of the grass on the chalk hills of Berkshire and Wiltshire. The **White Horse of Uffington** can be seen, on a clear day, immediately above the tower of St Mary's. The thin white streaks of chalk represent a very strange sort of horse. The animal measures 374' from nose to tail and is believed to have been first cut in the Iron Age, about 100 B.C. This and the Rude Man of Cerne are the only two pagan chalk monuments surviving in Britain. The animal may be a dragon rather than a horse. Nearby is a curious flat-topped mound called Dragon Hill – on which, it is claimed, St George slew the dragon. Nothing grows on top of the mound because, it is said, this is the very spot where the dragon's blood was spilled.

45 LONGCOT PARISH CHURCH is about a *R:l* mile north of the line. The tower was built in three stages in 1772, its ashlar faced and crowned with four stone urns.

46 SHRIVENHAM PARISH CHURCH has a *R:l* late-fourteenth-century tower; the rest of the church was rebuilt in the mid-seventeenth century.

47 BOURTON The site of Shrivenham Station is *L:r* at the east of a mile-long cutting. At the west end, just south of the line, is the small hamlet of Bourton. The large **Victorian mansion** in the trees is now a school.

At this point the line passes from **Berkshire** in the east to **Wiltshire** in the west.

48 SOUTH MARSTON PARISH CHURCH is *R:l* about half a mile from the line, in the village of South Marston. St Mary Magdalen is mostly Perpendicular, including the broad west tower, but the battlements were added by John Belcher in 1886.

49 SWINDON In the course of the last 150 years the town of Old Swindon has twice been completely transformed by waves of industrialisation. There were only 2000 inhabitants in

MAP 3

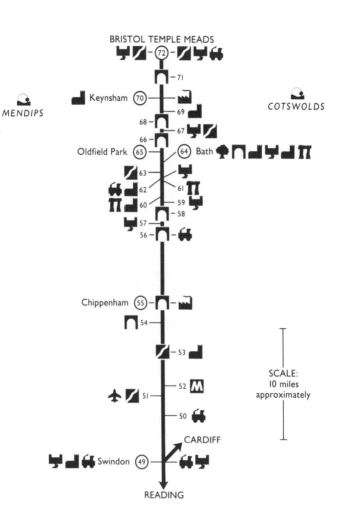

BRISTOL TEMPLE MEADS

Keynsham

MENDIPS

COTSWOLDS

Oldfield Park

Bath

Chippenham

SCALE:
10 miles
approximately

CARDIFF

Swindon

READING

1840, now there are 130,000, and the modern boom — unparalleled in present-day Britain — goes on. Each year nearly 1500 new houses are built in the borough.

The first boom was precipitated when Brunel made the decision to route the tracks of his railway immediately to the north of the town and, all-importantly, to establish repair and locomotive works there. The long grimy shells of these are all along the line, west of the station, backed by the tiny terraced cottages of the railway workers.

Faced with the decline of the railways, the town council encouraged growth and diversification of the town's economic base in the early 1950s. The result is a town which today not only services a vast rural hinterland, but also serves as an inexpensive and accessible alternative to London. The secret of Swindon's recent growth is the strategic position it occupies on the north—south axis between the Midlands and the South Coast and on the M4 between London, Bristol and South Wales. Acres of new and expensive housing now surround the petrified working-class town of the nineteenth century.

Swindon Station was the first part of the Victorian new town to be built. It consisted of two stone buildings 170' long on the two platforms, built between 1841 and 1842. Refreshment rooms occupied the ground floors; the first floors were connected by a bridge and used as a hotel and later banqueting rooms for Edward, Prince of Wales. When the station was opened, the refreshment rooms were run by the proprietor of the Queen's Hotel, Cheltenham:

every train passing through had to stop for ten minutes. Brunel found the coffee so nauseating he doubted whether real coffee beans were used – it tasted of 'bad roasted corn'. The evil brew in question was prepared in a coffee pot designed as a scale reproduction of a Daniel Gooch steam engine, with the percolator in the firebox – now in the Railway Museum at Swindon. All that remains of the original station is the **northern building**. The ground floor has *R:l* been completely modernised, but it is still possible to see the original honey-coloured Bath stone above.

The **railway works** west of the station were *R:l* completed in 1843. The main administrative building of the factory is now the headquarters of BR Engineering (Swindon) Ltd. The Chief Mechanical Engineer's building faces the line and above the entrance are two tablets carved in limestone depicting Gooch 'single' engines. George Jackson Churchwarden, who was responsible for locomotive design early in the twentieth century, had his office at the top of the building.

The **railway houses** which were to form the *L:r* beginnings of New Swindon followed the completion of the works; by 1853, 243 cottages had been erected. Tradition ascribes their design to Matthew Digby Wyatt. Six streets were laid out in the fields immediately south of the line. The **Parish Church** of **St Mark's** and the **Vicarage** were both designed by George Gilbert Scott. A new peal called 'Evening Star Delight Minor' was rung from the church bells in May 1960 for the last steam engine built at Swindon – called the 'Evening Star'.

Though the railway works and cottages are visible from the train, the overall impression of Swindon is of a modern city bristling with new office development. Tall office blocks and modern shopping precincts dominate the landscape. The tallest building in the centre is the **David** *L:r* **Murray John Tower**, a multistorey office and residential tower block, designed by Douglas Stephen and completed in 1978, which forms an integral part of the Brunel Centre. To the north of the station is **The Oasis**, a large *R:l* sports and leisure centre designed by Gillinson and Barnet and completed in 1976. The dome covers a lagoon-style swimming pool. The largest development is the **Princess Margaret** *L:r* **Hospital**, which covers about 22 acres on the hillside west of the city centre, designed by Powell and Moya.

About three miles west of Swindon, where the **M4** motorway crosses over the railway line, is the **Blagrove Employment Area**, a highly *R:l* imaginative industrial estate. The Anchor Butter Factory, designed by the Wyvern Partnership, is painted a suitable creamy-yellow and shaped not unlike a slab of butter. The brilliant blue and red factory belongs to the Water Research Council and was designed by the Architects' Design Partnership.

Travelling westward from Swindon, the railway moves beyond the upper reaches of the Thames valley, beyond the source of the Thames itself, and into a new river valley, the

Avon. Unlike the Thames, which flows east-wards and eventually enters the North Sea, the Avon flows west into the Severn, the Bristol Channel and the Atlantic.

50 WOOTTON BASSETT is situated close to *R:l* the junction of the lines to South Wales and Bristol Temple Meads; it is still possible to see some of the remains of the station.

51 WILTSHIRE AND BERKSHIRE CANAL *L:r* The Wiltshire and Berkshire Canal used to flow from Abingdon to Semington near Trowbridge and part of its course can be seen as a wide grassy ditch snaking through the fields and around the base of the hills south of the line between Swindon and Chippenham. The canal was built by William and Robert Whitworth between 1796 and 1810 and was some 51 miles long. Traffic was never very heavy on the canal (70,000 tons in 1830) but it was responsible for the use of Bath stone in buildings in Oxford. The stone was transported by barge from quar-ries at Box and Corsham. Ironically, the busiest period in the life of the canal was during the building of the GWR – the completion of which brought about its virtual extinction.

Low-flying aeroplanes are a familiar sight along this stretch of the line. **RAF Lyneham** is just *L:r* over the hills to the south.

52 M4 The M4 motorway – which has in its turn *R:l* threatened the railway – was constructed between 1971 and 1974 and runs parallel to the railway from just west of Swindon to Chippenham.

53 CHRISTIAN MALFORD The medieval church *R:l*
of **All Saints** (Post-Reformation tower) is on
the east bank of the Avon. The railway line
crosses over the Avon about a mile west of the
village.

54 MAUD HEATH'S CAUSEWAY Part of *L:r*
Maud Heath's Causeway can just be seen from
the train as it crosses the flood-plain of the
Avon, as a series of shallow brick arches supporting a footpath above ground level. Maud
Heath was a Wiltshire countrywoman who, in
1474, left her life's savings to build a path above
the marshy ground, around the Avon, which she
had struggled across to reach Chippenham market. She also left enough to maintain the causeway at the rate of £8 a year.

55 CHIPPENHAM (BR) The bright blue factory,
Westinghouse Brake and Signal Co. Ltd, *R:l*
part of the Hawker Siddeley group, dominates
the line at Chippenham Station. Since the 1870s
Westinghouse has supplied the braking systems
and signalling equipment for many railway lines
throughout Britain. The railway line passes over
Chippenham on a **viaduct** built in 1839 by
Brunel. Seen from below, the viaduct appears
to stride through the market town on formidable piers, dwarfing shops and offices.

56 BOX TUNNEL From Chippenham the
approach to Brunel's famous Box Tunnel is
through a cutting with increasingly steep sides,
first grass-covered and then revealing outcrops
of natural limestone rock with a stone wall built
along parts of the south side. The remains of

Corsham Station platform are glimpsed on *R:l* the north side of the line just before the train disappears into the tunnel, which took Brunel four years to complete. It is 3212 yards long (nearly two miles) and slopes towards Bath at an incline of 1 in 100. This last fact caused Brunel endless trouble when he was trying to get the plans for his line accepted. One critic calculated that if the brakes were to fail as the train entered the tunnel on the falling gradient it would emerge at the other end at 120mph, a speed at which no passenger would be able to breathe.

Three-quarters of the length of the tunnel passes through clay, blue marl and inferior oolite and is lined with brick. Half a mile at the east end was cut out by Brunel's navvies through the solid Bath stone in the shape of a Gothic arch. About 100 men died in the cutting of the tunnel but, when it was opened in June 1841, it was at last possible to travel by train from Paddington to Bristol in only four hours. Many travellers continued to be nervous of entering the tunnel and for some years after it was opened they could leave the train and travel over the top between Corsham and Box by horse. It is possible to see through the tunnel from either end — and on 9 April (Brunel's birthday) it is apparently possible to see the sun shining through the tunnel from the eastern end before it rises up over Box Hill.

57 **BOX** The village of Box appears briefly in *L:r* between Box and Middle Hill tunnels. The spindly **clock tower** to the east of **St Thomas**

of **Canterbury Church** (fourteenth century) belongs to the Victorian Gothic village school.

58 MIDDLE HILL TUNNEL is shorter than Box Tunnel but the entrances are more ornate. Brunel wanted to impress travellers on the nearby main road (A4), from where there is still a good view of the tunnel entrance.

59 SHOCKERWICK HOUSE is visible through *R:1* the trees just west of Middle Hill Tunnel. The house, which commands a fine view down the valley towards Bath, was built of honey-coloured Bath stone by John Wood the Elder in about 1750.

Shockerwick House

West of Shockerwick the line crosses from **Wiltshire** (east) to **Avon** (west). The county of Avon was established only in the early 1970s, and comprises parts of Somerset and Gloucestershire.

About three miles east of Bath, the railway line

enters the valley of the Avon between the villages of **Batheaston and Bathford.**

60 ST SWITHUN'S, BATHFORD, is a Vic- *L:r* torian church (tower 1879). Above the village and close to the top of the tree-covered hill is **Brown's Folly**. The square tower was built in 1840 by a local builder called Wade Browne and is on the border of Avon and Wiltshire.

61 The summit of **LITTLE SOLSBURY HILL**, a *R:l* flat-topped hill above **BATHEASTON**, is covered with the remains of a large iron-age fortification.

62 BATHAMPTON is a small village beside the Kennet and Avon Canal and the railway line, though its suburbs now reach to the edge of Bath.

St Nicholas's Church (Perpendicular *L:r* tower) and a fine Cotswold stone barn are close to the line. **Hampton Manor** is the *R:l* attractive early-eighteenth-century house just west of the small roadbridge which crosses over the line. The remains of **Bathampton** *L:r* **Station** can be seen where the line to Bradford on Avon and Westbury branches to the south.

63 THE KENNET AND AVON CANAL was *L:r* completed in 1810, connecting the ports of London and Bristol. It was designed by Robert Whitworth and John Rennie and extends for nearly 57 miles from Newbury to Bath, through 79 locks. Annual traffic on the canal was up to 300,000 tons before the GWR was built, and the canal was used extensively while the railway was being constructed. However, the active life of the canal came to an end once the line was completed. It was bought by the GWR Company in 1852 for £210,000 and was used less and less over the following decades. Now, however, it is being restored by an independent trust and sections are already open to traffic again. The canal continues close to the line and slightly above it as far as Bath, where it joins the River Avon immediately next to the station. The canal was diverted by the GWR along part of the eastern approach to Bath: the railway line itself runs along the old bed of the canal. The canal flows behind a massive retaining wall which is 5′ thick in some parts.

64 Approaching **BATH** The entry by train into Bath is, from either direction, one of the most spectacular surprises that British railway travel can provide. From the east, at the villages of Bathford and Batheaston, the line joins the Avon and with it cuts through the very southernmost tip of the Cotswolds, emerging into a basin filled to overflowing with the city, a multiplicity of towers, spires and terraces, ancient and modern, uniformly built of golden Bath stone.

Bath now has around 90,000 inhabitants. It is situated at the point where the Roman Fosse Way crosses the Avon: the baths built by the Romans to contain the constant supply of warm spa water have for centuries been one of the town's greatest tourist attractions. The centre of the city is mainly eighteenth-century, built with tremendous speed when it became fashionable to take the waters. Metalworking and engineering have also developed, making use of varied metal deposits in the surrounding hills, but with the revival of Bath's spa facilities, the tourist industry dominates as the city's source of wealth.

Brunel made the eastern approach through the city as unobtrusive as possible: the line passes through a cutting lined with Bath stone and crossed by elegant stone and iron bridges. The **Sydney Gardens** provide a border of *R:l* shrubs and trees and the back of the **Holburne of Menstrie Museum** (1797) appears through the foliage. The train then emerges on an embankment leading to a viaduct of 37 arches which carries the line over the Avon and into the station.

Bath Abbey stands out clearly above the *R:l* Avon. The Abbey was begun in 1499 by Bishop King, Chief Secretary to Henry VII. He was inspired by a dream in which he saw angels ascending and descending a ladder stretching up to heaven and heard a voice saying 'let a king restore the church'. The ladder and angels decorate the west front of the Abbey.

Just before the train crosses the Avon there is a clear view of **North Parade Bridge** (rebuilt *R:l* 1945) and, beyond, the elegant **Pulteney Bridge**. Robert Adam was commissioned by Sir William Johnstone-Pulteney in 1770 to design a complete new town at Bathwick, but only Pulteney Bridge and Pulteney Street were completed at the time. Pulteney Bridge was based on the Ponte Vecchio in Florence and still has shops on either side of the road.

Bath Spa Station originally had a roof completely covering the platforms and tracks. Now only the familiar awnings stretch over the platforms, supported by freshly painted iron columns of chocolate brown and red. Bath is one of the most popular tourist attractions in Britain and the immaculate station, with shrubs and flowers growing in containers between the tracks, reflects the international traffic. The façade of the station was designed by Brunel and is a curious mixture of Tudor and classical styles, reflecting Bath's Roman, medieval and Regency past.

Western Bath A viaduct of 73 arches carries the railway line over the Avon, across two main roads and out of the city towards Bristol. The bridge over the Avon is an extraordinary Gothic affair with arrow slit windows and crenellated turrets. The terraces, crescents and squares of Bath cluster on the hillside above the **Abbey**: closer to the summit are the spires and *R:l* towers of churches and schools. The highest, most easterly tower, which begins as a square but turns into an octagon, belongs to **St Stephen's Lansdown**, designed by James Wilson in 1840–5. The most westerly tower, just visible above the trees, is **Beckford's Tower,** which was built for William Beckford, the eccentric Gothic novelist and creator of Fonthill, by H. E. Goodridge in 1825–6. In his old age, Beckford lived immediately below the tower in Lansdown Crescent and could walk up to his eyrie through his garden. The Lysicrates Monument in Athens was the inspiration for the tower, which is 154′ high.

Beckford's Tower

65 OLDFIELD PARK (BR)

66 TWERTON TUNNEL The railway line passes over the 28-arch Twerton Viaduct, through a cutting lined with Bath stone and into the

Twerton Tunnel. The tunnel is 264 yards long and has two splendid Gothic entrances. A tessellated Roman villa pavement was unearthed when the Newton Cutting, just west of the tunnel, was dug.

67 KELSTON PARK was built in about 1770 by *R:l* John Wood the Younger on a fine site with views down the wooded slopes to the River Avon below.

68 SALTFORD TUNNEL is approached by deep cuttings at each end and is 176 yards long.

69 BITTON ST MARY'S CHURCH (late four- *R:l* teenth century, Perpendicular tower). It is just possible to see a bridge over the Avon which once carried a railway line to Bath Green Park Station (recently restored by Sainsbury's).

70 KEYNSHAM (BR) The valley of the Avon is wide and flat here as the river meanders over its flood-plain. There has been extensive industrial development since the nineteenth century. The **John Dickinson Paper Mill** is immediately *R:l* east of the station. The large red-brick factory belonging to **Cadburys** (formerly Fry's) is to *R:l* the west. The **Church of St John the Baptist** *L:r* has a Carolean tower, built in 1634, two years after the original tower collapsed 'by Tempestuous weather... Which contrived in a most fearfull manner, being inter-mixed with hideous Clapps of Thunder and flashes of Lightning'.

71 BRISLINGTON TUNNEL AND IVY MAN-TLED TUNNEL As the Avon Valley narrows, and the banks become increasingly steep, Brunel had to carry out extensive digging of cuttings and tunnels to take his railway line into Bristol. The Avon itself was diverted so that the railway line could run along the narrow shelf made by the river beneath the steep wooded bank to the south. Two short tunnels through the hillside were opened out by 1894 but the **Brislington Tunnel** is 1017 yards long. The shorter **Ivy Mantled Tunnel** is called after its western entrance, which resembles the entrance to an old ivy mantled castle.

72 **BRISTOL** is a regional capital, with over half a million inhabitants. It was a prosperous and important city in the Middle Ages, but the seventeenth century was the period of its chief prosperity, when Bristol grew to be the second largest city and port after London. Extraordinarily, its imports were ten times as high as its exports: it was not a manufacturing town and it failed to become an outlet for the industrial West Midlands. Its wealth came instead from the West Indies: sugar, tobacco, and cocoa were unloaded and processed for home consumption; slave ships stopped by on the journey west. The abolition of the slave trade severely reduced the wealth of the city. In the twentieth century, aircraft engineering has flourished, which made Bristol a focus of the German bombers' attentions in the Second World War. Rebuilding continues, with office blocks, shopping precincts and multistorey car parks evidence of continued prosperity and industry.

The train crosses over the **Avon** and then over

the **Feeder Canal** as it approaches Bristol
Temple Meads from the east. Immediately to
the south, and dominating the surrounding
buildings, is the unusual **Great Western Cot-** *L:r*
ton Mill (1837–8), a large castellated building
which is now partly used as a transport depot.
The bold Gothic tower of the **Wills Building**,
which stands out above the buildings of Bristol
directly ahead, is part of Bristol University and
was completed in 1925, paid for by Sir G. A.
and H. H. Wills (Sir George Oatley, architect).
Two more towers to be seen are the **Cabot
Tower** (1897–8 by W. V. Gough) and the
modern **Lead-shot Tower** which is still in use, *R:l*
employing a technique invented two and a half
centuries ago.

Just before entering the station, the train
crosses over the **Floating Harbour** which was
constructed in 1804 as part of improvements to
the port. The old sinuous course of the Avon
through the city was converted into a long wet
dock called 'The Float'. Brunel was employed
to help clear The Float of mud at the same time
as plans were being prepared for the GWR. The
railway line enters the station 15 to 20′ above
ground level on a series of arches, to give mast
room to the sailing ships which once filled the
harbour below.

Bristol Temple Meads The arrival at Bristol
Temple Meads station is memorable as the train
passes beneath the Gothic arch of Matthew
Digby Wyatt's train shed, which follows the
curve of the railway tracks and has a wrought
iron roof with a span of 130′. Wyatt's part of

the station is not the earliest structure. Temple Meads is a complex station: at one time it served three separate railway companies, each with its own station master.

The first station at Temple Meads was designed by Brunel for the GWR. The offices were built between 1839 and 1840 and their extraordinary mock-Elizabethan façade, complete with turrets and a centre oriel, face Victoria Street at the beginning of the station approach. Pugin found the offices horrible, nothing but 'architectural display... at once costly and offensive and full of pretension'. Behind the GWR offices and on the north side of the station is Brunel's masterpiece, his train shed with a wooden mock-hammerbeam roof wider than the roof of Westminster Hall. Left in a sad condition for years and partly used as a car park, it is now being restored to its former glory.

The Bristol and Exeter Railway (B & ER) shared the GWR facilities between 1840 and 1845 but then built its own station, linked to the GWR lines by an 'express curve'. The terminal building of the B & ER (built in 1852 by S. C. Fripp) is beside the raised station approach on the south side of the station and adds the neo-Jacobean style to the expanding terminus.

The Midland Railway (MR) arrived at Bristol in 1854, creating more congestion and confusion. Wyatt designed a joint station for the MR and the B & ER in 1865–75 along the line of the 'express curve', keeping Brunel's Gothic details and building the unusual curving Gothic-arched train shed. Wyatt's entrance hall is more like part of a Gothic university than a railway station, with red-brick walls and mullioned windows. Above the entrance rises a Gothic clock tower with exuberant decorations. *The Builder* magazine found Wyatt's work as appalling as Pugin had found Brunel's: 'Pseudo-Gothic of the commonest and most vulgar kind, utterly wanting in refinement and knowledge… who is the architect?… The shareholders ought to know who is wasting their money.' When P. E. Culverhouse came to design extensions to the station in the 1930s, he managed to fit in with Wyatt's 'vulgar' style. The result is a most unusual and characterful Victorian station.

PADDINGTON
TO
CARDIFF

Paddington to Reading (see pages 32-49)
Reading to Swindon (see pages 50-58)

MAP 4

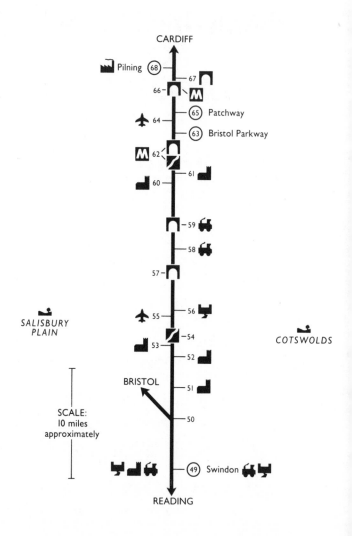

50 WOOTTON BASSETT is at the point where *R:l*
the Paddington line divides into two distinctive
courses: south-west to the port of Bristol and
north-west to the industrial belt of South
Wales. The stretch of line in between Swindon
and Cardiff takes passengers through four
counties, two countries and two of the most
ambitious tunnels created by nineteenth-
century engineering.

51 ST MICHAEL'S CHURCH, BRINKWORTH *R:l*
(Perpendicular embattled tower) is close to the
line and built of the local Cotswold limestone.

52 LITTLE SOMERFORD ST JOHN THE *R:l*
BAPTIST'S CHURCH (thin Perpendicular
tower) is close to the line. Nearby is an attractive red-brick timber-framed house and the
remains of the old station platform. Captain
Mark Phillips, the equestrian husband of Princess Anne, comes from here.

53 ST PETER AND ST PAUL'S CHURCH, *L:r*
GREAT SOMERFORD (ornate Early Perpendicular battlemented tower).

54 Crossing the **RIVER AVON** This is gently undulating countryside, ideal for the sheep which
brought so much wealth to the area in the fifteenth and sixteenth centuries. To the south
are the bleaker downs of **Salisbury Plain**, to the *L:r*
north the limestone ridge of the **Cotswolds**.   *R:l*

55 HULLAVINGTON The hangars and adminis- *L:r*
trative buildings of Hullavington Airfield can be
seen south of the line. This is the depot of the

79

RAF Balloon Regiment. Balloons are sent to Aldershot for use by paratroopers practising jumps.

56 BRADFIELD FARM On the other side of the R:l line, close to the old station platform for Hulla-vington, is Bradfield Farm, a rare fifteenth-century hall. A range of three storeys was added in the seventeenth century to create a fine Cotswold farmhouse with a stone barn nearby.

57 ALDERTON TUNNEL is approached through long cuttings from east and west. It marks the boundary between **Wiltshire** and **Avon**. The county of Avon was established only in the early 1970s, and comprises parts of Somerset and Gloucestershire.

58 BADMINTON STATION The old red-brick R:l station building survives, though rather forlorn, beside the railway line. The station was specially built for the Duke of Beaufort, who could demand that any train must stop at request until a private Act of Parliament put an end to his right — just before the station was closed. His family seat, Badminton House, is to the north of the line. The game of badminton was first played at the house and the Badminton Horse Trials are held annually in the grounds. To the south of the line is Dodington Park, built by James Wyatt for the wealthy plantation owner Christopher Bethell Codrington. Capa-bility Brown was employed to landscape the parks of both estates, which are now separated by the M4 as well as the railway.

59 **CHIPPING SODBURY TUNNEL** extends for 2 miles and 924 yards through the Cotswold limestone. There are cuttings at either end, obscuring the picturesque wool town of Chipping Sodbury to the north. The remains of the **station** can be seen west of the tunnel, a red *R:l* and blue-black building now used by a local coal merchant.

60 **WESTERLEIGH CHURCH** The line to Glou- *L:r* cester from Bristol leaves to the north. South of the line is the ornate Perpendicular tower of Westerleigh parish church. The church was largely rebuilt in the fifteenth century at a time when local wool merchants and clothiers were growing rich on the trade in undyed broadcloth. Churches were built, schools founded and country mansions erected. In the sixteenth and seventeenth centuries the merchants became landed gentry, acquiring land which had belonged to the monasteries before the Dissolution.

61 **COALPIT HEATH** The village and church are *R:l* below the railway line. Both church and vicarage were designed in the early fourteenth-century style by the Victorian architect William Butterfield.

62 A series of viaducts carries the train over the valley of the **RIVER FROME** with the village of **Winterbourne** to the north, over **Bradley** *R:l* **Brook** and the **M4**.

63 **BRISTOL PARKWAY** (BR) Seemingly insignificant in itself, Bristol Parkway is representative

of a new breed of stations, marrying the train to the car. Situated on the edge of cities, giving easy access to express routes, parkway stations put the car driver at a premium. For the Bristolean pedestrian there is a shuttle service from Bristol Temple Meads.

64 **FILTON AIRFIELD** The eau-de-nil hangars of *L:r* Filton Airfield are immediately ahead, as the train follows the line in a curve towards the north-west and the Severn Tunnel. Eric Ross designed the buildings for the Bristol Aeroplane Company — originally the Bristol Colonial Aeroplane Company, founded by Sir George White in 1910 — in the 1950s. The famous Bristol Fighter was produced at Filton during the First World War and the Blenheim, Beaufort and Beaufighter aeroplanes during the Second World War. In 1946 the Brabazon — then the largest aeroplane ever to be built in Britain — was built at Filton and in the late 1960s the airfield became famous as one of the sites where Concorde was part built.

65 **PATCHWAY** (BR)

66 **PATCHWAY** or **CATTYBROOK TUNNEL** The **M5**, joining Exeter, Bristol and Birmingham, passes over the top of the second shorter tunnel.

67 **SEVERN BRIDGE** On a clear day, there is a *R:l* good view of the towers of the Severn Bridge with the hills of Gwent in South Wales beyond. The bridge was designed by Sir Gilbert Roberts and opened in 1966 by the Queen. The main

Severn Bridge

span is 3240', the side spans are each 1000' and the towers are 400' high. The box girder design creates a breathtaking impression of lightness, grace and fragility, even though the bridge can carry vehicles up to 200 tons in weight. Professor James Sutherland described the bridge as being 'almost as far ahead of its forebears as the jet is in advance of the piston engine'. However, only 20 years on, it is now under threat. It has been calculated that if a wind only slightly faster than the strongest wind ever recorded were to sweep up the estuary, the bridge would be in danger of collapse — and with it, the Welsh economy. There is now lobbying for a second span across the Severn.

68 **PILNING** (BR) The Severn Estuary is heavily industrialised, with a vast **chemical works** just *L:r* to the south. Further south around Avonmouth are smelting works, docks and an oil depot.

69 **SEVERN TUNNEL** A tunnel under the Severn was first sketched out by Charles Richardson in 1865. The GWR took up his plans in 1872 and employed Sir John Hawkshaw and Richardson as the engineers. The works were flooded out twice. On the second occasion, in 1883, a tidal wave put back the work by three years. The tunnel was finally completed in 1886 at a cost of £1½ million. It is the largest mainline railway tunnel in Britain — 4 miles 628 yards. The tunnel takes the train from **Avon** into **Gwent**: **England** into **Wales.**

Wales can be divided into three areas: the borderland with England to the east; the high, bleak mountains of the north; and the industrial south — through which Brunel's line runs.

South Wales is accessible by sea, river, canal, railway, bridge, tunnel and road. It is a broad, flat, low-lying plain, flanked ten miles inland by green rounded hills and bordered in the south by the estuary of the River Severn and Bristol Channel. It is not, apparently, a momentous landscape, yet its contribution to the industrial wealth of Britain has been spectacular, the result of a fortuitous combination of location

MAP 5

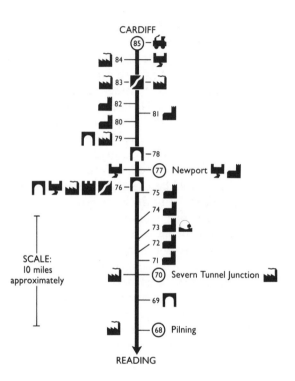

and natural resources.

The valleys which come into view to the north had long been mined for iron ore, but when smelting with coal was developed, the coalfield on which South Wales rests was there to be exploited, along with the limestone of the hills and the water from the valley rivers. An economically irresistible combination, it was nevertheless only the first stage of development. As the iron began to run out in the nineteenth century, coal came increasingly into world demand, and Newport and Cardiff, the principal cities on this stretch of the line, grew up as outlets for coal to a world hungry for power for its ships and steam engines. The iron and steel foundries too moved to the coast, where ore could be cheaply imported and coal easily shipped 10 or 20 miles downriver. Thus South Wales, only a tenth of the size of Wales as a whole, contains two-thirds of the country's population of two million. Newport and Cardiff mushroomed, overtaking the established port of Bristol across the channel in volume of trade. The rapidity of the development and the concentration of enterprise mean that the journey along the southern coast of Wales is full of contrasts: tiny medieval communities sit silently across the line from the noise and smoke of heavy industry.

70 **SEVERN TUNNEL JUNCTION** (BR) There is a complex of marshalling yards at Severn Tunnel Junction and a locomotive depot. Along the English and Welsh banks of the Severn are vast modern industries which have replaced the small firms established in the valleys at the

beginning of the Industrial Revolution. On the southern bank, the chemical smoke of **ICI** stains *L:r* the air; to the north lies one of the **British** *R:l* **Steel Corporation's** biggest plants.

71 **ST MARY'S CHURCH, ROGIET** (thirteenth- *R:l* century embattled tower). St Mary's is one of several medieval churches close to the line, all centrepieces of rural communities which have witnessed the noisy arrival of industry and its gradual decline. St Mary's even had an aisle added in 1903 to cope with the rise in the local population because of employment on the railway. Some of the cottages in the villages have the traditional Welsh lime-wash.

72 **ST MICHAEL AND ALL ANGELS, LLAN-** *R:l* **FIHAGEL ROGIET**

73 **ST MARY'S, MAGOR** Known as the 'Cathe- *R:l* dral of the moors', St Mary's is close to the railway line. Originally a Norman foundation, the church was lavishly rebuilt in the Middle Ages. Some of the fine carving may have been done by workmen from Tintern Abbey; the Cistercian Abbey owned St Mary's in the thirteenth century.

The rounded **green hills** of South Wales may *R:l* look peaceful and secluded in contrast to the smoky industrial activity near the river, but they contain the valley villages such as Tonypandy, Blaenavon and Abertillery, where the extracting of iron and coal first began to transform the economy of the area.

74 **ST CADWALADR'S, BISTON** St Cadwaladr *R:l*
was the last of the Welsh kings to assume the
title of chief sovereign of Britain. He fought the
Saxons in many battles and died of the plague in
664 A.D.

75 **ST MARY'S, LLANWERN** In the churchyard *R:l*
of St Mary's is a cross commemorating David
Alfred Thomas, Lord Rhondda, who lived at
Llanwern Park (demolished). He was Liberal
MP for Merthyr, a coal-owner and responsible
for introducing rationing in the First World
War. The Norman church, in its pastoral setting, contrasts dramatically with the industrial
might of the vast steelworks to the south.

76 **LLANWERN STEELWORKS** were establish- *L:r*
ed in 1962 after Caldicott Level was reclaimed
from the Severn floods by tipping lorry loads of
shale brought down from the valleys of South
Wales. The Llanwern plant stretches for $3\frac{1}{2}$
miles along the railway line and is three-quarters
of a mile wide, with 40 miles of internal railways. One of its most important products is the
steel used for car bodies in the motor industry.
Iron ore is brought from Port Talbot by rail,
coal comes from the South Wales collieries by
rail and limestone comes from Gloucestershire
by road. The largest blast furnace is capable of
producing 5000 tons of iron every day. The
steel is stretched out in the rolling mills, the
long buildings beside the railway line. It is also
possible to see the coke ovens where the coal
is converted into coke. For a few seconds the
characteristic smell of bad eggs (sulphur
hydroxide) fills the train.

Approaching Newport from the east
Approaching Newport there is a view of the
George Street Bridge, the new suspension L:r
bridge across the River Usk. Newport is situated at the point where the Rivers Usk and
Ebbw join the Severn. Canal and tramways followed the Usk River gap to reach the eastern
valleys and the Ebbw River gap to reach the
western valleys. Brunel chose to take the SWR
straight through the centre of Newport, which
involved building an expensive bridge over the
Usk and digging a tunnel. The town is still
divided by the railway line, with the most of the
commercial property seaward and the residential property landward of the line.

Crossing the River Usk The first railway bridge
over the Usk was burnt down during the construction of the line in 1848, which considerably delayed the completion of the SWR. The
Road Bridge was built in 1922. Immediately L:r
below the line are the ruins of **Newport** L:r
Castle on the west bank. The castle was
founded in the twelfth century to command the
crossing of the Usk, but only the east side of
the court remains. The river has the greatest
tidal rise and fall of any river in Britain, so the
castle is regularly surrounded by mud banks.
The grandiose towered building on the west
bank is the Victorian iron and glass **Market** L:r
Hall (by J. Linton and C. Kirby).

77 **NEWPORT** is the county town and commercial capital of Gwent (formerly Monmouth-
shire) and has been a centre of canal, tramroad
and railway activity for some 200 years. It is

now linked to England by the M4. Around 1900, foundries, iron works, timber yards, glass and brick works all contributed to the wealth of the town, although the main business was the export of coal, for which the town was ideally situated. Being so dependent on coal and steel, South Wales has suffered severely from the decline in world demand over the last 50 years.

Newport Station (BR; 1848–50 enlarged 1875–8 by Lancaster Owen and J. E. Danks; street frontage including large red-brick office block, 1923–30). The **Victorian Railway** *L:r* **Hotel**, in red brick and limestone, survives facing the station. On the upside, **Victorian** *R:l* **stone platform buildings** have limestone trimmed round-arched windows; the awnings have ornate valancing and are supported by bright red pillars.

The **Civic Centre**, a vast symmetrical building *R:l* with a clock tower, was begun in 1937 and designed by J. Cecil Howitt. **St Mark's Church** *R:l* has an ornate Perpendicular tower which is a striking landmark on the side of the hill called Gold Tops.

78 STOW HILL TUNNEL and **HILLFIELD TUNNEL** The tunnels are adjacent to one another. Stow Hill is 742 yards long and is the oldest. Hillfield is longer and was completed in 1911.

79 ALEXANDRA DOCK Beyond the sidings, *L:r* coal trucks and warehouses of **Pillgwenlly**

Junction are the cranes, transporter bridge and power station associated with Newport's Alexandra Dock. The Alexandra (Newport) Dock Company was incorporated in 1865 and named after Princess Alexandra, who had married the Prince of Wales two years earlier. The North Dock was opened in 1875, the South Dock in 1894. The transporter bridge was designed in 1902 by the French engineer Arnodin (who built the Marseilles transporter bridge). It is in essence a high-suspension bridge, supported on deceptively slender pylons which taper to points at their bases. Suspended from the main span a moveable carriage hovers above the Usk, able to carry people and up to six cars across the river. Like the Tower Bridge in London, it allows tall ships up river.

80 **ST BRIDE'S CHURCH, WENTLLOOG** The *L:r* Perpendicular tower of St Bride's rises above the flat marshy land of the Wentlloog Level, leaning slightly to the north-west because of the alluvial nature of the ground. The Wentlloog Level stretches between Newport and Cardiff, flat land reclaimed from the Bristol Channel and crossed by drainage ditches called reens. Reed Sweet Grass grows in the reens to a height of 6'.

81 **ST MARY'S CHURCH, MARSHFIELD** The *R:l* warm red local sandstone church with its tall embattled tower was restored early in the twentieth century and contains lavish Edwardian woodwork, glass and sculpture.

82 **ST PETER'S CHURCH, PETERSTONE** *L:r*

WENTLLOOG The pinnacled tower of St Peter's (rebuilt 1450) leans slightly – like St Bride's. It is surrounded by the desolate, water-logged Level and has only one grave in the churchyard – to a drowned man. A long embankment called Peterstone Great Wharf protects the land from the sea.

83 Crossing the **RIVER RHYMNEY** The River Rhymney is now on the outskirts of Cardiff: industrial and residential estates have swallowed up the villages and fields. Cardiff had a population of only 40,000 in 1870 but it expanded to over 150,000 in the next 30 years, and now stands at around a quarter of a million. There is much evidence of the industry which brought wealth and prosperity to the area in the nineteenth and early twentieth centuries – extensive **container sidings** and the **Rover** *R&L* **Way Industrial Estate**; **Williams's Alexandra Foundry**; **Leo's Moneysaver** in a large Victorian emporium of red and yellow brick. Further away to the south-west is **Bute East Dock**. The terraces of houses around the docks form Butetown but are traditionally known as 'Tiger Bay', a reflection of the exotic mixture of races attracted to the port in the nineteenth century.

84 **BUTE EAST DOCK** The cranes and brick *L:r* warehouses of Bute East Dock can be seen south of the line. At the beginning of the eighteenth century, Cardiff was a rural town with a declining population: in 1730 there was only one iron furnace making pig iron in the region. By 1839, however, there were 51 iron furnaces,

all situated on the narrow strip of iron-bearing limestone at the northern edge of the coalfield between Aberdare and Rhymni. The Glamorganshire Canal was opened in 1794 from Merthyr to Cardiff and the Penydarren Tramroad was opened in 1800 (to be used in 1804 for the trials of Trevithick's first steam locomotive to run on rails). From 1790 until the 1850s South Wales was the most important iron-producing area in Britain. The ironmasters had opened up the valleys but the immensely wealthy Scotch Bute family was responsible for the creation of Cardiff as a great port and modern city. The 1st Marquis married an heiress of the Herbert and Windsor families and then Frances Coutts, of the millionaire banking family. By the 1850s, the family owned 22,000 acres of land in and around Cardiff. The 2nd Marquis built Bute West Dock in 1830–9 and Bute East Dock in 1855–9, providing 120 miles of dock lines and sidings. The East Dock was designed by Sir John Rennie in association with W. S. Clarke, resident dock engineer. Clarke's Bute warehouse alongside the north wharf (1861) has survived as an outstanding example of industrial architecture, with an iron framework of beams and round cast-iron columns. The Butes continued to finance and manage their docks until 1922. The **Custom House** *R:l* immediately before Cardiff Station was built in 1845.

85 **CARDIFF** The boom in the production of iron (1790–1850) in South Wales was followed by the development of steamcoal production; by the beginning of the twentieth century, Cardiff

was the foremost coal-exporting port in the world. The railways were vitally important in promoting the prosperity of the area and connecting the port with the coal mines in the valleys to the north. The Taff Vale Railway was planned by Brunel and opened in 1841 between Merthyr Tydfil and Cardiff. Unlike Brunel's other railways, it was narrow-gauge in order to negotiate the floors of the narrow winding valleys. By 1900 the docks at Cardiff were surrounded by chemical, brick and steel works, with blast furnaces, copper works and a timber yard giving employment to the region.

Like all of the great nineteenth-century industrial centres, Cardiff has experienced decline since the Second World War. However, its position as capital of Wales, its expanding university and its importance as a commercial and tourist centre have given it new life — as well as the inevitable towering office blocks, concrete multistorey car parks and traffic problems. It has proved able to mediate the industrial shift that has left its enormous dock area paralysed and decaying.

Cardiff Station The SWR entered Cardiff in 1850. The River Taff was diverted to create the site for the station and in so doing provided the benefit of flood control and reclaimed land which was used to build the pub-less 'Temperance Town'. **Cardiff Central Station** or **Caerdydd Canalog** — it is now illegal not to give the public the option — was rebuilt in the 1920s in a restrained classical style. The gracious Portland stone building with its colourful clock tower is spoilt, however, by an enormous advertisement hoarding suspended across the front. The platform buildings and connecting tunnel under the tracks are elegantly clad in white and brown tiles with brown lettering, creating a 'between the wars' atmosphere.

PADDINGTON
TO
PENZANCE

Paddington to Reading (see pages 32-49)

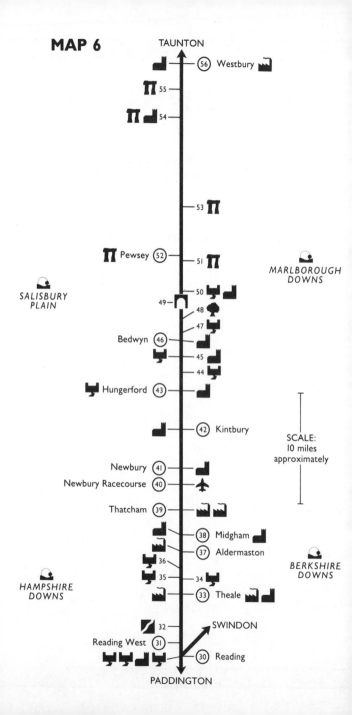

MAP 6

TAUNTON

(56) Westbury

55

54

53

(52) Pewsey   51

50

49

48

47

Bedwyn (46)

45

44

Hungerford (43)

(42) Kintbury

Newbury (41)

Newbury Racecourse (40)

Thatcham (39)

(38) Midgham

(37) Aldermaston

36

35   34

(33) Theale

32

Reading West (31)

(30) Reading

SWINDON

PADDINGTON

SALISBURY
PLAIN

MARLBOROUGH
DOWNS

SCALE:
10 miles
approximately

HAMPSHIRE
DOWNS

BERKSHIRE
DOWNS

Leaving Reading the train emerges into the countryside and begins its journey south-westward: one of the most varied, exciting and historical in Britain. One of the lengthiest, too: over five hours to Penzance, where the train waits for about forty minutes and then starts on the long haul back. From **Berkshire** in the east it cuts through **Wiltshire** and **Somerset** to Exeter, and then begins to trace the coastline, first of **Devon** and then **Cornwall**, arriving finally at the westernmost point of the line — from which the only extension is on to the Atlantic aboard the ferry to the Scilly Isles.

The journey west is also, geologically, a journey back through time. In Berkshire and Wiltshire, the landscape is young, made up of ocean-bed chalks and the clays deposited by the great ice-age rivers. In Somerset, the railway line passes over an older profile of limestone and marble and into the rich red of Devonian sandstone. But arriving in Cornwall, an eastern outpost of the ancient landmass of America, the contrast is dramatic. There the mood of the land changes, becomes unaccommodating, unyielding, pre-human, bound with granite and slate, lined with tin. Much of the joy of the journey is the sense of going into a wilderness. The train moves from the fertile built-up plains of the east to the open moors and wastelands of the west.

31 **READING WEST** (BR)

32 **KENNET AND AVON CANAL** The Kennet and Avon Canal is close to the railway line from Reading to Pewsey and it is possible to see

some of the locks and red-brick bridges over the canal. The digging of the canal began in 1794 at Newbury and, 40 miles further west, at Bradford on Avon. Now, the railway line and the canal appear to coexist peacefully enough, but 150 years ago the two routes wound about each other in a battle to the death. The canal was completed in 1810, forging a link between England's two booming ports, Bristol and London. But the waters of the Severn and the Thames had scarcely begun to mingle when Brunel's line was built. In 1852 the GWR actually bought the canal, only to run it down. The first great phase of the Industrial Revolution was over. The trains dash on still; only holiday-makers dawdle along the canal.

33 **THEALE** (BR) The imposing red-brick **Prest-** R:l
cold Factory is just east of Theale Station. On the other side of the line is the enormous **Stone Coating Plant** with a cement depot and R:l oil depot also on the site. The village of Theale sprawls to the north with the large **Church of** R:l **Holy Trinity** (1820–32) appearing just west of the station.

34 **ENGLEFIELD HOUSE** is the enormous Eliza- R:l bethan mansion just west of Theale. It was probably built between 1590 and 1600, but the pinnacles on top and the massive entrance towers were added by Richard Armstrong in the late nineteenth century after a fire. Elizabeth I's influential favourite, the Earl of Essex, owned Englefield for a brief period – until he was executed in 1601. The house then passed to his executioner, Elizabeth I. In 1832 Con-

stable was commissioned to paint a series of studies of Englefield for its owner Richard Benyon de Bouvoir and found the house 'very bright and cheerful'.

35 **SULHAMSTEAD HOUSE** is opposite Engle- *L:r* field House on top of the tree-covered hillside. The elegant white two-storey house was built early in the nineteenth century.

36 **PADWORTH HOUSE** is altogether more *L:r* sombre and ponderous than Sulhamstead. It was built around 1769 by J. Hobcraft on the hillside just east of Aldermaston Station and is now a private girls' school.

37 **ALDERMASTON** (BR) The former station building was built in 1846 of red brick with semi-circular arches over doors and windows. The 'chalet style' of the station with the roof extending to become a platform awning, was used on many GWR stations in the nineteenth century.

The 'William' pear and nuclear weapons are both associated with Aldermaston. The pear was developed by a local schoolmaster, John Stair; the nuclear weapons were the target of the famous protest march from London to Aldermaston at Easter, 1958. The Atomic Weapons Research Establishment has continued to be a focus of protest ever since. The large fuel depot just east of the station has a pipeline which carries aviation fuel to Heathrow Airport. **Sterling Cable** is on the site of the *L:r* headquarters of the GWR during the Second World War.

38 MIDGHAM (BR) The village immediately behind the station is called **Woolhampton**. The *R:l* station itself was opened in December 1847 and was called Woolhampton until 1873, when the name was changed to Midgham, because — according to local legend — of numerous confusions between the small rural station and the rather larger industrial centre of Wolverhampton. The last straw came when horses dispatched by Queen Victoria to Wolverhampton arrived at Woolhampton.

Midgham Church Spire stands out on the *R:l* hillside to the north. It was built of flint in 1869, designed by John Johnson. On the hillside opposite, almost lost in the summer foliage, is another church of Johnson's, **St Peter's,** *L:r* **Brimpton** (1872).

39 THATCHAM (BR) Thatcham has been a busy residential and industrial town for centuries. As early as 6000 B.C. Maglemosean hunter-fishers occupied a Mesolithic settlement to the west of the station site and developed a flint-knapping industry. Later the reeds growing along the banks of the River Kennet were sent to basket-makers in London: brushes and brooms are still made in Thatcham. At the beginning of the nineteenth century, the **Colthrop Paper Mills** *R:l* east of the station were run by Foudrinier, who invented the machinery for making paper in a continuous roll. The mills are now owned by the Reed Paper Group. The **Royal Ordnance** *R:l* **Depot** is also east of the station.

40 NEWBURY RACECOURSE (BR) Trains stop

here only on the days of race meetings. With both flat racing and hurdling at Newbury, races are held all year round. The course — laid out by John Porter and opened in 1905 — is nearly two miles long with a straight mile-long stretch 105′ wide. During the Second World War the course was used as a depot for locomotives. American trains, in particular, would wait on the course before being shipped to Europe.

Greenham Common Airbase is on top of the hill. Embedded in it are the silos containing the USAF cruise missiles which began arriving in December 1983. On 12–13 December 1982 thousands of women demonstrators made a human chain around the base as part of a continuing campaign of protest at the threat to humanity posed by nuclear weapons.

41 **NEWBURY** (BR) The station at Newbury is imitative of the late Perpendicular style of the early sixteenth century with red-brick platform buildings and limestone caps or lintels over the windows and doors. The attractive stained glass in the buffet — brightening up BR refreshments — is Edwardian.

The most famous character associated with Newbury is undoubtedly 'Jack of Newbury', whose real name was John Smallwood. Marrying his employer's widow helped him to become the wealthiest clothier in Newbury in the sixteenth century — so wealthy that he sent his own company of archers to the Battle of Flodden in uniforms he designed and made in his factory. Smallwood paid for the nave of **St** *R:I* **Nicholas**, the parish church, and his initials can be seen on the roof. St Nicholas is to the north of the station, a striking monument to the wealth of the town in the late Middle Ages.

42 KINTBURY (BR, 1847) The village is to the south of the line. The church of **St Mary's** has *L:r* a thirteenth-century flint tower. East of the village is the site of a Roman building.

43 HUNGERFORD (BR, 1847) The red-brick station has an arcade of yellow-brick arches over the doors and windows and the brackets steadying the support beams of the platform canopy have 'ear of wheat' motifs.

Hungerford is famous for its trout and crayfish and has been associated with fish ever since the fourteenth century, when John of Gaunt gave the burgesses the right to fish in the River Kennet. He also rented the Church Croft to the town for the annual rent of his family emblem: a red rose. The young Queen Elizabeth II was presented with such a rose in 1952 by the Constable of the Manor. The **Town Hall** (1870 *L:r* by Ernest Prestwick) has a distinctive tower. The parish church of **St Lawrence**, below the *R:l* line, was built in 1816 of Bath stone, brought to the site down the canal; its designer, John Finch, was also from Bath.

Between Hungerford and Froxfield the line crosses from **Berkshire** (east) to **Wiltshire** (west).

44 FROXFIELD It is just possible to glimpse the *R:l* attractive red-brick **Somerset Hospital** at

Somserset Hospital

Froxfield between grassy cuttings. The hospital, with its white tower and ashlar gateway and chapel, was built by Sarah Duchess of Somerset

in 1694, and subsequently enlarged in 1775 and
1813 to provide accommodation for 20 clergy
and 30 lay widows.

45 **LITTLE BEDWYN** is a delightful Wiltshire
village. The flint church of **St Michael** is R:l
approached by brick estate housing dating from
1860. Across the railway line and the canal is
the eighteenth-century **Manor Farmhouse** of L:r
chequer brick, with its own octagonal game
larder and square summer house.

46 **BEDWYN** (BR) The village is called Great Bedwyn and was once of considerable importance,
with 25 burgesses recorded in Domesday. The
large church of **St Mary's** has attractive open- R:l
work battlements decorating the top of its late-
twelfth-century tower.

47 **CROFTON PUMPHOUSE** The Crofton R:l
Pumphouse, built at the highest point of the
Kennet and Avon Canal, 401′ above the source
of the Kennet, pumped water from nearby Wil-
ton Water to keep the canal 'topped up'. The
brick house, with its round chimney, has been
restored by the Kennet and Avon Canal Trust
and is open to the public: demonstrations are
given throughout the year. The older of the
beam engines inside the pumphouse was
supplied by Boulton and Watt in about 1812.

48 **SAVERNAKE FOREST** The Savernake R:l
Forest has been royal since the Norman Con-
quest. Thomas Lord Bruce, Earl of Ailesbury,
was Warden early in the eighteenth century and
his son Charles employed Capability Brown to

landscape the forest and to plant avenues of beech trees which still flourish on the chalky soil. The forest now covers 2000 acres and is leased to the Forestry Commission, which maintains the mix of broad-leaved and coniferous trees.

49 BRUCE TUNNEL The Kennet and Avon Canal passes under the railway line between Bedwyn and Pewsey through the Bruce Tunnel, which is 500 yards long. Travelling towards the west, the **eastern entrance** can be seen below *R:l* the line. Travelling towards the east, the **western entrance** can be seen to the north of *L:r* the line. The tunnel was designed by John Rennie. There is no towpath, but chains hanging from the walls enabled bargees to pull their vessels through. An inscription above the eastern entrance reads 'The Kennet and Avon Canal Company inscribe this Tunnel with the name "Bruce", in testimony of their gratitude for the uniform and effectual support of the Right Honourable Thomas Bruce, Earl of Ailesbury, and Charles Lord Bruce, his Son, through the whole progress of this great National Work, by which a direct communication by water, was opened between the cities of London and Bristol, A.D. 1810.'

50 WOOTTON RIVERS is another attractive *R:l* village in the Kennet Valley with several timber-framed thatched houses. The **Manor Farmhouse** is particularly fine, built of soft red brick with ancient beams and a thatched roof. The church of **St Andrew's** behind the farmhouse was virtually rebuilt by G. E. Street in 1861 and has a wooden bell-turret.

51 MARTINSELL HILL, on the north escarpment *R:l*
of the Vale of Pewsey, is one of the highest hills
(947') in Wiltshire. The remains of a 32-acre
Iron Age hillfort cover the top. At a fair held
annually on the hill every Palm Sunday until
1860, boys slid down the hillside using horses'
jawbones as toboggans.

52 PEWSEY STATION was opened in 1862,
along with the line from Hungerford to
Devizes, and designed to match the neighbouring houses. Skilled local workmen were
employed to give the station attractive
diamond-patterned brickwork and stone trims.

Above Pewsey is the **Pewsey White Horse**, *L:r*
cut in 1785. It was restored in 1937 by volun-
teers from the local fire brigade to mark the
coronation of George VI.

**53 THE VALE OF PEWSEY, THE MARL-
BOROUGH DOWNS AND SALISBURY
PLAIN** The Vale of Pewsey has been worked
by farmers for over 5000 years. But for many
thousands of years before that, the dark clay
soil was ill-drained and heavily wooded, so prehistoric man lived on the more open, easily de-
fensible chalk uplands. The surrounding hills —
the **Downs** to the north and **Salisbury Plain** to *R&L*
the south — are studded with earthworks and
hillforts. **Knap Hill** has a Neolithic camp dating *R:l*
from about 2700 B.C. and part of **Wansdyke**
or 'Woden's Dyke' runs along the top of the
Downs. This long bank, with a ditch along the

north side, is thought to have been erected as a
defence against peoples from the north,
possibly Saxons threatening the Romano-
Britains in the fifth century A.D. or Thames
Saxons threatening Wiltshire Saxons in the
sixth century. Smaller earthworks and tumuli
are scattered over the hills. The stone circles of
Avebury and **Stonehenge** are further to the
south and west. The **Milk Hill White Horse** *R:I*
was cut early in the nineteenth century on the
hillside overlooking the Vale and is 165′ long.

The **Marlborough Downs** and **Salisbury
Plain** are composed of extremely porous chalk
which has eroded over the millennia leaving a
thick debris, with harder flints on the surface. It
is of these that so many of the local churches
are made. Sheep graze on the springy turf but
dense woodland of beech and pine probably
covered the hills before the earliest settlers
arrived. The clumps of woodland to be seen on
the hilltops may be the remains of these ancient
woods. Kenneth Grahame found a night spent
on the Downs a timeless experience: 'on the
downs where Alfred fought we lay and smoked,
gazing up at the quiet stars that had shone on
many a Dane lying stark and still a thousand
years ago'.

54 EDINGTON The church of **St Mary, St** *L:r*
Katherine and All Saints at Edington is in a
fine setting at the foot of Salisbury Plain with
Edington Hill rising 666′ to the south. The
church, an early example of the Perpendicular
style, was consecrated in 1361, three years
after it was transferred to the Bonshommes,

priests who followed the Augustinian rule. William of Edington, Bishop of Winchester, was responsible for its erection.

55 WESTBURY WHITE HORSE The Westbury *L:r* White Horse was cut early in the eighteenth century and is 166′ long and 163′ high. It was restored in 1873 and then, in 1957, recut and lined with cement at a cost of £4000. To the left of the White Horse is **Bratton Castle**, a starkly impressive Iron Age hillfort which encloses a Bronze Age long barrow. Tradition claims that Guthrum retreated to Bratton after being defeated by King Alfred at the Battle of Ethandun in 878.

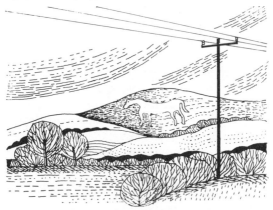

Westbury White Horse

56 WESTBURY (BR) Westbury Station was rebuilt in 1905 in preparation for the new direct line from Paddington to Exeter via Castle Cary. The fine iron brackets supporting the platform awnings date from 1899. Immediately east of the station is an early-twentieth-century signal

MAP 7

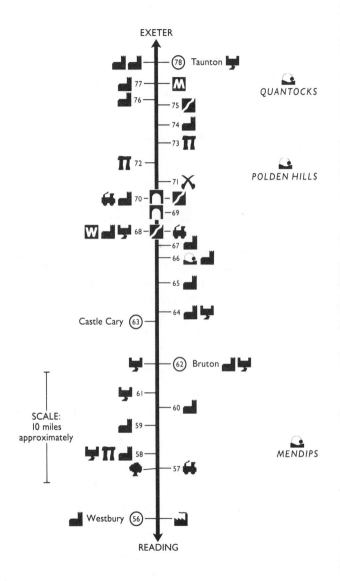

EXETER

(78) Taunton

77

76 75

74

73

72

71

70 69

68 67

66

65

64

Castle Cary (63)

(62) Bruton

61

60

59

58

57

Westbury (56)

READING

QUANTOCKS

POLDEN HILLS

MENDIPS

SCALE:
10 miles
approximately

box: the semaphore signals are still in use.

Westbury sprawls up the hillside to the south. *L:r*
All Saints Church, like Edington nearby, was
built at the period of the transition between
the Decorated and Perpendicular styles of
architecture. The tall chimney belongs to a
Blue Circle cement works.   *R:l*

57 **FROME** (BR) Fast trains bypass Frome Station
on a loop line which was opened in 1935 and
passes south of the town. The station is particularly interesting, however, as it has one of
the few remaining over-sheds so characteristic
of Brunel's stations. It was opened in 1850 as
part of the Wiltshire, Somerset and Weymouth
Railway, to which Brunel was nominally the
engineer. J. R. Hannaford designed the station,
engine shed and goods shed, using timber instead of iron for the columns as the company
was short of money.

The town (pronounced 'Froom') was
founded as a Christian missionary settlement in
the late seventh century. Its Christianity had
developed into Puritanism by the time of the
Civil War, when it took Cromwell's side.
Traditionally it has processed wool from the
Mendip sheep.

Between Frome and Bruton the railway line is
bordered on the east by a **line of hills** covered *L:r*
with extensive woodland, which means landmarks are easier to spot in the winter. To the
north-west are the limestone **Mendip Hills**, *R:l*
formed of marine sediment about 30 million
years ago. They are a steep-sided, flat-topped,

compact line of hills, rising to over 1000′. To the south they overlook the **Somerset Levels,** on which the train now travels towards Taunton. The wetness of the land − much of it below sea level − is its most apparent feature for most of the year. Up to 40 inches of rain fall annually, and the consequent heaviness of the soil makes it particularly suitable for cattle pasture − it is also one of the few remaining 'wetland' areas in Northern Europe.

58 **ST KATHERINE'S CHURCH, EAST** *L:r* **WOODLANDS** was originally built in 1712; John Loughborough Pearson rebuilt it in 1880, when he added a spire to the old tower. Immediately above the church on top of the hill is **Roddenbury Camp**, an Iron Age encampment 150 by 75 yards. Just out of sight on the far side of the hill is **Longleat**, a magnificent Elizabethan house, home of the Marquess of Bath, at the centre of an enormous park laid out by Capability Brown and Humphry Repton and now home to a pride of lions − the first of England's 'Safari Parks' to open in the 1960s.

59 **ST MICHAEL'S, GARE HILL** (1857 by *L:r* William Butterfield) has a thin bell-turret decorated with a tiny spire and is on the top of the same ridge of hills as St Katherine's.

60 **WITHAM FRIARY** Opposite Gare Hill on the *R:l* other side of the line is the church of **St Mary, St John the Baptist and All Saints**. It is all that remains of Witham Friary, the first Carthusian monastery in England. The church dates from the late twelfth century and was possibly

built by St Hugh of Lincoln, third prior of the monastery. Henry II founded the monastery in 1178–9 as a penance for the murder of Thomas à Becket.

61 **ALFRED'S TOWER** is a triangular brick *L:r* tower with three turrets, rising 150′ above Kingsettle Hill, and built by Henry Hoare in 1766 as a memorial to the victory of Alfred the Great over the Danes in 878 at Ethandun. Hoare was so impressed by what he read of Alfred's exploits in Voltaire's *Histoire Générale* that he paid for the tower to be built on the western edge of his family's property at Stourhead. The National Trust now owns both the tower and Stourhead, the exquisite Palladian villa designed by Colen Campbell for Henry's father, a wealthy banker.

62 **BRUTON** (BR) The fifteenth-century church *R:l* of **St Mary's** is immediately west of the station. It is built of Doulting Stone and has a tower $102\frac{1}{2}'$ high. It was originally part of the Augustinian Priory founded in Bruton in 1142 and made into an Abbey in 1511. Berkeley Square in London is named after the Berkeley family whose tombs are in the church: Bruton gave its name to Bruton Street, which adjoins Berkeley Square. West of the church is **King's** *R:l* **School**, founded by Edward VI in 1519. One of its famous pupils was the explorer Dampier, who was on board the ship that discovered Alexander Selkirk, Defoe's inspiration for Robinson Crusoe. Opposite the church and school on the other side of the line is the tower-like four-gabled **Abbey Dovecote**, now *L:r*

the property of the National Trust, and dating from the sixteenth century.

63 **CASTLE CARY** (BR, 1856) R. P. Brereton designed nearly all the stations between Frome and Maiden Newton. He used local stone from the quarries at Kineton and employed a simple rectangular design. The stations between Castle Cary and Taunton were all closed in 1962.

   Ansford is the village nearest the railway line. *L:r* Castle Cary itself is about two miles to the south. Charles II stayed at an inn there in 1651, when making his way secretly to France. Though disguised as a servant he was recognised – fortunately by a Royalist.

64 **ALL SAINTS CHURCH, ALFORD** (Per- *R:l* pendicular) can be seen in the trees. **Alford House** is a late Georgian house remodelled in a mock-Elizabethan style by F. C. Penrose in 1877: the porches have slated pyramid roofs.

65 **ST MARY'S CHURCH, EAST LYDFORD** *R:l* (1866 by Benjamin Ferrey) can be distinguished by its spire, immediately north of the line.

66 Much further away to the north is **GLASTON-** *R:l* **BURY TOR**, 500′ high and topped by the remains of the thirteenth-century chapel of **St Michael**. Nearby is where, according to one version of the Glastonbury 'legend', Joseph of Arimathea buried the Holy Grail. He thrust his thorn staff into the ground, from which grew the winter-flowering Glastonbury Thorn. When looking towards the horizon and the Tor it is

easy to miss the point at which the line passes over the Roman Road, the **Fosse Way**, now the A37.

67 **KEINTON MANDEVILLE** was the birthplace *R:l* of John Henry Brodribb, who changed his name to Henry Irving and became the most famous of Victorian actors. Between the village and the railway line is the Early English church of **St Mary Magdalene** (tower c. 1800).

68 **SOMERTON Somerton Erleigh** is the name *L:r* of the large ashlar-faced eighteenth-century house south of the line and visible just before the line curves southwards, crossing the **River Cary** and entering the village of Somerton. The medieval church of **St Michael** is of dark grey stone and *L:r* has a particularly fine roof with wooden tie-beams decorated with foliage. The red-brick remains of **Somerton Station** can be seen on *R:l* the west side of the line.

South of Somerton are the radio masts of **Blacks Moor Hill Wireless Station**. The *L:r* 187'-high masts were erected in 1927 and are now used by British Telecom as the main long-range receiving station for marine telephony.

69 **SOMERTON TUNNEL** is 1056 yards long.

70 **LANGPORT** was an important settlement *L:r* from Roman times until early in the nineteenth century. It grew up around a ford across the River Parrett: the remains of two Roman villas have been found at the crossing. The River Parrett provided a navigable waterway con-

necting Langport with the Bristol Channel; by the early nineteenth century Langport was a port for over 30 ships. The church of **All Saints** is late Norman.

The **Langport Viaduct** over the Parrett was built for the 1906 opening of the direct line from Paddington to Exeter. The red-brick re- mains of **Langport Station** can be seen beside *L:r* the line.

71 **SEDGEMOOR** The hills to the north and *R&L* south of the line turn away and the train crosses the flat marshy plain of Sedgemoor. The straight ditches draining the moor are called 'rhines'. The 'withies' or willows growing along their banks and in fields close to the rail- way line are used for making wicker-ware.

This bleak open land was the **site of the** *R:l* **bloody Battle of Sedgemoor** in 1685 between the armies of the Duke of Monmouth and James II. Monmouth tried to attack the King's army under cover of darkness – in the last battle on English soil against a reigning monarch – but the alarm was given and after Monmouth had fled the field, his loyal troops were massacred. 22 were hanged on the battle field and, of the 500 prisoners taken, most were executed after being tried in the 'Bloody Assizes' by the notorious Hanging Judge Jeffreys.

72 **BURTON PYNSENT** The Tuscan column on *L:r* the hillside to the south was built by Capability Brown in 1765 in memory of Sir William Pyn- sent. Pynsent left his Elizabethan mansion

Athelney Obelisk

nearby to William Pitt in 1765; Pitt retired to the house after rebuilding it. Now only Pitt's part of the house remains.

73 **ATHELNEY** As the line crosses over the **River** R:1
Tone, Athelney appears to the north, easily distinguished by the **obelisk** erected on the small hill in 1801. Now Athelney is turned into an island only in times of flood but in 877–8 it provided a safe refuge for King Alfred and his nobles, as they fled from the Danes. Alfred was able to rally the men of Somerset, Wiltshire and Hampshire and in the spring of 878 they defeated the Danish King, Guthrum, and his army at Ethandun near Chippenham. In 1693 'Alfred's Jewel' was found in the marshy ground near Athelney. Now in the Ashmolean Museum in Oxford, the jewel is inscribed with the words 'Alfred had me made.'

74 LYNG Immediately to the west of Athelney is *R:l*
the church of **St Bartholomew's, Lyng** which
was once the chapel of the monastery Alfred
founded in thanksgiving for his time of rest and
safety at Athelney. The Perpendicular tower is
built of local blue lias and Ham Hill stone.

75 THE BRIDGWATER AND TAUNTON *R:l*
CANAL flows parallel to the railway line between the junction with the line to Bridgwater
and Taunton, where it joins the River Tone
(Taunton means Tone Town). The canal, which
was prone to silting and needed frequent
dredging, can be distinguished by the hedges on
either side, occasional solitary fishermen on its
banks and the bridges crossing over the water.

76 CREECH ST MICHAEL'S CHURCH has a *L:r*
thirteenth-century tower.

77 RUISHTON CHURCH, immediately to the *L:r*
west, has a sixteenth-century tower which is
only 66′ high. The money left for its construction between 1530 and 1535 ran out and
the tower has stood, stunted, ever since.

The railway line passes under the **M5**, heading
to Exeter in the south and Bristol and Birmingham in the north, past the Creech Castle Hotel,
a wood yard and a car dump, through light
industrial development over the canal and into
Taunton Station.

78 TAUNTON is the county town of Somerset
with a population of about 40,000. Standing on
the River Tone, between the Quantocks to the

north and the scarp of the Blackdown Hills to the south, it seems a gateway to the south-western peninsula of England. It is a prosperous market town, serving the rich farmland around, and with one of the largest cattle markets in the West Country. It is a thriving industrial centre too, with light engineering and paper- and shirt-making. The most successful of the shirt manufacturers in the nineteenth century was the Dutch American Van Heusen.

Since King Ina of the West Saxons built its first castle over 1000 years ago, Taunton has been a stronghold in successive conflicts. Perkin Warbeck held it for a short time, before being driven out by Henry VIII; the Parliamentarians took it as a garrison, and their enthusiastic Protestant successors welcomed Monmouth and his rebellion against the Catholic James II.

Taunton Station was officially opened on 1 July 1842 when it was reached by the Bristol and Exeter Railway. Brunel's original station was one-sided. A more conventional station was built in 1868 with an overall roof but this was removed with further rebuilding in the 1930s. Taunton was once served by local trains from seven different routes but now most of the traffic is InterCity. All the stations between Taunton and Exeter except Tiverton were closed in 1964.

Two tall church towers can be seen from the train. The tallest belongs to **St Mary Magda-** *L:r* **lene** and is over 160' high. It was rebuilt from the ground in 1862 by Benjamin Ferrey and George Gilbert Scott in the late medieval style

MAP 8

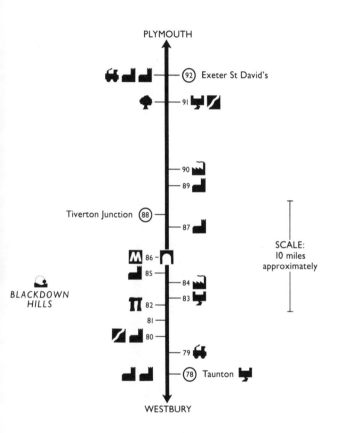

PLYMOUTH

(92) Exeter St David's

91

90
89

Tiverton Junction (88)

87

86

85
84
83
82
81
80
79

(78) Taunton

WESTBURY

BLACKDOWN HILLS

SCALE:
10 miles
approximately

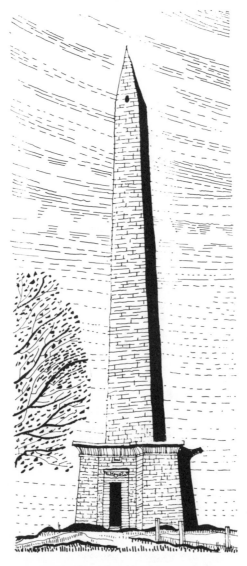

Wellington Monument

and dominates the town. The shorter tower is 120′ high and belongs to **St James's**, rebuilt 1870–5.

Taunton School, immediately west of the station, was founded in 1847 as the 'West of England and Dissenters' Proprietary School'. The main building is in the Gothic style and was built by Joseph James of London in 1867–70. *R:l*

79 **NORTON FITZWARREN** was once a larger settlement than Taunton, as the ancient rhyme testifies: 'when Taunton was a furzy down, Norton was a market town.' An Iron Age fort some 150 yards across covered the hill above the church and was used later by the Romans. The privately-run West Somerset Railway leaves from Norton Fitzwarren to Minehead on the coast to the north. *R:l*

80 **BRADFORD ON TONE** The River Tone flows close to the railway line: Bradford is the broad ford over it. **St Giles**, the village church, has a tenor bell which has been ringing from its embattled, Virginia-creeper-covered tower since 1520. *L:r*

81, **WELLINGTON** Isolated and unadorned, the
82 **Wellington Monument** is visible long before the town of Wellington comes into view. Arthur Wellesley chose Wellington for the seat of his dukedom in 1814, although his original family seat lies to the east at Wells, on the edge of the Mendips. The honoured townspeople elected to build the obelisk in 1815, 900′ up on one of the highest points of the Blackdown *L:r*

Hills. In 1817 the foundation stone was laid, but only in 1892, 50 years after the Duke's death, was it completed. 239 steps take one 175′ to the top. Its sister monument in Dublin, where the Duke was born, is 30′ taller.

83 **TONEDALE** Immediately west of the remains *R:l* of the old station of Wellington is an unusual group of nineteenth-century factory housing built round a square and called 'Five Houses'.

84 **ROCKWELL GREEN** In the course of the *R:l* First World War the woollen mill at Rockwell Green was given the biggest order ever for khaki material — over 850 miles of it.

85 **HOLY CROSS CHURCH, SAMPFORD** *L:r* **ARUNDEL** has an unusual carving on the wall of two carved hands holding a heart. The River Sand is a tributary of the Tone, through the vale of which the railway line now runs.

86 **WHITEBALL TUNNEL** is 1092 yards long and marks the boundary of **Somerset** and **Devon**. In the days of steam, 'hard snorting' would be heard as the powerful engine 'pounded its way up the rise', a gradient of 1 in 128. The building of the thickly brick-lined tunnel caused great disruption in the area: 14 shafts were sunk and filled in by 1000 navvies employed on the job.

The **M5** motorway is close to the railway line *L:r* from just west of the tunnel to a few miles east of Exeter.

Geologically the county of Devon is quite different from Wiltshire and Somerset. It is an upland block of primary rock that completely escaped glaciation. The topsoil has consequently remained on its river-dissected plateau, to the great advantage of its agriculture. The sparse rural population lives in hamlets and isolated farms. The little fields that nip at the edges of the moorland are now very largely cattle pasture, a feature which was determined only 150 years ago by the railways. Until then the isolation of Devon made the population dependent on its own locally-produced grain. But the railways were able to bring grain into the county and the Devon fields were given over to the beef and dairy production more suited to the heavy rainfall and steep-sided hills.

The railways also opened up enormous urban markets for the new agriculture. The Devon Red, almost the same colour as the Devonian Red sandstone, is the local beef animal. The Friesian makes up most of the dairy herd. Agriculture and tourism alike are favoured by the sunny summers and mild winters. Tourism is Devon's biggest industry – also initially made possible by the railways. It is hard to believe now that this picturesque county was the world's major source of copper and arsenic in the latter half of the nineteenth century.

87 **SAMPFORD PEVERELL ST MARY'S** *R:1* **CHURCH** (consecrated 1318) has an aisle added in 1498 by Lady Margaret Beaufort, who owned the manor and was the mother of Henry VII.

88 **TIVERTON JUNCTION** (BR; opened 1844)
The village of Tiverton is about five miles away
to the north-west; the Culm Valley Railway extends about ten miles in the opposite direction.
The Esso Oil Depot and large timber yard
reveal the industrial activity at the rural halt.
The elegant signalbox was built in the 1930s.
Willand is the village immediately to the south- *L:r*
east.

89 **CULLOMPTON** is an old market town astride
the once-busy A38. Now, however, with the
opening of the M5, the town has resumed a
more peaceful way of life beside the River
Culm. The church of **St Andrew**, with its *R:l*
100'-high tower, was built in 1545–9 out of the
local red sandstone. One of its aisles is known
as the Lane Aisle after John Lane, a wool merchant, who endowed it. The once-famous
horse-racing track at Cullompton is now
closed.

90 **HELE MILLS** The sidings and signal box are all *R:l*
that remain of the station 'Hele and Bradninch'
but the **Devon Valley Mills** are still in production. The Hele Paper Mills began the tradition
at the turn of the century of sending a bunch of
primroses to each of their customers in Britain
every spring.

91 **RIVER CULM AND RIVER EXE** The railway
line has been following the course of the River
Culm from Tiverton Junction. The Culm joins
the River Exe about three miles north-east of
Exeter. **Stoke Woods** cover the hillside to the *L:r*
south. The fine red-brick seventeenth-century

house on the opposite hillside is called **Pynes**.   *R:l*

92 **EXETER** was called Isca Dumnoniorum by the Romans and grew up at the west end of the Icknield Way. It remained one of the chief markets for south-west woollens until the seventeenth century. The trade declined thereafter and even the arrival of the railway in 1844 did little at first to stimulate new industry. But Measom's Railway Guide of 1861 noted an air of 'independence and gentility'. Today the appeal of a quiet cathedral city attracts undergraduates to the modern university (1956). The resident population is about 100,000.

Exeter Cathedral

Exeter Cathedral Exeter and Salisbury are the   *L:r*
exceptions to the rule that English cathedrals are an assortment of architectural styles. Exeter was the work of only three generations between 1275 and 1360: the work was begun by Bishop Branscombe. George Gilbert Scott carried out restoration work between 1870 and 1877. The spire to the east belongs to **St**   *L:r*
Michael's Church.

MAP 9

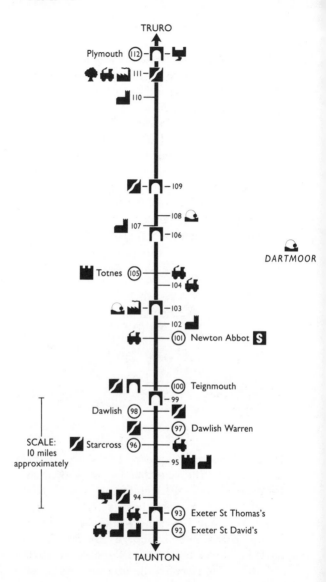

TRURO

Plymouth (112)

111

110

109

108

107

106

DARTMOOR

Totnes (105)

104

103

102

(101) Newton Abbot **S**

(100) Teignmouth

99

Dawlish (98)

(97) Dawlish Warren

Starcross (96)

95

SCALE:
10 miles
approximately

94

(93) Exeter St Thomas's

(92) Exeter St David's

TAUNTON

Exeter St David's Station, lying alongside the great igneous rock where the Norman castle was built, is the most important of the four stations at Exeter and has been rebuilt several times. **St David's** and **St Thomas's** belonged to the GWR; **Central** and **St James's Park** to the LSWR. Exeter was first reached by the Bristol and Exeter Railway (B&ER) on 1 May 1844, but nothing of Brunel's one-sided station now remains. A new station was designed for the B&ER by Henry Lloyd of Bristol and Francis Fox, the railway's engineer. The station was given an attractive façade of local stone with recessed Italianate arches, a disc frieze and 26 massive stone urns along the top of the wall. The urns have gone and the façade is obscured by modern offices, but the frieze can be seen from outside the station. Fox's station was rebuilt by the GWR in 1910–12 and his train shed removed. The towers carrying the footbridge at the eastern end of the station are part of this rebuilding. Passengers changing trains or alighting at Exeter might appreciate the impressively gloomy Edwardian waiting rooms, refreshment facilities and cloakrooms, with dark wooden panelling, sombre brown paint and period tiles.

93 **EXETER ST THOMAS** (BR) is one of the saddest and most neglected stations still in use. The station was designed by Brunel in 1846 with one of his overall roofs and a two-storey Italianate station building. The roof was removed in 1970 and now the station is only a halt with the windows of the elegant 'villa' boarded up or altered to form shops; the

ground floor is used as offices.

There are fine views of the city and cathedral from the viaduct which carries the line above the houses and sprawling industrial development to the west of Exeter.

94 **THE EXETER SHIP CANAL** flows between *L:r* the railway line and the River Exe, and was one of the first modern canals to be built in Britain: opened in 1566, it can still be used by ships of up to 400 tons. The low, white, modern **Marine Barracks** can be seen on the far side *L:r* of the estuary.

Powderham Castle

95 **POWDERHAM CASTLE** has been the home *R:l* of the Courtenay family – the Earl and Countess of Devon – since the fourteenth century and is now open to the public. The rich park-

land around the castle was created in the eighteenth century, when the marshes bordering the River Exe were drained. The herd of red deer can sometimes be seen among the trees. The small red sandstone church of **St** *R:l* **Clements** on the edge of the park and close to the line contains the Coat of Arms of Sir William Courtenay, who died in 1485. The oldest parts of the castle date from the fourteenth century but much was altered and added in the eighteenth and nineteenth centuries. Charles Fowler designed the entrance courtyard and the banqueting hall in 1840 in what was then the fashionable Gothic style.

96 STARCROSS (BR) The **red sandstone** *R:l* **building** at the south end of the platform with the inscription 'The Brunel Atmospheric Railway' is almost all that remains of Brunel's innovative railway system (see p.12). The building was one of the pumping stations and has Bath stone dressings, a red pantiled roof and a campanile-like chimney which gives it a distinctly Italianate appearance.

There is a fine view across the estuary of the **Exe** from Starcross. Sailing boats, fishing boats, wading birds and seagulls help to create the holiday atmosphere of this part of the country. The many small hotels and holiday houses at Starcross reveal the main source of income for local residents in the summer season. Starcross was named after a cross which once stood near the first landing-place for the town on the bank of the estuary.

97 DAWLISH WARREN (BR) The approach to Dawlish Warren from the north is across the flat marshy ground of the Warren. A special protective barrier of massive granite blocks protects the line from the sea. The station was opened in 1905 to accommodate the Edwardian enthusiasm for seaside resorts.

Between Dawlish Warren and Teignmouth there are magnificent views along the coast to east and west. This is one of the most exhilarating sections of any railway line in the country. The train passes along the base of red sandstone cliffs with the sea pounding against the wall immediately to the south. The wall itself, which carries the track, is all that separates the train from the sea. It stretches from the Exe to the Teign estuaries and the parapet is curved in order to deflect the waves.

98 DAWLISH has been an attractive and popular seaside town since early in the nineteenth century. The long stretch of lawn on either side of **Dawlish Water** (the stream which flows *R:l* through the town and into the sea) was laid out in 1803. Before fashionable society 'gentrified' Dawlish, it was the favourite haunt of Devon smugglers, who used the caves in the cliffs and the Warren to hide their contraband and evade capture.

Dawlish Station was opened on 30 May 1846. It has had a tempestuous history on this exposed site, but remains one of the best cared for of Brunel's stations. As recently as 1974 most of the 'down' platform was washed away after a fierce storm. The signal box had to be moved from its correct position on the down platform to the up because of the ravages of the sea. The working of the box is consequently contrary to normal practice on the Western Region, with the levers at the back instead of the front. A wall of limestone and red sandstone at the end of the station car park is all that remains of the pumping station for Brunel's atmospheric railway (see p. 26).

99 **FIVE TUNNELS** Between Dawlish and Teignmouth there are five tunnels through the red sandstone cliffs: **Kennaway**, **Phillot**, **Clerk's**, **Coryton**, **Parson's**. The prospect of the coastline and sea in between are breathtaking. Close to Parson's Tunnel, and cut off from the land by the crashing breakers, is the spindly, ever-diminishing **Clerk Rock**. In 1905 all the tunnels *L:r*

Clerk Rock

had to be widened to accommodate double tracks. The excavations were carried out without interrupting the train service, but the workmen suffered badly from the hot sulphur fumes: there were no ventilation shafts in the tunnels.

100 **TEIGNMOUTH** (BR) (pronounced 'Tinmouth'). Little can be seen of the town − a fashionable watering hole at the beginning of the nineteenth century − as the station is approached from east and west through deep cuttings. The **harbour** is protected by a long *L:r* spit which stretches across the mouth of the **River Teign**. The long **road bridge** across the *L:r* Teign connects Teignmouth with Shaldon on the west bank.

101 **NEWTON ABBOT** (BR), situated at the western end of the picturesque Teign estuary, is the centre of a productive farming area. However, the town's past importance as the locomotive headquarters of the south-west (since Brunel set up his atmospheric railway here) has given it a predominantly industrial character: with its sidings, warehouses and sheds it is a small, Devonian version of Crewe. The station was rebuilt in the 1930s with an imposing frontage to reflect its importance − an importance which ceased when the headquarters were removed to Plymouth. The publishers David and Charles, who specialise in railway books, occupy the **modern offices** *L:r* immediately next to the station. The train passes by the **racecourse**.   *R:l*

102 **ST AUGUSTINE'S PRIORY** The turrets and *R:l*

grey slate roof of St Augustine's Priory, Abbotskerswell, are visible in the trees covering the hillside west of the line. The Canonesses Regular of the Lateran arrived at Newton Abbot after a turbulent history. Originally from Buckinghamshire, they moved to France after the Dissolution of the Monasteries and then back to England with the French Revolution. Their priory was built in 1871: J. A. Hansom was the architect.

Abbotskerswell village is a little further away *R:l* from the line. The name of the village came from its patron, the Abbot of Sherborne, 'kers' (an old name for watercress) and the well in the village which was reputed to cure eye infections.

103 **DAINTON TUNNEL** The train climbs steadily from Newton Abbot to Dainton Tunnel; the incline immediately up to the tunnel is 1 in 37. East of the tunnel is **Stonecombe** *L:r* **Quarry**, where the red and pink stone of Dainton Hill is extracted. West of the tunnel the train enters lush countryside, the fields edged with hedges, but in the distance lie the impressive bleak hills of **Dartmoor** – outcrops *R:l* of its granite appear close to the line, in dark contrast with the pastel sandstone.

104 **DART VALLEY LIGHT RAILWAY** This *R:l* branch line from Totnes to Buckfastleigh was first opened in 1872 and flourished partly because of the woollen mills in the Buckfastleigh area. It was closed to passengers in 1958 and to freight in 1962 but reopened in 1969 by

the Dart Valley Railway Company. Now steam trains carry passengers from the new platform some distance to the east of Totnes main line station up the Dart Valley to the Abbey of Buckfastleigh on Dartmoor. The museum in the goods shed at Buckfastleigh houses 'Tiny', the only surviving locomotive built in 1868 for Brunel's broad-gauge railway (see p. 24), which remained in service until 1883.

105 TOTNES (BR) The remains of the pumping station for Brunel's atmospheric railway (see p. 26) have been incorporated into the **Unigate Creamery**, whose tall chimney is *R:l* visible immediately behind the station. The town grew up as a port, because of its strategic position at the highest navigable point of the Dart and the lowest fording point.

Totnes Castle can be seen in a group of trees *L:r* on a hill just west of the station. The walls of the keep are all that survives of the motte and bailey fort. The ditches around the bailey are now covered with gardens. The circular sandstone wall of the shell keep dates from the early fourteenth century.

It was at Totnes that Thomas Savery, in 1698, obtained a 21-year patent for one of the earliest examples of a piston working a cylinder. He leased the manufacturing rights to Thomas Newcomen, who produced the first steam pumping engines used in the tin mines of Cornwall.

106 THE MARLEY HEAD TUNNEL was built to

hide the railway from the view of a local land-owner, Sir Walter Carew, who lived at Haccombe — now Syon Abbey. When the line was doubled a new bore was cut, but no attempt was made to match the eastern portals: one is of stone, the other of red brick.

107 **ST PETROCK'S, SOUTH BRENT** is Nor- *L:r* man and a foretaste of the final phase of the journey. St Petrock is a Cornish saint who came back to life in his coffin. Brent Station was closed in 1964 and a further five stations between Brent and Plymouth were closed in 1959.

108 **BRENT HILL** rises to over 1000′ to the north *R:l* of the line and is a foothill of the 365 sq. miles of moorland which comprise **Dartmoor**, which rises to 2039′. In fact a granite 'batholith' underlies the whole south-west peninsula of England: an immense escape of molten rock deep in the earth.

109 **IVYBRIDGE VIADUCT** The viaducts are a feature of the GWR in the West Country — though difficult to appreciate from inside the train. It is possible to see the original stone piers of the **viaduct** at Ivybridge beside the line *R:l* as the train crosses over the valley of the **River Erme**. **Ivybridge** sprawls south of the line. *L:r* Stowford Mill in Ivybridge makes security papers for stamps, cheques and passports for governments all over the world.

After Ivybridge the train crosses the valley of

the **River Yealm** over the **Blatchford Viaduct** and the valley of the **River Piall** over the **Slade Viaduct**.

110 **PLYMPTON** was more important than its neighbour Plymouth in the early Middle Ages, possessing both a castle and a priory. The priory was founded early in the twelfth century by Bishop Warelwast for Augustinian canons. The castle was also built early in the twelfth century by Richard de Redvers, Earl of Devon: part of the walls remain. **St Mary's Church** L:r (fourteenth and fifteenth centuries) has a granite ashlar tower with big polygonal pinnacles. The old grammar school of Plympton records Sir Joshua Reynolds as its most famous pupil. Plympton is now part of Plymouth, their boundaries blurred by extensive industrial and residential development.

111 **SALTRAM** The train crosses over the **River** L:r **Plym** with its copious grey-white mud, passes the **Blue Circle Cement Factory**, and continues to L:r the north of the **British Rail Laira Depot**, the L:r main servicing depot in the West Country. On the other side of the estuary are the grounds of **Saltram**. The house, now owned by the National L:r Trust, was built by John and Lady Catherine Parker in the 1740s. The interiors were designed by Robert Adam and Reynolds was a frequent visitor.

112 **PLYMOUTH** and the neighbouring districts have been associated with the navy since 1287 when 325 ships assembled in the harbour. In 1588 the captains of the English navy waited on

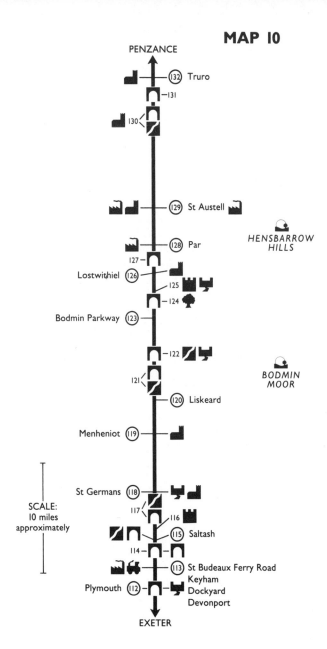

MAP 10

PENZANCE

132 Truro
—131
130

129 St Austell

128 Par
127—
Lostwithiel 126
125
—124
Bodmin Parkway 123

—122
121
120 Liskeard

Menheniot 119

St Germans 118
117
116
115 Saltash
114—
113 St Budeaux Ferry Road
Keyham
Plymouth 112 Dockyard
Devonport

EXETER

HENSBARROW HILLS

BODMIN MOOR

SCALE:
10 miles
approximately

Plymouth Hoe for the arrival of the Spanish Armada. (Drake, incidentally, knew he was losing nothing by finishing his game of bowls, as the port can be sailed from only with an ebb tide.) In 1608 the Puritans of the *Mayflower* sailed from Plymouth to North America. Connections with the army began when Charles II decided to build a citadel in the town which, during the Civil War, had been staunchly Parliamentarian.

Plymouth is a resort town with a population approaching a quarter of a million. It is the regional capital of the south-west, more centrally placed than Exeter, with a deep-water harbour, and Saltash Bridge and ferry services. A great naval base, commanding the western end of the English Channel, it has never developed as a mercantile port because of its remoteness from any centres of population and the lack of industrialisation of its hinterland.

Plymouth Station was opened as 'North Road' in 1877 and renamed Plymouth in 1958 after the closure of 'Plymouth Friary'. It is one of the dreariest of stations on the GWR, revealing some of the dullest aspects of twentieth-century design. The unprepossessing offices which dominate the platforms are occupied by British Rail.

Little impression of the town can be gained approaching from the east as the station is reached through a cutting and the short **Mutley Tunnel**. The **Royal Eye Infirmary** is the Vic- *R:l* torian building just east of the station.

**113 PLYMOUTH STATION TO THE SALT-
ASH BRIDGE** Immediately west of Plymouth
Station a **'buried bridge'** can be seen, marking *L:r*
the disused track of a branch line to the docks.
The train continues through a cutting and under
bridges passing **Devonport Station** (BR, 1859)
and **Dockyard Station** (BR, 1905). The train
then emerges above the houses, with views of
the town, docks and even Saltash Bridge in the
distance, and continues through **Keyham
Station** (BR, 1900), with a small marshalling
yard still in use, then over a viaduct and through
St Budeaux Ferry Road Station (BR, 1904).

The principal building to be seen from this section of the line — and again from the other side
of the Tamar Estuary — is the **Royal Naval** *L:r*
Dockyard of Devonport. The Dockyard was
founded by William II on Bunkers Hill in 1691
and steadily extended to include the site on
Keyham. It now covers some 3200 acres,
dominating the left bank of the Hamoaze for $2\frac{1}{2}$
miles. The Royal William Victualling Yard was
designed by Sir John Rennie (1826–35); the
Royal Naval Hospital was begun in 1762 and
the Royal Marine Barracks in 1784. Plymouth is
an amphibious town, bound on three sides by
water. With navies having assembled here since
the thirteenth century, military depots have
built up for troop embarkation. The city's
modern character reflects the damage inflicted
by German bombs in the Second World War.

114 ROYAL ALBERT BRIDGE, SALTASH
Crossing over the **River Tamar** on the Royal
Albert Bridge is one of the highlights of train

Royal Albert Bridge, Saltash

journeys in Britain. The bridge has never been widened: even modern high-speed trains slow down. Both approaches offer magnificent views of the bridge and surrounding scenery. Warships and submarines look like frail toys resting in the water 100′ below. Even the more recent suspension **roadbridge**, completed in 1951, *R:1* does not mar the impact of Brunel's masterpiece.

Work was delayed on the bridge from 1848 to its completion in 1859 because of the poverty of the Cornwall Railway Company. The two main spans, each 455′ long and weighing over 1600 tons, are supported by three piers, 100′ above the water. The spans consist of oval tubes arched to an extent equal to the fall of the suspension chains. The spans were constructed on the bank and floated into place on pontoons, then raised by hydraulic jacks. Brunel himself directed the raising of the first span on 1 September 1857, signalling from a platform high in the centre of the truss. An eye-witness recorded the event: 'as by some mysterious agency, the tube and rail, borne on the pontoons, travelled to their resting place, and with such quietude as marked the beginning of Solomon's temple. With the impressive silence which is the highest evidence of power, it *slid*, as it were, into its position without an accident, without any extraordinary mechanical effort, without a "misfit", to the eighth of an inch.' The floating of the second span was superintended by Brunel's assistant R. P. Brereton in July 1858 and the bridge was opened by Prince Albert in May the following year. Brunel was too sick to attend the opening – he had only four months to live. His name, however, appears on the Egyptian style approach to the bridge at the **Devon** (eastern) end: the western end is in **Cornwall**.

115 **SALTASH** (BR 1858) As the train follows the curve of the coast southwards through Saltash Station there are good views of the **bridge**, the *L:r* **Tamar Estuary** and **Plymouth**. The small fishing village below has been overpowered by the mighty bridge and viaduct, dominating its narrow streets.

Cornwall's projection into the temperate Atlantic gives it the most maritime climate in mainland Britain. The ocean's surface temperature continues to rise after midsummer, thus prolonging a tourist season now vital to the county's economy. The many fishing villages set on coastal inlets are now principally resorts, their small, irregularly-built houses offering a sleepy, antique charm.

Broadly speaking, Cornwall consists of four granite moorlands surrounded by a cliff coastline – the Scilly Isles, had the level of the sea not risen at the end of the last ice age, would be a fifth. From east to west the train passes most of them: Bodmin Moor, St Austell highland, Carnmenellis near St Ives, and then the St Just uplands north of Land's End.

116 **TREMATON CASTLE** is one of the largest *R:l* castles in Cornwall and has belonged to the Duchy of Cornwall since the fourteenth century. The main surviving structures are the high walls of the inner bailey and gatehouse and the shell keep on the mount. The castellated **pink-washed house** with Georgian windows below the mount was built in 1807 for the Surveyor General to the Duchy. One of its governors was Sir Richard Grenville, immortalised in Tennyson's poem: 'At Flores in the Azores Sir Richard Grenville lay/And a pinnace, like a fluttered bird, came flying from far away.'

117 **THE SHILLINGHAM** or **WIVELSCOMBE TUNNEL** is 450 yards long and was dug early in the twentieth century as part of improvements to the line. Emerging at the western end the train crosses the **River Lynher**, broad and meandering, and the **River Tiddy**, its small boats lying beached at low tide.

118 **ST GERMANS** (BR) The **village**, below the *R:l* line, is where the missionary St Germanus landed in 430. The **parish church** was consecrated in 1261 as part of the Priory of the Augustinian

Canons in St Germans. Before that, however, the village was a cathedral city, the seat of the Bishop of Cornwall. Even today there is a suffragan bishop of St Germans. Close to the line is a row of six seventeenth-century **alms-houses** divided in an imaginative way. The six gables project forward and are supported on tall stone piers. The space created gives the ground-floor flats a loggia and the upper floors a balcony reached by outer stone steps.

119 **MENHENIOT** (BR) The village of Menheniot is about a mile away to the north with the spire of **St Lalluwy** just visible. One of the rectors *R:l* was William of Wykeham, the founder of Winchester College. The station is in the Italianate style with round-headed windows, massive chimneys and projecting eaves. The buildings were leased to a private tenant but they were severely burnt in 1982 and still await rebuilding.

120 **LISKEARD** (BR) is a market town whose greatest prosperity was when the copper mines to the north were in full production. There are two parts to the station: through platforms on the main line to Penzance and the terminus building for the branch line to Looe in the south, carrying passengers to Looe and slates to Liskeard.

121 **LISKEARD VIADUCT** The seven-arched viaduct is just west of the station and carries the line over the **River Looe**. The ivy-covered **Gothic piers** which supported Brunel's original *L:r* timber trestles can be seen to the south.

122 **VALLEY OF RIVER FOWEY** (pronounced 'Foy') The train enters the thickly wooded valley of the Fowey and is carried across the intersecting valleys on viaducts. Prolific rhododendron bushes grow alongside the railway line and parkland surrounds **Glynn House**, the *R:l* handsome grey stone Georgian house on the opposite hillside, built in 1805 for Lord Vivian, one of Wellington's generals. The **St Pinnoc Viaduct** in the Fowey Valley is the highest of Brunel's viaducts — 151′. It was altered in 1882 by heightening the original stone piers and laying a steel girder frame across them.

123 **BODMIN PARKWAY** (BR) The station has recently been renamed, in line with British Rail's policy of establishing 'parkway' stations: out of town and accessible to the car driver. What was once the goods-yard is now a car park.

124 **BROWNQUEEN TUNNEL** is approached through tree-lined cuttings. Much of the surrounding countryside is owned by the National Trust, including the house and park of **Lanhyd-** *R:l* **rock**, immediately west of the line and north of the tunnel — the model for Endelstow House in Hardy's novel *A Pair of Blue Eyes*. The formal gardens and wooded parkland of the estate extend almost to the railway line and were laid out by George Gilbert Scott in 1857. The mansion itself — not visible from the train — was built by a wealthy Truro merchant in the seventeenth century.

125 **RESTORMEL CASTLE AND HOUSE** All *R:l* that remains of Restormel Castle is the massive

black granite circular wall of the shell keep, built c. 1200, on a natural hill above the Fowey. The ruined living quarters inside the wall were added by Edward Earl of Cornwall in 1280. Even in Cromwell's time the castle was in a dilapidated state: 'time and tirranie hath wrought desolation and the castle beginneth to mourne and wring out hard stories for tears.' Below the castle is Restormel House, a pretty battlemented house, built in the 1760s in the Gothic Revival style.

126 **LOSTWITHIEL** (BR) was the capital of Cornwall in the thirteenth century and belonged to Richard of Cornwall along with Restormel. Economically it was an important stannary town, a centre for the assaying of tin. **St Bartholomew's Church** has a thirteenth-century *R:l* tower with a spire added a century later. Lostwithiel means 'Lost-within-the-hill'.

127 **TREVERRIN TUNNEL**

128 **PAR** (BR) A palm tree flourishes on the down platform of Par Station: a first indication of the temperate climate of the Cornish peninsula.

The china clay industry dominates Par – an industrialised village permanently covered in the fine white dust from the **'English China Clays** *L:r* **Group' Works** which surround the harbour. China clay was first discovered in the Chinese mountain Kao Lin, hence its alternative name kaolin: the deposits in Cornwall and near Plymouth are among the largest in the world. William Cookworthy was the first to discover china clay in England in the Wheal Grey Tin Mine near Helston in 1746. He then found richer deposits on the moors near St Austell. China clay was first used for porcelain and pottery but is now used in talcum powder, as an alkaline in digestive biscuits, and as an additive in the manufacture of paper.

129 **ST AUSTELL** (BR) There are more palm trees at St Austell growing on the platform as well as an ornate lattice footbridge handsomely painted in black, cream and white with the initials 'GWR 1882'. The town is below the line and the tower of **Holy Trinity Church**, faced *L:r* with yellow Pentewan stone, was built in 1478–87.

China clay dominates the scenery. St Austell is the centre of the industry (Par the port) and the 'Cornish Alps' – white mounds of quartz – rise above the town. Powerful hoses break down the clay rock into liquid form. The quartz is trapped and sent by miniature trucks to the top of the pyramids. Mica and clay continue together until the stream slackens and the mica (another component of granite) sinks first as it is heavier. The clay is then collected, filtered and dried. The white pyramids are in their turn quarried for use in the building industry, for the construction of houses and roads: some of the modern local houses are built of a synthetic granite-like stone made from this.

St Austell to Truro The journey between St Austell and Truro gives a vivid impression of the length and the small population of Corn-

Probus Church (see overleaf)

wall. There are few villages to be seen from the train; only isolated farmhouses, cottages and barns. Dead elm trees add to the bleak atmosphere. The smoothness of the railway line is also apparent. With the aid of viaducts and embankments, cuttings and tunnels, the line seems to pass over the undulating countryside on a cushion of air.

The first of many disused tin-mine chimneys can be seen on this stretch. The steam engines which brought the railway to Cornwall also revolutionised the mining industry, replacing men in the crushing of the lode-bearing granite. Like the igneous granite, the tin is the product of the liquefaction of the rock in volcanic activity. Cornish tin-mining is now very expensive, and the falling world price of the metal threatens to close down all Cornish mines.

130 **PROBUS CHURCH** The sixteenth-century *L:r* granite tower of St Probus and St Grace stands out a mile to the south. It is 123′ high, the tallest in Cornwall, and is in three stages. In 1851 two skulls were found beneath the altar of the church and are believed to belong to two saints. In the churchyard is a monument to Sir Christopher Hawkins who lived at Trewithian nearby and, in 1827, used the first portable agricultural steam-engine. The **Tresillian River** is then crossed, to the west, over the **Tresagne Viaduct**.

131 **POLPERRO TUNNEL AND BUCKSHEAD TUNNEL** The Polperro Tunnel is 581 yards long.

132 **TRURO** (BR) The station is approached from the east on a viaduct 443 yards long, which offers an impressive panorama of the **city** and *L:r* **cathedral**. Truro is Cornwall's only city — its county town is Bodmin.

Truro Cathedral may look medieval but it was designed by John Loughborough Pearson

MAP II

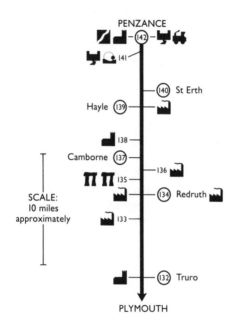

PENZANCE

142

141

140 St Erth

Hayle 139

138

Camborne 137

136

135

134 Redruth

133

SCALE:
10 miles
approximately

132 Truro

PLYMOUTH

and built between 1880 and 1910: the style is Early English except for the Normandy Gothic spires. Pearson's son completed the 250-ft towers after the death of his father. Truro appears with the pseudonym of Polchester in several Hugh Walpole novels set in Cornwall. Close to the cathedral is the old grammar school where Humphry Davy, the inventor of the miner's safety-lamp, was educated.

133 **CHACEWATER** Between Chacewater and *L:r* the line are the remains of the calciners and flues of the **Wheal Busy Mine Site**. These were used in the arsenic industry, a by-product of tin-mining, which was important to the economy of Cornwall from 1870 onwards. The calciners, or roasting ovens, burnt off the arsenical impurities in tin ore, which were then collected in long zig-zag 'lambreth' flues, refined and ground. Few precautions were taken and the land around the calciners was made infertile by the arsenic-bearing fumes — it is still infertile to this day. James Watt lived here, while supervising the first steam-pumping engine used in a Cornish mine.

134 **REDRUTH** (BR) is at the centre of Cornwall's tin-mining region: the tall stone **chimneys** of the *R&L* disused engine houses can be seen either side of the line. The Tolgus Mine just outside Redruth is a working museum and still produces tin with the machinery and methods of the early nineteenth century. Redruth, together with its neighbour Camborne, has a population of about 35,000 and is dependent now on light engineering and brewing.

135 CARN BREA Part is still visible of the great *L:r*
Iron Age hillfort of Carn Brea, 750′ above sea
level and covering about 36 acres. There is
evidence that Neolithic man lived here, also the
Romans and, more recently, the men of the
Middle Ages, who built a cliff-castle and chapel
on the site. Nearby is the 90′ monument to
Lord de Dunstanville, built in honour of the *L:r*
Cornish mine- and land-owner in 1836.

136 TUCKINGMILL The safety-fuse factory at *R:l*
Tuckingmill was developed after William Bick-
ford invented a safety-fuse in 1831.

137 CAMBORNE (BR) The station is approached
along a cutting with heather-covered sloping
sides. The Dolcoath Tin Mine at Camborne is
one of the biggest in the world. The School of
Metalliferous Mining is still world renowned.
William Brunton was living in Camborne when
his patent steam engine blew up during a
demonstration and killed 13 spectators.

138 GWINEAR The fifteenth-century granite
tower of **St Winierus** is to the south of the *L:r*
line in the village of Gwinear. Lanyon Farm
nearby was the home of William Lanyon until
he joined Captain Cook on his voyage round
the world.

139 HAYLE (BR) The station may be insignificant
but Hayle has been at the centre of Cornish industrial history for centuries, with its busy harbour, railway terminus, iron foundries, engine
works and copper and tin smelting works. It is
the only commercial port on the north Cornish

coast and ships bring in coal, sulphur and oil for local factories and depots.

The Copperhouse Foundry, to the east of Hayle at the head of the eastern of two inlets which make Hayle Harbour, made the original tension chains for Brunel's Clifton Suspension Bridge at Bristol, which were finally used on the Saltash Bridge. In 1834 the first steam railway in Cornwall was built at Copperhouse. It carried ore from the mines of Hayle to be smelted at Redruth. Copperhouse Foundry closed down in the 1870s but its rival, the **Hayle Foundry** of Harvey & Co., still survives as an importer of timber and fuel, builders' merchant and owner of Hayle Harbour. In the nineteenth century Hayle Foundry was known throughout the world for its pumping machinery. In the 1840s the foundry manufactured giant pumping engines for the Dutch government to drain Haarlem Meer. The viaduct which carries the railway across the estuary crosses the site of Hayle Foundry. *R:l*

It is possible to see **St Ives** across the estuary and just along the coast to the west. *R:l*

140 **ST ERTH** (BR) Leaving St Erth, the train cuts south-west across the peninsula towards Penzance: a few minutes' journey.

141 **ST MICHAEL'S MOUNT AND MARA-ZION** St Michael's Mount and the nearby harbour of Marazion appear immediately ahead and then to the south of the line. The remains of the disused stone station for Marazion can *L:r*

St Michael's Mount

still be seen beside the line. The Mount, rising 220′ out of the sea, can be reached by a causeway from Marazion at low tide.

St Michael's Mount has belonged to the St Aubyn family for over 300 years. The family bought the island in 1659 and the present appearance of the buildings is mostly the responsibility of Piers St Aubyn, an architect and cousin of the owner, who restored the property in the second half of the nineteenth century. The history of this granite rock is much older than the St Aubyn connection, however. As early as 495 A.D., fishermen had a vision of St Michael appearing on the summit; Milton referred to this in his elegy *Lycidas:* 'Where the great Vision of the guarded mount/ Looks towards Namancos and Bayona's hold.' Edward the Confessor granted the island to the monks of the Norman monastery Mont St Michel. It was a place of pilgrimage in the Middle Ages. Pilgrims were particularly attracted to the jaw-bone of St Apollonia of Alexandria, who refused to follow the local religion and whose teeth were pulled out before she was burnt – not surprisingly she became the patroness of toothache! Henry VI gave the monastery on the island to the Brigittine Nuns of Syon, near London: the medieval refectory is still intact. The National Trust now owns the property, which is open to the public.

142 **PENZANCE** There is a view of Penzance as *R&L* the train approaches the station. As a port it still does a little international trade, but the town is chiefly devoted to tourism. In the eighteenth century, when it was an important tin-assaying town, Daniel Defoe described it as being 'so rich in ore that veins of lead, tin and copper may be seen at low-water mark'. The

Penzance Harbour

granite tower of **St Mary's Church** dominates *R&L*
the town (1832–5, Charles Hutchins). In the
centre of the town the dome of the **Market** *R&L*
House (1836, W. Harris of Bristol) stands out
clearly: it is now a branch of Lloyds Bank. The
Scillonian **ferry** is sometimes visible from the *L:r*
train, waiting to begin its regular three-hour
journey further west to the Scilly Isles.

Penzance Station, opened to standard-gauge
trains on 11 March 1852 and broad-gauge trains
on 1 March 1867, was built by the West Cornwall Railway and has a rather bleak, unadorned
granite-sided train shed built c. 1865 and
covered with a shallow crescent-shaped iron
roof. Longer platforms extend eastwards
beyond the shed to accommodate the extra-
long holiday trains and the thousands of passengers who have made the journey from
London, the Midlands and even Scotland seeking the balmy summer climate of the Cornish
Riviera.

KING'S CROSS
TO THE NORTH

Contents

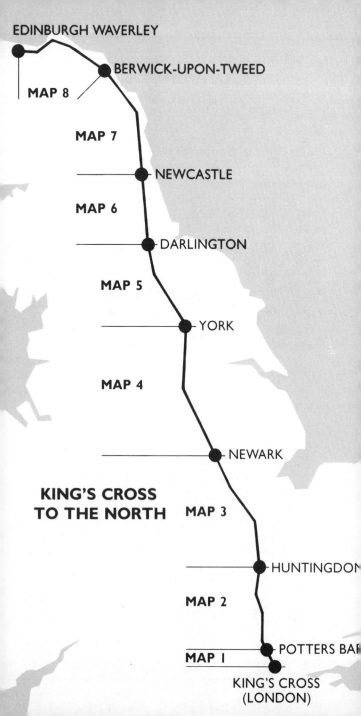

EDINBURGH WAVERLEY

BERWICK-UPON-TWEED

MAP 8

MAP 7

NEWCASTLE

MAP 6

DARLINGTON

MAP 5

YORK

MAP 4

NEWARK

**KING'S CROSS
TO THE NORTH**

MAP 3

HUNTINGDON

MAP 2

POTTERS BAR

MAP 1

KING'S CROSS
(LONDON)

Introduction

The line between King's Cross and Edinburgh has a much more complex history than those lines built by one engineer – the Great Western Railway of Brunel, for example, or the London and Southampton Railway of Joseph Locke. Parts were constructed by different railway companies, engineers, contractors and architects. Only in 1923 did the line become the responsibility of one company, the London and North Eastern Railway (LNER).

The first part of the line to be constructed was in the middle, at York, where one man, George Hudson, was busy making a fortune out of the railway mania. Hudson was the son of a Yorkshire farmer who quickly became a prosperous linen draper in York and, after inheriting £30,000 from a great uncle at the age of 27, invested his wealth and energy in the railways. He made friends with George Stephenson, became chairman of the York and North Midland Railway and set about building a network of lines around York and throughout the Midlands. In 1844 he became chairman of the first major amalgamation of railway companies, the Midland Railway. He was hailed as the 'railway king' and 'railway Napoleon' (see also p. 210).

Hudson's position was challenged by the setting up of a 'committee of direction' in May 1844 in York to consider a direct line between York and London. Hudson desperately fought the scheme using the Midland Railway's good relationship with the London and Birmingham Railway to offer his own rival route through the Midlands to the north. On 18 June 1844 the first train made the trip from London to Gateshead. It travelled on the London and Birmingham Railway from Euston to Rugby, on the Midland Railway from Rugby to York, on the York and Newcastle Railway from York to Newcastle. The journey of 303 miles was covered in 9 hours 32 minutes, including stops of 70 minutes.

The part of the line between York and Newcastle was originally the idea of Joseph Pease (the first Quaker MP and son of Edward Pease of the Stockton and Darlington Railway). Pease planned to connect Tyneside with Hudson's proposed York and North Midland Railway. The first sod of his Great North of England Railway was cut near Croft-on-Tees on 25 November 1837 and the line opened to Darlington in 1841. The Newcastle and Darlington Junction Railway was opened on 19 June 1844 and combined with the Great North of England Railway to form the York and Newcastle Railway.

The York 'committee of direction' proceeded with its own scheme. After 82 days in the House of Commons, some 20 days in the Lords, and at a cost of £590,355, the London and York Bill finally received Royal Assent on 26 June 1846. At the first meeting of the directors of the newly-named Great Northern Railway, on 1 July 1846, William Cubitt was confirmed as consulting engineer; John Miller was the engineer for the northern part of the line, Joseph Cubitt (William's son) the engineer for the south.

The first part of the GNR to be completed was between Maiden Lane (the temporary London terminus) and Peterborough. On 5 August 1850 a party of directors and their guests travelled along the line, leaving Maiden Lane at 9 a.m. and arriving at Peterborough at 1.30 p.m.

A reporter from the *Illustrated London News* described the journey: on emerging from Copenhagen Tunnel the train 'went skimming along a region of cornfields. This sudden transition from the busy haunts of life to quiet rural scenery, undisturbed even by the presence of a villa, is what chiefly strikes one.' A special stop was made at Southgate to view the recently opened 'large and handsome' lunatic asylum. Another stop was made at Welwyn and passengers were able to descend to the Mimram Valley to experience the full glory of Cubitt's Welwyn Viaduct.

The route to York at first involved a loop through Lincoln. The first train to use the new line travelled the 210 miles on 8 August 1850. Hudson, in the face of the railway slump at the end of the 1840s, had been forced to allow the GNR direct entry to York. The Lincoln loop was avoided when the stretch between Peterborough and Retford was opened on 1 August 1852. The GNR had met opposition on part of this last stretch from Lord Lindsey. In exchange for the use of part of his lands, he demanded not only a large sum of money but that trains were to stop at Tallington (his local station, just north of Peterborough) whenever he wished. The GNR had to agree and at one period were forced to stop an express train almost every day. The directors of the company finally rebelled in 1883 after a servant catching the Scotch Express at King's Cross demanded that it should make the unscheduled stop. Lord Lindsey was paid £1,000 to have the right extinguished.

Between Newcastle and Edinburgh, little has changed since the opening of the line, except the closure and demolition of many local stations. The Newcastle and Berwick Railway opened on 1 July 1847, though the bridges over the Tyne and the Tweed, both by Robert Stephenson, were not opened until 28 September 1849 and 29 August 1850. The North British Railway between Edinburgh and Berwick was initiated by a group of Edinburgh businessmen in January 1842. They were eager to reach England but also to open up the rich agricultural land of Haddington and East Lothian. Waverley Station in Edinburgh was opened on 12 June 1846, Berwick Station on 22 June.

Queen Victoria seems never to have missed an opportunity of experiencing the new inventions and advances of her reign. She made her first ever trip by train on the Great Western Railway between Slough and Paddington. The GNR offered a convenient alternative to the long coach journey to Balmoral and she made her first train journey north on 27 August 1851. A special train left Maiden Lane for Doncaster where Her Majesty spent the night at the Angel Hotel. The journey continued to Stonehaven where the Queen transferred to a coach. The special royal saloon was fitted out with silk linings and upholstery which cost over £800 – to the horror of the GNR – although the prestige was no doubt reward in itself. 'The floor [of the coach was] covered with a dark maroon carpet showing a scarlet figure of the House of Lords pattern, thus keeping before Her Majesty, even in a railway carriage, the highest House which represents the legislature of Her Kingdom.' A royal journey in 1855 ended in tragedy for one of the GNR employees. Greaser William Haigh, while on the footboard keeping the axle lubricated, was knocked off his perch by the girder of a bridge. The Queen awarded his widow a life pension of £30 per annum and the directors of the GNR gave each of his three children 2s a week. Charles Dickens was treated almost as well as the Queen by the GNR when travelling on the line in the late 1860s. He was already very sick – he died in 1870 – and was given one of the royal saloons.

The line to Scotland became the responsibility of the LNER from 1 January 1923 and it was then that the name 'Flying Scotsman' was officially given to the daily express train to Edinburgh. When the first expresses to Scotland began, in 1862, the journey to Edinburgh took $10\frac{1}{2}$ hours. The time taken now is 4 hours 35 minutes.

The trains now plying the 393-mile route between King's Cross and Edinburgh are known as the InterCity 125s. The first 125s to operate passenger services between London and Scotland were delivered in September 1977 and by May 1979 the fleet was complete on the East Coast Main Line.

The 125s now operate on numerous routes from London, cutting journey times from the capital to major cities in Yorkshire, Humberside, Cleveland, the North-East and Scotland. There are also some 125s on major cross-country routes. Their reduced weight and aerodynamic streamlining enables them to run over long distances at sustained speeds of up to 125 mph. Many of the trains cover journeys exceeding 1100 miles in a day.

Though the extra speed of today's travel does not favour attention to detail along the route, it does promote a large view, and the King's Cross to Edinburgh journey is of large landscapes and broad horizons. If the design of a church is hard to catch, the traveller is more than compensated by being presented, in speedy succession, with contrasting phases of the landscape of eastern Britain. The train crosses ten counties in England and three in Scotland. Out of London the train first crosses the suburbs; then into the commuter belt with its new towns, dormitory villages and golf courses; then into the Bedfordshire countryside beyond; on into black soil, market-gardening and brick-making; over the great clay plains of the Trent and Ouse and miles upon miles of sugar beet and power stations; past the great ecclesiastical centres of York and Durham; through the industry on the Tyne; into the hard grudging land of Northumberland; and along the clean abrupt coast-line of the North Sea towards Edinburgh.

MAP 1

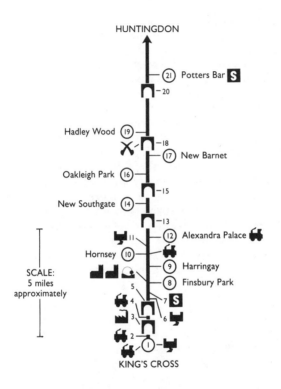

1 **KING'S CROSS STATION** Margaret Schlegel, the heroine of E. M. Forster's novel *Howards End* (1910) catches a train at King's Cross: 'to Margaret... the station of King's Cross had always suggested Infinity. Its very situation — withdrawn a little behind the facile splendours of St. Pancras — implied a comment on the materialism of life. Those two great arches, colourless, indifferent, shouldering between them an unlovely clock, were fit portals for some eternal adventure, whose issue might be prosperous, but would certainly not be expressed in the ordinary language of prosperity.' King's Cross may not suggest Infinity to every traveller, but it is still one of the more impressive of the London termini. It manages to keep much of the simplicity and elegance originally created by its architect, Lewis Cubitt, in 1852. It is quite small — there are only 8 mainline and 2 suburban platforms and it covers 16 acres — but once the traveller has arrived at the station the 'great, indifferent arches' still offer the prospect of 'some eternal adventure'.

The station and its neighbour, the Great

King's Cross Station

Northern Hotel, have recently been cleaned and modernised and their spotless yellow bricks gleam in the filth and air of decay which characterises this part of the Euston Road. The two great train sheds — originally one for arrivals and one for departures — loom up behind the brick frontage. The space in front was first used by a vendor of garden furniture who displayed rustic seats, arches and summer houses.

Cubitt completed the station in 1852. John Jay was the builder and it was opened on 14 October. The cost was £123,500 but the Great Northern Railway had to spend £65,000 buying and then demolishing the fever hospitals which occupied the site. The two sheds are 800 feet long, 105 feet wide and the glazed arched roofs rise to 71 feet. The arched ribs were originally timber — the finest examples at the time of laminated timber arches — but they have been replaced with iron. The roofs are now painted cream, the brick arches down the central platform are yellow and beige. The legend is now discounted which suggests that the design for the train shed roof was borrowed from the riding school in Moscow. Below there were originally only two platforms (1 and 8), separated by 14 tracks interconnected by turntables. When the station opened, two platforms were sufficient for the number of passengers. Bar, bistros and offices are situated along the west side of the platforms. With surprisingly subdued signs and tasteful use of the original arches and pillars BR has managed to retain many of the Victorian features: the offices of the station in 1852 were situated on this western side above waiting rooms, refreshment rooms and the booking and parcels office.

The clock between the arches of the train sheds is a useful feature of the station for passengers, although it invariably offers a different time from its rival on (the former) St Pancras Hotel. The clock was first exhibited at the Great Exhibition of 1851. E. B. Denison, son of the chairman of the GNR, was so impressed that he insisted the company should buy it for King's Cross. It was made by Frederick Dent of the Strand and cost the company £200. This included its installation in the tower and the fitting of three new 9-foot-long dials.

The Great Northern Hotel was also designed by Cubitt and built by Jay. Its opening was delayed until 17 May 1854 because of strikes by the bricklayers and plasterers. It cost £35,000 and J. Dethier of Brussels became the first tenant. He also managed the refreshment rooms in the station and remained in charge for the next 22 years. The hotel is built of yellow brick like the station and is in a quiet Italianate style. There could not be more of a contrast between the hotel and station and the extravagance of George Gilbert Scott's frontage to St Pancras Station immediately next door.

2 **ST PANCRAS TRAIN SHED** On passing *L:r* out from under the King's Cross train sheds there is a fine view of W. H. Barlow's even more spectacular shed at St Pancras. The glass and iron roof has a span of 243 feet and, when opened, was the widest in the world. It is 100 feet high, 689 feet long and covers nearly 17,000 sq.feet.

3 **MAIDEN LANE TUNNEL** (also known as Gasworks Tunnel) is 527 yards long and carries the train under the Regents Canal and York Way. Just before disappearing into its sooty depths, there is a view to the west of some of

the most elegant **gasholders** in London. They *L:r*
have recently been painted glossy black and red
and on close examination reveal delicate floral
decorations – picked out in white – on many of
the girders. They were constructed in about
1865 by the Imperial Gas Light and Coke Company, which provided gas to light King's Cross
Station.

4 **YORK WAY** Before the first train left King's *L:r*
Cross Station at 7 a.m. on 14 October 1852
passenger and goods traffic was handled at
Maiden Lane Station. After 1852, goods traffic
continued to be handled at the enormous
depot west of York Way, which contained
warehouses, granaries, sheep and cattle pens,
and premises for stabling and shoeing horses.
The GNR was one of the largest owners of
horses in the country (by 1867 they owned
879). Their animals were renowned for their
quality and health – there was an infirmary in
the goods yard for the sick.

5 **THE COPENHAGEN TUNNEL** has magnificent castellated entrances but they are hard to
make out through the black grime. The tunnel
passes under Copenhagen Fields in Islington. In
1855 the City Corporation moved their cattle
market from Smithfield to a new site on
Copenhagen Fields. The GNR had already built
a cattle siding just north of the Caledonian
Road Bridge and proceeded to construct a
private road from the siding to the cattle market. All that is left of the market buildings (designed by Bunning) is the extraordinary Italianate tower in the centre: the public houses at
each angle of the market square were also part
of the original design.

6 HIGHBURY FIELDS SCHOOL, BENWELL *R:l*
STREET The elegant cupolas on top of this
perfectly ordinary local school show just how
much care the Victorians took with their public
architecture.

7 ARSENAL FOOTBALL STADIUM The *R:l*
cannon of the Arsenal 'Gunners' – formerly at
Woolwich Arsenal – can be seen on the side of
the pink-washed stadium. Herbert Chapman,
manager of Arsenal in 1926, was responsible for
making football a fashionable sport to be enjoyed by all classes of the population. Arsenal
was the first southern club to win the Football
League Championship in 1930–1; it went on to
win the championship three years running. It is
the only club to have been in the first division
of the Football League since its inception. The
west stand (nearest to the railway) was opened
in 1932 by the Prince of Wales.

8 FINSBURY PARK (BR) There is a view of
Highgate Hill south of the station. The dome *L:r*
belongs to the **Roman Catholic church**, the
spire to **St Michael's** where Coleridge was
buried after spending the last 18 years of his life
in Highgate. Finsbury Park Station was first
opened on 1 July 1861 as Seven Sisters Road. It
was known as 'Pneumonia Junction' by suburban passengers because of its original draughty
wooden platforms built high on the embankment. The tea gardens in nearby Hornsey
Wood were an attraction and when the wood
was renamed Finsbury Park in 1869 after
becoming a public park, the station's name was
changed as well. The park is 120 acres, formerly
covered by a much more extensive Hornsey
Wood. Leaving the station to the north, one
passes from what was formerly the **County of**

London into **Middlesex**.

9 **HARRINGAY** (BR) Home of Harringay Greyhound Race Track, mecca of London's dog-fanciers.

10 **HORNSEY** (BR) When the line was being built, the local inhabitants of Hornsey petitioned against the construction of a station, but to no avail. In the 1850s Hornsey was a village four miles from London: 'the village is pleasantly situated amidst much picturesque scenery, the neighbourhood being enlivened with the villa residences of the merchant princes of London'. By the 1870s, however, extensive development had begun in Hornsey and Wood Green with terraces of yellow stock brick houses being built with slate roofs.

On the eastern side of the main line, opposite Hornsey station, is British Rail's **Hornsey** *R:l* **Maintenance Depot**. Opened in 1976, its main functions are to control power supplies, maintain electric traction equipment and service and clean the electric multiple-unit trains which operate suburban electrified services radiating from King's Cross and Moorgate to Royston, via Welwyn Garden City and Hertford North.

11 **ALEXANDRA PALACE** The charred ribcage *L:r* on the brow of Muswell Hill was once a People's Palace, an idea first proposed in 1860. Harrison Rhodes and other proprietors of the late Thomas Rhodes's Tottenham Wood Estate offered part of the estate for pleasure grounds and the erection of a palace. The grounds, laid out with a racecourse, were used for the World's Fair in 1864. In 1873 the palace was opened, but within a month it suffered the

Alexandra Palace

same fate as the Crystal Palace it was intended
to rival, and burned down. It was reopened two
years later (designed by J. Johnson) and has
since been used as government offices and, in
1936, as the first television centre of the BBC.
It is now a sad ruin after being re-engulfed by
fire in 1980. Redevelopment is under way, however: park and palace will continue to be used
by the public.

12 **ALEXANDRA PALACE** (BR: Victorian ticket *R:1*
office in yellow and red brick) was opened on
1 May 1859 as Wood Green Station. It was
built at the suggestion of Harrison Rhodes's
property company which recognised the value
of a local station for their development of the
Tottenham Wood Estate. The Rhodes's Estate
provided the land and contributed £4,000
towards the costs.

To the north east of Alexander Palace station,
situated in the 'elbow' of bank between the
main line and the branch line to Hertford
North, is British Rail's **Bounds Green Main-** *R:1*
tenance and Servicing Depot. Here BR's
modern fleet of main line passenger trains,
principally InterCity 125 high-speed trains, are
serviced and kept spick and span.

13 **WOOD GREEN TUNNEL** under Muswell
Hill is 705 yards long. It was originally called
Tottenham Tunnel.

14 **NEW SOUTHGATE** (BR) was originally
called Colney Hatch and Southgate and was
specially built to serve the new (c. 1850) lunatic
asylum nearby. The asylum authorities manufactured their own gas and supplied the station
with gas and water for many years. The asylum
was also one of the earliest GNR coal customers. Now New Southgate is in the centre of
anonymous industrial and urban sprawl with a
rubbish dump, gasholders and a builder's yard
south of the station.

15 **BARNET TUNNEL** is 605 yards long: it was
originally called the East Barnet Tunnel.

16 **OAKLEIGH PARK** (BR)

17 **NEW BARNET** (BR) was first extensively developed in the Edwardian period. Wealthy businessmen built villas on the surrounding high ground, enjoying the expansive views but also the speedy travel by train to the city. Less prestigious suburban development followed. On the high land to the north is Hadley, while on the rising ground to the south are the superior villas of Lyonsdown. To the east is Cockfosters; westward High Barnet and Totteridge.

18 **HADLEY SOUTH TUNNEL** was originally called South Enfield and is 384 yards long. Just to the west, is the **site of the Battle of Barnet** *L:r* where Edward IV defeated the army of Henry VI. Warwick 'the king-maker', who had assisted in restoring Henry VI to the throne, was killed.

19 **HADLEY WOOD** (BR) Immediately before entering the tunnel, the line passes from **Middlesex** in the south to **Hertfordshire** in the north.

20 **HADLEY WOOD TUNNEL** under Long Hill is 232 yards long and was originally called North Enfield Tunnel. **Potters Bar Tunnel**, originally called South Mimms Tunnel, is 1,214 yards long. There is a total of nine tunnels between King's Cross and Knebworth.

21 **POTTERS BAR** (BR: originally Potters Bar and South Mimms; rebuilt 1955) was called after an ancient bar on Enfield Chase, once a great hunting forest. It developed into a suburb of London between the wars and by 1939 the GNR was running 12 trains daily which terminated at the then expanding settlement. The car park is filled by daily commuters; the **golf** *R:l* **course** just to the north provides their week-

MAP 2

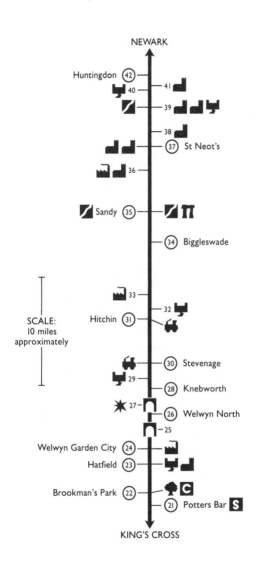

NEWARK

Huntingdon (42)

41

40

39

38

(37) St Neot's

36

Sandy (35)

(34) Biggleswade

33

32

Hitchin (31)

(30) Stevenage

29

(28) Knebworth

27

(26) Welwyn North

25

Welwyn Garden City (24)

Hatfield (23)

Brookman's Park (22)

(21) Potters Bar

KING'S CROSS

SCALE:
10 miles
approximately

end recreation. A new **industrial estate** to the *L:r*
west threatens the surviving green fields.

22 **BROOKMAN'S PARK** (BR) About a mile *R:l*
from the line are five of the BBC's earliest wireless masts. The park, running parallel with the
railway and the Great North Road, belongs to
Hatfield House.

23 **HATFIELD** (BR) **Hatfield House** was one of *R:l*
the most important Jacobean houses in England
and now must be one of the most well known
of the great ancestral houses open to the
public. It is situated on top of the hill above the
village of Hatfield. Most of the house is visible
in winter – just the clock tower in the summer
– above the tower of the parish church. Hatfield House was built by Robert Cecil, 1st Earl
of Salisbury, who was persuaded by James I to
exchange his home at Theobalds, which the
King coveted, for the old Bishop's Palace at
Hatfield. Cecil had the new house built in the
form of an 'E' to commemorate the fact that
the Princess Elizabeth was staying in the palace
when news was brought of her accession to the
throne. The oak still survives under which she
was sitting reading at the time.

When the railway arrived at Hatfield a special
approach was made from the station to the
house for the 3rd Marquis, Robert Gascoyne
Cecil, who was Prime Minister three times, and
the many celebrities who visited Hatfield by
train. They included Dickens, Gladstone, Lewis
Carroll, Edward VII, Balfour, Joseph Chamberlain
and Kitchener.

The parish church of **St Etheldreda** has a *R:l*
fifteenth-century tower built in four stages. The
Salisbury Chapel inside has a monument to the

Robert Cecil who built Hatfield. He died in 1612; below his effigy is a skeleton lying on a rough straw mat.

24 **WELWYN GARDEN CITY** (BR), the home of Shredded Wheat, was begun by a private company in 1919 and was taken over by the state in 1948. The garden city was designed by Louis de Soissons and A. W. Kenyon, inspired by the efforts of Sir Ebenezer Howard, who wrote *Tomorrow: A Peaceful Path to Real Reform* in 1898. Howard founded the Garden City Association in 1899: Letchworth, begun in 1903, and Hampstead Garden Suburb, begun in 1906, were the first 'garden cities' following his ideals. Welwyn extends on both sides of the railway: factories, offices and new housing surround the line. Some industrial development was planned as part of the original township: the striking green and white **Nabisco Shredded** *R:1* **Wheat factory**, designed by de Soissons in 1925, is an example. Expansion has been far

Nabisco Factory

beyond the dreams of the original planners, however. In 1921, Welwyn had a population of 950; today it is more than 40,000. Luton and Dunstable lie to the west; Hertford to the east.

25 **DIGSWELL OR WELWYN VIADUCT** This magnificent viaduct is all too easy to miss from the train as the wide valley below is crossed at high speed. Lewis Cubitt designed the viaduct using the same dramatic effects he achieved at King's Cross. Forty solid brick arches stride across the valley reaching 89 feet at their maximum height.

26 **WELWYN NORTH** (BR)

27 **WELWYN SOUTH TUNNEL** is 446 yards long and was originally called Locksley Hill Tunnel and also Digswell Tunnel. **Welwyn North Tunnel** is 1,046 yards long and was originally called Harmer Green. An accident occurred in this tunnel on the night of 9–10 June 1866. A train of empty coal wagons stopped in the tunnel with a burst boiler tube. It was first hit by a Midland goods train and then by a meat express train. All three were destroyed by fire – the smell of roast beef drifted for miles around. Two men were killed.

28 **KNEBWORTH** (BR) is the only settlement along this stretch of the GNR not to share in the dramatic expansion of population experienced by its neighbours – Hitchin, Stevenage, Welwyn and Hatfield – since the Second World War. A rambling old vine has been preserved in the new subway of the station: commuters can share the fruit harvest.

29 **KNEBWORTH HOUSE** The Victorian *L:r*
Gothic pinnacles and towers which decorate
the top of Knebworth House are just visible
about a mile from the line across a golf course
and amongst trees. The house is the home of
the Lytton family and was begun by Sir Robert
Lytton at the end of the fifteenth century.
Dickens was a friend of the writer Edward Bul-
wer Lytton and often visited Knebworth. In
1850 Dickens produced and acted in three
charity productions of Jonson's *Every Man in his
Humour* in the banqueting hall. The architect
Edwin Lutyens was the son-in-law of the 1st
Earl of Lytton, the Viceroy of India. He carried
out building work in the house, gardens and
villages, besides designing New Delhi for the
Viceroy. The grounds of the house were used
for rock festivals in the early 1970s.

30 **STEVENAGE** (BR) Just before entering
Stevenage the train passes over the remains of
troughs which were filled with water which the
steam engines would scoop up, spectacularly, at
speed, to replenish tanks almost exhausted
from the long haul out of London. These
troughs are the first of several on the line and
were over a third of a mile long. **Stevenage**
lies at the north-eastern end of the Chiltern
plateau. In 1921 its population was 5,038. However, after the Second World War it became
the site for the first development under the
1946 New Towns Act. The town expanded
dramatically and by 1971 had a population of
67,016. Industrial estates surround the station
which was built in 1973 to replace the old
station (now demolished) a mile to the north.
The station has an overhead passageway leading
to the town centre, which made an early
attempt to segregate people and cars.

31 **HITCHIN** (BR) From the train the impression
of Hitchin is of a large shapeless town reflecting
its considerable residential and industrial expansion since the Second World War. The market
town and centre for rose-culture has been in-
vaded by aero-engineering. The line officially
leaves suburbia at this point: the electrical overhead lines which power the suburban trains
from King's Cross go no further north.

But work has now started on a £306 million
scheme to electrify the East Coast Main Line
northwards from here to Edinburgh. Bridges
are being demolished or raised to provide
higher overhead clearances for the electric
wires and a start has been made on erecting the
masts which will carry the wires. The first
electric trains will reach Huntingdon and Peterborough in May 1987 and the line will be electrified all the way to Edinburgh by 1991.

Immediately north of Hitchin station a line
branches from the main line eastwards to Royston and Cambridge. This branch line is electrified as far as Royston and a connecting service
of diesel multiple-unit trains operates between
Royston and Cambridge.

32 **LETCHWORTH** is about two miles to the R:l
east of the line. This was the first garden city
ever built, on a site of 4,500 acres, in 1903. The
designers were Barry Parker and Raymond
Unwin, the team that went on to build Hampstead Garden Suburb.

The line passes from **Hertfordshire** in the
south to **Bedfordshire**, near the old **Three** R:l
Counties Asylum.

33 All the local stations between Hitchin and Peterborough, except Biggleswade, Sandy, St Neots and Huntingdon, have been closed to passengers – Three Counties, Arlesey, Offord and Buckden, Holme, Yaxley and Farcet in 1959; Tempsford in 1956; and Abbots Ripton in 1958. **Arlesey Brickworks** were opened in *L:r* 1852, a direct result of the coming of the railway.

34 BIGGLESWADE (BR: Victorian yellow stock brick buildings). Before the train came to Biggleswade, the town was an important stop on the coach route to the north. James Boswell described his journey by coach from Scotland to London (four days and nights) in 1762. Nearing Biggleswade 'I was a good deal afraid of robbers. A great many horrid ideas filled my mind... However, I affected resolution, and as each of us carried a loaded pistol in his hand, we were pretty sure. We got at night to Biggleswade.'

35 SANDY (BR: neat Victorian yellow-brick 'house', one of the original GNR stations designed by Henry Goddard) is on the Roman Road between Godmanchester and Verulamium (St Alban's) and remains of an important Roman settlement have been found around the town. When the GNR was built, ancient coins, armour and a skeleton were unearthed. There is a hillfort, **Caesar's Camp**, which looks like *R:l* an earthwork, on a spur overlooking the River Ivel just north-east of the station. More recently, since the coming of the line, Sandy and Biggleswade have established themselves as important centres for growing fruit and vegetables. The railway has provided a vital link with the London markets.

Between Sandy and St Neot's the line is built up on almost continuous embankments. The **River** L:r **Ivel** and then the **River Great Ouse** meander close to the line to the west. The landscape has pylons striding across the wide cornfields, with few hedges and trees to break up the vista: rich productive land for the farmers.

36 **ST DENIS'S, LITTLE BARFORD** is about L:r half a mile from the line. It is a mixture of Norman and Decorated styles with Victorian restoration work by G. E. Street. Its tower appears insignificant when compared with the vast proportions of the power station just to the north. **Little Barford Power Station** was L:r built by Farmer and Dark in 1955–7. It is in brown brick and in the tradition of Scott's Battersea Power Station.

The train crosses the former border of **Bedfordshire** and the old county of **Huntingdonshire** to the north: now part of an extended **Cambridgeshire**.

37 **ST NEOT'S** (BR: yellow-brick buildings; attractive footbridge) was named after the learned Christian missionary who died c. 880. His remains were brought here from Cornwall and a monastery founded in his honour. The bones were moved again in 1003 to Coryland to be safe from the Danes. Just west of the station beside the River Great Ouse is the **site** L:r **of the Benedictine Priory** which was founded c. 972–5. The highest church tower visible to the west, rising above the houses, belongs to **St** L:r **Mary's**, one of the largest late medieval churches in the county. The tower is 130 feet high and was begun in 1489. The unusually tall pinnacles on top were added in 1526–35. A

saline spring rises in the town and the waters from it are similar to those at Cheltenham and Leamington.

38 HOLY TRINITY, GREAT PAXTON is very close to the railway line. It is built of grey stone and brown cobbles and has a Perpendicular tower. It is a very unusual church because although on the outside it appears to be Perpendicular, the interior is of Romanesque proportions, presenting an 'architectural shock of a high order' (Pevsner). Close to the church is a pleasantly solid **Edwardian vicarage**. *R:l*

39 OFFORD D'ARCY CHURCH AND OFFORD CLUNY CHURCH are close to each other and the railway line. St Peter's, Offord D'Arcy, is built of cobbles and has a fourteenth-century tower with a recessed stone spire. The **manor house** just south of the church dates from the seventeenth and eighteenth centuries. All Saints, Offord Cluny, is also built of cobbles and has a Perpendicular tower. The name Offord Cluny came from Cluny Abbey in Burgundy, which owned the manor from the eleventh to the fifteenth centuries. There is a fine view of the **River Great Ouse** on the other side of the railway line. *R:l* *L:r*

40 HINCHINGBROOKE HOUSE is now part of Hinchingbrooke Comprehensive School and pupils will give visitors conducted tours. The house began as a nunnery but was given to Sir Richard Cromwell in 1538 when the monasteries were dissolved. Sir Oliver Cromwell (uncle of the Protector Oliver Cromwell) was forced to sell the property to Henry Montagu, Earl of Manchester, in 1627. Sir *L:r*

Oliver had married an heiress but spent all her money on entertaining. The house remained in the Montagu family until 1962. Samuel Pepys, cousin of Edward Montagu, was a visitor and wrote 'the house do please me infinitely beyond Audley End'. Horace Walpole found the house 'old, spacious, irregular, yet not vast or forlorn'.

41 **GODMANCHESTER** was an important *R:1* Roman station and traces of buildings have been found, including a suite of bathrooms. The tower of the large church of **St Mary's** was built in 1623 with a Perpendicular recessed spire on top. The **River Great Ouse** passes under the line here, a fording point on the Roman Ermine Street, now the A14. Rabbit-bitten pastures and ancient willows line the broad lazy river: a picture of slow ease and tranquillity.

42 **HUNTINGDON** (BR, opened 1850; rebuilt 1959–60) The small proportions of the country station with some of the original Victorian yellow-brick buildings are overshadowed by the **concrete flyover** which carries the A14 over the line just to the north. Around the time the station was rebuilt, Huntingdon was designated an overspill area from London. Since then the town population has markedly increased: hundreds of business commuters use the station in the mornings and early evenings. Huntingdon has been an important settlement since Saxon times. Huntingdon Castle was built at the orders of William the Conqueror in 1068 and the earthworks still remain in the centre of the town. The town cemetery is on the site of the Augustinian monastery. In 1200 the town had 16 parish churches, but with the constant

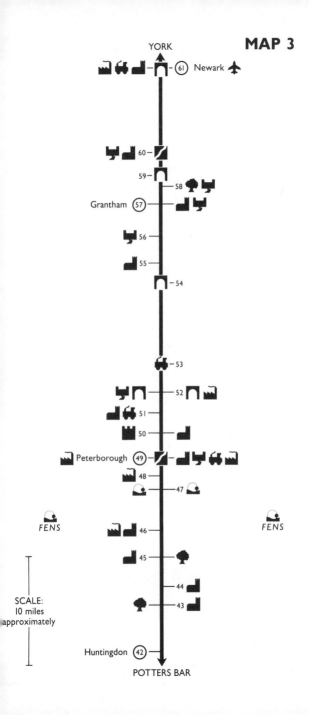

MAP 3

YORK — 61 — Newark

60

59

58

Grantham — 57

56

55

54

53

52

51

50

Peterborough — 49

48

47

FENS

FENS

SCALE:
10 miles
approximately

46

45

44

43

Huntingdon — 42

POTTERS BAR

flooding of the River Ouse and the Black Death the population declined: by the sixteenth century there were a mere four parish churches left. However, the town has maintained its importance as an agricultural centre with a manure works and large steam mills developed at the end of the nineteenth century. Oliver Cromwell was born in Huntingdon and attended the Grammar School: both his house and school survive. William Cowper's house is also standing. He lived in Huntingdon from 1765–7.

43 ST ANDREW'S, ABBOTS RIPTON has a *R:l* Perpendicular tower and appears in the trees just before a long grassy cutting. One of the bells in the tower was made by William Dawe c. 1400. The other side of the line, a little to the north, is **Monk's Wood**, a nature reserve and *L:r* experimental area. The British Antarctic Survey Biological Unit has laboratories here.

44 ST ANDREW'S, WOOD WALTON is very *R:l* close to the line and all on its own: the village of Wood Walton is about a mile to the south. The church has a Decorated tower and an attractive soft-red tiled roof. **Castle Hill**, more of a

St Andrew's, Wood Walton

sloping field than a hill, immediately north-east of the church, was a motte and bailey castle.

The Fenlands are the region of England most deliberately and profoundly transformed by man. They also constitute the largest expanse of continuous flat land, the most continuous tillage, and the richest agricultural soils in the country. They extend southwards from the Wash and rarely rise 50 feet above sea level. The earliest local settlements were made on the few slight hillocks of solid rock or gravel — Ely and Boston are such examples. The Fenlands are essentially reclaimed swamp, formed by the silting of the Wash which created an inland lagoon which in turn was filled with silt and peat, making great shallow meres which provided the inhabitants with the industries of wildfowl and fish until Dutch engineers began drainage work in the early seventeenth century. Since then the level of the land has dropped, in some places by as much as ten feet, as the peat has shrunk. The rivers, in their silt-lined channels, have remained at their original levels and are thus heavily embanked to reduce flooding.

45 The cluster of **GIDDINGS** is just off the line to *L:r* the west: Great Gidding, Steeple Gidding and Little Gidding, where T. S. Eliot lived. **All** *L:r* **Saints, Connington** can be seen from the train and has a monumental tower, ashlar faced and crowned with enormous pinnacles which were rebuilt by Sir Thomas Cotton in 1638. Cotton was not only responsible for the upkeep of the church but followed the example of the Earl of Bedford and began to drain Connington Fen in 1639. The Cotton family had lived at Connington since 1460 and the church contains the

family monuments. Sir Robert Cotton, who died in 1631, was a famous antiquary: his collection of manuscripts is now in the British Museum. The church also contains monuments to the Kings of Scotland, including King David and Prince Henry. Members of the Scottish Royal family were lords of the manor in the twelfth and early thirteenth centuries.

The silver birches along the railway line are part of the nature reserve of **Holme Fen**. *R:l*

46 ST PETER'S YAXLEY is a large medieval *L:r* church, its spire supported by delicate flying buttresses. It contrasts with the stark simplicity of the chimneys of the **brick works** further to *L:r* the west. Inside the church is an unusual heart burial, an arched panel with a carving of two arms holding a heart. A box was found behind the panel containing a heart which is believed to have belonged to William de Yaxley, Abbot of Thorney, who died in 1293.

After the arrival of the railway, the fine soil in this area was planted with celery to satisfy the newly fashionable demand for it in London. The landscape here has a special beauty in spring, when the young corn covers the black fields with a haze of shimmery green.

47 WHITTLESEY MERE The Fens caused the *R&L* builders of the GNR considerable problems: the worst area was Whittlesey Mere, about three miles south of Peterborough. It was known as the 'quaking bog' and Thomas Brassey declared the whole area shook when he stamped on it. Ballard, the agent for Brassey and a fen drainage expert, solved the problem of crossing the bog by sinking alternate layers of faggots and peat to displace the moisture. He made simultaneous bulk purchases of timber over a wide area of the countryside before the prices could be raised against him and so saved the company a large sum of money.

48 OLD FLETTON is now an industrial suburb of Peterborough and the individual parishes of Fletton, Woodston and Stanground have become lost in the residential and industrial development which extends to the west and east of the railway line. The name Fletton is famous for the Oxford clay bricks which have been made here for centuries but which the railway turned into a universal brick, in use throughout Britain. There is a clear view from the train of the **claypits, rows of kilns, tapering chimneys** *L:r* **and stockpiles of baked red Fletton bricks**. The railway offered the means to distribute the bricks all over the country and this in turn dramatically increased the population of the area as the works expanded. From a population of 3,580 in 1801 Peterborough rose to a population in 1967 of 80,000. As late as the 1930s, the brickworks were the largest in the world, but now many of the old pits are being filled in by power station waste, brought by special 'piggy-back' trains, and finally covered with topsoil.

49 PETERBOROUGH (BR) When Samuel Sidney wrote his *Rides on Railways* in 1851 he described Peterborough as 'a city without population, without manufactures, without trade, without a good inn, or even a copy of The Times, except at the railway station . . . The cathedral viewed, nothing remains to detain the traveller in this peculiarly stupid city.' The railway has since transformed Peterborough from being simply an agricultural centre into a city of some industrial importance. It is a major crossroads for British Rail, serving as the gateway to East Anglia and providing cross-country connections between the Northwest, the Midlands, Norwich, Ipswich and the port of Harwich Parkeston Quay.

As the train crosses over the **River Nene** there is a brief view of the **Cathedral**. It was built of *R:l* Barnack stone between the tenth and fourteenth centuries. A Benedictine monastery was founded at Peterborough by Peada, King of Mercia, in 650; Henry VIII elevated it to cathedral rank and the town to a city in 1541. The famous Anglo-Saxon Hedda Stone is inside – a large grey stone with rather stiff-looking apostles carved around the sides. Henry VIII's first wife, Catherine of Aragon, is buried here.

Peterborough Station was formerly called North Station. It has recently been rebuilt in red-brick with enclosed corrugated footbridge and ramps. This is in contrast to the **Great** *R:l* **Northern Hotel** which survives at the south end of the station, built in 1852 of yellow brick. The architect, Henry Goddard of Lincoln, was responsible for all the original GNR stations from London (except King's Cross) to Doncaster. He used local bricks for the stations: yellow stock near London, red in Hertfordshire and Bedfordshire, grey-white north of Newark.

Just north of Peterborough Station, on the eastern side of the main line is British Rail's **Peterborough Electrification Construction Depot**. This is the centre for maintaining and *R:l* storing the construction machinery and materials – such as steelwork, wire and cement

– used in electrifying the East Coast Main Line. There is further industry to the east and west: the red-brick factory of **Baker Perkins Ltd** *L:r* **Westwood Works**, the **Rail Express Parcels Peterborough Depot** and the extensive **engineering works of Peter Brotherhood** *R:l* **Ltd.** Peterborough has been an important centre of engineering and metal manufactures. Agricultural machinery has been produced for use on the highly-tilled farmland of the area and rolling stock has been built for the railway.

50 **WOODCROFT CASTLE**, almost hidden by *L:r* trees, consists of a fragment of the original late-thirteenth-century castle and much later additions. Opposite is the spire of **Glinton** *R:l* **Church**, taller than the tower on which it is built. A little further north is the village of **Etton**, home of Daniel Defoe.

51 **HELPSTON VILLAGE AND CHURCH** are *L:r* about half a mile from the line and can be seen just before the Stamford line branches to the west. The **remains of the platform of Helpston** *L:r* **Station** – which belonged to the Midland Railway and not the Great Northern – are on the west side of the line. **St Botolph's**, Helpston, is a limestone church. The Norman tower was re-built in 1865 and topped with a short spire. In 1869 a monument was erected in the village to the poet John Clare, who was born in Helpston and buried there after dying in Northampton Lunatic Asylum in 1864. He came from a poor rural background – his father was a labourer, his mother illiterate – but he managed to educate himself and achieved a considerable reputation with his poems of the English countryside. He struggled to keep a wife and seven children on the pitiful wages of an agricultural labourer and

with a little help from patrons but finally collapsed, mentally and physically. He spent most of the last 25 years of his life in asylums.

52 **LOLHAM BRIDGES** About a mile after the *L&R* Stamford line branches to the west, the train crosses the Roman Road known as King Street (a branch of Ermine Street) over a level crossing. This area was liable to severe flooding and there are still areas of water to right and left of the line, though some has collected in sand and gravel pits. In the seventeenth and eighteenth centuries five bridges were built on King Street to carry the road up over the surrounding meadows. One bridge is just south of the line; four are just to the north. It is also possible to see a **water mill** on the **River Welland** and *L:r* opposite the **West Deeping Cement Works**, *R:l* where railway sleepers are made.

53 **FROM LOLHAM BRIDGES TO STOKE TUNNEL: THE MALLARD** This is a particularly fast stretch of line – almost straight – which carries the train through rolling sedimentary land from **Cambridgeshire** into **Lincolnshire** at Lolham Bridges, then across a couple of miles of **Leicestershire** and back into **Lincolnshire**. It has been associated with high speeds for many years. It was here that the bright blue 'Mallard' achieved the world steam speed record of 126 mph in 1938. The main lines to Scotland from Euston (LMS) and King's Cross (LNER) were competing for the fastest time to the north the moment they were completed. In July 1938 the LNER ran brake tests on No. 4468 'Mallard' and the engine reached 126 mph racing down Stoke Bank. The engine's streamlined shape, similar at the front to the modern 125, was reckoned to be worth 500

extra horsepower when travelling at 90 mph.
'Mallard' is now one of the principal exhibits at
the National Railway Museum in York and
money is being collected to try to put it back
on the railway line for the 50th anniversary in
1988 of the record-breaking run.

54 **STOKE TUNNEL** is 880 yards long. To the
south of it the train reaches the highest point of
the Great Northern line; immediately to the
north, the train crosses over **Ermine Street**. Just
before the tunnel the line used to pass through
the tiny county of **Rutland**. Now the boundary
is between **Leicestershire** and **Lincolnshire**.

55 **HOLY CROSS, GREAT PONTON**, about a   *L:r*
mile north of Stoke Tunnel, is in the village
down in a hollow. The large tower was built in
1519 by a wool merchant called Anthony Ellis
and is 80 feet high.

56 **LITTLE PONTON HALL** is below the line,   *L:r*
built in the eighteenth and nineteenth centuries.
The octagonal **dovecote** is Georgian.

57 **GRANTHAM** (BR) The prosperity of Grantham in the Middle Ages was great and its parish
church — **St Wulfram's** — is one of the love-   *R:l*
liest in England. The slender spire rises 272 feet
above the houses and factories of the town.
Close to the church is the Victorian **town hall**
with its frivolous clock tower rising above
French Renaissance slate roofs. The town is the
birthplace and childhood home of Margaret
Hilda Roberts, better known as Margaret
Thatcher. A local rhyme declares 'Grantham,
two rarities are thine, A lofty steeple and a
Living Sign': in fact the line refers not to the
Prime Minister but to an old elm tree inn sign.

58 BELTON PARK, just bought by the National *R:l*
Trust, is about a mile to the east of the line.
Though it is not possible to see the magnificent
late-seventeenth-century home of the Brownlow family, the **Bellmount Tower** is visible, *R:l*
close to the top of the hill just north of
Grantham with trees behind. It was built by
Christopher Wren in 1750 for Sir John Brownlow, and is an observatory with a wooden roof
opening to the stars. The 1st Earl of Belton was
a particularly progressive landowner and early
in the nineteenth century he built three-
bedroom cottages for his labourers. His bene-
ficence apparently pleased no one. The local
gentry were shocked, the farmers thought the
labourers were being spoilt and the labourers
were annoyed because they were forbidden to
let out what they considered to be unnecessary
extra bedrooms.

59 PEASCLIFFE TUNNEL is 968 yards long.

60 MARSTON The train crosses over the **River** *L:r*
Witham which then meanders close to the line
to the west. The medieval church of **St Mary's**
has the largest laburnum tree in its graveyard.
The church is built of ironstone, has a slender
broach spire and contains the Elizabethan
monuments to the Thorold family who built
nearby **Marston Hall**. The Georgian hall is to
the south of the church and has a red roof.

At the village of **Barnby-in-the-Willows** the *R:l*
River Witham, flowing from east to west
under the line, marks the boundary of **Lincolnshire** in the south and **Nottinghamshire** in the
north.

61 NEWARK (BR), like Grantham, was a rich

town in the Middle Ages and has a magnificent parish church. The spire of **St Mary Magda-** *L:r* **lene** was built in the fourteenth century and rises up, needle-sharp, to a height of 252 feet. Wool merchants were largely responsible for the wealth of the town, dealing with local sheep-breeders and Flemish clothiers. Newark is situated on the River Trent and the ruins of Newark Castle are close to the old bridge over the river. King John died there, surfeited on new ale and unripe peaches. Newark was defended by the Royalists during the Civil War but finally fell to the Parliamentarians in 1646, after a siege which lasted some six months. About 1,500 men defended the town against 7,000 Scottish and 9,000 English soldiers.

Newark Northgate Station buildings are of golden-yellow brick with limestone trims above the windows. North of the station is the **sugar** *L:r* **beet factory**, one of the largest in Europe, and an indication that the railway line has passed from the rich soil of the fens to heavy clay.

Immediately north of Newark the train crosses over **Winthorpe Rack** on a bridge which was the principal engineering feat of the line between Peterborough and Retford. The **Newark Dyke Bridge** crosses the water on a skew, with a span of 262 feet. It was designed by Joseph Cubitt using the 'Warren Truss' design unique to Britain, though there was one example in the USA. Beyond the expanses of water alongside the **Trent** is one of the river's many **power stations**. Opposite, nearer the *L:r* line, is the Second World War RAF station of **Winthorpe**. *R:l*

Churches from Newark to Retford The

speed of the modern train makes it difficult to identify all of the parish churches to the west and east of the line but the following are those most easily seen.

62 **ST WILFRID'S, SOUTH MUSKHAM** is near *L:r* to the line and built of limestone. The bottom of its tower dates from the thirteenth century, the top is Perpendicular. **Sand and gravel pits** *R:l* are opposite the church on the other side of the line.

63 **ST GILES'S, CROMWELL** has an insignificant *R:l* Perpendicular tower built in 1427 and is about half a mile from the line in the small village of Cromwell. Ralph, Lord Cromwell, a fifteenth-century inhabitant of the village, was Constable of Nottingham Castle, Treasurer to Henry VI and Keeper of Sherwood Forest.

64 **ST MARY'S, CARLTON ON TRENT** is a *R:l* Victorian church. The spire appears just after the train passes over a level crossing beside the **Great Northern Inn**.

65 **ALL SAINTS, WESTON** has a thirteenth- *L:r* century tower: the battlemented parapet and needle-sharp spire were added in the four-teenth century. **High Marnham Power** *R:l* **Station** on the Trent can be seen to the east. Just north of Weston the train passes close to the base of an old **windmill** at Stone Road End *L:r* Farm. **Lincoln Cathedral** is not one of the *R:l* parish churches along the line, but it can be seen on a fine day to the east, looming on its hill. **Dukeries Junction**, now closed, was so *L:r* called because of the preponderance of noble seats in the area: Clumber Park, belonging to the Duke of Newcastle; Thoresby, the resi-

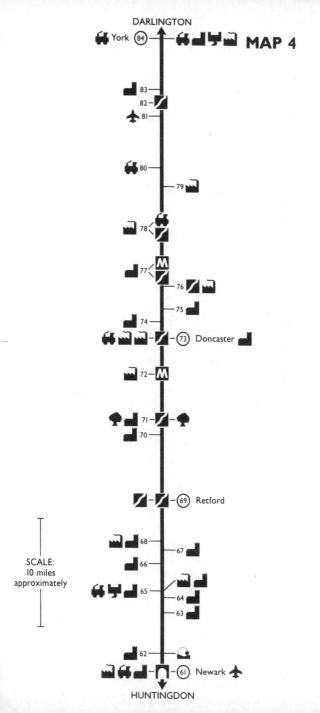

DARLINGTON

York ⑧④

MAP 4

83

82

81

80

79

78

77

76

75

74

⑦③ Doncaster

72

71

70

⑥⑨ Retford

68

67

66

65

64

63

62

⑥① Newark

SCALE:
10 miles
approximately

HUNTINGDON

dence of Earl Manvers; Welbeck Abbey, seat of the Duke of Portland.

66 ST JOHN THE BAPTIST, EAST MARK- L:r
HAM is a fifteenth-century church with a tower crowned with eight pinnacles. Inside is the tomb chest to Sir John Markham, who died in 1409. It is inscribed *Orate pro anima Johis Markham justiciarii* ('pray for the soul of John Markham, judge') and Nikolaus Pevsner comments: 'well may he ask; for he drew up the document deposing Richard II'.

67 ST NICHOLAS'S, ASKHAM has a tower R:l crowned with eight pinnacles and is a mixture of Norman, medieval and Victorian work.

68 ST PETER'S, GAMSTON was restored by L:r George Gilbert Scott in 1855 and has a medieval tower. There is an enormous **coalmine** close L:r to Gamston, west of the line, part of the Notts-Derby coalfield.

69 RETFORD (BR) The train crosses the **River Idle** and enters the town. Retford Station was opened in 1849 when the Lincolnshire extension of the Manchester, Sheffield and Lincolnshire Railway was built. It is built of yellow bricks in the Italianate style with black-brick trims. The river divides the town into east and west. The town's main industry is engineering.

Leaving Retford Station for the north the train crosses over the **Chesterfield Canal**, which L:r then continues parallel to the line on the west side for a short distance. The landscape between Retford and York consists of huge fields, unbroken by trees or hedges; north of Doncaster loom increasing numbers of power stations.

70 **ST WILFRID'S, SCROOBY** is barely a *L:r*
quarter of a mile from the line. It has an unusual
Perpendicular steeple which turns from a
square into an octagonal spire. Scrooby is the
village from which the Pilgrim Fathers first de-
parted on their journey to Holland and finally
America. Both their leader, William Brewster,
and the Governor of Virginia, Sir Edwin Sandys,
who provided them with the land, were
Scrooby men.

71 **ST NICHOLAS'S, BAWTRY** is very near the *L:r*
railway line and dates from the twelfth to the
fourteenth centuries. It is a small limestone
church – the tower was rebuilt in 1712–13.
South of Bawtry, along a bank of the **River
Idle**, is the boundary of **Nottinghamshire** and
South Yorkshire, formerly the **West Riding**.
Just to the north the train passes through
Bawtry Forest. The birch and coniferous trees
are the property of the Forestry Commission.

72 **NEW ROSSINGTON New coalminers'** *L:r*
houses stretch to the west of the line; to the
east is the original village of **Rossington** and *R:l*
Rossington Hall. The train is travelling above
the vast Notts, Derby and Yorkshire coalfield
and **tips and pitheads** can be seen behind the *L:r*
houses to the west. There has been continuous
coalmining in this area since the fourteenth century. Just north of New Rossington the train
passes under the **M18**.

73 **DONCASTER** (BR) The industrial town of
Doncaster is approached between sidings and
past the large **BOC International Harvester** *L:r*
Factory at Carr Hill, a mixture of red- and yellow-
painted brick. The **British Ropes Factory** is
on the same side and just before the station

the Victorian red-brick **offices of British Rail Engineering**, with flag flying, proclaim *L:r* Doncaster's long-standing connection with the railway. Doncaster was the site of the former Great Northern locomotive works and there are still extensive workshops to the south and west of the station where diesels are maintained and stored.

Doncaster is in the heart of British Rail's 'merry-go-round' country – the continuous system of moving coal between pits and power stations. A typical merry-go-round train consists of 30–40 wagons, permanently coupled together, carrying a payload of about 1,000 tonnes. These trains are loaded and discharged on the move and, depending on the distance involved, can make up to four round trips in a day. Throughout British Rail some 250 trains each day carry 80 per cent of the coal used to produce electricity. Virtually every time a light is switched on in home or factory the consumer is relying on the merry-go-round train.

Immediately north of the station and east of the line is **St George**'s designed by George *R:l* Gilbert Scott and built in 1854–8. The earlier church was destroyed by fire in 1853 and subscriptions were collected for the rebuilding. Queen Victoria gave £100; Lord Palmerston 20 guineas. St George's is in the Early Decorated style and has a tower 170 feet high crowned with 16 pinnacles. J. F. Bentley, who designed Westminster Cathedral, was inspired to become an architect by the experience of seeing the church built.

The population of the town is around 90,000. The Corporation Books show that there was a stand on the racecourse here before 1615. The most famous race, the St Leger, began in 1778. The racecourse is right over to the south-east.

The first flat race of the season, the Lincoln, has been run here since the closure of Lincoln racecourse.

North of Doncaster Station the train passes through scrap-iron yards, rundown allotments and scrappy waste land to cross the **River Don Navigation** and the **River Don** over impressive girder bridges. The Don has the dubious distinction of being Britain's most polluted river.

74 **BENTLEY CHURCH** The smoke-blackened *L:r* church of **St Peter's** (1891 by J. Codd) sums up the atmosphere here: coalmines, power stations, canals and pylons.

75 **ALL SAINTS, ARKSEY** is a Norman church *R:l* with a spire added in the thirteenth century. It is surprisingly clean – a contrast to St Peter's – particularly as there is an enormous coalmine just across the railway line.

76 **THORPE MARSH POWER STATION** is on *R:l* the River Don to the east of the line.

77 **HAYWOOD CHURCH**, close to the line, is *L:r* of limestone, with a red-brick Victorian rectory beside it. When Barnsdale Forest stood near here, Robin Hood raided travellers on the Great North Road from it.

The train crosses the **River Went** passing from **South Yorkshire** on the south bank to **North Yorkshire** on the north. The train almost immediately crosses about half a mile of **Humberside** before continuing through **North Yorkshire** and over the **Aire and Calder Navigation** and the **M62** to Leeds, Manchester and Hull. The heavy clay soil of this area is ideal for sugar beet and wheat.

78 **EGGBOROUGH POWER STATION** is *L:r* west of the line between the Aire and Calder Navigation and the River Aire. The power station, with its eight massive cooling towers, is an impressive site on the flat plain. It was built in 1972–3 and has four 500-megawatt generators. The stack, 800 feet high, used to be one of the tallest in the country. Power stations are popular attractions with the public. When Eggborough was opened recently, 26,000 visitors came in one day. Ferrybridge C Power Station is further away to the west. This was the first of the big 500 stations, commissioned in 1967. An unusual method of handling the coal is used at Ferrybridge. Coal arrives by barge on the canal. An enormous 'grab' lifts up the barge and empties its contents into a hopper, then returns the barge to the water.

Eggborough Power Station

The line crosses the **River Aire** close to *R:l* **Temple Hirst**, a former house of the Knights Templar.

It's here that the train leaves the Old East Coast route which went through Selby and enters on a new high-speed stretch of line known as the 'Selby Diversion'. The 15-mile-long diversion was completed in 1983, avoiding subsidence caused by the new Selby Coalfield, which is the largest and most modern coalfield in the world. It was the first major stretch of new main line to be built in this country to take speeds of up to 125 mph. The project included the building of 12 bridges carrying roads over the railway, one bridge carrying the railway over a road, a three-span bridge over the River Aire and another over the Selby Canal. Other bridges include one to carry the Leeds—Selby railway over the diverted main line and multi-span viaducts over the Selby Dam and River Wharfe. About $1\frac{1}{2}$ million tonnes of rock-fill and 345,000 tonnes of ballast were used to build the embankments and track formation.

79 **DRAX POWER STATION** is some miles *R:l* away from the line to the east and close to the River Ouse. The first half was commissioned in 1975 and has three 660-megawatt generators. When the second half is completed in 1987, Drax will be the largest station in Europe, capable of using 10 million tonnes of coal a year — the entire output of the new Selby coalfield. The land around has been artificially landscaped using the fuel ash which is a by-product of power stations. Sheep graze contentedly on the grassy slopes, watched by visitors from Japan, America and Australia who come to study the reclamation of wasteland. Drax also has a 26-acre greenhouse heated by excess heat from the station. The tomatoes, aubergines and other fruit and vegetables are marketed by EXEL, the Express Dairies and the Electricity Board. Drax is known to be a major source of acid rain over Norway.

80 **HAMBLETON** Close to the line (just north of *L:r*

the village) is a small **commemorative stone** *L:r* at the point where the new railway is crossed by the Leeds–Selby–Hull line. This stone, marking the start of work on the Diversion in 1980, was dedicated by the Bishop of Selby, the Rt Rev. M. H. St John Maddocks, in the presence of 200 invited guests. All their names, along with a commemorative scroll and other representative items of the late twentieth century, were deposited in a time-capsule within the stone.

81 **RAF CHURCH FENTON** On this part of the *L:r* journey the vast expanse of sky stretching to the west is frequently broken up by jet trails from the jet pilot training school whose runways and hangars are clearly visible from the train. Sometimes, smaller light aircraft from the nearby private Sherburn Aeroclub can also be seen.

82 The line crosses the **RIVER WHARFE** which in winter frequently floods the surrounding fields.

83 **BOLTON PERCY CHURCH** Built from *L:r* white stone in 1423, it dominates the village.

About a mile further north is the northern end of the Diversion. The line joining from the west is the route to Leeds and Sheffield. The junction is the first 125 mph turnout to be built on British Rail.

84 **YORK** (BR) is historically England's second city. Constantine the Great was proclaimed Emperor here. The Romans called it Eboracum, the Saxons who followed them Jorvik, from which it derives its present name. In the Middle Ages it was a great wool market and the next city to London. Side by side with Norwich it

MAP 5

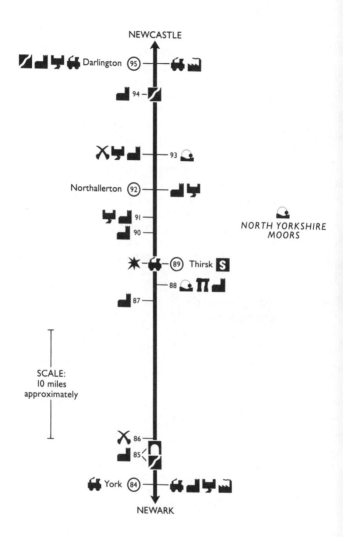

was the second biggest city in England, with a population of well over 100,000. It still has 19 parish churches, though in the Middle Ages the total was over 40. The reasons for its importance are simple: it sits on the east coast route to the north, commanding the gateway between the Pennines and the Yorkshire Wolds, and has been protected from invasion by marshland to north and south. In fact, the city suffered a depression in Tudor times, but in the eighteenth century became a fashionable resort, a development accelerated by the railways.

There is a clear view of **York Minster** from *R:l* the north of York. The Minster was founded by Edwin King of Northumbria in 627, after he had been converted to Christianity by Paulinus. The Archbishop of York is Archbishop of England, as opposed to the Archbishop of Canterbury, who is Archbishop of All England. The present building is nearly all Gothic, dating from the thirteenth to the fifteenth centuries. It is 485 feet long and built of oolitic limestone from Tadcaster. The roof was recently partially destroyed by lightning following the controversial appointment of the Bishop of Durham.

The **railway buildings** at York are a magnificent display of decades of railway history. The first railway station at York was built in 1841–2 to the design of George Townsend Andrews. As Sheriff of York in 1847 he assisted the nominees of George Hudson, 'the railway king', to become Members of Parliament. His first job for Hudson was to cut an arch through the city wall for Hudson's York and North Midland Railway to enter the city. He then built a U-shaped terminus with an Italianate façade in grey brick. The elegant train shed of iron and glass was

York Station

supported by tapering columns and designed by
the engineer Thomas Cabrey. The immaculately
kept station buildings are now British Rail
offices on Tanner Row. Andrews also designed
a hotel — the first railway station hotel — in
1853, which is part of the same block.

A new railway station was begun in 1866 and
completed in 1877. This was for the North of
England Railway. The original design was by
Thomas Prosser, architect for the NER
between 1854 and 1874. His work was completed by Benjamin Burley and William Peachey.
The front of the station is of yellow brick with
a nine-bay porte-cochère (gateway). Behind is

the magnificent train shed, which must be one of the finest in Britain. Travellers from the south are unfortunately often taken through York on more recent lines outside the Victorian train shed, but those from the north pass through it. It is 800 feet long and built on a curve. The iron structure is prefabricated, the spandrels have heraldic details and there is a subtle gradation of the light filtering through the glass sections of the roof.

The station, which is a listed building, is now reaping the benefits of a £950,000 modernisation scheme which includes a new travel centre, a new waiting-room, a new left luggage office and lock-up shops leased out to businesses. Both inner and outer concourses have been resurfaced with terrazzo while a lot of insensitive work carried out in the 1930s and the effects of major bomb damage — sustained during a German air-raid in 1942 — have been rectified.

The travel centre, heart of the new scheme, has been designed to combine the very latest — and best — in customer care facilities with the station's architectural splendour.

By way of acknowledgement to the long-standing importance of York as a rail centre, a 100-year-old North Eastern Railway Distant Signal from nearby Haxby has been erected on the outer concourse of the station.

The **headquarters** of BR's Eastern Region *R:l* are close to the station. They were built in 1900–6 by Horace Field in an exuberant red-brick 'Edwardian William and Mary' style. The BR flag now flies from the roof.

The **National Railway Museum** is to the *L:r* west of the line and close to the station. A large hall was constructed from the former North Loco Shed and inside, grouped around the turntables, are the 'Rocket', the 'Mallard' and many other famous engines. The museum is free and some of the exhibits displayed outside can be seen from the train.

Lines leave York for Scarborough and Leeds as well as Thirsk and Darlington.

North of York Station is **St Peter's School**, *R:l* founded in 732, with a red-brick castellated façade set back behind playing fields. Guy Fawkes was a pupil. The large white house is the school sanatorium. On the same side of the line are the **County Asylum** with its square tower, and **York Waterworks**.

85 **NETHER POPPLETON** The train crosses the **River Ouse** immediately north of York at the quiet retirement village of Nether Poppleton. The small Norman church of **St Everilda**, *L:r* with its heavy bellcote, is just south of the crossing, which is over the **Skelton Bridge**.

86 **MARSTON MOOR** Immediately to the west, *L:r* about five miles away, is the site of the Battle of Marston Moor. The battle was the biggest of the Civil War of 1641–6. A mixed army of Scots, Yorkshiremen and East Anglians routed the Royalists, led by the king's nephew Prince Rupert, on 2 July 1644. The Roundheads gained control of the north and Cromwell was able to demonstrate his outstanding abilities as a cavalry leader.

87 **ST JOHN THE EVANGELIST, DALTON** *L:r* was designed by William Butterfield in 1868. It is a small church, rockfaced, with a thin west

tower with a polygonal top and spirelet.
William Morris designed the stained glass.

88 A sign beside the railway line marks the halfway
point of the journey: $196\frac{3}{8}$ miles to London and
to Edinburgh. Rising to the north-east of the
Vale of York are the limestone and sandstone
North Yorkshire Moors. This beautiful area *R:l*
of heather and rough pasture rises to over
1,000 feet and is cut into by deep, steep-sided
dales. The **Hambleton Hills** are closest to the
line and it is possible to see a **White Horse**, cut *R:l*

White Horse

in 1857, on the scarp slope rising sharply from the Vale of Mowbray. There are few towns or villages on the moors and little ground is cultivated. The spired church of **Sessay** contains a *R:l* brass engraving of Thomas Magus, Henry VIII's chaplain at the Field of the Cloth of Gold.

89 **THIRSK** (BR) cannot be seen clearly from the train. The **racecourse** lies between the line and *R:l* the town. An unfortunate railway accident took place here in 1892. A signalman fell asleep during the night and accepted a train when he already had another train in his section of the line. The Scotch Express ran into a Middlesbrough to Starbeck goods train and 8 passengers were killed with 39 injured. The signalman had fallen asleep because he had spent the preceding day (when he would normally be resting) looking for a doctor for his sick child. He was quite unfit for night duty but there was no relief to take over. The child later died.

Just north of Thirsk, at milepost 25, on 12 June 1973, the prototype version of the InterCity 125 high-speed train, heading north from York, reached a world record speed for diesel trains of 143.2 mph — a mile in 25 seconds! The record-breaking run was part of a series of tests to establish the power car performance and the riding, braking and air-conditioning properties of the new train. The new world record was, in fact, repeated just two hours later when the train headed north on an even more spectacular run, maintaining an average speed in excess of 140 mph over a distance of 12 miles. The train again reached 143.2 mph, this time at milepost 28.

90 **&91 SOUTH AND NORTH OTTERINGTON** *L:r*

The small churches of South and North Otterington are close to each other and the railway line. **St Andrew's** may appear to be Norman but was designed by Anthony Salvin in 1844–7. **St Michael's** has a Victorian spire but Norman walls. **Otterington House** (c. 1800) is between the churches and has a castellated front.

92 **NORTHALLERTON** (BR) The Great North of England Railway employed navvies to tip 252,641 cubic yards of soil to build the embankment on which the train travels to Northallerton from the south. The dark imposing church of **All Saints** is mostly Perpendicular. The **County Hall** – the town is the administrative centre of North Yorkshire – was designed by an architect from nearby Darlington in 1873. *R:l* *R:l*

93 **DANBY WISKE** There is a glimpse of the *L:r* Norman **church** of Danby Wiske and its Perpendicular tower as the train passes into a cutting. Immediately east of the church is the mid-seventeeth-century **Lazenby Hall**. Nearby is the **battle site** of the Battle of the Standard, fought between England and Scotland in 1138. Nineteen years of confusion were to follow the death of Henry I in 1135 as Henry's daughter Matilda and Stephen competed for the crown. King David of Scotland took the opportunity to invade England but was defeated by Stephen near Danby.

The **Cleveland Hills** rise up to the east. *R:l*

94 **CROFT-ON-TEES** The train crosses over the **River Tees** at the delightful village of Croft-on-Tees in the Yorkshire Dales, passing from

North Yorkshire on the south bank to **County Durham** on the north. In the eighteenth century there was a spa at Croft and when the GNER made its crossing of the Tees at Croft, Croft Spa Station was opened. This has since gone, like many of the local Victorian stations on the line. South of Croft it is still possible to see the red-brick station building for **Cowton**. There was also a station at *L:r* Otterington, south of Northallerton.

St Peter's, Croft-on-Tees, is a red sand- *L:r* stone church, close to the river and near the old road bridge with seven pointed and ribbed arches, which was built in the fifteenth century. When Byron and his wife spent their honeymoon nearby, they worshipped here. Charles Dodgson (better known as Lewis Carroll) spent his childhood in the vicarage at Croft: his father was Rector of St Peter's from 1843. Charles had ten brothers and sisters and their favourite game was 'trains'. The rules were elaborate and carefully drawn up. Rule 3: 'Station master must mind his station and supply refreshments: he can put anyone who behaves badly to prison, while a train goes round the garden.'

95 **DARLINGTON** (BR) is exceptional among the large towns of the north-east in that it lies inland. It was chosen as a site for railway workshops because of its strategic position in relation to the nineteenth-century railway system. The site of BR's Engineering Works, which once announced the train's arrival at Darlington from the south, is now an **industrial estate**. The town has been *R:l* associated with the railways since their beginnings and only began to develop as a modern city with the arrival, in 1825, of the Stockton and Darlington Railway. This 27-mile-long railway

MAP 6

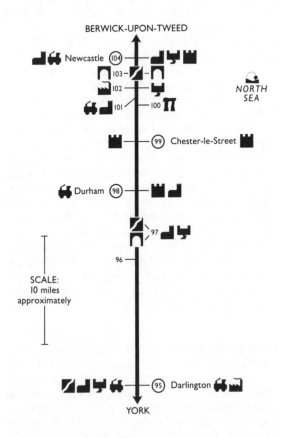

BERWICK-UPON-TWEED

Newcastle ⑩④

⑩③

⑩②

⑩① —⑩⓪

NORTH
SEA

⑨⑨ Chester-le-Street

Durham ⑨⑧

⑨⑦

⑨⑥

SCALE:
10 miles
approximately

⑨⑤ Darlington

YORK

was the result of the combined talents of George Stephenson and the Darlington citizen Edward Pease and became the first to secure powers to operate both passenger and goods traffic by means of locomotives. George Stephenson's engine 'Locomotion' hauled the passenger trains on the opening day, 27 September 1825. From a population of 4,700 in 1801, Darlington increased to 11,600 by 1850 and 44,500 in 1901. The original terminus of the Stockton and Darlington Railway was replaced in 1842 with the Georgian-style North Road Station. This has now been restored as a railway museum and houses 'Locomotion'.

Darlington Station was built in 1887 for the North Eastern Railway. It was designed in red brick by William Bell. The large porte-cochère facing down the approach road cannot be seen from the train, but there is a good view of the majestic double-arched **train shed**. Fast trains *L:r* travelling northwards bypass the train shed. Inside, supporting the roof, are solid iron columns with foliated capitals painted grey and white, their bracket spandrels decorated with the triple arms of the railway company. The woodwork in the station is painted cream and there is much fine iron work on the platforms.

Looking west over the town it is possible to see the **parish church** and the tower of the *L:r* **Covered Market** built by Alfred Waterhouse *L:r* in 1864 and restored in 1978–9.

After leaving Darlington the line runs alongside the **River Skerne** to **Aycliffe** with its industrial *L:r* estate. London is now about 250 miles away.

96 FERRYHILL The convent of Durham once had *L:r*

a chapel at Ferryhill with a court-house, swannery and fish pool. In the nineteenth century the town had its own station and was a centre of industrial production. Now, grafted on to an unfriendly, limestone landscape, it presents a gloomy picture of northern industrial decay.

97 SUNDERLAND BRIDGE The train enters a deep cutting at Sunderland Bridge to emerge from the hillside and cross over the **River Wear**. The tower of **Sunderland Bridge** *R:l* **Church** can be seen on the south bank. It is also possible to see, from the north bank, the red-brick **viaduct** over which the train crosses the Wear. There are clear views to east and west along the tree-lined river valley. The old **road** *R:l* **bridge** over the Wear is to the east, as is **Croxdale Hall** in the distance, south of the river.

98 DURHAM (BR) is approached from the south through the first really dramatic countryside since King's Cross: the train crosses over steep-sided river valleys which have cut deep into the landscape. Durham itself has a spectacular site in a loop of the River Wear. The castle and cathedral are tactically placed on the high ground in the centre of the loop and dominate the town. The train passes through the city on a stone viaduct built in 1857 which offers magnificent views of the **city** to the east. *R:l*

Durham Station was opened in 1857 by the *L:r* North Eastern Railway and designed by G. T. Andrews in a Tudor-Gothic style to harmonise with the surroundings. Mullioned windows, heavy-angled buttresses and hexagonal chimney shafts adorn the stone station buildings. The broad platform awnings are conspicuous, supported by broad curved brackets.

The **castle** and the **cathedral** are the most *R:l* prominent of Durham's buildings and were built at about the same time in the late eleventh century. The castle began as a key fortress in the defence of the border with Scotland and then became an imposing but also comfortable palace for the Bishops of Durham. The present buildings were begun by Waltheof, Earl of Northumberland, in 1072. William the Conqueror gave the castle to Walcher, Bishop of Durham, and it remained a Bishop's Palace until 1836 when it was adopted for use as a hall of residence by Durham University. The cathedral is unusual among English cathedrals in that almost all of its architecture belongs to the same period, 1093–1133. The foundation stone was laid by Bishop William of St Carileph in 1093.

Durham Cathedral and Castle

Coal has been the county's main industry since the nineteenth century and the Durham miners' gala (pronounced 'gayla') is held here each July.

Just outside the city lies the ancient suburb of **Framwellgate**, actually founded as a suburb in *L:r* the twelfth century.

99 CHESTER-LE-STREET (BR) Just before

Chester-le-Street is **Lumley Castle**, once the *L:r*
seat of the Earl of Scarborough, but now converted
into a luxury hotel. The train passes through
Chester-le-Street and its red-brick station on a
viaduct 90 feet high and just under half a mile long.
There is a good view of the town to the east and
across the valley **Lambton Castle**. The architect *R:l*
Bonomi (the elder) designed Lambton Hall at the
end of the eighteenth century. It was renamed
Lambton Castle in 1833, when it was enlarged and
embellished with towers and turrets. The fanciful
biscuit-coloured stone castle is now an educational
establishment.

Immediately north of Chester-le-Street is the
border of **County Durham** with **Tyne and
Wear**.

100 **PENSHAW MONUMENT** is a strange, in- *R:l*
congruous structure, set on a hill to the east. It
was erected to the memory of the 1st Earl of
Durham in the mid-nineteenth century. The
design, of 18 pillars, 70 feet high, is from the
Temple of Theseus.

101 **ST ANDREW'S, LAMESLEY** is dwarfed by the *L:r*
surrounding extensive sidings which make up the
British Rail Tyne Marshalling Yard where
freight traffic to and from Tyneside is handled.

102 The line now begins its dissection of the Tyneside conurbation: South Shields, Tynemouth,
Newcastle, Gateshead and Jarrow. The train
passes through the many factories and warehouses, sidings and yards of the **Team Valley** *L:r*
Trading Estate, Gateshead. The massive
Dunlop Factory is part of the 700-acre trading
estate which originated in 1936. It was a pilot

scheme following the passing of the Special Areas Act of 1934 and was intended to help relieve the high unemployment in Tyneside. Sir W. Holford designed the estate with its long straight avenues and low red-brick factories which later in the decade were producing clothing, tools, foodstuffs, plastics, glass and radio components. The **terraces of red-brick** *R:l* **houses** with slate roofs to the east of the line are evidence of the enormous expansion of Gateshead following the Industrial Revolution. Until 1800 Gateshead was no more than a few streets around its parish church; Dr Johnson described it as no more than, 'a dirty lane leading to Newcastle'.

Tyne Bridge

103 Crossing the **RIVER TYNE** The crossing of the Tyne and arrival at Newcastle Central Station is one of the most spectacular events on InterCity journeys. Even though the old Redheugh Bridge has now gone, there are still **six bridges** to be seen from the train. The line passes over the King Edward Bridge and over the High Level Bridge in an emergency. The bridges, from west to east (L:r to R:l) are:

1. the **new Redheugh Bridge**, opened to traffic in 1983, which was designed by the engineering consultants Mott, Hay and Anderson.

2. the **King Edward Bridge**, consisting of one deck carrying four tracks of railway.

3. the new Metro (a local underground railway) Bridge, called the **Queen Elizabeth Bridge**.

4. the **High Level Bridge**, designed by Robert Stephenson. It was the first major bridge-building work on which the power-driven pile-driver — James Nasmyth's steam hammer — was used. Stephenson supervised the driving of the first pile on 24 April 1846. For the super-structure he used cast iron: the bridge is now the only surviving bridge in which cast iron is used extensively. The ironwork has a total weight of over 5,000 tons, produced locally by Hawkes, Crawshay and Co. of Newcastle. The High Level Bridge is also the earliest example of a dual-purpose structure, having two decks, the top for the railway and the bottom for a road-way 20 feet wide and two 6-foot-wide foot-paths. The girder design is known as 'bow and string'. The cast-iron arch forms the bow and the ends are tied by horizontal wrought-iron strings. The railway is supported on the crowns of the girders 120 feet above the Tyne: the roadway is slung beneath and carried by the strings. Tolls were collected on the roadbridge by North Eastern Railway employees wearing special livery: in winter 'Ticket Collectors Double Breasted Frock Coat Suit', in summer 'Ticket Collectors Double Breasted Jacket Suit'.

5. the **Swing Bridge** is the smallest of the bridges and was built in 1876.

6. the **New Tyne Bridge** was built in 1925–6 and designed by Mott, Hay and Anderson together with the architects Cackett, Dick and

McKellar. One large arch of steel (Britain's largest steel arch span – 531 feet) is anchored far below the roadway to massive concrete pylons.

104 **NEWCASTLE** (BR) was the third richest provincial town in England in the fourteenth century. The New Castle was built in the twelfth century and the city grew up within the medieval town walls, with the grander merchants' houses concentrated around the riverside quays. Expansion coincided with the Industrial Revolution at the end of the eighteenth century and the walls practically disappeared as the houses spread out in every direction. The Victorian period was Newcastle's golden age: the city was established as the commercial and cultural capital of the north east. The city centre with its classically proportioned streets was laid out by Richard Grainger, John Dobson and John Clerk, the parish church of St Nicholas becoming a cathedral. The principal industries which brought the city so much wealth were coal, shipbuilding, engineering, milling and the manufacture of optical instruments.

Newcastle Station was designed by John Dobson. He began work in 1848 but the station was not finally finished until 1865, after Thomas Prosser completed Dobson's original design. The station has an imposing exterior with a massive grey-ochre stone porte-cochère which seems to sum up the power and wealth of this northern city. From the train the impressive features of the station are the three train sheds built on a sharp curve. Dobson was the first to devise long wrought-iron ribs rolled to a designed curve which, with a span of 55 feet, arch over the tracks and platforms to create three elegant roofs.

The **Cathedral of St Nicholas** is visible before *L:r*
and after the station. It was built in the fourteenth and fifteenth centuries but only became
a cathedral in 1882. The fifteenth-century spire
is striking, rising above the arched roofs of the
train sheds. Large polygonal buttresses support
the crown on top of the tower. Four flying
buttresses reach up from the crown to support
a spire which is an open lantern with its own
four pinnacles and a further, higher recessed
spire. The steeple is $193\frac{1}{2}$ feet high.

Leaving Newcastle Station for the north, the
centre of the city still reveals much of the *L:r*
dignity and orderliness which Richard Grainger
and John Dobson brought to it early in the
nineteenth century. Grainger, the son of a
quayside porter, became a builder and joined
forces with Dobson to give Newcastle the
classical style which can be seen from the train.

All Saints Church (1786–96) was designed by *R:l*
David Stephenson, architect to Newcastle Corporation, and is one of the finest eighteenth-
century churches in the country. It cost over
£27,000, much of which was used for the tower
and spire. In the distance beyond the church is
the colourful and eccentric **Byker Wall** *R:l*
Housing Scheme.
    When Dobson built Newcastle Station he cut
through part of the medieval city including its
castle. Only the **keep**, the **Black Gate** and *R:l*
some fragments survive below the railway line.
The keep was built by Henry II in 1172–7 and
cost £911 10s 9d. The battlements were added
during later restoration work. The gatehouse,
Black Gate, was built by Henry III in 1247. It
was in ruins by early in the seventeenth century
and a brick house with mullioned windows was

EDINBURGH

MAP 7

Berwick-upon-Tweed ⑬¹

130—

129

128

127

126

125

Chathill ⑫⁴

123

122

Alnmouth ⑫⁰

119

118

Acklington ⑪⁷

116

Widdrington ⑪⁵

114

Pegswood ⑪³

Morpeth ⑪²

111

Cramlington ⑪⁰

109

108

Manors ⑩⁶

105

Newcastle ⑩⁴

DARLINGTON

NORTH SEA

NORTH SEA

CHEVIOTS

121

107

SCALE:
10 miles
approximately

erected on the site. This now houses the Museum of the Society of Antiquaries of Newcastle.

105 HOLY JESUS HOSPITAL is below the rail- *L:r* way line. It was built of brick in 1683 (though the top storey was added later) and is distinguished by the 30 brick arches around the ground floor.

106 MANORS (BR) Manors Station was rebuilt in *L:r* 1909 with a giant gable and cupola-cum-clock tower. It followed the electrification of the North Eastern's suburban lines north of the Tyne in 1904 — the first open-country electrified line in the United Kingdom.

107 THE OUSEBURN VIADUCT carries the line over the busy city streets and the industrial development along the north bank of the Tyne. It was designed by the Newcastle architect John Green, who also designed the Scotswood Suspension Bridge over the Tyne. Green used a technique originally devised for road bridges — using a laminated timber arch in which the laminations were bent into position. They lasted until 1869, when they were replaced with iron.

108 WILL'S FACTORY, producing cigarettes and *L:r* tobacco, is in Cochrane Park, a suburb of Newcastle. The enormous red-brick building was begun in 1947: the factory opened in 1950.

109 KILLINGWORTH was at the centre of the Tyne district mines and part of the Grand Allies — one of the wealthiest and most powerful commercial partnerships to emerge during the Industrial Revolution. In 1804, the young

George Stephenson was employed at West Moor Pit, Killingworth, as a brakesman. Such was his skill and inventiveness that by 1812 he was in charge of all the Grand Allies' colliery machinery. West Moor was one of the most dangerous pits and Stephenson invented the Geordie Safety Lamp at the same time as Humphry Davy invented his own safety lamp. **Dial Cottage**, Great Lime Road, West Moor is *R:l* about half a mile to the east of the railway line. It was Stephenson's home when he worked in the pit. To the west is **Gosford Park Race-** *L:r* **course**.

110 **CRAMLINGTON** (BR) The **blackened tower** *R:l* to the east of the sandstone station is the base of an old windmill.

111 **RIVER BLYTH** The line between Newcastle and Berwick crosses several beautiful tree-lined steep-sided river valleys. The port of Blyth, sited where the river joins the North Sea, was once an important coal-exporting port. Now it is the outlet for Northumbrian grain and imports Scandinavian timber products. **Nether-** *R:l* **ton Hall** can be seen amongst the trees.

112 **MORPETH** (BR) The new **red-brick offices** *L:r* immediately south of the station are the headquarters of Northumberland County Council. Morpeth is below the railway line and much of the town is hidden by trees. It is possible to see the top of the **castle** which consists of the *L:r* remains of a Norman motte and bailey with a fifteenth-century tower house built in the form of a gatehouse. Away to the east is the **Lyne-** **mouth Aluminium Factory**. Morpeth Station *R:l* was built in 1847 and designed by Benjamin Green. It is one of the finest of the stations he

designed for the Newcastle and Berwick Railway, of rock-faced stone and built in the Tudor style.

River Wansbeck The railway line crosses the steep-sided valley of the Wansbeck. The old **County Asylum** on the hill was built in 1859. *L:r*

113 **PEGSWOOD** (BR) is a mining village. There are open-cast coalmines throughout the area, and as far north as Chathill, all part of the Northumberland and Durham coal field. One of the most impressive pieces of equipment used in the coal fields is 'Big Geordie', a vast excavator with a bucket big enough to hold a double decker bus.

114 **LYNEMOUTH** is on the coast about $4\frac{1}{2}$ miles *R:l* to the east. It is at the centre of a heavy coal-mining area and has a large power station and aluminium works. **Lynemouth Colliery** is slightly nearer the railway line.

115 **WIDDRINGTON** (BR) is another of Benjamin *R:l* Green's stations with patterned bargeboards. Though there is a first view of the **North Sea** *R:l* away to the east, the area appears predominantly industrial, with brickworks, extensive sidings, coal trucks and pitheads dotting the landscape. The village was the first halt of James VI and I after leaving Berwick on his way to London to assume the English Crown in 1603. Had he passed along the future track of the railway he would have had a further $291\frac{1}{2}$ miles to travel.

116 **ACKLINGTON AIRFIELD** was an RAF base *R:l* during the Second World War, then became an air-sea rescue station but is now the site of an open prison.

117 **ACKLINGTON** (BR) has a symmetrical *L:r*
Tudor-style station building by Green in
brownish-yellow stone with mullioned windows and a canopy over the platform. **Coal** *R:l*
trucks can be seen from the train, apparently
stranded in open fields. A network of railway
lines criss-crosses the countryside serving the
open-cast coalmines. Mining in the vast Northumberland and Durham coal field began as
early as the thirteenth century, but expanded
after 1800. Though many of the pits have a
doubtful life expectancy, there are seams of
coal under the North Sea offering potential
supplies for the future.

118 Crossing the **RIVER COQUET** The Coquet
flows down a deep tree-lined valley from the
Cheviots to join the sea at Amble. **Coquet** *R:l*
Island is immediately off the coast and can be
seen from the train a little further north.

119 **WARKWORTH CASTLE** The remains of *R:l*
Green's **Warkworth Station** can be seen beside
the line. The castle is across the fields towards
the coast in a loop of the River Coquet. It became an important military base in the twelfth
century and in 1332 passed to Henry, 2nd Lord
Percy of Alnwick. It remained the second house
of the Percys (Alnwick Castle is their main
residence) until 1922, when the 8th Duke of
Northumberland handed it over to the state.
The 3rd Lord Percy of Warkworth was created
Earl of Northumberland in 1377 by Richard II.
He and his son Harry Hotspur spent much of
their lives plotting against the monarchy and
after helping to put Henry IV on the throne
they then conspired to dethrone him. Three
scenes of Shakespeare's *Henry IV Part One* take
place in Warkworth Castle, that 'worm-eaten

hold of ragged stone', where the Earl defended himself after the failure of his conspiracy and after his son Hotspur had been killed by Prince Hal at the Battle of Shrewsbury.

120 **ALNMOUTH** (BR) The sea is very close at this point and the seaside village of **Alnmouth** *R:l* (once pronounced 'Alemouth') can be seen at the mouth of the River Aln just south of the station. Alnmouth was the gateway to Northumberland for the Anglo-Saxons and was used to establish their settlements in the Aln Valley. The names they gave to the two heights which command the view over the bay still persist: Spy Law and Look Out. To the east is the profile of the **advance-warning radar station** *R:l* at Lesbury.

121 **ALNWICK** As the train crosses over the **River** *L:r* **Aln** it is just possible – on a clear day – to see the town of Alnwick to the west, together with **Alnwick Castle**. The castle has been the residence of the Percys since 1309. After their defeat by Henry IV, the family remained quiet for over a century. However, they were a strong Catholic family: in 1568, along with the Dacres, they rose against the Protestant Elizabeth I. Thomas the 7th Earl of Northumberland was beheaded in 1572 but beatified by Rome. He had carried out extensive restoration work on the castle but it was Hugh, the 1st Duke of Northumberland (Sir Hugh Smithson), who restored the whole estate. He employed Robert Adam to turn the castle into a comfortable home in 1755–66. **Brislee Tower** was *L:r* erected in 1781.

122 **HOWICK ESTATE** is visible from the train. *R:l* Lord Howick bitterly opposed George

Stephenson's planned route for the Newcastle and Berwick Railway which was to pass immediately to the west of his house. Stephenson wrote to a friend: 'I am rather astonished at Lord Howick's observations about the line passing Howick. It does not go through any of their pleasure grounds ... there is a turnpike road between the house and the intended railway ... it is compensation they want, nothing else.' What Lord Howick really wanted was for Stephenson to build the line through the limestone quarries on the estate. Stephenson was furious: 'I have never taken any part in politics, but I think I now will and become a Tory, and I shall buy a piece of land in Northumberland to oppose Lord Howick.'

123 **DUNSTANBURGH CASTLE** is now a dis- *R:l* tant but spectacular ruin perched on the coast above the North Sea. Most of it was finished in 1314, but the barbican was added in the late fourteenth century. Dunstanburgh experienced fighting in the border wars and in the Wars of the Roses when the castle was besieged by an army of 10,000.

124 **CHATHILL** (BR) is another attractive station *L:r* in local stone by Green. The branch line to Seahouses on the coast used to leave from here. The **Cheviot Hills**, rising to 2,176 feet, lie to *L:r* the west. They are based mainly on volcanic rocks and granite.

125 **BELFORD** was one of Green's most pic- *L:r* turesque stations with a distinctive lancet-arched porch. Now it is closed and stands beside the line, boarded up, forlorn and in need of a new owner. Surtees based his comic hunting stories on the people he knew around here.

126 **BAMBURGH CASTLE** On a clear day it is *R:l* possible to see Bamburgh Castle on the coast. The castle is in a dramatic position perched on a basalt outcrop overlooking the North Sea. The site has been occupied since the 1st century BC when it was in the territory of the Votadini tribe. The keep was built by the Normans and the castle remained a military stronghold of the crown until the fifteenth century. Though defended by Henry VI, the castle finally fell to the gunfire of Edward IV during the Wars of the Roses. One of its famous prisoners was Piers Gaveston, favourite of Edward II. The castle fell into decay until the 1st Lord Armstrong bought it at the end of the nineteenth century and carried out extensive restoration and reconstruction work. Now the castle is a home for the Armstrongs as well as providing leasehold flats: parts are open to the public. From the **Longstone Lighthouse** on **Farne Island**, a *R:l* little further up the coast, Grace Darling and her father made their famous rescue.

127 **HOLY ISLAND AND LINDISFARNE** *R:l* **CASTLE** There is a clear view of Holy Island from the train, as the railway line passes close to the coastline. Holy Island is one of the outcrops which are part of Whin Sill, a massive volcanic feature which stretches across the Pennines. The basalt outcrops on which Lindisfarne and Bamburgh Castle were built were formed by molten rock forcing its way between the sedimentary rocks (limestone and sandstone on Holy Island). Part of Hadrian's Wall is built along the top of the sill as it crosses Britain.

Aidan and his Irish monks settled on the island in 634 AD and proceeded to evangelise Northumberland. The Lindisfarne Gospels, now in the British Museum, were written in this period. Cuthbert, one of the most famous bishops of Lindisfarne, is buried in Durham Cathedral. The Venerable Bede recorded Cuthbert's work on the island: 'he handed on the monastic rule by teaching and example . . . He became famous for miracles, for his prayers restored sufferers from all kinds of disease and affliction.' The island was abandoned between 875 and 1082 because of constant threats from the Danes, but in 1082 the Bishop of Durham established a Benedictine Priory on the island which he renamed Holy Island. The Priory survived until its dissolution in 1537 and the ruins can still be seen.

Lindisfarne Castle dates from the sixteenth century, when the occupants of the island were famous for their wrecking activities: 'the common people ther do pray for shippes which they sie in danger. They al sit down upon their

Lindisfarne Castle

knees and hold up their handes and say very devotedly, Lord, send her to us, God send her to us.' The castle was bought in 1901 by Edward Hudson, the founder of *Country Life*, who employed Edward Lutyens and Gertrude Jekyll to turn it into a comfortable country house.

128 **HAGGERSTON CASTLE** All that remains of *L:r* Haggerston Castle is a tall tower with a yet higher stair-turret. The castle was rebuilt in the eighteenth and early nineteenth centuries, renovated by R. Norman Shaw at the end of the nineteenth century; but all was later de-molished except for the water tower.

For about a quarter of an hour after leaving Holy Island behind, heading north the train makes an exhilarating passage along the edge of the North Sea. To the west is the rough, hillocky windswept border country, to the east the vast expanse of sea, bordered by arable land up to the very point where the rock shelves into the sea.

129 **TWEEDMOUTH** The Newcastle and Berwick Railway reached Tweedmouth on 1 July 1847, but until Stephenson's Royal Border Bridge was opened in 1850 passengers had to cross the Tweed by ferry. Excursions between Edinburgh and Newcastle were popular even before the bridge was opened. The North British Railway put an advertisement in *The Scotsman* in 1849 entitled 'Excursion to England: the Parties who have arranged this trip to England announce it with perfect confidence, on account of the complete nature of the Travelling arrange-ments, and because the district of country through which the Party will pass is famed for

its varied and picturesque scenery. Each passenger, on Purchasing his Ticket, will be furnished with a Card, which will inform them of all that is to be seen in Newcastle.' First class return fare from Edinburgh to Newcastle was 15s. Not only tourists caught the train. Every weekday live animals were sent to the London markets: the fare for a sheep was 3s 6d and for a lamb 2s 6d.

130 Crossing the **RIVER TWEED** The train crosses the Tweed on Robert Stephenson's magnificent **viaduct** which was opened by Queen Victoria on 29 August 1850. The view of **Berwick-** *L:r* **upon-Tweed** and the **Tweed estuary** is spec- *R:l* tacular as the train follows the sweeping curve of the viaduct. Over 2,000 men helped to build the bridge, which is 2,160 feet long and consists of 28 red-brick semicircular arches, each of 61 feet 6 inches span, carrying the rails 126 feet above the river bed. The Nasmyth steam piledriver was used to construct the coffer dams and the foundations of the elegant tapering stone piers. The river has given its name to the cloth, the production of which, from local hill sheep, began in the valley in the eighteenth century.

The **Royal Tweed Road Bridge** was con- *R:l* structed in 1925–8 by L. G. Mouchel and Partners. It is 1,410 feet long with four reinforced concrete arches and parapets of sandstone. Beyond the road bridge is the oldest surviving bridge at Berwick, the **Old Bridge**, com- *R:l* pleted in 1634. It consists of 15 arches, is 1,164 feet long and 45 feet high and cost the large sum (in those days) of £15,000.

George Borrow described his impression of

crossing the Tweed to Berwick early in the nineteenth century in *Lavengro*. 'Before me, across the water, on an eminence, stood a white old city, surrounded with lofty walls, above which rose the tops of tall houses, with here and there a church or steeple. To my right hand was a long and massive bridge, with many arches and of antique architecture, which traversed the river. The river was a noble one, the broadest that I had hitherto seen. Its waters, of a greenish tinge, poured with impetuousity beneath the narrow arches to meet the sea, close at hand, as the boom of the billows breaking distinctly upon the beach declared.'

131 **BERWICK-UPON-TWEED** (BR) Whether Berwick was Scottish or English was a matter of dispute for centuries of the town's history. Between 1174 and 1482 the town changed hands no fewer than 14 times. It then became a 'free town' owing allegiance to neither country; as a result it failed to grow large either as an English outpost against the Scots, or as a Scottish focus for the Tweed basin. Finally, in 1885, Berwick became one of the parliamentary constituencies of Northumberland and the northernmost town in England. Its population approaches 15,000.

Murray's *Handbook for Travellers in Scotland* of 1875 warned travellers that the town 'is best seen from the railway and is not worth entering'. This is hardly fair, particularly since the local Preservation Trust has restored many of the fine classical buildings in the town. The promenade along the top of the town walls (fashionable in the eighteenth century), with views looking across the Tweed estuary and out to sea or over the attractive red pantiled roofs of the town, offers a unique experience.

MAP 8

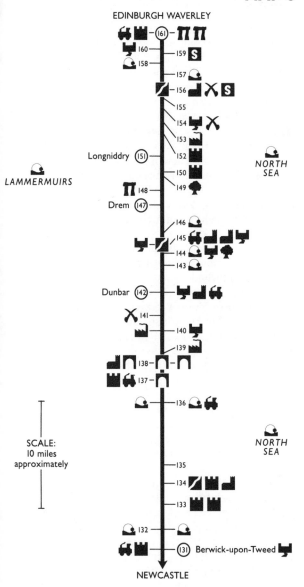

EDINBURGH WAVERLEY

161

160
159 S
158
157
156
155
154
153
152 Longniddry 151
150
149
148
Drem 147

LAMMERMUIRS

NORTH
SEA

146
145
144
143

Dunbar 142

141
140
139
138
137

136

SCALE:
10 miles
approximately

NORTH
SEA

135
134
133

132

131 Berwick-upon-Tweed

NEWCASTLE

One of the chief features of the town's skyline is the octagonal cupola crowned by a short spire on the **Town Hall**. The Town Hall was *R:l* built in the mid-eighteenth century and originally had a gaol on the top floor.

The Elizabethan defences around Berwick help to make it a special town. Though the first castle was built in the twelfth century, it was Elizabeth I – worried by threats from Scotland – who built entirely new fortifications based on the Italian plan of Lucca in Tuscany. The bastions were designed by Italians, Portinari and Jacopo a Contio. The walls are nearly 1½ miles long, 22 feet high, 12 feet thick at the base and 10 feet thick at the top. With the accession of James VI of Scotland as James I of England, the defences became redundant and were never completely finished.

Berwick-upon-Tweed Station was sited in 1844 by the North British Railway on the remains of Elizabeth I's castle. Part of the original **medieval walls and turrets** can be seen *L:r* immediately to the west of the station, from where they run down to the river bank. The station consists of a two-storey red sandstone building with a central clock pediment and platform awnings. The elegant timber waiting rooms and offices are Edwardian; now painted chocolate brown, cream and red.

132 **LAMBERTON** The train crosses the border *L:r* between **England** and **Scotland** about three miles north of Berwick-upon-Tweed and near the village of Lamberton. The **sign** by the rails *L:r* also signals the crossing from **Northumberland** to **Berwickshire**. Lamberton Bar on the Great North Road was a popular spot for runaway couples from England – Scottish

marriages could be performed there. The **red** R:l
sandstone soil farmed below the line along the
sea's edge is particularly suited to potatoes.

133 **BURNMOUTH** The line curves inland at R:l
Burnmouth, which is a small fishing village. It is
possible to see its harbour at the foot of the
steep ravine immediately below the railway line.
Looking south-east from this point, **Lindisfarne** R:l
and Bamburgh Castles are plainly visible.

134 **AYTON** The line follows the valley of the
River Eye for several miles and there is a good
view of **Ayton Castle** on the opposite side of R:l
the valley. Though there was an older castle on
the site, the present red sandstone building is
thoroughly Victorian. It was built in 1851 in the
Scottish baronial style. **Ayton Church** is also R:l
Victorian: its spire can be seen below the line to
the west of the castle.

135 **RESTON** and Ayton both had railway stations R:l
which are now closed. Reston may appear to be
little more than a small isolated village, but it is
an important animal market for the area. The
animal pens can be seen from the train. The
market is owned by Berwick Auction Company
and there are weekly sales of cattle and sheep.
The best-known sales are in the autumn, however, when top quality suckled calves are sold.

136 **PENMANSHIEL MOOR** Reston is in a bleak
situation, with the **Lammermuir Hills** stretching
to east and west, blackened by their dense
covering of heather. The desolation of the area
even begins to impinge on the cocooned comfort inside the train, as the line cuts deeper into
the hills to pass through Penmanshiel Moor.
The train used to pass through Penmanshiel

Tunnel until a fall in the tunnel in 1979. Two men working in the tunnel were killed and the line was rerouted. The tunnel was sealed up as a permanent tomb. The train runs between black granite cuttings together with **Eye Water** and the **A1**. It is now 350 miles from London.

137 **COCKBURNSPATH** The remains of the old *L:r* station are to the west of the line. After Cockburnspath the line crosses the county border between **Berwickshire** in the south and **East Lothian** in the north, formerly **Haddingtonshire**. The coastal plain of East Lothian has some of the finest agricultural land in Scotland: cereals, potatoes, oil-seed rape and vegetables are the chief crops.

The train crosses the 125-foot high bridge over **Thornton Burn**; to the west is the ruined **Hamilton Fortress of Innerwick**. *L:r*

138 **DUNGLASS** The train crosses **Dunglass Burn** over a viaduct built in 1840 by Thomas Grainger and John Miller with a main span of over 120 feet. To the east the A1 crosses over a reinforced **concrete bridge** built by Blyth *R:l* and Blyth in 1932. The oldest bridge over the burn is to the west, a **single-span bridge** with *L:r* a battlemented parapet which was built in 1798. Just beyond this bridge is the fifteenth-century church of **St Mary's**, Dunglass. The church is in the grounds of the now demolished Dunglass House which was designed for the antiquary Sir James Hall. Hall (1761–1832) was a geologist and a chemist – the first geologist to apply laboratory experimentation to geological hypotheses.

139 **TORNESS NUCLEAR POWER STATION** *R:l*

is newly built, a very clean and inoffensive looking building compared with the coal-fired stations of Nottinghamshire and Yorkshire.

140 **BARNS NESS LIGHTHOUSE** is close to a *R:l* restored limekiln. The modern cement works opposite still makes use of the lime.

141 **BATTLE OF DUNBAR** The site of the Battle *L:r* of Dunbar is just south-west of Dunbar in **Broxmouth Park**. On 3 September 1650, Cromwell defeated the Scottish Covenanters who had earlier crowned Charles II King of Scotland at Scone. Cromwell then spent £300 carrying out repairs to the pier in Dunbar Harbour.

142 **DUNBAR** (BR) is an ancient seaport and royal borough. The harbour is sheltered between two headlands, with the remains of Dunbar Castle on the northernmost headland. Dunbar has seen much fighting and the coming and going of kings and queens. Edward II left from Dunbar harbour for England in some confusion after his defeat at the Battle of Bannockburn in 1314. 25 years later 'Black Agnes', the Countess of Dunbar, defended the town against the English. Mary Queen of Scots stayed in Dunbar Castle twice, once with her second husband, Lord Darnley, after he had killed her lover Rizzio, and once with her future husband, Bothwell, after he had murdered Darnley.

The **Belle Vue Hotel** is at the eastern end of *R:l* the town. It was built in 1900 in the 'Queen Anne Baronial style' and its grand pretensions reveal the town's importance as a resort. There are two golf courses and a distillery. Dunbar also maintained a garrison from the late eighteenth century until 1945.

Between the hotel and the station is the **parish church** with its 108-foot tower. It was *R:l* built in Dunbar red sandstone in 1818–21 by James Gillespie.

Dunbar Station is bypassed by fast trains. It *R:l* was built in 1845 in sandstone in the Tudor style and has an iron footbridge which was originally at Ayton Station.

The line now follows the coastline along the *R:l* **Firth of Forth**.

143 **THE BASS ROCK** can be seen immediately *R:l* north of the coastline. This huge inhospitable mount is 313 feet high, seven acres in extent and composed of hard volcanic rock. It is now the home of a vast bird colony including some 23,000 gannets, kittiwakes, razorbills, guillemots, puffin, shag and Solan geese. Humans once lived on the rock. St Baldred had a cell there early in the seventh century. A castle was built in the sixteenth century and in 1671 it was used to imprison Covenanters. Some of the prisoners seized control of the prison and held it for nearly three years until they were granted amnesty and walked out free men. The Rock thus became the last place in Britain to surrender to the government. R. L. Stevenson imprisoned David Balfour, the hero of his novel *Catriona*, in the castle.

144 **BERWICK LAW** is composed of volcanic rock *R:l* like Bass Rock. It rises 614 feet behind the town of North Berwick and can be seen from the train across the fields to the north. A watchtower on the Law dates from Napoleonic times. There is also an archway formed by the jawbone of a whale. Nearer the line, **Tyning-** *R:l* **hame House** is set in **Binning Wood**, planted

by the Earl of Haddington in the early
eighteenth century.

145 EAST LINTON The train crosses the **River** *R:l*
Tyne at East Linton over a bridge built in 1845.
The station for East Linton is closed, but the
battlemented **station house** remains beside *R:l*
the line. The chief landmark of the town is the
spire of **St Andrew's**, formerly the Free *R:l*
Church, close to the line and built mostly in
1879. Further away is the tower of the
Georgian parish church of **St Baldred**. A head- *R:l*
stone in the churchyard marks the grave of
Andrew Meikle, who invented the threshing
machine. The **water mill** is owned by the *R:l*
National Trust; on the other side is a Norman *L:r*
beehive **dovecot**.

146 TRAPRAIN LAW is a strange hill shaped like *R:l*
the back of a whale and rising to 724 feet. An
excavation on the Law in 1919 revealed a hoard
of native and Roman silver. It is composed of
the neck of an extinct volcano, but is now being
quarried away. Nearby is **Haddington**, once a
county town and the birthplace of John Knox
and Jane Carlyle.

147 DREM (BR; 1845) has an attractive iron lattice
footbridge. A wall-mounted fountain in the
station is inscribed 'NBR (North British Railway) Keep the Platform Dry'. Drem is in the
centre of some of the best farming land in East
Lothian. The area has been settled since the
Iron Age and there is an Iron Age multivallate
fort just to the south. The Knights Templar
established a chapel in Drem in the fifteenth
century: the shell of the chapel still stands.

148 THE HOPETOUN MONUMENT was *L:r*

erected in 1824 on the edge of the Garleton Hills to the 4th Earl of Hopetoun, by his 'affectionate and grateful tenantry'. The Earl became a hero of the Peninsular Wars after taking command of the British Army when Sir John Moore fell at Corunna.

149 **GOSFORD HOUSE** The trees to the north of *R:l* the line and close to the coast surround Gosford House, the home of the Earl of Wemyss, designed by Robert Adam in 1790. When the railway arrived, the family erected a lodge on the west side of their estate for access to Longniddry Station.

150 **SPITTAL** The ruined sandstone castle close to *R:l* the line, after crossing a small river, is the sixteenth-century **Redhouse Castle**, in the village of Spittal.

151 **LONGNIDDRY** (BR) has had a long association with coalmining and weaving. Mining continued in the area for five centuries until 1924. Weaving declined early in the nineteenth century and by 1836 there were only 200 inhabitants in the village. Even though the station was opened in 1845, the village remained undeveloped until 1916, when the Scottish Veterans' Garden Cities Association built 20 cottages and 2 shops. Looking out into the Firth of Forth it is possible to see **oil tankers** *R:l* and **oil rigs** waiting to be towed out to sea.

152 **SETON HOUSE** is actually a castle. It was *R:l* built on the site of Seton Palace, and the Chapel of St Mary and Holy Cross, dating from the thirteenth century, remains within the old palace walls. The palace was bought as a ruin by the Edinburgh lawyer Alexander Mackenzie. He

kept the seventeenth-century garden walls with their round corner towers and employed Robert Adam, in 1789, to design his three-storey castle in grey, yellow and brown stone.

153 **COCKENZIE POWER STATION** was built *R:l* by Kennedy & Donkin and Strain & Robinson, consulting engineers, and Robert Matthew, Johnson-Marshall & Partners, consulting architects. The two chimneys are 500 feet high. The power station is beside the old fishing village of **Cockenzie**, which was once a port for the export of coal. The first railway line in Scotland was built in 1772 to carry coal to Cockenzie.

154 **PRESTONPANS** (BR) is the seaward part of the borough of Preston and was named after the saltpans which were the foundation of its prosperity from as early as the twelfth century. The railway line is next to **Preston**, meaning *R:l* Priest's town: the monks of Newbattle and Holyrood owned lands here.

The site of the **Battle of Prestonpans** is *R:l* immediately east of the station. A cairn marks the site where the Hanoverian army of Sir John Cope was defeated by Prince Charles Edward's Highlanders in 1745. To the south is the monument to Colonel Gardner, killed in the battle. His house, where the wounded of both sides were taken afterwards, is just behind it.

Preston Towers is the shell of the fifteenth- *R:l* century tower house of the Hamiltons of Preston. The initials of Sir John and Dame Katharine Hamilton on the windows record the enlarging of the tower in 1626, when a house was constructed inside. It has been burned out three times, once by Cromwell. The dovecot nearby can house almost 1,000 birds.

155 **THE KINGDOM OF FIFE** is north of the Firth of Forth and can be seen rising up in the distance ahead of the train as it travels towards Edinburgh. The earliest inhabitants of the beautiful peninsula were the mysterious Picts, then the Scots. St Andrew's, once the ecclesiastical capital of Scotland and still the seat of the country's oldest university, is in Fife.

The line now passes from **East Lothian** to **Midlothian**.

156 **INVERESK** The train crosses the **River Esk** R:l and the extensive golf links reveal the recreational pursuit of the residents and visitors to Inveresk. Across the golf links is the spire of **St** R:l **Michael's**, the parish church, built in 1805 and designed by Robert Nisbet.

The **Battle of Pinkie** took place just east of R:l the river – the last battle between the English and Scottish crowns. The Duke of Somerset, Lord Protector of England, defeated the Scots led by the Earl of Arran, Regent for Mary Queen of Scots, in September 1547. Somerset hoped Mary would marry young Edward VI of England, but she went to France and married the Dauphin instead.

157 **PORTOBELLO** This seaside resort (which has R:l the largest open-air swimming pool in Europe) was named early in the eighteenth century after a Scottish sailor who assisted in capturing the Spanish fortress of Puerto Bello in the isthmus of Darien and called his Scottish home 'Porto Bello'.

158 **ARTHUR'S SEAT AND SALISBURY** L:r **CRAGS** As the train approaches the outskirts of Edinburgh, the strange-shaped volcanic hill known as Arthur's Seat rises up 822 feet in

front with the Salisbury Crags behind. The train passes through extensive light industrial development with sidings for the Freightliner Terminal.

159 MEADOWBANK SPORTS COMPLEX, with *R:l* facilities for over 30 sports, was opened in 1970 after much controversy and was first use for the Commonwealth Games. It covers 25 acres and the Highland Games take place here every August. Meadowbank Football Club is also based here.

160 PALACE OF HOLYROODHOUSE Just *L:r* before the train disappears into **Calton** tunnel to emerge in Waverley Station it is possible to see the towers and roofs of the Palace of Holyroodhouse below the Salisbury Crags. Holyrood is the official residence of the Queen when she visits Scotland. The present palace is mainly the work of Charles II, who began rebuilding in 1671. Mary Queen of Scots spent six years of her reign in the palace; her lover Rizzio was murdered here. The last Stuart to occupy the palace was Prince Charles Edward, who held a ball at the palace in 1745, just before his defeat at Culloden.

Palace of Holyroodhouse

161 **EDINBURGH** (BR) was first called the 'Athens
of the North' by the painter 'Grecian' Williams
because of the Grecian-style buildings on
Calton Hill and the nearby old Royal High *R:1*
School, now the City of Edinburgh Art Centre.
The **National Monument** on Calton Hill was
begun as a copy of the Parthenon though it was
never finished. The **Nelson Monument**,
shaped like a telescope and rising to 108 feet,
was erected on Calton Hill in 1806–16 in
honour of Nelson. The Grecian style was continued by W. H. Playfair in his designs for the
Royal Scottish Academy (1823) and the
National Gallery of Scotland (1845), which is in
Princes Street Gardens immediately opposite
the entrance to Waverley Station.

Edinburgh's 'golden age' was in the
eighteenth century, when it became a literary
metropolis. Tobias Smollett, Oliver Goldsmith,
Adam Smith and David Hume made it their
home: Samuel Johnson and Boswell were
visitors. Sir Walter Scott was born in Edinburgh
in 1771 and is commemorated by the extraordinary Gothic spire of the Scott Monument
designed by George Meikle Kemp in 1844. It is
200 feet high with 287 steps to the top and
dominates East Princes Street Gardens.

The nineteenth century brought the Industrial Revolution and the railways to Edinburgh.
The university achieved fame through the work
of Sir James Simpson, who discovered the use
of chloroform in 1847, and Lord Lister in his
work with antiseptics. Alexander Graham Bell,
the inventor of the telephone, was born in
Edinburgh in 1847 and attended the university.
By the end of the century Edinburgh was an
important centre of banking and insurance.
Robert Louis Stevenson, Kenneth Grahame and
Arthur Conan Doyle were all born in the city.

Conan Doyle studied medicine in Edinburgh and used one of his teachers – Joseph Bell – as a basis for Sherlock Holmes. Now Edinburgh is also the biggest industrial centre in Scotland after Glasgow.

Edinburgh Castle can be seen clearly from *L:r* the entrance to Waverley Station. It is in a magnificent site on top of the volcanic Castle Rock, 443 feet high. The oldest building still in use is the Norman Chapel which was built by Queen Margaret in 1076. Margaret was the wife of Malcolm III, the son of King Duncan, who was murdered by Macbeth and immortalised by Shakespeare. The House of Stuart began in 1371 and the castle became the family's residence but also sometimes their prison.

Waverley Station was opened on 12 June 1846. The station was confined by its geographical situation, in a narrow valley between the old and new towns of the city. The station buildings had to keep to a maximum of 30 feet above the level of the rails. Congestion was appalling: 'on the platforms... may be witnessed every evening in summer a scene of confusion so chaotic that a sober description of it is incredible to those who have not themselves survived it. Trains of caravan length come in portentously late from Perth, so that each is mistaken for its successor; these have to be broken up and re-made on insufficient sidings, while bewildered crowds of tourists sway up and down amongst equally bewildered porters on the narrow village platform reserved for these most important expresses... while the hands of the clock with a humorous air survey the abandoned sight, till at length, without any obvious reason and with sudden stealth, the shame-stricken driver hurries his passengers off into the dark' (1889).

Expansion was authorised to the west and east in 1892 and in 1900 was completed at a cost of £1,400,000. The tunnel was cut through Calton Hill and the station was rebuilt round a central island containing the booking hall and administrative offices. This, together with the 19 platforms, covered 23 acres. The booking hall has been replaced by a BR travel centre. However, the glazed rotunda above the central waiting room is still in place, with its attractive decorative frieze of garlands, cherubs and fruit in pale blue and gold. The yellow-brown stone walls are decorated with classical arches and pilasters which are repeated throughout the station so that it has become the perfect introduction to the 'Athens of the North'.

VICTORIA
AND WATERLOO
TO THE SOUTH

(Brighton · Dover · Southampton)

Contents

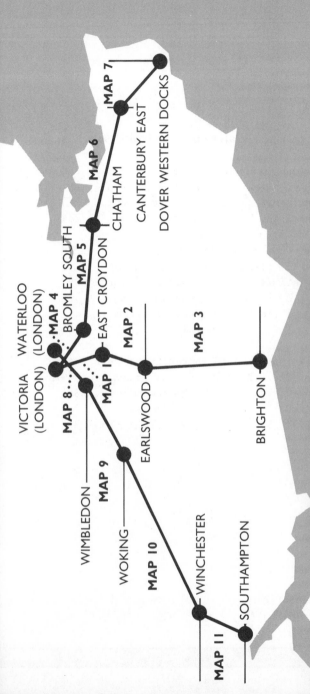

VICTORIA AND WATERLOO TO THE SOUTH

WATERLOO (LONDON)
VICTORIA (LONDON)
MAP 4
MAP 8
BROMLEY SOUTH
MAP 5
MAP 1
EAST CROYDON
MAP 2
MAP 6
CHATHAM
MAP 7
CANTERBURY EAST
DOVER WESTERN DOCKS
EARLSWOOD
MAP 3
BRIGHTON
WIMBLEDON
MAP 9
WOKING
MAP 10
WINCHESTER
SOUTHAMPTON
MAP 11

VICTORIA
TO
BRIGHTON

Introduction

The line from London to Brighton was first suggested in 1823 by William James, who wrote a pamphlet supporting a horse-operated line from Waterloo Bridge to Brighton. Sir John Rennie surveyed a line from Kennington Common straight across the Weald to a terminus at Brighton on the hillside above the Royal Pavilion. Rennie's line was placed before Parliament in 1835 alongside four rival routes. The chief rival was Robert Stephenson's 'natural' route, which was longer than Rennie's but less expensive because it avoided the High Weald and crossed the South Downs by the Adur Gap, thus needing few earthworks. Rennie's route was finally chosen, however, and the London and Brighton Railway Company was incorporated by Act of Parliament on 15 July 1837 to build a railway line from just south of Norwood Junction to Brighton.

On 12 July 1838 the first sod was cut north of Merstham Tunnel. John Urpeth Rastrick was the engineer, David Mocatta was the company's architect. On 21 September 1841 the line from London Bridge to Brighton was ceremonially opened. Massed bands, choirs and jubilant crowds assembled at Brighton. The *Brighton Herald* described how 'up to Clayton the county poured forth its inhabitants. Hurst and Ditchling sent out their populations, in holiday array, to meet the train at Hassocks station; and Patcham, Withdean and Preston all lent their quota to make up our general sum of joy'.

The London and Brighton Railway and the London and Croydon Railway (the line north of Norwood Junction) amalgamated on 27 July 1846 to form the London, Brighton and South Coast

Railway – the LBSCR. The London terminus continued to be London Bridge until the LBSCR helped to promote the West End of London and Crystal Palace Railway, which built a temporary terminus in Battersea and joined up with the LBSCR at Crystal Palace. In 1860 Grosvenor Bridge was completed and Victoria opened (see p. 263).

Even before the line was built 'stock-jobbers' were living in Brighton and commuting to their work in London. But the journey by coach was slow and expensive. In 1836, for example, 36 coaches ran daily between London and Brighton, carrying over 100,000 passengers, but the time taken was six hours, the 1st class fare was 21s (on the inside) and the fare outside was 12s. In 1846 the 1st class fare by train was 14s 6d, 2nd class 9s 6d. By 1875, the City Limited, the best train for businessmen, with all Pullman coaches by 1881, could reach London in 65 minutes.

But the service declined while other lines across the country improved. There was no competition, and 'creeping paralysis' overcame the LBSCR. The leisurely trips to and from the seaside were notorious, the subject of continuous satire. In September 1895 *The Times* described 'The Crawl to the South': 'It was a light train running on a lovely afternoon. We swept on so rapidly the speed could not alarm the most timid. We did not escape a single stop, yet steamed into Victoria so proudly at 5.30 pm I felt sure we must have arrived unexpectedly early. The Time Table (a work of fiction) indeed made us arrive at 4.37, but this seems merely to be a printer's error.' The situation is very much improved now: the fastest scheduled time between Victoria and Brighton is currently 51 minutes, and commuters have even been offered language classes to pass the time on their journeys to and from work.

One of the best known of all trains ran on the line from 1908 to 1972 – the Southern Belle, renamed the Brighton Belle with electrification in 1934. In Edwardian times it was particularly luxurious as Arnold Bennett's character Edwin Clayhanger discovered in *Clayhanger*: 'Everybody who came towards this train came with an assured air of wealth and dominion ... All the luggage was luxurious; handbags could be seen that were worth 15 to 20 pounds apiece. There was no question of first, second or third class; there was no class at all on this train ... When he sat down in the vast interior of one of these gilded vehicles, he could not dismiss from his face the consciousness that he was an intruder, that he did not belong to that world.'

After the First World War the Southern Belle introduced 2nd and 3rd class cars. In 1952 the Brighton Belle starred in the breathtaking film 'London to Brighton in Four Minutes'. The Brighton Belle was a favourite of the 'Railway Club' which was formed in 1923 by a group of talented Oxford undergraduates including Evelyn Waugh, Harold Acton and John Sutro. Meetings were held on the railways; private dining-cars were hired and attached to regular trains. The last meeting took place on the London to Brighton line in 1963. Evelyn Waugh described the elaborate proceedings: 'chefs were ... recruited from London restaurants and fine wine added to the fare. Silver cigarette boxes were presented to astonished engine-drivers and reception committees met us at our destinations.'

MAP 1

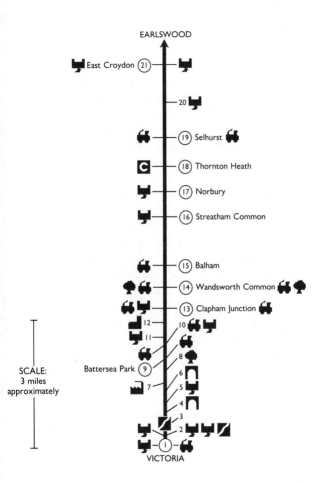

EARLSWOOD

East Croydon ㉑

20

⑲ Selhurst

⑱ Thornton Heath

⑰ Norbury

⑯ Streatham Common

⑮ Balham

⑭ Wandsworth Common

⑬ Clapham Junction

12

11

10

Battersea Park ⑨

8

7

6

5

4

3

2

SCALE:
3 miles
approximately

①

VICTORIA

1 **VICTORIA STATION** Throughout the summer months thousands of visitors to Britain arrive at Victoria from either the Channel Ports or Gatwick Airport. Their first impressions of a major London terminus and the capital itself could hardly be less inviting. Compared with the termini of Rome and Munich, Victoria appears to be a confusing jumble of oddly assorted, grubby buildings belonging to different, equally outrageous architectural styles. The smooth image of 1970s British Rail clashes awkwardly with earlier Edwardian Baroque frills. Outside, the busts of the famous high up on the Grosvenor Hotel stare down on the drab bus station and swirling traffic of Victoria. More building works are proceeding on top of the Brighton lines and there are plans to brighten up the station with bistros and boutiques. Meanwhile it is all very different from the days of the Brighton Belle with its Pullman carriages called Vera, Doris, Hazel, Gwen, Audrey and Mona. The Golden Arrow service to the continent has been revived by private enterprise but the Orient Express of the 1980s looks out of place with its Edwardian elegance amid the shoddiness of present-day Victoria.

The station has a complex and confusing history. Basically its design problems have been caused by the presence in one station of two railway companies. The terminus for the London, Brighton and South Coast Railway (LBSCR) and the terminus for the London, Chatham and Dover Railway (LCDR) were built alongside one another. Both companies had financial difficulties so were far less interested in creating favourable impressions in their London termini than wealthier companies such as the Great Western Railway. It was sometimes hard enough merely keeping their trains running, and there were constant criticisms for slowness, bad rolling stock and poor treatment of passengers.

In 1858 the LBSCR ended at a temporary terminus on the south bank of the Thames opposite Pimlico. The terminus was built by the West End of London and Crystal Palace Railway and opened on 29 March 1858. The Chelsea Suspension Bridge had been opened on 26 March so passengers had direct access across the Thames and into the West End. The LBSCR was joined by the East Kent Railway which changed its name to the LCDR in 1859.

The Victoria Station and Pimlico Railway approached the LBSCR for financial assistance to build a bridge across the Thames and a station close to Buckingham Palace, and received two-thirds of their capital from the Brighton line. In return the LBSCR had its own section of the terminus and its own access lines to the west. The LCDR and the GWR jointly rented the eastern side.

The terminus covered 14 acres on the site of the basin of the obsolescent Grosvenor Canal. The first part to be built was for the LBSCR and covered 8½ acres on the western side of the site. Robert Jacomb Hood, resident engineer of the company, designed the station which was covered with a 40-foot-high ridge and furrow roof and opened on 1 October 1860. Grosvenor Bridge, designed by Sir John Fowler, had been completed in June 1860.

The Brighton half of the station was dwarfed by the enormous **Grosvenor Hotel** which extended 262 feet down Buckingham Palace Road. The 300-room hotel was completed in 1861. The railway companies were too poor to erect such a colossus, which still dominates the western side of the terminus, so it was owned by an independent company attracted by the prospect of custom from the railways. James T. Knowles was the architect. The first and top floors are decorated with portrait busts set in medallions – unfortunately most are too high to identify clearly – of eminent Victorians including Palmerston, Lord Derby, Queen Victoria and Prince Albert.

None of the Victorian grandeur and pomposity displayed by the Grosvenor Hotel appeared in the LCDR's terminus on the eastern side, which was opened on 25 August 1862. John Fowler designed the 740-foot-long iron roof in the form of two tied lattice arch spans of 124 feet and 117 feet. These are still in position over platforms 1–8 which are used by the continental services.

The frontage of Victoria was an eyesore right from the beginning with no relationship between the designs of the two companies. The ends of the train sheds were closed off with 'untidy wooden structures ... in appearance more in keeping with those of some new town of mushroom growth in the wilds of Canada or Australia than with that of the leading railway station of London' (Harold Clunn, *London Rebuilt*). Inside, the Brighton half was hardly improved when, in February 1884, the Fenian Brotherhood left a home-made bomb in a Gladstone bag. It exploded and demolished the cloakroom and ticket office. Perhaps this inspired Oscar Wilde to place the infant hero of *The Importance of Being Earnest* in a Gladstone bag beside the Brighton line.

The LBSCR was the first to begin rebuilding when the company experienced mild prosperity in the 1890s. The Grosvenor Hotel was bought, redecorated and newly furnished and let to Gordon Hotels Ltd. A vast 150-room wing was added to the hotel across the front of the terminus. It was built in red brick and Portland stone in the 'free Renaissance' style and dominated by an illuminated clock flanked with recumbent figures. Behind this, the old station roof was removed and five new louvred ridge roofs were erected, the ridges 64 feet above rail level and supported on cast-iron columns 18 inches in diameter. Inside the station there was an impressive booking hall tiled in pale green and off-white with art nouveau motifs in green and gold mosaic. Outside, all along Buckingham Palace Road, the LBSCR was forced by Parliament to build an ornamental screen wall. This was designed by C. L. Morgan in Portland stone and red hand-made sand-faced Reading bricks – but the niches are still waiting for busts.

Soon after the new Brighton terminus began to emerge, the LCDR – renamed the SECR – began work on their new terminus. The style chosen has been called 'French Second Empire' and 'Edwardian Baroque'. Sir Arthur Blomfield was the architect and used Portland stone, decorating the front with a broken pediment carried by large busty mermaids. J. Lyons and Co. managed the 1st, 2nd and 3rd class refreshment rooms which were included in the new building.

The Railways Act of 1921 created the Southern Railway and made the two Victorias into one. Three years later a hole was broken open in the wall between the two termini. In 1930 the whole of platform 8 – the main continental arrivals platform – was roofed over to give passengers a more congenial setting in which to wait for their customs examination and even heating facilities were provided. Other forms of transport were eager to make use of Victoria's continental links and can be seen in, around and above the station. The cab yard in front of the station was the site for the London General Omnibus Company's bus station, opened in July 1926. In 1939 Imperial Airways opened its London terminal in Buckingham Palace Road. This was extended in 1963 under BOAC and an eight-storey block was built over the ends of platforms 15 to 17. In 1962 the first rail-air terminal in London was opened above the north end of platforms 15 and 16, designed by Clive Pascall in steel and glass.

Victoria is still changing. Work is in progress to create a separate rail-air terminal for passengers travelling to Gatwick Airport. Over platforms 9 to 19 a concrete 'raft' has been constructed upon which new terminal facilities will be built. A 200,000 sq. ft. office block is also being built by British Rail and Greycoat London Estates Group and will help offset the cost of the terminal – some £50 million. Passengers can now enjoy a fast service to Gatwick in air-conditioned coaches. Perhaps the surviving Victorian and Edwardian parts of Victoria Station will also be given a face-lift so that their incongruous styles and decorative details can be enjoyed to the full.

2 VICTORIA STATION TO GROSVENOR ROAD (NORTH BANK OF THE THAMES)

When, in 1860, the Victoria Station and Pimlico Railway Company completed the short stretch of line between Victoria and the temporary terminus on the south bank of the Thames, they were forced to disguise their line to the satisfaction of the influential and aristocratic landowners whose land they crossed. Almost all the way from the beginning of the line to the river the track was covered by a glazed roof supported on iron columns and arcaded brick walls. It must have created a more pleasing effect on arriving or leaving Victoria than the present views of the grubby utilitarian **blocks** *L:r* **of flats** and the cumbersome **British Airways** *R:l* **Terminal Building**.

Western Pumping Station

However, there is a clear view of the magnificent **Pumping Station** on the north bank of the *R:l* **River Thames**. The French chateau-like building with its ornate chimney was built as part of Joseph Bazalgette's system of sewers under London. The pump house raised the flow of sewage from the low western sewer – the Fulham branch – up to the level of the northern low-level sewer.

It is also possible to see the entrance to the **old Grosvenor Canal** between Grosvenor Bridge *R:l* and Chelsea Bridge.

3 **GROSVENOR BRIDGE** The railway line crosses the **Thames** on the Grosvenor Bridge. John Fowler, engineer of the Victoria Station and Pimlico Railway Company, designed the first bridge (see p. 263). The present bridge was built in 1963–7 by Freeman, Fox and Partners and carries ten tracks across five open-spandrel steel arches. It was constructed with virtually no interruption to the flow of traffic across the river – around 1000 trains a day.

4 **CHELSEA BRIDGE** The first Chelsea Suspen- R:l sion Bridge was opened on 26 March 1858 and provided direct road access to the West End from the temporary terminus in Battersea of the London to Brighton line, before the Grosvenor Bridge was built. The present bridge was designed by G. Topham Forrest, architect of the LCC, and built in 1934–7 by Rendel, Palmer and Tritton. It is a self-anchored suspension bridge and the pull at the ends of the cables is taken by a thrust through the stiffening girders. The main span is small for a modern suspension bridge, only 352 feet. The girders are an early use of high-tensile steel.

5 **ROYAL HOSPITAL CHELSEA** There is a R:l brief glimpse of Christopher Wren's Royal Hospital through the trees on the north bank and beyond Chelsea Bridge (although summer foliage does get in the way). After the establishment of a standing army during Cromwell's Commonwealth the country was faced with the problem of how to provide for invalided and veteran soldiers. Charles II laid the foundation stone of the hospital in February 1682 and when it was opened ten years later nearly 500 noncommissioned officers and men moved into

their new barracks. Christopher Wren received £1000 for the design. The Chelsea Flower Show is held annually in the grounds.

6 ALBERT BRIDGE The fanciful Albert Bridge is *R:l* beyond Chelsea Bridge. It was designed by R. W. Ordish on his rigid suspension principle, and built in 1871–3. Diagonal wrought-iron stays radiate from the towers: the light suspension chains merely take the weight of the stays. In 1971–3 the main span of 400 feet was propped up to allow heavier traffic loads.

7 BATTERSEA POWER STATION was built in *L:r* two stages: the western half in 1929–35 with its innovative water sprays used to clean the chimneys; the eastern half in 1944–55 also supplying heating to the Churchill Gardens Estate just across the river. Sir Giles Gilbert Scott, the architect of Liverpool's Anglican Cathedral, was the consultant on the exterior. His details – the elaborate parapet and the decorations to the chimneys – created one of the most exciting industrial buildings of this century, as well as setting the pattern for the design of power stations for the next two decades. Battersea Power Station closed down completely in 1983 but the building is to be saved. Its most likely fate is to be used as a 'leisure theme park' (see also p. 356–7, Waterloo to Southampton).

8 BATTERSEA PARK was laid out in 1858 on the *R:l* site of Battersea Fields where, in 1829, the Duke of Wellington fought a duel with the Earl of Winchelsea. The Fields were popular not only for duels but also for gaming, sports and generally pleasurable pursuits. One Puritan visitor declared: 'surely if ever there was a place out of hell that surpassed Sodom and Gomorrah in ungodliness and abomination, this was it'. The present Festival Gardens are a little more sober with a 15-acre boating lake, a sub-tropical garden and sculptures by Henry Moore and Barbara Hepworth. The site was landscaped with earth which was brought up-river from Victoria Docks and then used to raise the surface of the open marsh on the site.

9 **BATTERSEA PARK** (BR, opened 1867 as York Road) The attractive two-storey **brick** *R:l* **booking hall** below the line (the top storey is visible from the train) cost £15,403. The Italianate-style building is decorated with leafy columns and female heads. Fortunately it is listed and much-needed restoration work has recently been carried out.

10 **RAILWAY LANDSCAPE – POUPARTS** *R&L* **JUNCTION** The lines to Brighton and to Dover are carried over the lines from Clapham to Waterloo on impressive brick viaducts. There are extensive views to west and east over this extraordinary wasteland of criss-crossing railway lines, viaducts and bridges, abandoned goods yards and sheds, old and new factories and warehouses and, further away, the endless roofs and chimneys of Victorian and Edwardian suburban London, broken up by tower blocks built since the Second World War.

The **Dodington Estate** is just such a high-rise *R:l* development: grey concrete slabs along the Battersea Park Road, just north of the railway line as it curves west towards Clapham. Emberton, Frank and Tardrew designed the council estate for

Wandsworth and it was built in 1967–71, a time when, unfortunately, the quantity of housing was considered a higher priority than the quality.

Pouparts Junction, just east of Clapham Junction, was named after the Pouparts family who were market gardeners in the area.

11 **SHAFTESBURY ESTATE, CLAPHAM** The *L:r* two-storey Victorian terraced houses south of the line approaching Clapham Junction from the east are part of an estate completed in 1877 and built on the site of the Pouparts' market gardens. The estate was built by the Artisans, Labourers and General Dwellings Company, founded by Robert Austin in 1867. Austin was a builder and he designed the modest cottages for respectable artisans. The estate was deliberately built without a public house and apparently very quickly earned a reputation for the inebriation of its desperate residents. Originally there was an open space in the middle of the estate but this was built over when the company ran into financial difficulties. Now the cottages are being bought by 'Sloane Rangers' venturing across the Thames from Chelsea.

12 **LAVENDER HILL CHURCH** Above the *L:r* Shaftesbury Estate on the skyline is the red-brick Church of the Ascension, without spire or tower. It was designed by James Brooks and begun in 1876. J. T. Micklethwaite and Somers Clarke finished it in 1898 but the tower was never built and its bellcote was destroyed in a fire.

13 **CLAPHAM JUNCTION** (BR) The large department store **Arding and Hobbs** with its *L:r* baroque cupola dominates Clapham Junction. The

271

store was founded in Wandsworth in 1876 but rebuilt in 1910 after a fire. Its Edwardian grandeur was designed by James Gibson.

Clapham Junction Station was opened in 1863. It is the junction for trains from Waterloo and Victoria and was steadily enlarged over the years to become the world's busiest railway station. In 1882 1100 trains were passing through every day. It is still one of the busiest junctions in the world with a complex interweaving of tracks. The many platforms are connected by a very long enclosed brick viaduct under which the trains pass. The **oldest buildings** which belonged to the *L:r* LSWR (the line to Southampton) are on platforms 9 and 10, of dirty yellow stock brick with red brick trims, Gothic arches and fine iron columns and brackets. A new entrance is being built on St John's Hill, part of a larger development which will include offices and a shopping centre. The old **Edwardian entrance**, sadly derelict, can just be *L:r* seen at the western end of the station above a dirty black brick wall and close to Barclays Bank.

14 **WANDSWORTH COMMON** (BR) There is an attractive **red-brick station building** erected *L:r* in 1869 on the side of the line; on the other an **Edwardian station building** which cost exactly *R:l* £4481 5s 2d!

The railway line cuts **Wandsworth Common** in half. The common has been a preserved piece of ground since the Wandsworth Commons Act was passed in 1871. There is a sail-less weather-boarded windpump on the common which was erected in the late 1830s to restore the water supply which had been broken by the railway cutting.

15 BALHAM (BR; Northern line station by Charles Holden, 1926)   Balham was never a proper village, just a settlement on the main road between Clapham and Tooting. It expanded with the arrival of the railway. Victorian and Edwardian houses back on to the railway line, their gardens reaching almost to the track. The fine brick walls with recessed panels which run alongside the track were built by the railway company and extend for miles through the suburbs of southern London.

The **signal box** south of the station is in the *L:r* 'Odeon' style which is common to almost all the signal boxes on the line to Brighton.

16 STREATHAM COMMON (BR)   Just before Streatham Common Station is the fanciful **Streatham Common Pumping Station**. It was *L:r* built in 1888 for the Southwark and Vauxhall Water Company and its copper domes give it a Moorish appearance.

17 NORBURY (BR)   The elegant stuccoed house with a central bow window which can be seen across parkland at Norbury Station is **Norwood** *L:r* **Grove**, on Gibson Hill, Upper Norwood.

The Impressionist painter Camille Pissaro (1830–1903) fled to London during the Franco–Prussian War and painted the expanding suburb of Norbury. Norbury, Streatham to the north and Thornton Heath to the south are virtually indistinguishable from one another as residential areas. They were created around their railway stations (which were all rebuilt in 1902–3 in red brick when the line was widened). The most sought-after areas to live in were on higher ground such as around the Crystal Palace. Smaller, cheaper houses filled in the

surrounding low ground of Norbury, Tooting and
Balham.

18 THORNTON HEATH (BR)   There are good
views of the **television mast at Crystal Palace** *L:r*

Crystal Palace Television Mast

from Norbury and Thornton Heath. The mast is close to the National Recreation Centre which is on the site of the Crystal Palace. This was a vast, entirely pre-fabricated iron and glass palace designed by Joseph Paxton for the Great Exhibition of 1851. It was first erected in Hyde Park, then moved to Sydenham in 1852–4. The poet John Davidson described the 'Victorian temple of commercialism ... like some immense crustacean's ganoid skeleton, unearthed, and cleansed and polished'. It was destroyed by fire in 1936 except for two towers and these were demolished during the Second World War in case they might provide a landmark for enemy aircraft. The stadium and sports hall of the Recreation Centre were designed by the LCC Architect's Department in 1956–64. Lifesize ferro-concrete prehistoric monsters roam around the lake.

19 **SELHURST** (BR)   Just south of Selhurst Station is the complex **Gloucester Road Junction** where *R&L* the lines divide to Brighton, Sutton and West Croydon.

20 **DAVIDSON LODGE, FORMERLY THE** *L:r* **FREEMASONS ASYLUM** faces the railway line just before East Croydon Station. S. W. Daukes designed the almshouses in 1852 for the use of 'worthy, aged and decayed freemasons'. The attractive red brick building has a big Dutch gable in the centre, blue diapering and stone trims.

21 **EAST CROYDON** (BR)   Until the last century Croydon was an identifiably individual market town. The Archbishop of Canterbury has had a palace in the town since the Middle Ages and some

of the 14th- and 15th-century buildings survive.
The palace was one of several on the route from
Canterbury to Lambeth and was used as the
administrative centre for the Archbishop's estates
in Surrey, Middlesex and Hertfordshire.

Now Croydon has been swallowed up by the
relentless southern spread of London, and its
modern centre of shopping precincts, multi-storey
car parks and office blocks is indistinguishable from
other town centres built since the Second World
War. Since the end of the war Croydon has been a
popular business centre attracting companies from
central London with the lure of lower rates and fast
communications with the capital. In 1981 the
population was 317,980, the highest of all London
boroughs. Even in the recession office development
continues at an apparently reckless pace. **N. L. A.** *L:r*
House, the octagonal office block of 23 storeys,
was designed by R. Seifert and Partners and built in
1968–70, sited in the middle of a roundabout. **The
Law Courts** are immediately south of the station *R:l*
and behind them, contained in one block, are the
Ashcroft Theatre, the **Fairfield Concert Hall**
and the **Arnhem Gallery**, all designed by Robert
Atkinson and Partners.

East Croydon Station was first opened in 1841.
Extra platforms were added in 1860 when the line
was opened to Victoria. The new platforms were
treated as a separate station and called New
Croydon – no doubt to the confusion of the
passengers. In 1897–8 the two stations were
amalgamated and three island platforms built. East
Croydon has always been a spacious station, coping
with thousands of commuters. In 1931, for example, 1.3 million passengers booked tickets and
20,000 season tickets were issued. Now the fast

MAP 2

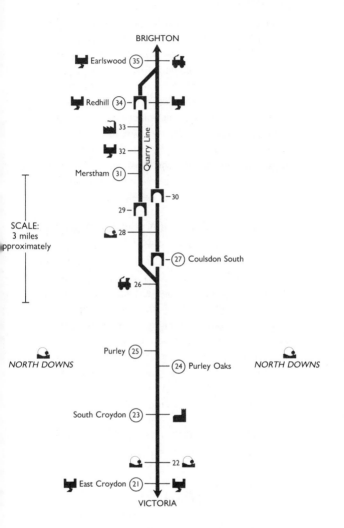

BRIGHTON

Earlswood ㉟

Redhill ㉞

33

32

Merstham ㉛

Quarry Line

30

29

28

㉗ Coulsdon South

26

SCALE:
3 miles
approximately

Purley ㉕

㉔ Purley Oaks

NORTH DOWNS

NORTH DOWNS

South Croydon ㉓

22

East Croydon ㉑

VICTORIA

trains to Brighton stop only at East Croydon.

D. H. Lawrence lived in Croydon from 1908–12, working as a school teacher and writing *The White Peacock*, *The Trespasser* and the beginning of *Sons and Lovers*. Tuberculosis forced him to give up teaching and return to his native Nottinghamshire. The contrast between suburban London and the countryside around his place of birth affected Lawrence deeply and he wrote in *The White Peacock*: 'there is no night in a city. How can I lose myself in the magnificent forest of darkness when night is only a thin scattering of the trees of shadow with barrenness of lights between?'

22 **CROYDON TO COULSDON: THROUGH THE NORTH DOWNS** Between Croydon and Coulsdon the train passes through a series of dark tree-lined cuttings as it ascends the steep slope of the North Downs. Though the surrounding countryside has long since disappeared beneath residential and commercial development there is still a sense of the land undulating naturally beneath the man-made covering of asphalt and concrete. South Croydon, Purley Oaks and Purley Stations are all situated in a deep dry valley which was used to advantage by the builders of the railway line.

23 **SOUTH CROYDON** (BR) Following its residential expansion caused by the arrival of the railways, Croydon set about building churches, a waterworks and, in the 20th century, its own power station. **St Peter's** is the church visible *R:1* from the train at South Croydon Station. It was designed by Sir George Gilbert Scott and built in 1849–51. The spire was completed in 1864 and rebuilt the following year after a fire. St Peter's is a

Commissioners' church, specially built to cope with
the rapidly increasing population.

24 PURLEY OAKS (BR)

25 PURLEY (BR) Both Purley Oaks and Purley
Stations were opened in 1899, catering for the
improved suburban services and consequent increase in the number of railway commuters. The
electrification of the line offered faster, more
frequent and cheaper trains.

   On the hillside opposite Purley Station is the
Thomas More High School which as the Russell *R:l*
Hill Schools was designed by John G. Bland and built
in 1863–4 for the children of warehousemen,
clerks and drapers. The red-brick building is in an
extravagant 'Venetian Gothic' style with many
gables and a spike on top of the raised centre.

26 THE QUARRY LINE Quadrupling of the London to Brighton line began in the 1860s and in 1864
two extra lines were opened from London Bridge
to South Croydon. By 1899 quadrupling had
reached a point just north of Coulsdon South. A
new line was then built from Coulsdon North
(closed 1983) to Earlswood Junction. This line, 6½
miles long, is known as the Quarry Line and avoids
Merstham and Redhill. It was opened to goods
trains on 8 November 1899 and to express trains
on 1 April 1900. It is now used by the fast trains to
Brighton.

27 COULSDON SOUTH (BR) The fast line
bypasses the station through a tunnel.

28 FARTHING DOWN The chalk ridge above *L:r*

the railway lines which extends to the south of
Coulsdon South Station and tunnel is Farthing
Down. Romano–British fields have been discovered
on the ridge and some pottery dating from the 1st
to 2nd centuries AD. The remains of a large
cemetery of 30 burial mounds have also been
found, dating from the 6th to 7th centuries AD,
together with a skeleton, iron knives, a sword and
shield boss. A slightly more recent and prominent
feature on the Down are the anti-aircraft trenches
dug during the Second World War.

29 **QUARRY TUNNEL**   The tunnel is 1 mile 353
yards long and takes the fast trains to and from
Brighton through the North Downs.

30 **MERSTHAM OLD TUNNEL** is 1 mile 71 yards
long and was the first tunnel dug by the London and
Brighton Railway Company through the Downs.
The company experienced some labour problems
while it was being dug. The navvies threatened to
strike because their supply of beer was two miles
away. To keep the workforce contented, the
company employed boys to fetch the beer, paying
them ½d a journey. When the tunnels were
opened they were whitewashed and lit by gas. The
tops of the ventilating shafts are marked by a line of
brick drums across the countryside. The stopping
trains use this tunnel.

31 **MERSTHAM** (BR)   The fast trains bypass the
station to the east. Since the Middle Ages Merstham has been famous for its stone which was used
to build Westminster Abbey. In the 19th century
the town also became an important centre for lime.
Royal Assent was given on 17 May 1803 for the

Croydon, Merstham and Godstone Iron Railway Company to extend the Surrey Iron Railway in the Wandle Valley up the dry valley south of Croydon to the Merstham Gap in the North Downs and on to Reigate. The railway was to carry local stone and fuller's earth from the quarries at Merstham and came into operation in 1805 with horses pulling the wagons along the tracks. The line never got further than the Greystone Lime Works at Merstham (now a gash in the face of the Downs alongside the tunnel entrances) and was closed in 1838. However, when the London and Brighton Railway Company planned the route of their railway they built their track close to the earlier line which is still used in parts as a country footpath.

32 **GATTON PARK** The south front of Gatton *R:l* Park is visible from the fast and slow lines though the house appears to be a long way off. It is now the Royal Alexandra and Albert School. Originally built in the early 19th century, it was rebuilt by Sir Edwin Cooper in yellow limestone in the Classical Revival style after a fire in 1934. The borough of Gatton was one of the most notorious of the rotten boroughs. When it returned two Members of Parliament in 1832, the borough contained only 23 houses. Now there is one house, one church and no MP. The 'Town Hall' in the grounds of Gatton Park was built in 1865. It is nothing more than a small open Doric temple under which the so-called 'elections' were held. The inscription (in Latin) reads, somewhat ironically:

> When the lots have been drawn the urn remains
> Let the well-being of the people be the supreme law
> The place of assembly of Gatton 1746
> Let evil deception be absent.

33 HOLMETHORPE INDUSTRIAL ESTATE *L:r*
stretches to the east of the fast line with the
extensive quarries of Holmethorpe British Industrial Sand. The clay vale of Holmesdale lies between
the North Downs and the greensand ridge on
which Redhill has developed. The vale is made up of
clay and sand washed down from the greensand
outcrops to the south. One of the old quarries,
known as Mercers Lake, is now used for water
sports.

34 REDHILL (BR) The fast trains bypass Redhill
through the **Redhill Tunnel** which is 649 yards
long and passes under Redstone Hill. Redhill grew
up at a natural gap in the greensand ridge – the
point at which first the Brighton Road (1807) and
then the Brighton Railway (1841) followed the
easiest route through the hills. The ridge has
provided many stones for building including the
Kentish ragstone used in the eastern part of the
Weald, in particular for the tall towers of churches.

On the slow line, just before the station, it is
possible to see **St Anne's**, the rambling red brick *L:r*
19th-century house which is now empty but once
housed elderly mental patients.

Development of the **centre of Redhill** is in *R:l*
progress, and a new library, civic centre and
shopping centre were opened in 1986.

35 EARLSWOOD (BR; two-storey **red-brick sta-** *R:l*
tion building 1905) The fast and slow lines join
up again north of Earlswood Station. This was an
important junction in the early years of the railway.

South of the station is the extraordinary Victorian building designed by W. B. Moffat for the
mentally handicapped – the **Royal Earlswood** *L:r*
Hospital. The rambling building is in red brick

Royal Earlswood Hospital

with limestone trims, in a sort of Jacobean style with a central tower. Dr Andrew Reed formed a charity in 1847 to provide an institution for the 'cure and care of idiots'. The hospital was opened in 1855 by Prince Albert (the station at Earlswood was built by the LBSCR specifically for the opening). It was first known as the Asylum for Idiots, then the Royal Earlswood Institution, and finally, in 1948, when it became part of the National Health Service, the Royal Earlswood Hospital. Now the 'hospital' part of the title may be dropped. The patients, once called inmates, are now known as residents – a reflection of the move to avoid identifying the mentally handicapped as 'sick'.

36 **SALFORDS** (BR) A halt was first constructed at Salfords in 1916 for the use of the Ministry of Munitions and the local Monotype works. The

MAP 3

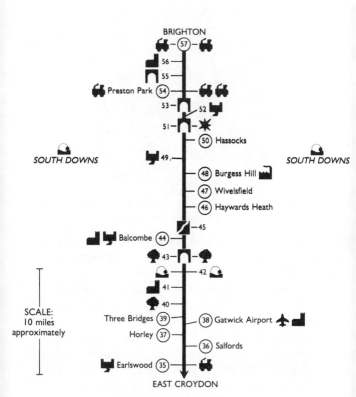

BRIGHTON

57

56

55

Preston Park 54

53

52

51

50 Hassocks

49

SOUTH DOWNS

48 Burgess Hill

47 Wivelsfield

46 Haywards Heath

45

Balcombe 44

43

42

SOUTH DOWNS

41

40

Three Bridges 39

38 Gatwick Airport

Horley 37

36 Salfords

Earlswood 35

EAST CROYDON

SCALE:
10 miles
approximately

station was opened in 1932 and serves the housing estates, farms, riding schools and golf courses which cover the level clay plain of the Weald. The heavy sodden soils of the Low Weald have created rather a featureless landscape and, until the railways came, few settlements. Drainage has led to the conversion of the land into orchards and pasture for cattle.

37 **HORLEY** (BR)   The old village of Horley has changed dramatically since the arrival of the railway and is now predominantly mid-20th-century housing and light industry. The original 1841 Tudor-style cottage station building designed by David Mocatta has not survived: most of his work on the Brighton line has gone.

38 **GATWICK AIRPORT** (BR)   The station for Gatwick Airport was opened in 1958 and has three broad island platforms linked to the airport buildings by overhead bridges.

Gatwick Airport is still in the process of *R:1* expanding. The buildings close to the station were designed by Yorke, Rosenberg and Mardall in 1958 and added to ever since. Sensible planning has made the best use of the junction of road, rail and air to create an efficient functional style. The new North Terminal of Gatwick is almost complete. It is due to open in summer 1987 and will raise the capacity of the airport from 16 million to 25 million passengers a year. The North and South Terminals will be linked by a new, unmanned rapid transit shuttle which will transport passengers between the terminals.

A mile to the south is a circular white building, the **old terminal building**, popularly known as *R:1* the beehive, designed by Hoar, Marlow and Lovett in 1936 and built beside the railway. It gives a touch of nostalgia to the expanding modern airport.

West of the old control tower and across the airfield it is just possible to spot **St Michael's Church, Lowfield Heath**. This is a small church *R:l* of yellow sandstone with a pyramid spire on its tower. It was designed by William Burges (the architect responsible for the 'medieval' features of Cardiff Castle) in 1867, in his very individual and inventive Gothic style.

The train crosses the border between **Surrey** to the north and **Sussex** to the south.

39 **THREE BRIDGES** (BR) The station was opened in 1841 to serve the small market town of **Crawley** to the west. In 1947 Crawley was *R:l* designated a New Town, one of six satellite towns to be built beyond the green belt ring round London (Crawley, Basildon, Harlow, Hemel Hempstead, Hatfield and Stevenage), and its population increased from 10,000 to 60,000. Unlike many of the New Towns Crawley has kept its original centre. The new development has been built at right angles to the old High Street.

40 **CRABBET PARK** Only the mass of trees on *L:r* the estate of Crabbet Park is visible about a mile east of Three Bridges. The soft rose-coloured brick house was built in 1873 in the neo-Queen Anne style, designed by its owners, Wilfred and Anne Scawen-Blunt. They established an Arabian stud at the park which is now a school of equitation. Scawen-Blunt was a diplomat, poet and traveller and an expert in the politics of the Near East; his

wife Anne, the grand-daughter of Byron, became
an Arabic scholar.

41 **ST NICHOLAS'S, WORTH** is about a mile to *L:r*
the east on the edge of Worth Forest. The trees
make it difficult to see except in winter. The
church is mostly Anglo-Saxon, dating from the 11th
century although the tower and spire were added
in 1871. The journalist and political writer William
Cobbett wrote *Cottage Economy* (1821) while
staying at Worth Lodge (since demolished).

42 **THE HIGH WEALD**   Between Three Bridges
and Balcombe the railway line crosses the wooded
hilly countryside of the High Weald. This is an area,
stretching from Horsham to Hastings, of broken
upland which rises to as much as 800 feet in places.
The mostly sandy soil was once covered with dense
woodland but intense deforestation took place
providing timber for the local iron industry. In the
16th century there were 32 furnaces and 38 forges
in Sussex. When adequate supplies of wood
declined, the workers moved on to areas such as
South Wales.

43 **BALCOMBE TUNNEL** is 1,141 yards long and
reaches a maximum depth of 60 feet below the
surface. It is lined with bricks and has given endless
trouble because of damp continuing to seep
through. It is approached from the north through
Worth and Balcombe Forests, remnants of the *L&R*
forests which covered the Weald before deforestation began.

44 **BALCOMBE** (BR)   The station was opened in
1841 and there is a quaint timber '**Gentlemen's**' *L:r*

on the down side. Just north of the station is a brief glimpse of **St Mary's**, the Victorian parish church. *L:r*

45 **OUSE OR BALCOMBE VIADUCT** Travelling south, the train appears to shoot out into space as it leaves the side of the hill, supported by brick arches it is impossible to see. The viaduct carries the railway high above the **River Ouse** and is one of the few surviving works designed by David Mocatta, architect for the London and Brighton Railway Company. It is 1475 feet long and reaches a maximum height of 100 feet. It has 37 brick arches, each pier arched at the bottom as well as the top, an elegant classical balustrade and four mock Italianate pavilions at each end. It was completed in March 1841 and has offered travellers a magnificent view of the unspoilt Sussex countryside ever since.

46 **HAYWARDS HEATH** (BR) Haywards Heath is a chiefly residential town which has developed since the opening of the London to Brighton railway line. It has a good shopping centre, the attractive Beech Hurst Park and some modern estates around the centre.

47 **WIVELSFIELD** (BR) The station opened in 1886 as Keymer Junction and was renamed in 1896. South of Wivelsfield the line to Seaford and Eastbourne branches to the east.

48 **BURGESS HILL** (BR) The plain white **station** *R:l* **master's house and warehouses** were built in the late 19th century and are in a bad state of repair (1985). South of the station and to the west is the huge modern office block which is the

headquarters of **Stork Margarine**. The embank- *R:l*
ment which begins about a mile south of the station
is over a mile long and crosses an extensive area of
low-lying land. Nearly a million tons of soil were
used to build it.

Jack and Jill Windmills

49 SOUTH DOWNS   The scarp slope of the South
Downs stretches across the horizon to the south.
The chalk downs have been used for grazing by
sheep farmers for centuries. The **two windmills** *L:r*
on top of the hills are called Jack and Jill. Jack is a
brick tower-mill of 1876 and Jill is a wooden
post-mill with four sails of 1821, brought from
Dyke Road, Brighton, in about 1850.

   Ditchling Beacon, the highest point on the *L:r*
Downs, is just to the east. Richard Jefferies
descended from the train at Hassock's Gate in the
1880s to climb to the top. He wrote that looking
down into the Weald 'it seems as if the mighty blast
rising from that vast plain and glancing up the slope
like an arrow from a tree could lift me up and bear
me as it bears a hawk with outspread wings'.

50 HASSOCKS (BR)   The original station was called Hassock's Gate (1841–81) after the tollgate on

the nearby turnpike road. The gasworks at Hassocks which now supply the town were built to provide gas lighting in the Clayton Tunnel. It was thought lights would give passengers a 'feeling of confidence and cheerfulness' as well as enabling the driver 'to see the road throughout as well almost as in broad day'.

Hassocks Station was rebuilt in 1880 in the Norman Shaw style by Terence Harrison Myers. When it was demolished, the same firm of builders erected the present effort.

51 CLAYTON TUNNEL is 1 mile 499 yards long and reaches a maximum depth of 270 feet below the surface. The extraordinary **north entrance** *R:1* can be seen (if the train isn't going too fast) just before the train disappears into the darkness. It is in the shape of a pointed Gothic arch with castellated turrets on either side. A small cottage is perched directly above the entrance: hardly an ideal spot for peace, quiet and fresh air, particularly in the days of steam. The south entrance is comparatively plain, with a brick parapet capped with stone.

The tunnel was the scene of a severe **accident** on 25 August 1861. 23 people were killed in a triple collision. Faulty hand signalling based on time intervals allowed three trains to enter the tunnel almost at once: they had been dispatched from Brighton at 8.28, 8.30 and 8.35 but caught each other up in the tunnel. The accident led railway companies throughout the country to abandon such a risky method of signalling.

52 South of the tunnel the line passes through the **SOUTH DOWNS** in a grass-covered chalk-sided cutting which is a natural valley through the hills. A

Clayton Tunnel

tower mill can be seen, complete with sails, just *R:1* before Patcham Tunnel.

53 **PATCHAM TUNNEL** is 492 yards long. It was specially extended at the north end to protect the estate of a Major Paine. He lived at Patcham Place, a mid-18th-century house faced with black mathe-matical tiles which cannot, of course, be seen from the railway! From Patcham to the sea the railway line continues through the suburbs of Brighton.

54 **PRESTON PARK** (BR)   Between Preston Park and Brighton it becomes all too clear how much Brighton has owed to the railway in terms of employment and trade. Sidings and sheds jostle

alongside the line. Just to the south of Preston Park Station is a fine **signal box** of brick and timber *R:l* with arched windows. The **Preston Carriage Sheds** were built in 1899 and became the *R:l* workshops of the former Pullman Car Company in the 1920s. They are now a 'steam workshop', the home of steam locomotives awaiting restoration. There are also the **Maintenance Depot**, the **Carriage Sheds** and the **Paintshops** of the *R:l* Brighton Locomotive Works. Brighton was the headquarters of the LBSCR and the **car park** to *L:r* the west of Brighton Station was the site of the main engineering works.

55 LONDON ROAD VIADUCT There is a view *L:r* of the London Road Viaduct below the line just north of Brighton Station. The viaduct is 330 yards long and has 27 brick arches, the highest 67 feet. It was built to carry the line to Lewes and the East Coast and curves effortlessly above the terraced streets on the outskirts of Brighton.

56 ST BARTHOLOMEW'S, BRIGHTON This *L:r* magnificent Victorian church is easily distinguished by its lack of tower or spire and its exceedingly high, steeply pitched slate roof. It is the tallest parish church in Britain. The height from ground level to the roof ridge is 135 feet. The church was completed in 1874 at a cost of £18,000. It is one of several churches built in Brighton by the Rev Arthur Douglas Wagner who inherited a considerable fortune and was determined to bring religion to the residential areas of the town newly expanding with the impact of the railway.

St Bartholomew's was positioned so that it could easily be seen by passengers arriving at and leaving

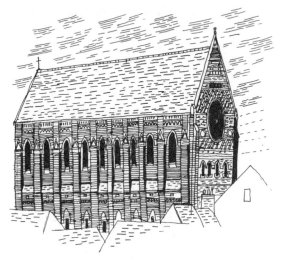

St. Bartholomew's, Brighton

Brighton Station. The neighbourhood objected to the size of the church, calling it Noah's Ark and Wagner's Folly. They also complained that it caused a downdraught and made their chimneys smoke. The architect was Edmund Scott and the designer of many of the internal features was Henry Wilson, an exponent of the Arts and Crafts Movement.

57 BRIGHTON (BR) Brighton was originally a small insignificant fishing village called Brighthelm-stone. By 1821, however, it was a thriving seaside resort of over 24,000, all because a Lewes doctor called Richard Russell had advocated sea bathing as a cure for a range of illnesses. George, Prince of Wales, made his first visit to Brighton in 1783 to enjoy the entertainments which were a feature of the town: assemblies, balls, gambling and promenading. His home was the Royal Pavilion which began as a 'superior farmhouse' in which the Prince and Mrs Fitzherbert could indulge in the simple life. Henry Holland turned the 'farmhouse' into a Palladian villa and, in 1815–22, John Nash turned the villa into the present fantasy palace.

The Prince Regent brought his friends to Brighton and established the town as a fashionable resort but it was the arrival of the railway in 1840 which turned Brighton into a sprawling, wealthy industrial town and brought employment and prosperity to the local inhabitants.

Brighton Station's most notable feature is the curved double train shed supported by elegant, slender iron columns and wide-arched elliptical spans, all painted maroon. The train shed is a late addition to the station. It was designed by J. A. Rastrick to the designs of H. E. Wallis and S. D. Bannister – the ironwork was supplied by the Patent Shaft and Axletree Company – and erected in 1883 over the original 1840 platforms. The pride of the LBSCR in their train shed is still obvious (notice the hanging baskets). It is a rival to the great termini of London and the north of England. The company arms decorate the ornate cast-iron columns and brackets. There is also an elaborate four-faced clock suspended over the concourse with intricate ironwork, c.1883.

The original station building designed by David Mocatta is also intact. It is the long building south of the concourse containing the ticket offices and travel information desk, built in 1840 and now painted cream. When opened the *Illustrated London News* called it 'an elegant structure in the Roman style with commodious portico'. Mocatta's frontage is obscured by an elaborate metal and glass canopy added in 1883 which covers the taxi rank in front of the station.

The Departure Board in the station is of particular interest. It is built to Howell's patent, displaying simultaneously the departure times, platforms and stopping stations of 18 trains. It was first erected at Victoria Station for the 1900 rebuilding of the LBSCR's half but it was replaced and sent to Brighton in 1927.

The underground exit to Trafalgar Street is also worth investigating. It has a Byzantine atmosphere to it – the floors covered in mosaic tiles and the walls covered in multi-coloured tiles. So many aspects of the station have been affectionately preserved, helping to create a memorable start to a day by the sea.

VICTORIA
TO
DOVER

Introduction

The London, Chatham and Dover Railway had a less than perfect reputation in its early decades. In 1877 the MP for Whitstable outlined the railway company's standards by which it earned its nickname of 'smash 'em and turnover'. 'Its trains are formed of unclean cattle trucks propelled at snail-like speed with frequent stops of great length by Machiavellian locomotives of monstrous antiquity, held together by pieces of wire, rusty bolts and occasionally by lengths of string, which clanked, groaned, hissed and oozed a scalding conglomeration of oil, steam and water from every pore.'

The main reason for the poor quality of the service, particularly for 3rd class passengers, and for the ancient engines and carriages, was the poverty of the LCDR. This was partly caused by the nature of the land the line crossed. Like its rival the SER, the LCDR was constructed in a piecemeal way, a short section at a time. There were problems buying land, much of which was unsuitable for level railway lines. The need for excavations, bridges and viaducts constantly threatened the company with bankruptcy. The LCDR has remained a difficult route to operate, with fierce gradients and appalling curves. Between Bickley and Rochester Bridge the line crosses the plateau of the North Downs against the grain of deep-sided valleys. East of Canterbury there is a steady climb up from the Stour Valley to Shepherd's Well and then a descent of 7¾ miles down towards Dover. There are three short tunnels just between Rochester and Gillingham, the Lydden Tunnel south of Shepherd's Well and a further three short tunnels through the chalk hills at Dover.

Though Kent is called the Garden of England and

the LCDR was guaranteed the carrying of fruit and hops as well as serving local industries such as brickmaking, the railway line crossed sparsely populated countryside so that passenger numbers were low. The collieries which opened on the East Kent coalfield during the First World War brought a welcome influx of new residents as well as the carrying of coal for the railway company. But the uncertain future of the coalfield again threatens the economics of the line.

The South Eastern Railway (SER) was the first to reach Dover via Tonbridge, Ashford and Folkestone. William Cubitt was the engineer-in-chief. His main work was on the Great Northern Railway (see **King's Cross to the North**). The SER's line reached Folkestone Junction on 18 December 1843 after Cubitt's magnificent Foord Viaduct of 19 arches was opened across Folkestone. Dover was reached on 7 February 1844. Three tunnels had to be dug through the cliffs: the Martello, Abbotscliff and Shakespeare. To avoid digging a fourth tunnel through Round Down Cliff, Cubitt proceeded to blow the cliff face away with 18,500 pounds of gunpowder. On the SER route express trains (no 3rd class) could reach Dover from London New Cross in three hours.

The LCDR came late to railway building, after the railway mania and the crash of the 1840s. Financial backing was harder to find and the company began in a small way as the East Kent Railway Company, receiving Royal Assent on 4 August 1853 to build a line of 48½ miles from Strood at Rochester to Canterbury. By 1858 the company had obtained permission to extend their line from Canterbury to Dover in the east and from Strood to St Mary Cray in the west. At St Mary Cray they linked up with the Mid Kent Railway to Bromley (Shortlands) and from Bromley connected with the West End of London and

Crystal Palace Railway all the way to its temporary terminus in Battersea. On 1 August 1859 the East Kent Railway became the LCDR and, by 22 July 1861, the route was complete between Dover and the newly opened terminus at Victoria.

The SER was furious and a feud lasted for the next three decades. Some sort of union was inevitable, however, and on 1 August 1899 the SER and the LC&D (Working Union) Act was passed. When the new Marine Station was built at Dover in 1915 the initials SECR appeared above its portentous arch: the South Eastern and Chatham Railway.

The amalgamation resulted in the concentration of continental services at Victoria and the development of the luxurious Golden Arrow service to the continent. The first time a Pullman carriage was used on the line to Dover was in 1882 but it was not followed until after the First World War under the Southern Railway. The first all-Pullman train left Victoria for Dover in November 1924. The engines used were the King Arthur class designed by R. Maunsell. They were given names connected with King Arthur and the Knights of the Round Table: Excalibur, the Green Knight, Sir Urre of the Mount. These were romantic years, particularly when in 1926 the Pullman service was extended to Paris and the French section called *Flèche d'Or* gave its name to the Golden Arrow. On 14 October 1936 ferries went into service which carried the train across the Channel so that it was possible to travel in Pullman luxury all the way to Paris without leaving the carriage. The service was interrupted by the Second World War but reintroduced in 1946. It lasted until 30 September 1972. Private enterprise had to reintroduce an equivalent service – the Orient Express – in 1982. However, on the Orient Express passengers are obliged to leave the train to cross the Channel by Sealink Ferry – an ignominious break in their Pullman opulence.

Note

For historical reasons there are several possible variations to the route from London to Dover. This section covers the route from Victoria to Dover via Herne Hill, Bromley South, Chatham and Canterbury East. Passengers catching the Dover train at Victoria may however find themselves travelling via Maidstone East and Ashford or via Sevenoaks, Tonbridge and Ashford missing out Chatham altogether. There are often such variations on Sundays when engineering works proliferate throughout BR's network. To add to this confusion it is possible to travel to Dover from Charing Cross via Ashford. This is also the route often taken by the boat trains from Victoria to Folkestone and Dover.

MAP 4

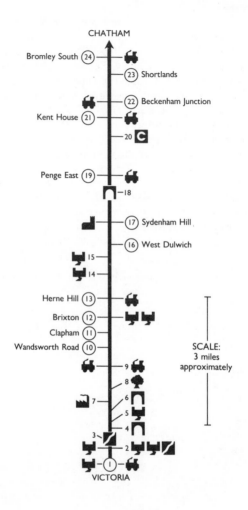

CHATHAM

Bromley South ㉔

㉓ Shortlands

㉒ Beckenham Junction

Kent House ㉑

20 **C**

Penge East ⑲

—18

⑰ Sydenham Hill

⑯ West Dulwich

15

14

Herne Hill ⑬

Brixton ⑫

Clapham ⑪

Wandsworth Road ⑩

9

8

7

6

5

4

3

2

①

VICTORIA

SCALE:
3 miles
approximately

I **VICTORIA STATION** Throughout the summer months thousands of visitors to Britain arrive at Victoria from either the Channel Ports or Gatwick Airport. Their first impressions of a major London terminus and the capital itself could hardly be less inviting. Compared with the termini of Rome and Munich, Victoria appears to be a confusing jumble of oddly assorted, grubby buildings belonging to different, equally outrageous architectural styles. The smooth image of 1970s British Rail clashes awkwardly with earlier Edwardian Baroque frills. Outside, the busts of the famous high up on the Grosvenor Hotel stare down on the drab bus station and swirling traffic of Victoria. More building works are proceeding on top of the Brighton lines and there are plans to brighten up the station with bistros and boutiques. Meanwhile it is all very different from the days of the Brighton Belle with its Pullman carriages called Vera, Doris, Hazel, Gwen, Audrey and Mona. The Golden Arrow service to the continent has been revived by private enterprise but the Orient Express of the 1980s looks out of place with its Edwardian elegance amid the shoddiness of present-day Victoria.

The station has a complex and confusing history. Basically its design problems have been caused by the presence in one station of two railway companies. The terminus for the London, Brighton and South Coast Railway (LBSCR) and the terminus for the London, Chatham and Dover Railway (LCDR) were built alongside one another. Both companies had financial difficulties so were far less interested in creating favourable impressions in their London termini than wealthier companies such as the Great Western Railway. It was sometimes hard enough merely keeping their trains running, and there were constant criticisms for slowness, bad rolling stock and poor treatment of passengers.

In 1858 the LBSCR ended at a temporary terminus on the south bank of the Thames opposite Pimlico. The terminus was built by the West End of London and Crystal Palace Railway and opened on 29 March 1858. The Chelsea Suspension Bridge had been opened on 26 March so passengers had direct access across the Thames and into the West End. The LBSCR was joined by the East Kent Railway which changed its name to the LCDR in 1859.

The Victoria Station and Pimlico Railway approached the LBSCR for financial assistance to build a bridge across the Thames and a station close to Buckingham Palace, and received two-thirds of their capital from the Brighton line. In return the LBSCR had its own section of the terminus and its own access lines to the west. The LCDR and the GWR jointly rented the eastern side.

The terminus covered 14 acres on the site of the basin of the obsolescent Grosvenor Canal. The first part to be built was for the LBSCR and covered 8½ acres on the western side of the site. Robert Jacomb Hood, resident engineer of the company, designed the station which was covered with a 40-foot-high ridge and furrow roof and opened on 1 October 1860. Grosvenor Bridge, designed by Sir John Fowler, had been completed in June 1860.

The Brighton half of the station was dwarfed by the enormous **Grosvenor Hotel** which extended 262 feet down Buckingham Palace Road. The 300-room hotel was completed in 1861. The railway companies were too poor to erect such a colossus, which still dominates the western side of the terminus, so it was owned by an independent company attracted by the prospect of custom from the railways. James T. Knowles was the architect. The first and top floors are decorated with portrait busts set in medallions – unfortunately most are too high to identify clearly – of eminent Victorians including Palmerston, Lord Derby, Queen Victoria and Prince Albert.

None of the Victorian grandeur and pomposity displayed by the Grosvenor Hotel appeared in the LCDR's terminus on the eastern side, which was opened on 25 August 1862. John Fowler designed the 740-foot-long iron roof in the form of two tied lattice arch spans of 124 feet and 117 feet. These are still in position over platforms 1–8 which are used by the continental services.

The frontage of Victoria was an eyesore right from the beginning with no relationship between the designs of the two companies. The ends of the train sheds were closed off with 'untidy wooden structures . . . in appearance more in keeping with those of some new town of mushroom growth in the wilds of Canada or Australia than with that of the leading railway station of London' (Harold Clunn, *London Rebuilt*). Inside, the Brighton half was hardly improved when, in February 1884, the Fenian Brotherhood left a home-made bomb in a Gladstone bag. It exploded and demolished the cloakroom and ticket office. Perhaps this inspired Oscar Wilde to place the infant hero of *The Importance of being Earnest* in a Gladstone bag beside the Brighton line.

The LBSCR was the first to begin rebuilding when the company experienced mild prosperity in the 1890s. The Grosvenor Hotel was bought, redecorated and newly furnished and let to Gordon Hotels Ltd. A vast 150-room wing was added to the hotel across the front of the terminus. It was built in red brick and Portland stone in the 'free Renaissance' style and dominated by an illuminated clock flanked with recumbent figures. Behind this, the old station roof was removed and five new louvred ridge roofs were erected, the ridges 64 feet above rail level and supported on cast-iron columns 18 inches in diameter. Inside the station there was an impressive booking hall tiled in pale green and off-white with art nouveau motifs in green and gold mosaic. Outside, all along Buckingham Palace Road, the LBSCR was forced by Parliament to build an ornamental screen wall. This was designed by C. L. Morgan in Portland stone and red hand-made sand-faced Reading bricks – but the niches are still waiting for busts.

Soon after the new Brighton terminus began to emerge, the LCDR – renamed the SECR – began work on their new terminus. The style chosen has been called 'French Second Empire' and 'Edwardian Baroque'. Sir Arthur Blomfield was the architect and used Portland stone, decorating the front with a broken pediment carried by large busty mermaids. J. Lyons and Co. managed the 1st, 2nd and 3rd class refreshment rooms which were included in the new building.

The Railways Act of 1921 created the Southern Railway and made the two Victorias into one. Three years later a hole was broken open in the wall between the two termini. In 1930 the whole of platform 8 – the main continental arrivals platform – was roofed over to give passengers a more congenial setting in which to wait for their customs examination and even heating facilities were provided. Other forms of transport were eager to make use of Victoria's continental links and can be seen in, around and above the station. The cab yard in front of the station was the site for the London General Omnibus Company's bus station, opened in July 1926. In 1939 Imperial Airways opened its London terminal in Buckingham Palace Road. This was extended in 1963 under BOAC and an eight-storey block was built over the ends of platforms 15 to 17. In 1962 the first rail-air terminal in London was opened above the north end of platforms 15 and 16, designed by Clive Pascall in steel and glass.

Victoria is still changing. Work is in progress to create a separate rail-air terminal for passengers travelling to Gatwick Airport. Over platforms 9 to 19 a concrete 'raft' has been constructed upon which new terminal facilities will be built. A 200,000 sq. ft. office block is also being built by British Rail and Greycoat London Estates Group and will help offset the cost of the terminal – some £50 million. Passengers can now enjoy a fast service to Gatwick in air-conditioned coaches. Perhaps the surviving Victorian and Edwardian parts of Victoria Station will also be given a face-lift so that their incongruous styles and decorative details can be enjoyed to the full.

2 VICTORIA STATION TO GROSVENOR ROAD (NORTH BANK OF THE THAMES)

When, in 1860, the Victoria Station and Pimlico Railway Company completed the short stretch of line between Victoria and the temporary terminus on the south bank of the Thames, they were forced to disguise their line to the satisfaction of the influential and aristocratic landowners whose land they crossed. Almost all the way from the beginning of the line to the river the track was covered by a glazed roof supported on iron columns and arcaded brick walls. It must have created a more pleasing effect on arriving or leaving Victoria than the present views of the grubby utilitarian **blocks** *L:r* **of flats** and the cumbersome **British Airways** *R:l* **Terminal Building**.

However, there is a clear view of the magnificent **Pumping Station** on the north bank of the *R:l* **River Thames**. The French chateau-like building with its ornate chimney was built as part of Joseph Bazalgette's system of sewers under London. The pump house raised the flow of sewage from the low western sewer – the Fulham branch – up to the level of the northern low-level sewer.

It is also possible to see the entrance to the **old Grosvenor Canal** between Grosvenor Bridge *R:l* and Chelsea Bridge.

3 **GROSVENOR BRIDGE**   The railway line crosses the **Thames** on the Grosvenor Bridge. John Fowler, engineer of the Victoria Station and Pimlico Railway Company, designed the first bridge (see p. 304). The present bridge was built in 1963–7 by Freeman, Fox and Partners and carries ten tracks across five open-spandrel steel arches. It was constructed with virtually no interruption to the flow of traffic across the river – around 1000 trains a day.

4 **CHELSEA BRIDGE**   The first Chelsea Suspen- *R:l* sion Bridge was opened on 26 March 1858 and provided direct road access to the West End from the temporary terminus in Battersea of the London to Brighton line, before the Grosvenor Bridge was

built. The present bridge was designed by G. Topham Forrest, architect of the LCC, and built in 1934–7 by Rendel, Palmer and Tritton. It is a self-anchored suspension bridge and the pull at the ends of the cables is taken by a thrust through the stiffening girders. The main span is small for a modern suspension bridge, only 352 feet. The girders are an early use of high-tensile steel.

5 **ROYAL HOSPITAL CHELSEA** There is a *R:1* brief glimpse of Christopher Wren's Royal Hospital through the trees on the north bank and beyond Chelsea Bridge (although summer foliage does get in the way). After the establishment of a standing army during Cromwell's Commonwealth, the country was faced with the problem of how to provide for invalided and veteran soldiers. Charles II laid the foundation stone of the hospital in February 1682 and when it was opened ten years later, nearly 500 noncommissioned officers and men moved into their new barracks. Christopher Wren received £1000 for the design. The Chelsea Flower Show is held annually in the grounds.

6 **ALBERT BRIDGE** The fanciful Albert Bridge is *R:1* beyond Chelsea Bridge. It was designed by R. W. Ordish on his rigid suspension principle, and built in 1871–3. Diagonal wrought-iron stays radiate from the towers: the light suspension chains merely take the weight of the stays. In 1971–3 the main span of 400 feet was propped up to allow heavier traffic loads.

7 **BATTERSEA POWER STATION** was built in *L:r* two stages: the western half in 1929–35 with its

innovative water sprays used to clean the chimneys; the eastern half in 1944–55 also supplying heating to the Churchill Gardens Estate just across the river. Sir Giles Gilbert Scott, the architect of Liverpool's Anglican Cathedral, was the consultant on the exterior. His details – the elaborate parapet and the decorations to the chimneys – created one of the most exciting industrial buildings of this century, as well as setting the pattern for the design of power stations for the next two decades. Battersea Power Station closed down completely in 1983 but the building is to be saved. Its most likely fate is to be used as a 'leisure theme park' (see also pp. 356–7, Waterloo to Southampton).

8 BATTERSEA PARK was laid out in 1858 on the *R:l* site of Battersea Fields where, in 1829, the Duke of Wellington fought a duel with the Earl of Winchelsea. The Fields were popular not only for duels but also for gaming, sports and generally pleasurable pursuits. One Puritan visitor declared: 'surely if ever there was a place out of hell that surpassed Sodom and Gomorrah in ungodliness and abomination, this was it'. The present Festival Gardens are a little more sober with a 15-acre boating lake, a sub-tropical garden and sculptures by Henry Moore and Barbara Hepworth. The site was landscaped with earth which was brought up river from Victoria Docks and then used to raise the surface of the open marsh on the site.

9 RAILWAY LANDSCAPE The lines to Dover *R&L* and Brighton are carried over the lines from Clapham to Waterloo on impressive brick viaducts. There are extensive views to west and east over this extraordinary wasteland of criss-crossing railway lines, viaducts and bridges, abandoned goods yards and sheds, old and new factories and warehouses and, further away, the endless roofs and chimneys of Victorian and Edwardian suburban London, broken up by tower blocks built since the Second World War.

Stewarts Lane Depot, formerly the Long- *L:r* hedge Locomotive and Carriage Works of the LCDR, is below the line close to the point at which the Brighton line branches west towards Clapham Junction. Several of the original Longhedge buildings remain, designed by Joseph Cubitt from 1860 onwards, with distinctive lancet-like windows in their gable ends. The Orient Express is now housed in the depot. It is maintained by BR who naturally do not want it breaking down on their rail network.

10 **WANDSWORTH ROAD** (BR) Wandsworth Road, Clapham, Brixton and Herne Hill stations were all opened by the LCDR when the stretch of line was completed on 24 August 1862.

11 **CLAPHAM** (BR) Early in the 19th century Clapham was the centre of the 'Clapham Sect'. Its leaders, William Wilberforce, Zachary Macaulay and the Thorntons, all lived in the area. They were devoted to the abolition of the slave trade and published their views in the *Christian Observer*.

12 **BRIXTON** (BR) **Two decorative towers** *R:l* can be spotted above the jumble of shops and houses which form the centre of Brixton. The angle tower of the **Town Hall** is elaborately adorned with allegories depicting Justice, Science, Art and Literature. The Town Hall was designed by Septi-

mus Earwick and H. Austen Hall in 1906–8. The tower of **St Matthew's Church** is finished off with Greek Doric columns. It was designed by C. F. Porden in 1822 and is one of the Church Commissioners' 'Waterloo' churches. There are four Waterloo churches, all in Lambeth, and named after the site of one of them, St John's Waterloo. They were built with the intention of bringing religion to the poorer inhabitants of the new urban residential areas of London – areas which grew up around the spreading railways.

The viaduct which carries the railway line through Brixton dominates the streets below. There is a good view of the top of the **Railway** R:l **Tavern**, built in 1880, with its attractive clock turret – perhaps designed to entice commuters off their trains?

The railway line is parallel to **Railton Road** R:l between Brixton and Herne Hill. This was the centre of the riots in 1981 and 1985.

13 **HERNE HILL** (BR) The unusual station was designed by C. H. Driver in 1862. The **booking office** is built of yellow, red and black bricks and R:l has a fanciful Italianate tower attached, designed to hold the water tank.

John Ruskin, the influential Victorian art critic and historian, moved to Herne Hill at the age of four. His house was 'embowered in leafy seclusion and commanding from its garret windows a notable view, on one side, of the Norwood Hills, and, on the other, of the valley of the Thames'.

14 **OLD COLLEGE, DULWICH** The 'College of L:r God's Gift' was founded in 1619 by Edward Alleyn, the actor who made his reputation playing in some

of the great Elizabethan and Jacobean revenge tragedies. He had bought land in Dulwich in 1605 and built a chapel, a school for 12 poor scholars, and 12 almshouses. These have been much rebuilt, covered in stucco and given mock Tudor windows. They are known as the Old College and can be seen across playing fields, well before West Dulwich Station.

15 DULWICH COLLEGE, NEW BUILDINGS *L:r* are on a level with West Dulwich Station across playing fields. The red-brick buildings were designed by Charles Barry the Younger and built in 1866–70. They are in the North Italian Renaissance style. *Building News* commented on the particularly ornate roof: 'Chinese pagodas are temperate in comparison.' The Dulwich governors could afford to be lavish. They had received £100,000 compensation from the railway company which took its line through their estate.

Dulwich College, New Buildings

16 WEST DULWICH (BR) The stretch of line between West Dulwich and Kent House was opened by the LCDR on 1 July 1863.

17 SYDENHAM HILL (BR) Surrounded by mature trees and shrubs, set in a deep cutting, with

Sydenham Hill rising up to the south, Sydenham Station has an unusual rural atmosphere. Even the station buildings are wooden. (The original Victorian buildings were bombed during the war.)

The spire of **St Stephen's Church, Dulwich**, *L:r* can be seen on the hillside before Penge Tunnel (above the entrance to the tunnel). It is a Victorian church (1867–75) built of ragstone with a slated spire. Inside are paintings by Sir Edward Poynter depicting the trial and stoning of St Stephen.

18 **PENGE TUNNEL** is 1 mile 381 yards long. The north entrance was designed by Joseph Cubitt. The LCDR was forced to design elegant railway structures for this stretch of the line by the local landowners – who happened to be the governors of Dulwich College.

19 **PENGE EAST** (BR; 1863 **yellow- and red-** *R:l* **brick station building**).

20 **CRYSTAL PALACE**   The tall **television mast** *R:l* is close to the National Recreation Centre which is on the site of the Crystal Palace. This was the vast entirely pre-fabricated iron and glass palace designed by Joseph Paxton for the Great Exhibition of 1851. It was first erected in Hyde Park, then moved to Sydenham in 1852–4. The poet John Davidson described the 'Victorian temple of commercialism ... like some immense crustacean's ganoid skeleton, unearthed, and cleansed and polished'. It was destroyed by fire in 1936 except for two towers and these were demolished during the Second World War in case they might provide a landmark for enemy aircraft. The stadium and sports hall of the Recreation Centre were designed

by the LCC Architect's Department in 1956–64. Life-size ferro-concrete prehistoric monsters roam around the lake.

21 **KENT HOUSE** (BR; 1884 **2-storey brick book-** *R:l*
   ing hall below the line)   The railway line passes
   through a jumble of residential styles as it crosses
   the furthest extension of south London: Victorian
   brick villas and terraces, between-the-wars semis
   with mock-Tudor trims, blocks of flats of the last
   decade. The network of railway lines attracted
   Londoners southwards throughout the 19th century and with the electrification of the Southern
   Railway travelling times into the centre were
   shortened and a new generation of suburban
   residents moved in. By 1939 the 'Southern Electric'
   system had grown into one of the largest electrified systems in the world. More recently soaring
   rates and rents and the absence of green spaces in
   the centre of London have encouraged those in
   search of better standards of living to move further
   out along the tentacles of the Southern Region.

22 **BECKENHAM JUNCTION** (BR; 1857; 19th- *L:r*
   century **yellow-brick station building** and
   bargeboarded railway cottages) Beckenham
   was once a village surrounded by fine mansions in
   their own parks. The arrival of the railway turned it
   into a residential suburb of London. Even in 1830,
   however, William Cobbett found it already tainted
   by the capital: 'When you get to Beckenham, which
   is the last parish in Kent, the country begins to
   assume a cockney-like appearance; all is artificial,
   and you no longer feel any interest in it.'

23 **SHORTLANDS** (BR)   The Victorian novelist

Mrs Craik lived in Shortlands Road. Her house, which is still there, was specially designed for her by Norman Shaw.

24 BROMLEY SOUTH (BR; modernised 1958 but still 19th-century **yellow- and red-brick station buildings** – like Shortlands – and **engine shed**) *R:l* When the railway arrived at Bromley in 1858 the market town was quite independent of London. In the next ten years its population doubled and by 1914 Bromley had become swallowed up by the capital. H. G. Wells was born in Bromley High Street on 21 September 1866. He was the son of an unsuccessful shopkeeper and was apprenticed to a draper before turning to literature. His background of 'shabby gentility' appears in novels such as *Kipps* and *The History of Mr Polly*.

The main line from Victoria to Dover was made up of several short stretches built or paid for by individual companies (see pp. 298–300). The Mid Kent (Bromley and St Mary Cray) Railway Company opened the line from Bromley to St Mary Cray on 5 July 1858.

25 BICKLEY (BR) Immediately east of Bickley Station the line divides at a complex meeting of lines known as **Bickley Junction**. The line to Dover via Sevenoaks continues southwards; the line to Dover via Chatham continues eastwards.

26 PETTS WOOD At last there are signs of the *L:r* countryside. Petts Wood is the property of the National Trust and stretches away north of the line. Even the **houses to the south** appear to have *R:l* larger gardens, more of the precious 'room to

MAP 5

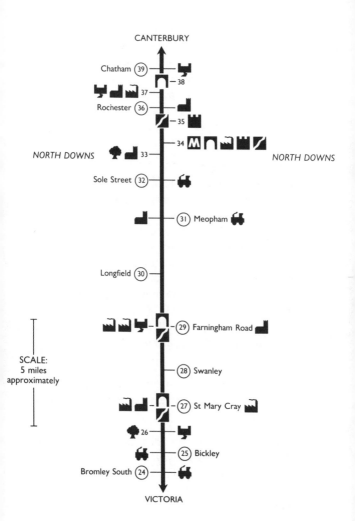

CANTERBURY

Chatham (39)

38

37

Rochester (36)

35

34

NORTH DOWNS   33   NORTH DOWNS

Sole Street (32)

(31) Meopham

Longfield (30)

(29) Farningham Road

SCALE:
5 miles
approximately

(28) Swanley

(27) St Mary Cray

26

(25) Bickley

Bromley South (24)

VICTORIA

breathe'. The garden suburb of Petts Wood was created in the 1930s. The mock-Tudor style of the houses became a hallmark of the development. The estate company described the square of shops as 'the beautiful Elizabethan Shopping Square'. The houses had mock beams, leaded lights, oak front doors with iron hinges and ring knockers, and, inside, inglenook fireplaces and oak-panelled 'baronial' halls.

27 **ST MARY CRAY** (BR)   The countryside over which the train travels to the east of St Mary Cray was hardly ideal for building a railway on. A series of deep steep-sided valleys had to be crossed involving expensive viaducts and embankments. St Mary Cray and the **River Cray** are crossed on a **viaduct** of nine brick arches. **St Mary's** is below *L:r* the line, a mostly 13th-century church with a flint tower and shingled spire. More obvious, however, is the post-war industrial expansion in the once-rural Cray Valley. **Small factories**, warehouses *L&R* and housing estates spread north and south beside the river.

East of St Mary Cray the line crosses the boundary between the outer London borough of **Bromley** and **Kent**.

28 **SWANLEY** (BR)   An Edwardian writer, George Dewar, described railway embankments in Kent before the First World War: 'I have heard that nightingales haunting wooded places by railway lines will sing persistently all night, and I seem to have noticed how long and choicely the railway nightingales sing in Kent. A friend says he thinks it is because they cannot sleep through the noise of the goods trains crashing and thundering all night.'

29 FARNINGHAM ROAD (BR)   On the down platform of the station the brick base of an **old** *L:r* **water tower** has been turned into a small waiting room.

In the distance, to the north of the station, is the **Littlebrook Power Station**, a reminder of the *L:r* intensive industrial development on the banks of the **River Thames** which here flows roughly parallel to the railway line about seven miles away.

To the east of Farningham Road Station, the line crosses the valley of the **River Darent** on a high **viaduct**. Below, to the north, are **paper mills** *L:r* beside the river. To the south is the Early English flint church of **St Mary's Horton Kirby** with a *R:l* brick tower.

30 LONGFIELD (BR)   The train now passes through gently undulating fields broken by small coppices. Cows graze close to the line.

31 MEOPHAM (BR; yellow stock brick **station** *R:l* **master's house** 1860)   The parish church of **St John the Baptist** stands out clearly across the *L:r* fields. It was dedicated in 1325 and has flint walls, a red-tiled roof and a stately tower.

32 SOLE STREET (BR)   The station is the typical LCDR design of 1860 consisting of a **plain Victorian villa** of two storeys with a single- *R:l* storey booking hall attached.

Sole Street is at the highest point of the line as it crosses the plateau of the North Downs between Bickley and Rochester. To the east, the train begins a long descent to sea level at Rochester Bridge. The 'Sole Street Bank', as this stretch is called, consists of a series of cuttings five miles in length and falling at 1 in 100.

33 **COBHAM CHURCH**   The flint church of **St Mary Magdalene** can be seen about a mile east of *L:r* Sole Street Station. The church was mostly built in the 13th century but the ragstone tower was added in 1362. Inside is one of the largest groups of brasses in the country. The finest brasses are of members of the De Cobham and Brooke families, lords of the manor. **Cobham Park** stretches to the east of the church but only the southern edge of mature trees is visible. Cobham Hall, on the other side of the hill, is now a private girls' school. It was begun in 1580 by William, 10th Lord Cobham, but the work was interrupted when he was sent to the Tower for treason. A favourite walk of Charles Dickens was through the woods of Cobham Park. His country residence, Gadshill Place, was just over a mile to the north-east. Pickwick also enjoyed Cobham: 'a delightful walk it was ... They emerged upon an open park, with an ancient hall, displaying the quaint and picturesque architecture of Elizabeth's time.'

34 **VIEW OF THE MEDWAY VALLEY AND** *R:l* **ROCHESTER**   The train emerges from the dry valley through which it has been descending from Sole Street. From here there is a dramatic view of the bustling Medway Valley. The banks of the **River Medway** are densely packed with remnants of older industries, quarries and abandoned warehouses but also thriving new factories and sprawling industrial estates. Below the line is the village of **Cuxton** and across the Medway on the east side *R:l* stretch the **Wouldham Marshes**.   *R:l*

As the train drops down to sea level it passes under the **M2** which crosses the Medway on a concrete **road bridge** (central span 500 ft; consulting engineers Freeman, Fox and Partners); then past large **cement works**. The magnificent keep of **Rochester Castle** rises up ahead. *R:l*

Rochester Castle

Strood is the name of the settlement on the west bank of the Medway immediately opposite Rochester. The railway line passes through it on a high brick viaduct. Strood is one of the Medway Towns – Strood, Rochester, Chatham and Gilling-ham – and has benefited from the commercial and industrial development of the area. Between the railway line and the river and almost buried by an industrial estate is Temple Manor, the remains of an overnight stopping place for high-ranking officials of the Knights Templar travelling between London and Dover on Watling Street (east of Rochester the railway line runs roughly parallel to the Roman road to Dover). But even before the Knights Templar and the Romans there was a settlement beside the Medway crossing.

This part of Kent was familiar to Dickens as a boy and again when he returned in middle age to buy Gadshill Place. *David Copperfield* and *Great Expectations* make use of the landscape. Pickwick began his travels from Rochester and described the busy banks of the Medway: 'the principal productions appear to be soldiers, sailors, Jews, chalk, shrimps, officers and dockyard men. The commodities chiefly exposed for sale in the public streets are marine stores, hard-bake, apples, flat fish and oysters.'

35 CROSSING THE MEDWAY – ROCHESTER CASTLE As the train crosses the Medway there is a fine view of the **keep of Rochester Castle** R:l rising above the bridges, still guarding the strategi-cally and economically important crossing. The castle was begun by Gundulf, Bishop of Rochester, in 1087–9 for William Rufus. The keep dominates the city. It was built by William of Corbeuil,

Archbishop of Canterbury, in 1127 and is the tallest keep in England – 120 feet.

36 ROCHESTER (BR) Rochester is the second oldest see in England. In 604 AD St Augustine ordained Justus as the first bishop. However, the **Cathedral** largely dates from the 12th century. *R:l* The original cathedral had fallen into disrepair by 1075, 'utterly forsaken, miserable and waste, from lack of all things within and without'. Money was collected for the building from offerings made at the shrine of St William of Perth. William was a baker who had been murdered at Rochester in 1201 while on pilgrimage to the Holy Land. Living, he had given every tenth loaf he baked to the poor; after his death, miracles began to take place in the neighbourhood and grateful worshippers made offerings at his tomb.

37 CHATHAM DOCKYARDS There are glimp- *L:r* ses of the dockyards and barracks between Rochester Station and Fort Pitt Tunnel and again between Chatham Tunnel and Gillingham Tunnel.

The navy first anchored in the Medway in 1547. Elizabeth I ordered the building of Chatham Dockyard and many of the ships which defeated the Spanish Armada were built here. In 1667 the Dutch Admiral Micheil de Ruyter sailed up the Medway, bombarded the docks and towed away the *Royal Charles*, the pride of the English fleet. However, the Medway was still considered a safer anchorage than Portsmouth, the defences were strengthened, new dockyards were laid out in 1685 and new administrative buildings and storehouses were built early in the 18th century.

Daniel Defoe visited the dockyards in 1720: 'the

buildings here are indeed like the ships themselves, surprisingly large, and in the several kinds beautiful. The warehouses, or rather streets of warehouses, and store houses for laying up the naval treasures are the largest dimension, and the most in number that are anywhere to be seen in the world.' The long brick buildings on the waterfront of four and five storeys are the 18th-century **ropeworks**. The large shed-like buildings in the distance are the **dry docks** which still retain their original timber roofs. HMS Victory was launched from Chatham in 1765. Her future captain, Horatio Nelson, joined HMS Raisonnable at Chatham as a twelve-year-old 'captain's servant'. The Royal Navy ended its long relationship with Chatham in 1984 when the docks closed. They have now been re-opened as a tourist attraction, and visitors may take paddle steamer trips from here down to the **River Medway**.

The church tower is **St Mary's**, the medieval *L:r* church of rock-faced ragstone which was rebuilt in 1884–1903 by Sir Arthur Blomfield. The tower with the green dome is part of **Chatham Town** *L:r* **Hall**, designed by George E. Bond, 1898–9.

38 FORT PITT TUNNEL is named after Fort Pitt, a 19th-century defensive structure under which it passes.

39 CHATHAM (BR)   Just before the station, which is squeezed into the valley between the two tunnels, there is a glimpse of the **terrace of houses** high above the line, in which Dickens lived *R:l* as a boy. His father, John Dickens, worked in the Navy Pay Office in 1816.

When Dickens made a pilgrimage to visit his old school he found the station had completely swamped the playing fields: 'it was gone. The two beautiful hawthorn trees, the hedge, the turf, and all those buttercups and daisies, had given place to the stoniest of jolting roads; while, beyond the station, an ugly dark monster of a tunnel kept its jaws open, as if it had swallowed them and were ravenous for more destruction.'

40 CHATHAM TUNNEL Between Chatham and Gillingham Tunnels there is a brief glimpse of the dockyards and barracks. The **Naval War Memorial** *L:r* can also be seen on the hillside. The column was erected in 1920–4 and added to after the Second World War by Sir Edward Maufe. The sculptures of soldiers are by William McMillan and Sir Charles Wheeler.

41 GILLINGHAM TUNNEL

42 GILLINGHAM (BR; rebuilt 1920s) A branch line was opened in 1877 to carry naval stores and materials for shipbuilding down to the docks and this is still used for freight.

East of Gillingham the railway line re-enters agricultural landscape but **oil refineries** on the Isle of Grain and the **Kingsnorth Power Station**, all *L:r* to the north, are a reminder of the industry which extends along the estuary of the Medway.

43 RAINHAM (BR) In the station yard is a fine old *L:r* **maltings**, recently restored and now used as a community centre.

Eight people were killed in a **railway accident** just east of Rainham during the Second World War. A flying bomb was shot down on its way to London and hit an underbridge on the line. An express train

MAP 6

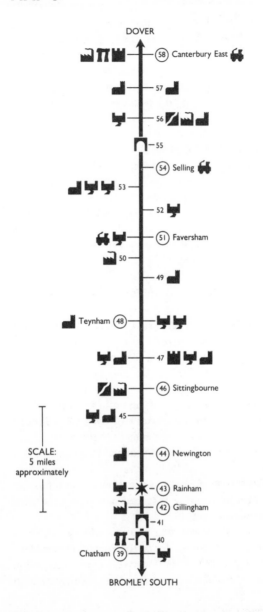

DOVER

58 Canterbury East

57

56

55

54 Selling

53

52

51 Faversham

50

49

48 Teynham

47

46 Sittingbourne

45

44 Newington

43 Rainham

42 Gillingham

41

40

Chatham 39

SCALE:
5 miles
approximately

BROMLEY SOUTH

Rainham Maltings

approaching the bridge had no time to stop and went off the track.

The train has now entered Kent's rich fruit and hop growing area known as **The Garden of England**. Orchards, fields of hops, some magnificent farm-houses and their oasthouses are scattered over the countryside. The villages of Rainham, Newington, Teynham and Selling were particularly important stops on the railway line for the LCDR because they were all centres of the fruit and hops industry.

Hops are an essential part of the production of beer. The female flowers give flavour and clarify the beer by precipitating the protein materials that cause turbidity. Also the active principles of the hop help to prevent spoilage in beer by retarding the growth of bacteria. The hops are dried in the oasthouses.

44 NEWINGTON (BR; rebuilt 1970) There is a

fine view of the Perpendicular parish church of **St Mary's** which has a characteristically Kentish-style L:r tower, with diagonal buttresses and a south-east polygonal turret rising above the battlements.

45 BOBBING CHURCH The flint church of **St** L:r **Bartholomew's** has a 14th-century tower. Inside are some fine brasses and a very old Romanesque sculpture, c.1190, of St Martial ordaining a deacon. The handsome red-brick 18th-century house near the railway line is **Bobbing Court**.   L:r

46 SITTINGBOURNE (BR) Sittingbourne expanded dramatically in the 19th and early 20th centuries with the establishment of brick- and paper-making industries. It was in an ideal position on Milton Creek, off the Swale waterway.

Bowaters were largely responsible for the development of the paper industry and there is an attractive **red-brick warehouse** of the com- L:r pany's close to the station. To the north of Sittingbourne there is a large industrial estate which stretches to and includes the village of Kelmsley, about two miles away. Kelmsley was built for the workers of Bowaters. It was designed in a neo-Georgian style in 1925–6 by Adams, Thomson and Fry. A light railway connects Kelmsley and Sittingbourne, built to link the paper mills with Ridham Dock on the River Swale. The section of the line between Kelmsley and Sittingbourne has been preserved and steam trains run at weekends.

As the train leaves Sittingbourne Station for the east, the masts and spars of sailing barges may be seen rising above the rooftops, moored at the **Dolphin Barge Museum**. The barges were a L:r common sight in the Thames Estuary as late as the

1930s. They tied up at the wharves on the creeks along the banks of the Medway and the Swale: Otterham Quay for Rainham; Lower Halstow Wharf for Newington; Conyer Wharf for Teynham. Their chief cargo was fruit which they still carried to London after the railway was built. The journey was slow, however, compared with the train – twelve hours with a good wind and tide.

47 BAPCHILD CHURCH AND TONGE CHURCH are opposite one another on either side of the railway line just east of Sittingbourne. **St Lawrence's** Bapchild is partly Norman and has a tower with a tall shingled spire. **St Giles's** Tonge dates from the Norman period through to the 19th century and has a tower of flint walls patched in brick. It looks rather like a barn with the tiled roof of the nave sweeping down over the narrow aisles almost to the ground. *R:l & L:r*

Between the two churches, close to the railway line, is the site of **Tonge Castle**. Close by is a **stock-brick mill** of 1837 and a weatherboarded **millhouse** of 1759. *R:l*

And almost immediately east of Tonge Church is one of the finest farmhouses to be seen from the train – **Bax Farm**. It stands on its own, built of flint, stone and timber, with parts dating from 1567. The huge stone chimney breasts have brick lozenge-shaped stacks on top. *L:r*

48 TEYNHAM (BR) Teynham has been called 'the cherry orchard and the apple orchard' of Kent. Orchards stretch to north and south of the line and there are particularly fine farmhouses and manor houses to be seen from the train. **Frognal** is just west of the station, one half timber-framed and *R:l* built in 1668, the other half added in the early 18th century in red brick. **Lower Newlands** is to the east of the station, another early half-timbered house. The parish church of **St Mary's** is about half a mile away on a hill, built of flint with the red-tiled roof common to churches in Kent. Richard Harris, fruiterer to Henry VIII, lived in Teynham and is reputed to have been the first man to grow cherries in Kent. *R:l*

L:r

49 **OSPRINGE CHURCH St Peter and St Paul** has a Victorian tower built in 1866 and designed by E. L. Blackburn. The original round tower fell down in 1695 and now there are no round towers in the county. *R:l*

50 **FAVERSHAM BRICKWORKS** The tall chimneys which can be seen just west of Faversham belong to the kilns of brickworks. Kent has produced some of the finest bricks ever made with a surprising range of colours. The alluvial clays and brick-earths of North Kent around Sittingbourne, Rainham, Faversham and Crayford have produced red- and yellow-brown stock bricks. The Medway Valley has a belt of stiff bluish clay overlying the lower greensand and this produces pale yellow 'white' bricks. Before the railway arrived at Faversham in 1858, bricks were taken away in barges from Faversham Creek just north of the town. *L:r*

51 **FAVERSHAM** (BR; rebuilt c.1900: **smart yellow and red brick buildings**) Faversham received its charter in 1225 as a limb of the Cinque Ports and was granted a mayor. It developed into a flourishing port and many fine houses survive from

the 18th century. The red-brick mansion **Del-** *L:r*
bridge House is an example, just next to the
station. The house of Thomas Arden also survives
in the town. It gained notoriety from an Elizabethan play based on the true story of the
murder of Arden by his wife and her lover, their
discovery and execution.

Faversham was the centre of the explosives
industry until the First World War and the remains
of the gunpowder mill have been preserved.
Extensive goods yards and sidings were necessary
to cope with the fruit, bricks and explosives sent by
train to the capital. The old **marshalling yards** *L:r*
are now used as a lorry park. The railway also
brought employment to locals and one Faversham
train driver is memorialised in the churchyard:

His last drive is over, death has put on the brake,
His soul has been signalled its long journey to take,
When death sounds the whistle, the steam of life falls,
And his mortal day shunted till the last trumpet calls.

52 COLKINS is another magnificent Kent farmhouse. *R:l*
Red brick, built early in the 18th century, it has a
17th-century red-brick barn close by.

53 BOUGHTON UNDER BLEAN The attrac- *L:r*
tive group of houses on the hill about half a mile
from the line consists of a converted **oasthouse**,
an early 18th-century **vicarage** and the parish
church of **St Peter and St Paul**. The church is
13th century and built of flint. The Perpendicular
tower was restored by St Aubyn in 1871. Inside is a
monument to Thomas Hawkins who died in 1617
leaving seven sons and six daughters. He mournfully
clutches at a handkerchief, his grief-stricken family
beneath him, carved out of alabaster.

54 SELLING (BR)   The **signal box** at Selling was   R:l
built by Saxby and Farmer, the large signalling
contractors who are now part of Westinghouse.

The train climbs to Selling through gently
undulating countryside scattered with orchards and
hop-fields. There are tantalising glimpses of the
verdant landscape in between the cutting dug
through the chalk by Victorian railway engineers.

55 SELLING TUNNEL extends through the chalk
for 405 yards.

56 East of Selling Tunnel, the train emerges above the
VALLEY OF THE RIVER STOUR and begins
its gradual descent to Canterbury. Below the line is
the village of **Chartham**. It is just possible to make   R:l
out the large **paper mill** in the centre of the
village and the stately grey **parish church**, begun
in the 13th century, with a tower of knapped flints.
The lakes beside the **River Stour** have been
formed by gravel extraction which continues
nearer to Canterbury.

On the other side of the line is **Tonford**   L:r
Manor, a brick and flint moated manor house built
in the mid-15th century with a low semi-circular
turret. Henry VIII stayed at the manor: 'to
Tonferde at which Manor the Kyng chaunged hym
self'.

57 CANTERBURY CATHEDRAL   There is a   R:l
clear view of the silvery-grey towers of Canter-   then
bury Cathedral as the train approaches the city   L:r
along the Stour Valley. The present building was
begun by Archbishop Lanfranc in 1070, three years
after the much older buildings had been destroyed
by fire. It was extensively rebuilt and extended

Canterbury Cathedral

between the end of the 14th and the mid-15th centuries.

The central tower is called Bell Harry and rises to just under 250 feet including the pinnacles. It was built by John Wastell in 1494–1503. Inside the cathedral are the tombs of Edward, the Black Prince, Henry IV and Queen Joan of Navarre.

The cathedral was the setting for the violent murder of Archbishop Thomas à Becket, who was hacked to death by four knights of Henry II on 29 December 1170. For over 300 years the body of St Thomas rested in a magnificent shrine in the Trinity Chapel. The pilgrims of Chaucer's *Canterbury Tales* were a few of the thousands who flocked to the cathedral. In 1538 the shrine was dismantled and the jewels which had adorned it were added to Henry VIII's treasury. In 1888, however, a box of bones was discovered in the crypt. Some experts believe the contents came from the shrine, hidden before the servants of Henry VIII could destroy them.

58 CANTERBURY EAST (BR; modernised 1960; **yellow- and red-brick Victorian platform buildings**)   When bombs destroyed a third of the old city of Canterbury during the Second World War the foundations of the city were revealed and archaeologists were able to establish all the stages of occupation from the Iron Age through to Roman and medieval times.

The Normans built Canterbury Castle and the **keep** is just west of the station. It is built of flint and Caen stone and has walls nine feet thick.   *L:r*

East of the station is **Dane John Mound**. The *L:r* original purpose of the mound is not known. It lies just inside the medieval city walls and was transformed into a pleasure garden for the citizens of Canterbury in 1790 by a philanthropic alderman, James Simmons. Simmons spent £1500 on the site, planting lime trees. A stone obelisk crowns the top of the mound.

One of the earliest railways was built from Canterbury to Whitstable, a distance of six miles. At the opening ceremony on 3 May 1830 the Invicta, made by Robert Stephenson & Co., hauled two trains along the line. The Invicta is now preserved in Canterbury: the line was closed in 1931.

On the outskirts of Canterbury is **St Martin's Tower Mill**, built in 1816 and just visible above *L:r* the roof tops. It is easier to see approaching Canterbury from Dover.

59 BEKESBOURNE (BR)   Less than half a mile north of Bekesbourne Station is **Howletts** (now *L:r* set in Howletts Zoo Park), a splendid mansion designed by the architect and lawyer John Leach in

MAP 7

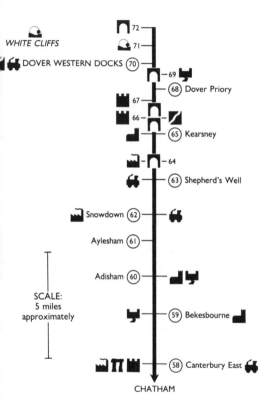

WHITE CLIFFS

DOVER WESTERN DOCKS (70)

72

71

69

(68) Dover Priory

67

66

(65) Kearsney

64

(63) Shepherd's Well

Snowdown (62)

Aylesham (61)

Adisham (60)

(59) Bekesbourne

SCALE:
5 miles
approximately

(58) Canterbury East

CHATHAM

1787. It has a lofty and impressive Ionic portico facing south.

St Peter's Bekesbourne is south-east of the *R:l* station, mostly medieval but with a Victorian tower. The Archbishops of Canterbury had a palace at Bekesbourne and part remains, close to the church. The initials of Archbishop Cranmer and the arms of Archbishop Parker are carved on one of the walls.

From Bekesbourne to the coast the landscape is very different from the fruit-growing areas of the Stour Valley and around Sittingbourne. The chalk downs created enormous difficulties for the railway engineers and contractors and the line passes through a series of cuttings, embankments and tunnels, with only glimpses of some dramatic landscape.

60 ADISHAM (BR) **Holy Innocents** can be seen *R:l* before Adisham Station. The flint church was built between the 12th and 14th centuries, and restored in the 19th century by W. White who added the tiled pyramid to the tower. **Adisham Court** is *R:l* the nearby elegant 17th-century brick house.

61 AYLESHAM (BR; rebuilt 1970s) Aylesham village was built for the miners of Snowdown Colliery. The station was first opened as Aylesham Halt in 1918; the village was laid out in 1926–7 by the architects J. Archibald, C. T. F. Martindale and Sir Patrick Abercrombie.

62 SNOWDOWN (BR) Snowdown Station was first opened in 1914 as Snowdown and Nonington Halt and used by the miners who travelled by train from Canterbury and Dover to work on the East

Kent coalfield. Snowdown Colliery was the first and most successful of the four collieries which were opened. Mining began in earnest in 1913 and the **winding gear and coal tips** extend to the *L:r* north and south of the station. There are now only three collieries open on the coalfield: Snowdown, Betteshanger and Tilmanstone. The union has appealed against the proposed closure of Betteshanger and Tilmanstone. Snowdown is also threatened with closure and is being worked only on a development basis by a skeleton workforce (1985).

Between Snowdown and Shepherd's Well stations a **branch line** leaves the main line to the *L:r* east, cutting through the chalk downs by way of the impressively named Golgotha Tunnel, to reach the colliery at Tilmanstone.

63 SHEPHERD'S WELL (BR)   The station build- *L:r* ings consist of a **two-storey 'villa'** with a one-storey booking hall attached, brick-built and covered in beige-coloured stucco.

The climb up to Shepherd's Well was difficult for heavily laden steam trains but from Shepherd's Well to the east is a 7¾ mile descent through the scarp slope of the North Downs, by way of the Lydden Tunnel and the Dour Valley.

64 THE LYDDEN TUNNEL is 1 mile 609 yards long and the entire length is brick-lined. Just south of the tunnel are the remains of old quarries at **Stonehall**. Chalk was little used for buildings but it *L:r* was quarried for the flint which is found in the upper layers of the chalk formation.

65 KEARSNEY (BR)   Kearsney Station was opened

as Ewell in 1862 and renamed in 1869. Ewell belonged to the Knights Templar in the 12th century and the church to the north of the station is **St Peter and St Paul**, Temple Ewell. It is a flint *L:r* church with a small west tower, originally Norman but largely rebuilt in 1874 by Talbot Bury.

66 As the train approaches Dover down through the narrow **Dour Valley** it is easy to imagine the problems for the Victorian railway engineers cutting their way through the chalk. There are glimpses of **Dover Castle** on top of the hill, *L:r* coming closer as the train passes through **Charlton Tunnel** (264 yards) and **Dover Priory Tunnel** (158 yards) to emerge at **Dover Priory Station**.

Dover Castle

67 **DOVER CASTLE** is on a magnificent site high *L:r* above the Channel and Dover Harbour on the edge of the White Cliffs. Iron Age man was the first to enclose the site with massive earth ramparts. The Romans built the Pharos lighthouse inside the ramparts and the Saxons added a church, St Mary in the Castro. The Normans began the stone castle and stationed a permanent garrison at Dover. The most prominent part of the castle is the keep which was built in c.1180 for Henry II at a cost of £7000.

68 DOVER PRIORY (BR)   Dover was first reached by the LCDR on 22 July 1861 and the station was named after the nearby St Martin's Priory. The station is dwarfed by the hills to the north and south and reached by tunnels from both directions. It is a busy station serving the residents of Dover all the year but large numbers of tourists in the summer months.

William Cobbett, early in the 19th century, declared Dover 'a most picturesque place, to be sure'. Dickens was less complimentary: 'the little narrow, crooked town of Dover hid itself away from the beach, and ran its head into the chalk cliffs like a marine ostrich ... The air among the houses was of so strong a piscatory flavour that one might have supposed sick fish went up to be dipped in it, as sick people went down to be dipped in the sea.'

69 HARBOUR TUNNEL is 684 yards long and takes the train through the last barrier of chalk hills and on to the edge of **Dover Harbour**. The *L&R* extension to the harbour was opened on 1 November 1861 and trains from London Victoria on the LCDR line now joined their competitors from London Bridge via Folkestone on the SER line. There was just room for a double pair of rails on the Admiralty Pier but rough weather brought waves crashing over the pier and the trains – to the horror of the passengers.

The **Lord Warden Hotel** was built at the point *R:1* where the rival lines met. The hotel is now BR Southern House, a gleaming white Italianate villa designed by S. Beazley in 1850–3. Visitors in the hotel could watch for the rival trains racing along from their respective tunnels through the cliffs and roaring past the hotel, one on each side, to be first on the pier.

70 **DOVER WESTERN DOCKS** (BR)   In the early 1900s improvements were vital to the station on the pier. Dover Marine was built on reclaimed land inside the Admiralty Pier and was first opened to military traffic in 1915. Continental traffic began to use the station in 1919. Dover Marine is now called **Dover Western Docks** though there is still a sign *L:r* with the original name. It is approached past the busy harbour with glimpses of cranes, ships loading and unloading their goods, car parks, the motorail depot and, towering above, Dover Castle. After **Dover Marine signal box** the train glides under *L:r* the gloomy imposing arch of the war-time station. The arch is built of massive rusticated blocks of light grey stone with the initials 'SE&CR' and a First World War Memorial above (556 men of the South East and Chatham Railway died during the First World War). Inside, the train shed is light and airy and supported by white painted girders and white and black painted iron columns. The platform buildings are of red and black brick. The end platform has an elaborate **war memorial** with sculptures of a soldier, sailor and an angel of peace; there are more carvings on the **red-brick buffet bar**.

71 **THE WESTERN HEIGHTS OF DOVER** *L:r* tower directly above Western Docks Station – on the west side of Dover and across the valley from the castle. Excavations began on top of the Western Heights in 1793 when it appeared that Napoleon might be intending to invade Britain.

Dover was to provide the last stronghold for the British army with the castle and the Western Heights as the two vantage-points. Work went on until the Treaty of Paris was signed in 1814 by which time, as William Cobbett pointed out, the quantity of brick buried in the hill would have built a cottage for every labourer in Kent and Sussex. The Citadel on the highest point is now used as HM Borstal.

72 SHAKESPEARE CLIFF TUNNEL Looking along the bottom of the cliffs towards the west it is possible to see where the railway line to Folkestone disappears into the Shakespeare Cliff Tunnel (part of *King Lear* is set in Dover). The tunnel is 1387 yards long and has two separate bores, each taking a single line of track.

The best views of the White Cliffs and Dover Harbour are from a cross-Channel ferry. When the Admiralty Harbour was built in 1900 it was designed to accommodate the whole of the Grand Fleet, but it was used only once for this purpose. It was the largest man-made harbour in the world when it was built and before the First World War Atlantic liners docked beneath the White Cliffs.

During the First World War the town was the centre of the Dover Patrol whose job it was to safeguard the straits. During the Second World War the town suffered bombing and shelling from the long-range guns in France. The strategic importance of Dover, its cliffs and harbour have brought the town prosperity as well as danger in time of war. Now, plans to dig a cross-Channel tunnel must seriously concern the locals whose employment is connected with the ferry port.

WATERLOO
TO
SOUTHAMPTON

Introduction

The initiative for a railway connecting London and Southampton came not from the capital but from Southampton. The businessmen of Southampton wanted a railway to connect their town with London because the port had declined as a commercial and residential centre. Southampton had been the focus of cross-Channel traffic since the Middle Ages but with the discovery of the New World and the development of the Atlantic trade, its position altered dramatically: 'It boasted a population of only 19,000; its shipping accommodation was of the poorest description, unsightly mud banks surrounded the town, and shipmasters were often heard to declare that instead of being called upon to pay port dues, they themselves should be paid for coming thither.' (Sam Fay, *A Royal Road*)

The Southampton, London and Branch Railway and Dock Company was formed in 1831 and at the first public meeting Colonel Henderson outlined the importance of the development of both railway and docks: 'The docks and the railways were intimately connected, and of such paramount importance to each other that the one without the other would be unproductive; for were the docks to be constructed without the railway, the cargoes of vessels could not be transported into the interior, nor the return brought to the coast; and if the railway were to be called into existence without the docks, there would not be sufficient traffic to produce a beneficial return.' Three years later, on 25 July 1834, the London and Southampton Railway Bill was passed by Parliament. The construction of the railway began almost immediately and the whole line was completed and opened on 11 May 1840.

The railway would have been finished earlier if the company had not appointed Francis Giles as the engineer. His estimates for building the line were wildly optimistic and he himself showed little faith in the railway, a lack of confidence which spread to the shareholders. The line 'would be used only for the conveyance of parsons and prawns, the one from Winchester, the other from Southampton'. 'To be connected with the Southampton Railway is to make the choice of being considered a fool or a rogue.' Giles was replaced by Joseph Locke in 1837 and the work finally began. Locke employed Thomas Brassey as the contractor for the line and they proved a formidable team. Brassey was to become the greatest of railway contractors, amassing a personal fortune of £5¼ million and, by the time he died in 1870, building one in every twenty miles of railway across the world.

The first section of the line to be opened was between London (Nine Elms) and Woking, on 19 May 1838. Each passenger was given a handbill stating the company regulations. Passengers were not allowed to alight without the assistance of a servant of the railway. The guard had to blow his whistle each time the train approached a crossing or a habitation – which suggests how sparsely populated the route was in the first half of the 19th century.

The company was eager to make money as soon as possible and special excursion trains were introduced. The company miscalculated the potential traffic when an excursion was organised from Nine Elms to Surbiton for the Derby at Epsom. Five thousand hopeful passengers turned up at Nine Elms, the station was overrun and police had to restore order.

Like most railway companies, the London and South West Railway (LSWR) tried to save money by treating their 3rd class passengers like cattle rather than humans. Third class carriages were open goods trucks attached to goods trains: 'in some of the trucks was the swinish multitude, in others a multitude of swine'. Most companies improved conditions for poorer travellers after the injury and loss of life inflicted on passengers being hauled in goods trucks on the GWR in Sonning Cutting. The chairman of the LSWR reported in 1842: 'The Goods Trains were not so secure from danger as the passenger trains and therefore we have adopted a third class conveyance by an early morning train, which gives the industrious poor not only a greater sense of security, but also encouragement for early rising.'

The completion of the line to Southampton was celebrated by a party of directors and 'bands of music' leaving Nine Elms at 8 a.m. in the morning of 11 May 1840, arriving at Southampton at 11 a.m. A 'cold collation' was served near Micheldever and the resulting inebriation caused the train to decapitate a dog and destroy the level crossing gates at Northam.

The original London terminus was not at Waterloo but at Nine Elms in Vauxhall. The architect for Nine Elms, the Southampton terminus and most of the stations on the line was Sir William Tite. Little now remains of his work and Nine Elms (see p. 355) has been demolished. Tite's Southampton terminus remains intact, though InterCity trains no longer call there. The station was closed in 1966. The facade is rather like a simple Italian palazzo. The lowest stage is pierced by five arches. The two upper storeys are topped by a balustrade with a clock in the centre.

The arrival of the railway did succeed in making an immediate and long-lasting change to Southampton's fortunes. The docks were developed alongside the railway throughout the 19th and 20th centuries: the railway company owned the docks.

The White Star Line moved to Southampton from Liverpool in 1907 and Cunard followed in 1921. The Southern Railway (the LSWR was absorbed by the SR in 1921) speeded up the construction of the New Docks and in 1933 opened the King George V Graving Dock, big enough to take the *Queen Mary*.

In recent years, Southampton's fortunes have again changed with the competition from air travel. However, the town has seen extensive residential and commercial development since the war and has a university partly designed by Sir Basil Spence. Few of the present passengers using the line would share in the criticism hurled at the originators of the scheme who were 'met with ridicule in all directions ... their scheme was regarded as the outcome of disordered imaginations'. And in the immediate future British Rail plan to introduce new faster rolling stock, bringing the villages of Hampshire and the recreational facilities of the Solent and the English Channel ever nearer to London.

1 WATERLOO STATION When work began in 1902 to rebuild Waterloo the station was notorious for its inconvenience and the appalling regularity with which passengers got lost. Jerome K. Jerome pilloried the station in *Three Men in a Boat*: a train driver is bribed to take the three heroes and dog to Kingston-on-Thames. Much of the confusion at the station was caused by the existence of three separate main-line stations and three underground stations. Unlike the London termini of Paddington, St Pancras and Kings Cross, Waterloo had been extensively altered and extended over the years and presented a very confused overall design by the turn of the century.

Nothing now survives of the first Waterloo Station which was reached by the LSWR in 1846 after the line was extended along a two-mile curving viaduct from Nine Elms. Joseph Locke designed the station. He extended Waterloo in 1862 and one wall of this survives – the wall of yellow stock bricks alongside platform 16.

The north section of the station – platforms 16 to 21 – was added in 1885 and the ridge and furrow roof over the tracks is original. It is supported by girders with attractive curly brackets attached to the old brick wall on platform 16. The south section of the station – platforms 7 to 12 – was added in 1879 but the roof is not original.

The major part of the station was built between 1902 and 1922 and opened by Queen Mary in March 1922. The dominant feature of Waterloo is the roof – acres of ridge and furrow glass and iron – which gives the impression of being inside an enormous greenhouse. J. R. Scott was the designer of the station; the engineers were J. W. Jacomb Hood and A. W. Szlumper. The curved concourse

MAP 8

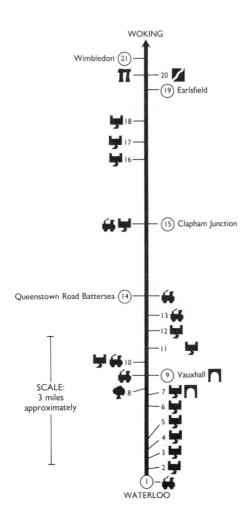

WOKING

Wimbledon (21)

20

(19) Earlsfield

18

17

16

(15) Clapham Junction

Queenstown Road Battersea (14)

13

12

11

10

(9) Vauxhall

8   7

6

5

4

3

2

(1)

WATERLOO

SCALE:
3 miles
approximately

is one of the simpler and more efficient to be found in British Rail's major stations. It is well lit, 120 feet wide, 770 feet long and serves all 21 platforms. It is relatively easy to find the ticket office, waiting rooms and bars and buffets; there are clear views of the functional departure boards and easy access to the platforms. The 'back wall' of the concourse is particularly fine. Built of red brick and limestone, it is decorated with classical arches and pilasters. The whole station is built on transverse arches with the parcels office below ground. Parcels and mail reach the platforms by lifts from a long tunnel underneath.

The dramatic potential of the exterior of Waterloo is ruined by the confused and haphazard development in the area. No railway hotel was built for Waterloo because even in 1900 the area was run down. Few passengers using Waterloo pass through the splendid art deco Victory Arch, cleaned up in 1985. The classical entrance built in Portland stone and bronze is opposite platform 19. The viaduct of the original London and South Eastern Railway carrying trains from Charing Cross to London Bridge via Waterloo East cuts straight across the arch and destroys the potential views both of the entrance itself and of London looking out from the Victory Arch.

The arch is flanked by Bellona Goddess of War (1914) and Peace 'enthroned on earth' (1918) with an enormous Britannia sitting proudly on the crown above, a memorial to the employees of the LSWR who died in the First World War. James Robb Scott was the designer. With the current fashion for art deco design Waterloo has come into its own. The clock above the arch and the lights on either side are fine examples and there are more details to discover in the station, particularly the ironwork between the platforms with lions' heads on the railings and gates.

Waterloo is a busy commuter station serving the southern suburbs of London and Surrey as well as providing InterCity services to Southampton, Portsmouth and Weymouth. Some 180,000 passengers use the station every day and in the course of a year several die from heart attacks trying to catch their trains.

Waterloo Station has long been associated with the prestigious express trains connecting with ocean-going liners at Southampton but those days have gone and the station conveys little sense of such adventures. However, the train journey from the terminus to Clapham Junction offers some fascinating views of London and the Thames – views best appreciated approaching rather than leaving Waterloo. For railway architecture enthusiasts there is a fine **signal box** just west of the station built of reinforced concrete in the 'International Modern' style of the 1930s.

2 **COUNTY HALL** (distinguishable by its central R:1 green tower)   Ralph Knott won a competition in 1908 with his design of County Hall but the building work was interrupted by the First World War and not completed until 1933. Additional wings were completed in 1963 and further additions were made when the London County Council made way for the Greater London Council, constituted in 1964. The frontage of the building on the south bank of the **River Thames** is 700 feet long with a concave giant colonnade in the centre – a familiar landmark along the river. Now (1986) a question mark hangs over County Hall: with the

abolition of the GLC rumours are rife about just what will happen to it. Perhaps it will become the railway hotel Waterloo has lacked.

3 **THE PALACE OF WESTMINSTER** In 1834 *R:1* faulty firing of the heating apparatus under the House of Lords caused a fire which burnt down the old Houses of Parliament. Sir Charles Barry and Augustus Pugin won a competition for the new Palace of Westminster the following year with their submission of a romantic Gothic design. Incorporated in the building is the oldest surviving part of the palace, **Westminster Hall**, built by William Rufus in 1099. Towering above the hall, and clearly visible from the train, are Barry's two gothic towers. The **clock tower of Big Ben** is 320 feet high and the **Victoria Tower** is 336 feet high: between them is the **flèche** over the central lobby.

4 **ST THOMAS'S HOSPITAL** St Thomas's *R:1* Hospital covers the land on the south bank of the Thames between Westminster Bridge and Lambeth Palace. The newest part is to the north; the oldest Victorian part is close to Lambeth Palace. The hospital was named after Thomas à Becket when it was founded late in the 12th century close to the Borough High Street, Southwark.

Queen Victoria laid the foundation stone of the present hospital in 1868 beside the Lambeth Palace Road. Three of the original seven pavilions designed by Henry Currey still remain with their tiers of arcades and corner cupolas visible from the train. Currey used the pavilion layout with 'Nightingale wards' (inspired by the French Hôpital de Lariboisière visited by Florence Nightingale) to allow the maximum ventilation and the dispersal of foul air.

The foundation stone of the new hospital was laid by the Archbishop of Canterbury on 24 July 1963. The northern section – massive smooth white cubes – was designed by Yorke Rosenberg and Marchall and completed in 1976.

Lambeth Palace

5 **LAMBETH PALACE** The Palace of the *R:1* Archbishop of Canterbury is largely medieval. The red-brick gatehouse was built by Archbishop Morton in 1495. The red-brick hall has a magnificent hammerbeam roof. It was rebuilt in the 17th century after being damaged by the Puritans, converted into a library in the 19th century and restored this century after being damaged during the Second World War.

6 **TATE GALLERY** The Tate Gallery can just be *R:1* seen across the Thames by peering through the office blocks which jostle each other on the south bank. The gallery was named after Henry Tate (of

Tate and Lyle) who offered some sixty modern English paintings to the trustees of the National Gallery in 1890. There was at the same time a move for creating a British Art Gallery in London. A suitable site was found – once occupied by the Millbank Prison – and the Tate was opened on 21 July 1897 by the Prince of Wales. It has since expanded and houses not only the important British collection – Turners, William Blakes, the Pre-Rapaelites – but also modern sculpture (Lord Duveen's sculpture gallery was opened in 1937) and an extensive modern foreign collection comprising Picassos, Matisses and contemporary art from all over the world.

7 **MILLBANK TOWER** The tall office block *R:l* dominating the north bank of the Thames and towering over and just to the east of the Tate is the Millbank Tower, designed by Ronald Ward and Partners and built in 1960–3 for the Vickers Group. *R:l* **Vauxhall Bridge** is just to the west.

8 **VAUXHALL GARDENS** The original site of *L:r* the Vauxhall Gardens was between the Embankment and Kennington Lane. No trace of the gardens has survived and part of the site is covered by the LCC Vauxhall Gardens Estate of the 1950s. John Evelyn and Samuel Pepys visited the gardens in the 17th century when they were known as the New Spring Gardens. They were refounded in 1732 and became one of London's chief places of open-air entertainment. There were walks, intimate supper boxes, the Grand Gothic Orchestra, Roubiliac's statue of Handel and an abundance of Regency rakes and pretty ladies seeking seclusion and seduction.

9 **VAUXHALL** (BR; 1848; **red- and yellow-brick station buildings of 1880–90**) There is a fine view of **Vauxhall Bridge** as the train approaches *R:1* the station from Waterloo. Sir Alexander Binnie designed the bridge and it was built in 1895–1906. It has five steel two-pinned arches. Binnie re-used the footings of the abutments of the earlier Regent Bridge which was demolished in 1898.

10 **NINE ELMS AND NEW COVENT GAR-** *L:r* **DEN** The original terminus for the LSWR was at Nine Elms. When the site was developed it was low and marshy, with windmills and willow trees. The terminus was an elegant affair, a partner to Sir William Tite's station at Southampton. It had an Italianate front with a giant loggia of pillars and arches. It survived as a local passenger halt after the line was extended to Waterloo and the surrounding area was developed as an important depot with locomotive and carriage workshops. However, in the 1960s the goods and locomotive depots were closed, plans to preserve Tite's station came to nothing, and decay and desolation descended on the site.

Redevelopment of the disused railway land began in the 1970s and in 1974 **New Covent Garden** fruit and vegetable market was opened. The market covers 65 acres, with buildings designed by Gollins, Melvin, Ward and Partners. The old Covent Garden, a mere 12 acres, has undergone its own redevelopment and is now one of the most popular shopping centres in London.

11 There is a fine **PANORAMIC VIEW OF LON-** *R:1* **DON** to the north. The Italian-style campanile of **Westminster Cathedral** rises 284 feet and can

easily be seen from the train. The Roman Catholic cathedral was designed by John Francis Bentley and built in 1895–1903. It is on the site of Westminster's Bridewell. Cardinal Manning bought the site in 1867 and Bentley was employed to design an early Christian-style cathedral. He went to Italy for inspiration and the campanile is similar to the one on Siena Cathedral.

A much higher and more recent tower is the **Post Office Tower** which is used for television and radio-telephony and is now part of British Telecom's empire. It was completed in 1964 and rises 619 feet.

Battersea Power Station

12 BATTERSEA POWER STATION The ex- *R:1* terior of Battersea Power Station was designed by Sir Giles Gilbert Scott. He managed to humanise industry by using fine Blockley bricks laid with straw-coloured mortar, placing 'sparse ornament beautiful in its design . . . just where it is needed and nowhere else'. The architect Curtis Green commented at the time: 'the great Power Station at

Battersea has, by the intelligent co-operation of the architect ... with the engineers, been transformed into something that gives pleasure by its dignity and expression of power' (Gavin Stamp, *Britain in the Thirties*). (See also p. 269, Victoria to Brighton.)

13 **STEWARTS LANE DEPOT**, formerly the Long- R:l
hedge Locomotive and Carriage Works of the LCDR, is below the line before (east of) Queenstown Road Battersea Station, close to the junction with lines to and from Victoria. Several of the original Longhedge buildings remain, designed by Joseph Cubitt from 1860 onwards, with distinctive lancet-like windows in their gable ends. The Orient Express is now housed in the depot. It is maintained by BR who naturally do not want it breaking down on their rail network.

14 **QUEENSTOWN ROAD BATTERSEA** (BR; 1877; **two–storey brick booking hall** below line) The station is snugly fitted in between railway viaducts carrying lines across the river to and from Victoria Station. This is a railway wasteland of tracks, viaducts, bridges and sidings. Before the arrival of the railways, however, the area was well known for its market gardens. Pouparts Junction, just east of Clapham Junction Station, was named after the Pouparts family who were the principal market gardeners.

15 **CLAPHAM JUNCTION** (BR) The large de- L:r
partment store **Arding and Hobbs** with its baroque cupola dominates Clapham Junction. The store was founded in Wandsworth in 1876 but rebuilt in 1910 after a fire. Its Edwardian grandeur

was the creation of James Gibson.

Clapham Junction Station was opened in 1863. It is the junction for trains from Waterloo and Victoria and was steadily enlarged over the years to become the world's busiest railway station. In 1882 1100 trains were passing through every day. It is still one of the busiest junctions in the world with a complex interweaving of tracks. The many platforms are connected by a very long enclosed brick viaduct under which the trains pass. The **oldest buildings** which belonged to the *L:r* LSWR are on platforms 9 and 10, of dirty yellow stock brick with red brick trims, Gothic arches and fine iron columns and brackets. A new entrance is being built on St John's Hill, part of a larger development which will include offices and a shopping centre. The old **Edwardian entrance**, *L:r* sadly derelict, can just be seen at the western end of the station above a dirty black brick wall and close to Barclays Bank.

16 ROYAL VICTORIA PATRIOTIC ASYLUM *L:r*
FOR GIRLS The yellow-brick Gothic building, with its turrets, bow windows and central tower, stands in the grounds of Spencer Park School, Wandsworth, and can be seen looking up from the train. The asylum was founded in 1859 to give an education to the daughters of soldiers, sailors and marines killed in the Crimean War. Rhode Hawkins designed the school which was opened on 1 July, admitting 150 girls. To begin with, the management of the institution was far from satisfactory. A girl was burnt to death while in solitary confinement and in 1875 an epidemic broke out as a result of a pipe being connected to the rainwater cistern instead of the drinking-water cistern. The building

has recently been converted into rehearsal rooms, studios and flatlets.

17 **ROYAL VICTORIA PATRIOTIC ASYLUM** *L:r* **FOR BOYS,** now **EMANUEL SCHOOL**   The second Victorian building also seen looking up from the train, of red brick and designed by H. Saxon Snell in 1872, was intended to house the boys' section of the asylum. However, the money ran out and the building was sold to Emanuel School. Emanuel was founded in 1594 by a bequest of Anne Sackville, Lady Dacre, though the school did not become established until the 18th century. Nearly 300 boys moved into the Wandsworth building in 1883. The school became independent in September 1977.

18 **WANDSWORTH PRISON**   There is the *L:r* briefest glimpse of the top of the prison. It was designed by D. R. Hill of Birmingham and built in 1849–51 as the Surrey House of Correction to relieve the overcrowding at Brixton Prison where there had been a severe outbreak of gaol fever in 1846. By 1860 there were 640 male and 190 female prisoners in Wandsworth. Their diet was sparse and monotonous. Prisoners on hard labour for more than four months were given 1 pint of oatmeal gruel for breakfast and supper, occasionally varied by 1 pint of cocoa for breakfast, plus 8 oz of bread for men and 6 oz of bread for women. Dinner consisted of 4 oz of cooked meat (3 oz for women) or 1 pint of soup with 6 oz of bread and 1 lb of potatoes (½ lb for women). The prisoners had to wear masks over their faces with eyelet holes except in chapel and when confined to their cells. One of the tasks for hard labour consisted of

operating a crank handle against a 7–12 lb pressure on a machine installed in the cell. Each prisoner had to perform about 1200 turns a day on this utterly useless machine.

19 **EARLSFIELD** (BR; 1884)   The station is approached from the north-east (Clapham Junction) past the vast **Wandsworth Cemetery**, opened in *L:r* 1878.

20 **RIVER WANDLE**   Immediately west of Earls- *R:l* field Station is the **River Wandle**, visible for a fraction of a second below the line. The Wandle was full of fish in the 17th century but in the 18th, with the development of water-powered industry, it became the centre of an important manufacturing area. The Surrey Iron Railway, the first public railway in the world, was built parallel to the river and opened in 1803 between Wandsworth and Merstham. Horses pulled wagons along the tracks. The light industry which grew up alongside the river and railway dramatically altered the area, and in a hundred years Wandsworth expanded from a population of 1455 (in 1801) to a population of 68,332.

21 **WIMBLEDON** (BR)   The station was opened in 1838 but the present unattractive concrete Southern Railway buildings suggest little of the wealth and prestige attached to Wimbledon as a residential and recreational centre. Wimbledon was a salubrious place to live as early as the 16th century. The Cecil and Spencer families had manor houses here and in the 18th century Sarah Duchess of Marlborough built herself a house. The All England Lawn Tennis Club was established in Wimbledon

MAP 9

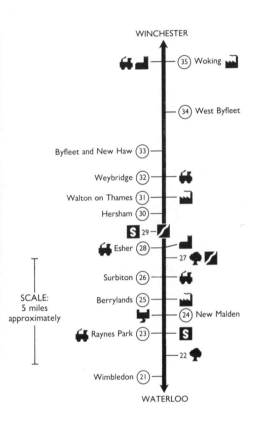

WINCHESTER

(35) Woking

(34) West Byfleet

Byfleet and New Haw (33)

Weybridge (32)

Walton on Thames (31)

Hersham (30)

S 29

Esher (28)

27

Surbiton (26)

Berrylands (25)

(24) New Malden

Raynes Park (23)

S

22

Wimbledon (21)

WATERLOO

SCALE:
5 miles
approximately

Park in 1922. The first championships had been held in 1877 at the original location in Worple Road, Wimbledon.

22 **WIMBLEDON COMMON** cannot be seen from *R:l* the train but stretches beyond the line of trees along the skyline. The preservation of the common was threatened by the Spencers, lords of the manor in the 19th century, but their ambitions were thwarted by Act of Parliament in 1871 and commoners have been enjoying its recreational facilities ever since: golfing; riding; walking. Caesar's Camp is on the common, a 14-acre Iron Age hillfort defended by a single bank and ditch. There is also a windmill, a combined smock and post mill which was restored in 1957.

23 **RAYNES PARK** (BR; 1870) With the coming of the railway, exclusive low density housing began to develop beyond Earlsfield and Wimbledon. Villas were built with large gardens, golf courses were laid out and patches of heathland preserved for recreation. The LSWR did its utmost to provide fast regular trains for the new residents of suburbs which gradually engulfed Guildford, Dorking and Windsor. **Malden Golf Course** and **Coombe Hill Golf Course** beyond are examples of the *R:l* amenities which have made 'villages' along the LSWR attractive to those rich enough to afford the season tickets, club subscriptions and exclusive housing: movie stars and pop singers in Weybridge; city financiers and stockbrokers in Esher.

West of Raynes Park Station and just before the junction with the line to Epsom is a **Southern Railways signal box** with the massive brick base *L:r* which was put round it as a protection against bombing during the Second World War.

24 NEW MALDEN (BR; 1846)   The town of New
Malden has been extensively developed in the last
few decades to attract businesses out of more
expensive office accommodation in central London.
Two massive sixteen-storey **office blocks** are *L:r*
close to the station (designed by Martin Richmond
of Planning and Development Ltd, 1963–8)
together with a dreary multi-storey car park. The
old village of Malden is away to the south-west.

25 BERRYLANDS (BR; 1933)   The large **sewage** *R:l*
farm behind the station adds to the bleakness of
the site.

26 SURBITON (BR)   The first station at Surbiton,
called Kingston New Town, was opened in 1838.
Within a few years it was known as Kingston-on-
Railway, then officially renamed Surbiton, an apt
name for the new suburban town created by and
around the railway.

Under Sir Herbert Walker Southern Region
undertook a massive programme of electrification
in the 1930s. Part of the 'Southern Electric' image
involved the reconstruction of stations. The design
of Surbiton, by J. R. Scott of Southern Region's
Architect's Department, was a response to the
imaginative London Transport stations designed by
Charles Holden. The high cubic **booking hall** has a *R:l*
distinctive clock tower which can be seen from the
train. Not all commuters approved of the Thirties
style, known also as the 'Odeon Cinema' style or
'super wireless sets'.

The name Surbiton sums up the character of this
railway line as far as the border with Hampshire.

This part of Greater London/Surrey has become an endless garden suburb of London with the individuality of villages lost amid housing and industrial estates, office blocks and shopping centres.

West of Surbiton the railway line crosses the border between **Greater London** and **Surrey**.

27 **HAMPTON COURT PARK**   The palace is not *R:l* visible from the train but Hampton Court Park reaches to the **River Thames** which is only a short distance from the railway line, to the north-west.

   When Cardinal Wolsey built Hampton Court in 1514 it was the grandest house to be constructed in England at the time: evidence of his meteoric rise from being the son of an Ipswich butcher to having a larger household than the Archbishop of Canterbury. Henry VIII was not amused by his servant's wealth. Wolsey tried to make amends by giving Hampton Court to the king in 1529, but he was deprived of all his land and belongings and died a year later under arrest for high treason.

28 **ESHER** (BR; 1838; **cream-painted wooden station building** of 1887)   The village of Esher is to the south. This is an area of fine old trees, large gardens and large houses, beginning of the 'stockbroker belt'.

   Just to the east of the station is the white- *R:l* washed church of **All Saints, Weston Green**, designed by Sir Edward Maufe in 1939.

29 **SANDOWN PARK RACECOURSE** is to the *L:r* south of the line just west of Esher Station. One of the most important races held at Sandown Park is the Eclipse Stakes, over a distance of 1¼ miles.

The **River Mole** is crossed immediately after the racecourse.

30 **HERSHAM** (BR; 1936)

31 **WALTON ON THAMES** (BR; 1838) The station is dominated by the enormous **Liptons** R:I **Factory** (Birds Eye Foods). The three-storey block was designed in 1960–1 by Sir John Burnet, Thomas Tait and Partners with an extension added in 1967–8. The two upper floors have a rapid flickering rhythm to their walls, created by bands of projecting hexagons of aluminium set against dark blue panels.

32 **WEYBRIDGE** (BR; 1838; **red-brick station buildings** c.1890s) Weybridge has experienced distinct stages of residential development. With the arrival of the railway came employees of the railway seeking new houses; by the end of the 19th century better-off middle-class professionals had settled in the village, commuting into London; from the 1930s onwards, with the expansion of suburban London, Weybridge became known for its new exclusive properties, often built within the grounds of older mansions. The trees alongside the roads and the railway hide the famous and the rich.

33 **BYFLEET AND NEW HAW** (BR; 1927 as West Weybridge)

34 **WEST BYFLEET** (BR; 1887) A railway traveller in the 1850s described the landscape west of Weybridge: 'Here we dip into a cutting, down whose bushy slopes the wild convolvuli twine their snowy flowers; and coming out again upon the

level, we see the heath stretching away in a wild expanse of undulating swells, and blue and solitary distances.' Allotments and pylons have tamed the 'wild expanse' considerably since then.

Shah Jehan Mosque, Woking

35 WOKING (BR) Approaching the station from the east is a striking advertisement for the **Shah** *L:r* **Jehan Mosque** which can itself be seen to the south of the line. The mosque was built in 1889 by W. I. Chambers for Dr Gottlieb Leitner, who founded the centre for oriental studies in Woking which has since become the centre for Muslims in England. The mosque was built to face Mecca though an unkind critic at the time commented: 'a captain of a P&O boat kindly went to Woking and took the bearings'.

On the same side of the track as the mosque is the red-brick **Southern Railwaymen's Home** *L:r* **for Children**, an example of the philanthropic side of the railways.

Woking Station has something of an international atmosphere. There is a connecting service to Heathrow by coach and the station notices are printed in three languages. When the station was opened in 1838 it was situated in open heathland two miles from the village. Since then the village has become a large residential town with a flourishing industrial and commercial centre. The **Woking Business Park** east of the station *R:l* emphasises the continuing expansion. The architecture of the station reflects some of the stages in Woking's development with a footbridge of c.1885 and buildings in the 'Odeon' style of 1936.

Between Woking and Farnborough the railway line crosses infertile countryside of sandy heaths, scrubland and woodland. The army has been able to make more use of the land than have the farmers.

36 **BASINGSTOKE CANAL** There are several *R:l* glimpses of the Basingstoke Canal as it flows close to the line between Weybridge and Farnborough, particularly just west of Woking below the line and

MAP 10

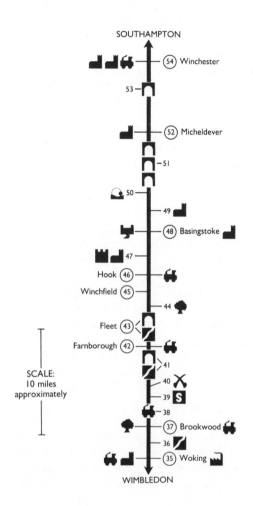

again just west of Brookwood. The canal was completed in 1796 and is supplied with water from the **River Loddon**.

37 BROOKWOOD (BR; 1864; **Dutch-style station buildings** c.1900) Brookwood Station is dominated by the **Brookwood Cemetery**, its *L:r* mature trees so thick it appears more like a park than a place of the dead. The cemetery, which covers over 2400 acres of heathland to the south of the line, was founded in 1854 by the London Necropolis Company to help solve the problem of disposing of increasing numbers of dead Londoners. Sir William Tite and Sydney Smirke designed the cemetery, planting the fine wellingtonias and conifers between the graves. The London Necropolis Company paid for the construction of the station at Brookwood and also built their own station adjacent to Waterloo. The 'Necropolis' train (from the Greek 'nekros' meaning corpse) left daily. The two platforms were distinctly signposted – one for mourners and one for coffins. George Measom, the writer of Victorian railway guides, found the cemetery an extraordinary place to visit: 'We are reminded of the final terminus which awaits us all at the close of life's swift railroad journey ... but ... we *cannot* despair here; heaven is too visible, God's holy influence too palpable in all we see and hear; the buzzing bee, the flitting butterfly, the singing birds ... the blossoming heather amidst which the graves lie.' There used to be a short branch line from Brookwood into the cemetery, ending at Cemetery Station.

38 PIRBRIGHT JUNCTION is about two miles *L:r* west of Brookwood. This is where the line to

Aldershot leaves to the south. This section of the line was heavily used during the First and Second World Wars. During the First World War, for example, in a period of 48 hours, the LSWR managed to convey 25,080 troops, 6722 horses and 1174 guns while still maintaining the flow of busy holiday traffic.

39 BISLEY Beyond the trees, in the heathland to *R:I* the north of the line, are the **Bisley Rifle Ranges**. The National Rifle Association's 116th annual shooting competiton was held at Bisley in 1985. The Association was founded in 1859 because of the fear of a French invasion of the country and the first meeting was held on Wimbledon Common in 1860. The move to Bisley was made in 1890 as too many buildings were being erected around the common and rifles had a much greater range.

40 PIRBRIGHT CAMP is to the north of the line. The Guards Division of the Infantry have their depot at Pirbright. This division includes the Grenadier, the Coldstream, the Scots, the Irish and the Welsh Guards.

41 THE VALLEY OF THE RIVER BLACK- WATER Immediately before the train crosses over the **River Blackwater** it passes under the **Basingstoke Canal** – carried across the line on a four-arched brick aqueduct. The River Blackwater marks the boundary between **Surrey** to the east and **Hampshire** to the west. Hampshire used to be covered by vast expanses of forest – of which the New Forest is a survivor – and still has more woodland cover than other areas of England.

42 **FARNBOROUGH** (BR; 1838; **red-brick station buildings** 1904 when line widened) A Victorian traveller, arriving at Farnborough in the mid-19th century, found the station well equipped with 'extra engines, fuel, force pumps for replenishing the boilers, and all the requisite appurtenances of an efficient engineering establishment, in case of any emergency arising on the journey'. The station was used extensively by the military from Aldershot before more convenient branch lines and stations were built. Now Farnborough is virtually indistinguishable from Aldershot with the expansion of their residential areas. The army arrived in 1855 when Queen Victoria opened the permanent North and South Camps outside what was then the small and remote village of Aldershot.

The Empress Eugenie came to live at Farnborough Hall in 1881, dying there in 1920.

43 **FLEET** (BR; 1847–69 known as Fleet Pond) The railway line crosses over more of a lake than a pond on a causeway.

44 West of Fleet there is an unusual quantity of rhododendrons beside the line which culminates in **RAILROAD HEATH**, an area of heath, wood- R:l land and a profusion of the purple flowers.

45 **WINCHFIELD** (BR) There are more rhododendrons at Winchfield, growing on the sides of the cutting west of the station.

46 **HOOK** (BR; 1883; **red-brick station buildings** – also at Winchfield) Hook suddenly became famous after the Second World War as the site of the LCC's proposed New Town – a proposal

squashed by the Conservatives in the period before New Towns became all-party policy. The LCC plan was published posthumously in 1960: 'the most influential urban planning document of its generation, transforming the dispersed low-density polynuclear forms of the first New Towns into the concentrated high-density linear forms since adopted elsewhere' (Nicholas Taylor, *Architectural Review*).

47 OLD BASING The brick cottages of Basing *L:r* village are in the marshy valley of the **River Loddon**. Both the church and the castle remains can be seen from the train, about three miles before Basingstoke Station.

St Mary's is a large late Perpendicular church (1519), built almost entirely of brick and with a tower. Inside there are monuments to the Paulet family who took over **Basing Castle** (immediately south-west of the church) in 1428. The original motte and bailey castle was probably built by Hugh de Port who was granted the estate by William the Conqueror. Sir William Paulet, 1st Marquess of Winchester, began building a house inside the walls in 1530 but it was destroyed in the Civil War. During the 1645 siege, Inigo Jones, the famous architect and designer, was one of the prisoners taken by the Roundheads. Queen Elizabeth I stayed twice at the Paulets' house. The second visit proved so expensive that to pay for her entertainment her host had to economise by demolishing part of his house.

48 BASINGSTOKE (BR; 1839; largely rebuilt 1903) The Victorian station at Basingstoke was famous for its refreshment rooms: 'Every article of excellent food, from a bun or a sandwich to mock turtle soup, every assuager of thirst, from tea . . . or bottled beer to iced lemonade or aristocratic champagne, is provided with express-train rapidity by civil, efficient waiters.'

Basingstoke began its 20th-century expansion after the LCC and Hampshire jointly planned to increase its population from 2500 to 80,000 in the fifteen years from 1963. The population has continued to increase as more offices and industries have established themselves in the centre of the town and in the bustling estates on the edge. The Civil Service Commission and the Headquarters of the Automobile Association are in Basingstoke. There is a large **IBM office** just by the station; also *L:r* the office of **Providence Life Insurance** which is *L:r* contributing part of the cost of renovating the station.

Part of medieval Basingstoke can be seen from the train. **Holy Ghost Chapel** is on Chapel Hill in *R:l* the cemetery just north of the station. The roof was pulled off the chapel to make leaden balls for the assault of Basing Castle (see p. 372) but the 13th-century flint tower still stands. The Guild-chapel of Holy Trinity was added to the Holy Ghost Chapel by Lord Sandys in 1524. Now also in ruins, it is built of brick with a chalk turret.

49 WORTING is a small village on the edge of *R:l* Basingstoke. The Victorian church of **St Thomas's** was designed by Henry Woodyer and has a thin shingled bell-turret with a spire. Immediately next to the line is a **terrace of red-brick cottages** with an extraordinary collection of signs from old railway stations displayed in the garden.

50 JANE AUSTEN'S COUNTRYSIDE A tree- *L:r*
covered hill is between the railway line and
Steventon, the birthplace of Jane Austen. But the
gently rolling **Hampshire landscape** through
which the train passes features in her novels. Jane
Austen was born in the rectory at Steventon in
1775 and lived there for the first 25 years of her
life. She died at 8 College Street, Winchester; the
house is now owned by Winchester College.

**51 LITCHFIELD TUNNEL
POPHAM NO 1 TUNNEL
POPHAM NO 2 TUNNEL**

52 MICHELDEVER (BR) **Micheldever Station**
is one of the most interesting stations on the line. It
was opened in 1840 as Andover Road and has
remained practically unaltered. The plain rectangular **station building** on the up side was designed *R:l*
by Sir William Tite. It is of flint with yellow bricks
for the corners, windows and door surrounds,
stone for the sills and keystones of the windows,
and a slate roof. The canopy is on all four sides and
is supported by plain iron columns. Plain, domestic
and rather intimate, it is the perfect station building
for a Hampshire village.

The vast cutting in which the station is situated is
really a quarry. It was made when chalk was
removed between the wars and transported by the
Southern Railway to Southampton to build the
Southampton Docks extensions. The sidings and
sheds in the cutting were erected during the
Second World War for the movement of soldiers
and military equipment.

The **village of Micheldever** is about two miles
south of the station. **St Mary's Church** is clearly *L:r*

visible on the edge of the village. It is an unusual church. The flint and stone tower is medieval but the octagon was inserted into the medieval church in 1808 by George Dance the Younger (the architect of Newgate Gaol).

53 WALLERS ASH TUNNEL

54 WINCHESTER (BR) The train approaches Winchester from north and south through a cutting so that it is difficult to see much of the city, which is sited in a hollow. William Cobbett described Winchester in *Rural Rides*: 'The city is . . . in one of the deepest holes that can be imagined. It never could have been thought of as a place to be defended since the discovery of gunpowder; and, indeed, one would think that very considerable annoyance might be given to the inhabitants even by the flinging of the flint-stones from the hills down into the city.' The Romans called the city Venta Belgarum and from the reign of Egbert in 829 until the accession of William the Conqueror (who was crowned in Winchester and London) it was the capital of Wessex and the second capital of England. Winchester public school is one of the oldest in England, founded by William of Wykeham in 1382.

Winchester Station was opened in 1839 and Sir William Tite's **original building** survives on *L:r* the down side, painted creamy white.

Winchester Cathedral can be seen to the *L:r* south of the station. The view is best approaching from the south. The rather squat building was constructed 1079–1500. Walkelin, the first Norman bishop, began the work and brought stone from the Isle of Wight. The vault of the nave is only

Winchester Cathedral

78 feet high but the length of the nave is 556 feet, the longest in Europe.

St Paul's Church is close to the station. It was R:1 designed by Colson in the late 19th century.

Further along the line towards Southampton is a deep cutting. When the railway navvies excavated the cutting they discovered hundreds of skeletons – the bodies of prisoners of war who fell victim to typhus while they were kept in Winchester during the Napoleonic Wars. Their bodies were thrown into a ditch and only brought to the surface because of the construction of the railway.

MAP 11

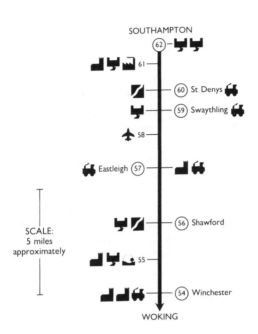

SOUTHAMPTON

62

61

60 St Denys

59 Swaythling

58

Eastleigh 57

SCALE:
5 miles
approximately

56 Shawford

55

54 Winchester

WOKING

Just after the cutting is **Christ Church**, de- L:r
signed by Ewan Christian and built of grey stone in
1861.

55 ST CATHERINE'S HILL, ST CROSS HOS- L:r
PITAL AND CHURCH Still on the southern
edge of Winchester, **St Catherine's Hill** is the
first distinct hill to be seen from the train. It has a
group of trees on top. An Iron Age hillfort covers
23 acres of the hill. There is also the site of St
Catherine's Chapel – early 12th century – and a
strange maze cut in the turf. The maze may have
had a religious significance or may simply have been
designed for amusement at the local fair.

Immediately beneath the hill – and between the
hill and the railway line – are **St Cross Hospital** L:r
and Church. The hospital was founded in 1136 by
Bishop Henry of Blois for thirteen poor brethren.
Cardinal Beaufort rebuilt the hospital in 1445
adding an 'Almshouse of Noble Poverty'.

56 SHAWFORD (BR; 1882) The **River Itchen** is L:r
below the line to the east and it is just possible to
see **Shawford House** (built of stone in 1685) L:r
through the trees in a fine position beside the river.
William Cobbett described the 'vale of Itchen' in
his *Rural Rides*: 'There are few spots in England
more fertile or more pleasant; and none, I believe,
more healthy . . . the vale contains about 5000 acres
of meadows, a large part of which is regularly
watered. The sides of the vale are, until you come
down to within about six or eight miles of
Southampton, hills or rising grounds of chalk,
covered more or less thickly with loam.'

57 EASTLEIGH (BR) Present-day Eastleigh was

created by the LSWR. The station was built in c.1840 in open country and the Victorian community of railway workers which grew up around it took the name Eastleigh from a nearby farm.

The **Church of the Resurrection**, immediately north of the station, was built for the railwaymen in 1868; G. E. Street was the architect. It was added to first by John Loughborough Pearson in 1884, then by Sir Arthur Blomfield in 1899–1905 to become a larger church able to cope with the expanding population. *R:l*

The expansion of Eastleigh increased with the arrival of the LSWR carriage works from Nine Elms in 1891 and the engine repair sheds and locomotive workshops in 1910. The town is still an important railway depot with the red-brick building '**British Rail Engineering Ltd Eastleigh Works**' just south of the station proclaiming the site of the carriage and locomotive works of BR's Southern Region. BR's parcels depot was originally opened in 1852 as a cheese market serving the railway community. Other industries have developed in the town making use of the good communications, in particular the manufacture of cables and confectionery. *L:r*

Eastleigh Station was designed by Sir William Tite in c.1840 in a simple Italianate style with unusual chimney stacks joined at the tops, the spaces below shaped into round arches. His building survives on the up side. Attractive curly brackets support the platform awning and there is a footbridge painted green and white with rosette designs. *R:l*

58 SOUTHAMPTON AIRPORT (BR) The station was opened to serve the **airport** which is *L:r* immediately to the east. The airport, now owned by the British Airport Authority, offers scheduled and chartered flights to other parts of the British Isles and the continent.

59 SWAYTHLING (BR; 1883, **red brick with** _L:r_
neo-Flemish details on facade)   Immediately south of the station is **South Stoneham House**. _L:r_ This was the manor house of South Stoneham, built of red brick in 1708 by Nicholas Hawksmoor. Now it is a hall of residence for Southampton University and can just be seen among the modern additions to the university's residential complex – which includes a 17-storey tower block.

60 ST DENYS (BR; 1861, **red-brick Italianate-** _R:l_
style station building)   St Denys is close to the **River Itchen** and just south of the station there is _L:r_ a fine view of the river with many sailing boats and water birds. The Rivers Itchen and Test both flow into Southampton Water. In geological terms the appearance of the landscape along the south coast is relatively recent. There used to be much more land to the south – the Isle of Wight was only divided from the mainland by a river and Bourne-mouth Bay was land up until the New Stone Age – but the lowering of the level of the land or the rise of sea level drowned the southern river system, creating new expanses of water. The lower valley of the **River Test** was thus flooded to become Southampton Water.

61 NORTHAM is a suburban and industrial area of Southampton which expanded in the mid-19th century around the **gas works**. The gas works _L:r_ were moved to the site in 1819 at what was considered a safe distance from the centre of Southampton. The area was heavily bombed during the Second World War and has been extensively redeveloped since then. The 16-storey block of flats called **Millbank Tower** is at the centre of the *L:r* rehousing scheme. It was designed in 1959–65 by the City Architect, L. Berger. The church in front of the tower is **St Augustine's**, designed by *L:r* Henry Woodyer and built in 1881–4 in a neo-Early English style.

Immediately next to the gas works the train turns west towards the city. The railway line used to continue southwards to Southampton Terminus (see p. 346) and Sir William Tite's elegant station – a suitably grand building at which to transfer from train to cruise liner.

Southampton Civic Centre

62 SOUTHAMPTON (BR) The station is approached through a **long cutting** between houses and light industrial development, then through a **long tunnel** under the city centre. Between the western entrance to the tunnel and the station there is a view of part of the **Civic Centre** above the line. The centre was designed *R:1* by E. Berry Webber and built in 1929–39 in a 'free Classical' style. It is faced throughout with Portland stone. The site was originally medieval common land and is called West Marsland.

Southampton Station is hardly an architectural delight for the end of the journey. The original station buildings (opened as Southampton West in 1895) were built in the 'Domestic Revival' style popularised by Eden Nesfield and Norman Shaw, with banded brick gables and a clock tower topped with an ogee-shaped cupola 100 feet in height. All this was gradually destroyed throughout the 20th century, finally to be replaced with a characterless **office block** on the up side and an ugly enclosed *R:1* concrete footbridge across the tracks.

South of the station is a wasteland of cranes, warehouses and factories, the usual commercial and industrial development associated with docks. Southampton was heavily bombed during the Second World War and redevelopment continues. It was made a city in 1964 but has no cathedral.

Southampton has been a flourishing port since Saxon times. Canute was proclaimed king here in 1017 and reputed to have ordered the waves to retreat. During the two world wars over ten million troops left Southampton for the battlefields of France. The docks were built at the same time as the railway to London. Ocean Dock, part of the Eastern Docks, has been the home of the great liners *Queen Mary* and both the *Queen Elizabeth*s.

EUSTON
TO
THE MIDLANDS
AND
NORTHWEST

(Birmingham · Liverpool · Manchester)

Contents

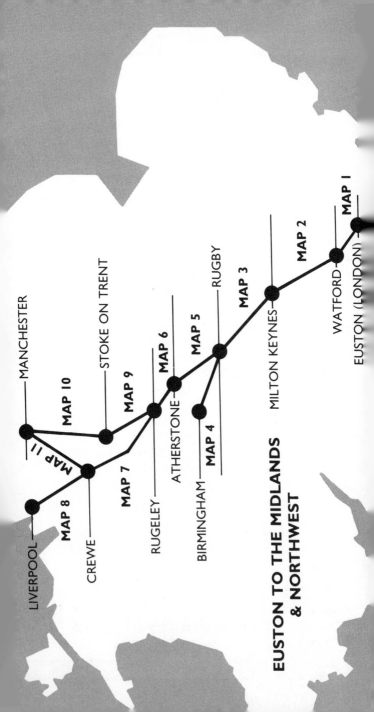

EUSTON TO THE MIDLANDS & NORTHWEST

MANCHESTER

STOKE ON TRENT

MAP 10

MAP 11

MAP 9

LIVERPOOL

MAP 8

CREWE

MAP 7

RUGELEY

ATHERSTONE

BIRMINGHAM

MAP 4

MAP 6

MAP 5

RUGBY

MAP 3

MILTON KEYNES

MAP 2

WATFORD

MAP 1

EUSTON (LONDON)

EUSTON
TO
BIRMINGHAM

Introduction

The industrialists and businessmen of Birmingham put forward the idea of a railway line connecting their rapidly expanding Midland empires with the markets and port of London. Birmingham was increasing its wealth and population at a tremendous rate. In 1801 the population was 86,000; by 1831 it was 147,000. A variety of small industries were established – the largest was Boulton and Watt's Soho Manufactory. Nearby Coventry was also experiencing the effects of the Industrial Revolution and its textile industry – still based on home weaving – was expanding. However, the only forms of transport available were canal barge and coach. Twenty-six fast flyboats a day transported light and perishable goods on the Grand Junction Canal to London and there were 16 coaches a day carrying sheep and cattle (8,000 head a week) to London. But these methods were slow and uneconomic and Midland industries were faced with increasing competition from the continent.

The London and Birmingham Railway Bill passed through Parliament in May 1833 but not without a struggle. Canal and coach owners were not unnaturally afraid of the competition from the railway for, as was the case wherever a railway was built in Britain, they would inevitably be put out of business. Some of the landed gentry, through whose parks and estates Robert Stephenson proposed to run his line, were also far from happy about the intended line. Sir Astley Cooper of Hemel Hempstead went so far as to declare: 'if this sort of thing be permitted to go on, you will, in a very few years, destroy the *noblesse*'.

The result of the opposition was that the L&BR Co. had to pay £750,000 to buy off the interested parties. Just to get the Bill through Parliament cost the company £72,000. Some landowners were able to make a tidy sum out of the railway: 'A reverend gentleman complained that his privacy had been ruined, that his daughter's bedroom windows were exposed to the unhallowed gaze of the men working on the railway, and that he must remove his family to a watering-place, to enable him to do which he must engage a curate. All this was considered in the compensation demanded, and paid; yet no curate has been engaged, no lodgings at a watering-place taken. The unhappy family have still dwelt in their desecrated abode, and borne with Christian-like resignation all the miseries heaped upon them. The gilding of the pill, it seems, has rendered it palatable, and we have no doubt that if his daughter's rooms have a back window as well as a front one, he would be exceedingly glad if a railroad was carried across at the same price' (C. B. Andrews, *The Railway Age*, 1937).

Robert Stephenson was employed by the L&BR as engineer. He decided on a maximum gradient between Camden Town and Birmingham of no more than 1 in 330 which forced him to undertake some enormous earthworks. Nearly 20,000 navvies were employed to carry out works which one contemporary writer compared to the building of the Great Pyramid of Egypt. Peter Lecount calculated that the labour of the Great Pyramid was equivalent to lifting 15,733,000,000 cubic feet of stone one foot high. To build the railway 25,000,000,000 cubic feet of a similar weight of material had to be lifted one foot – 9,267,000,000 cubic feet more than for the Great Pyramid. Charles Dickens described the effect of such efforts in Camden Town in *Dombey and Son*: 'The first shock of a great earthquake had . . . rent the whole neighbourhood to its centre. Traces of its course were visible on every side. Houses were knocked down; streets broken through and stopped; deep pits and trenches dug in the ground; enormous heaps of earth and clay thrown up; buildings that were undermined and shaking propped by great beams of wood ... Everywhere were bridges that led nowhere; thoroughfares that were wholly impassable; Babel towers of chimneys wanting half their height; temporary wooden houses and enclosures in the most unlikely situations; carcases of ragged tenements, and fragments of unfinished walls and arches, and piles of scaffolding, and wildernesses of bricks, and giant forms of cranes, and tripods straddling above nothing. There were a hundred thousand shapes and substances of incompleteness wildly mingled out of their place, upside down, burrowing in the earth, aspiring in the air, mouldering in the water, and unintelligible as any dream ... the yet unfinished and unopened railroad ... from the very core of all this dire disorder trailed smoothly away upon its mighty course of civilisation and improvement.'

Thirty main contractors undertook to build sections of the line and ten of these failed completely. Jackson and Seeldon lasted only a few months on the contract for the Primrose Hill Tunnel (see p. 402). Stephenson had to take over the work which cost £286,000, over twice the original estimate.

T. Townsend worked for a year on the cutting north of Tring until giving in. One and a half million cubic yards of chalk had to be removed to create a cutting through the Chilterns ¼ mile long and up to 57 feet deep. The cutting between Roade and Blisworth took 800 men 3,000 barrels of gunpowder to remove 1 million cubic yards of spoil. Later over 100 iron girders had to be placed across the line to keep back the retaining walls, following slips along the cutting.

The Kilsby Tunnel (see p. 427) caused the greatest problems, bankrupting the contractor –

who then died – killing 26 men and holding up the completion of the line. It is 2,423 yards long and when completed was the largest railway tunnel in the world. Its position was soon overtaken by further engineering feats as a writer pointed out in 1851. '... once one of the wonders of the world; but ... reduced to the level of any other long dark hole'. A hidden spring was discovered soon after work on the tunnel began and 13 pumping engines had to work for 19 months to pump out the water (1,800 gallons a minute). The navvies who built the tunnel had a reputation for strength and recklessness. Three were killed while competing at jumping over the mouth of one of the ventilation shafts. Stephenson was praised by an early railway historian for giving his men the extra willpower to complete Kilsby: 'Stephenson infused into the workmen so much of his own energy that when either of their companions were killed by their side they merely threw the body out of sight and forgot his death in their own exertions.' When the tunnel was completed costs amounted to £291,030: the estimate had been for £98,988.

Stephenson confessed to a friend his unease about the work on the L&BR. With such heavy earthworks the cost per mile was far higher than many other lines: 'I sometimes feel very uneasy about my position. My courage at times almost fails me and I fear that some fine morning my reputation may break out under me like an eggshell.' However, one of his pupils, F. R. Conder, revealed the enormous power of the engineer: 'It is rare that a civilian has so free and almost martial an address, it is still more rare for such features to be seen in any man who has inherited them from a line of gently nurtured ancestors ... He knew how to attach people to him; he also knew how to be a firm and persistent hater.'

The first section of the line to be completed was

from Euston to Boxmoor (for Hemel Hempstead) and it was opened on 20 June 1837. The sections from Boxmoor to Denbigh Hall (just north of Bletchley) and from Birmingham to Rugby were opened on 9 April 1838. Passengers had to travel by coach between Denbigh Hall and Rugby until the earthworks in between were completed and the line was eventually opened on 17 September 1838. The break in the line caused irritation and delay and some people were unable to fit on the coaches. Bletchley was said to be (c. 1838) 'a small miserable village, where those disappointed in getting on from Denbigh Hall must not expect to find accommodation even for their dog'.

The service opened with six trains each way. The fastest journey time was 5 hours 37 minutes. The 1st class fare to Rugby was 24s 6d one way; 2nd class, 15s. This was not particularly cheap and 2nd class passengers had to travel in coaches 'open at the side, without linings, cushions or divisions in the compartments', but large numbers still flocked to use the railway. Osborne, in his L&BR Guide of 1838, commented on the immediate social effects: 'It has already begun to produce great and material changes in society. Many who, but a few years since, scarcely penetrated beyond the county in which they were born are now induced to visit places far more remote ... and become acquainted with customs, manners and habits which previously were unknown to them.'

The traffic in goods and livestock was equally heavy. For the Christmas cattle market in London in 1843 the L&BR carried, in two days, 1,085 oxen, 1,420 sheep and 93 pigs in 263 wagons. In 1859 the up line between Primrose Hill and Bletchley was duplicated, in 1874 a new tunnel at Watford was opened and by 1882 the whole of the line had been quadrupled.

A new town was established at Wolverton

around the locomotive and carriage workshops of the L&BR. Wolverton is halfway between London and Birmingham and in 1831 was a small hamlet with a population of 417. Seven years later the locomotive works opened with a workforce of 400. Houses were built by the railway company together with a church, schools and supplies of gas and water. From 1854 housing developed to the east of Wolverton, at Bradwell, as the original landowner refused to sell any more of his land to the company. The peak of the works was from 1886 to 1900 when 5,000 men were employed and the workshops covered 35 acres. In 1851 Samuel Sidney commented in his *Rides on Railways* on the workforce he found at Wolverton, their conditions and opportunities: 'we have here a body of mechanics of intelligence above average regularly employed for 10½ hours, during five days, and for eight hours during the sixth day of the week, well paid, well housed, with schools for their children, a reading-room and mechanics' institution at their disposal, gardens for their leisure hours, and a church and clergyman exclusively devoted to them. When work is ended, Wolverton is a pure republic – equality reigns.'

At the London end the goods station at Camden Town was developed with facilities for building and repairing wagons and trucks. In the 1850s the yard had enough passenger carriages to give 11 miles of seat room or to seat 40,196 individuals. There were arrangements for building wagons and trucks, conveying coals and other merchandise and live-stock. A newspaper reporter in the 1860s described the scene: 'in the grey mists of the morning, in an atmosphere of a hundred conflicting smells, and by the light of faintly burning gas, we see a large portion of the supply of the great London markets rapidly disgorged by these night trains: fish, flesh and food, Aylesbury butter and dairy-fed pork, apples, cabbages and cucumbers.' The Roundhouse remains the last surviving memorial to the depot.

The L&BR merged with the Manchester and Birmingham Railway and the Grand Junction Railway (which had absorbed the Liverpool and Manchester Railway) to form the LNWR in July 1846. The great steam engines which ran on the LNWR were designed and built at the Crewe workshops which originally belonged to the Grand Junction Railway. David Joy created the 'Jenny Lind' class and John Ramsbottom the 'Lady of the Lake' class.

Steam running ended in 1968 on British Rail. The lines from Euston to Birmingham, Manchester and Liverpool had been electrified two years before: by 1974 electrification was extended as far as Glasgow, creating the longest stretch of electrified line in Britain. The trials of the Advanced Passenger Train took place on the line between Glasgow and Euston. Designed and built at Derby, the APT was the latest development in electric rail transport, aerodynamically shaped to reduce wind resistance and aid stability. The APT, however, has not been the success BR hoped and is off the tracks for the foreseeable future. Nevertheless, some of its new technological and design features are being incorporated in BR's rolling stock.

A newspaper article in 1982 revealed that the track between Euston and Birmingham was so worn out that on 25 occasions trains had to reduce their speeds from 100/75 mph down to 20/5 mph with the result that trains averaged 10 minutes late. The signalling system was apparently also worn out; there had been derailments, a serious land-slip, and structural faults in the Primrose Tunnel – yet more headaches for an already over-burdened British Rail. But since then there have been extensive engineering works on the line, for example improvements to the approaches to Birmingham

New Street. For the better-off passenger there is the opportunity to travel to Liverpool and Manchester in luxury Pullman carriages. However, all passengers will benefit from the new coaches and the locomotives now being built by BR for their InterCity services.

MAP I

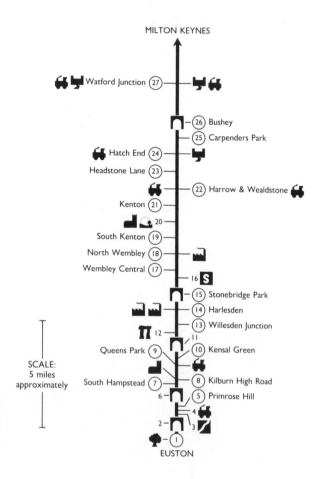

MILTON KEYNES

Watford Junction (27)

(26) Bushey
(25) Carpenders Park
Hatch End (24)
Headstone Lane (23)
(22) Harrow & Wealdstone
Kenton (21)
20
South Kenton (19)
North Wembley (18)
Wembley Central (17)
16 S
(15) Stonebridge Park
(14) Harlesden
(13) Willesden Junction
12
11
Queens Park (9)
(10) Kensal Green
South Hampstead (7)
(8) Kilburn High Road
6
(5) Primrose Hill
4
2
3
(1)
EUSTON

SCALE:
5 miles
approximately

1 EUSTON STATION was London's first main line terminus, planned by Robert Stephenson and designed by Philip Hardwick. Its two great features were the Doric Triumphal Arch or Propylaeum, 72 feet high and built of Bramley Fall stone, and the Great Hall by Philip Charles Hardwick. Both were destroyed amid a storm of protest in 1961. Little remains of the Victorian station. The small entrance lodges faced with Portland stone which stand on either side of the approach used by buses from Euston Road were designed by J. B. Stansby as part of improvements to the station in 1869–74. Gilded letters on the quoin stones proclaim the names of the principal stations of the LNWR. The statue of Robert Stephenson by Baron Carlo Marochetti, presented to the LNWR by the Institute of Civil Engineers, now stands in the piazza of the station, dwarfed by the office blocks towering above it.

Objections to the Doric Propylaeum were made when it was first erected in 1838. Augustus Welby Pugin commented 'this piece of Brobdingnagian absurdity must have cost the Company a sum which would have built a first rate station.' The Arch, together with attendant lodges and 300-ft screen cost £35,000 but the Directors of the L&BR considered the money well spent. 'It may be said that the Railway is a great national undertaking, and that the national character is, in some respects, involved in the execution of the whole. All spectators are impressed by magnitude or mass, or by highly enriched detail in public buildings; and it is often remarked by critics that the English are too parsimonious and calculating to produce either the one or the other.' Parsimony ruled, however, when it came to rebuilding Euston. Though the LCC insisted the portico should be re-erected, the

Minister of Transport, Ernest Marples, announced its preservation did not justify the expenditure it would involve. The Ministry produced questionable figures of £12,000 for the demolition of the Propylaeum and £190,000 to move and rebuild it. Ernest Marples and the Prime Minister, Harold Macmillan, were unmoved by protests and demolition began on 6 November 1961. With the new terminus completed it is obvious that the portico could have been sited along Euston Road. It would have provided welcome relief to the coldly efficient, functional and characterless terminus behind.

Euston had two hotels, opened in September 1839 and designed by Philip Hardwick. The Victoria was for 2nd and 3rd class passengers, a 'dormitory and coffee room'; the Euston was for 1st class passengers. These were linked in 1881 by a new block, designed by J. Maclaren, which completely destroyed the view of Hardwick's screen from the Euston Road. Further expansion of the station in the 1880s involved disturbing the dead of St James's churchyard immediately west of the station. Considerably more care was taken over the removal of the bodies because of the criticism which had accompanied the loose treatment of corpses at St Pancras. Each corpse was given a new coffin and taken to St Pancras Cemetery in Finchley. 'A doctor and an inspector were constantly present at either end on behalf of the company, to see that nothing was done which might offend against either due reverence for the dead or due regard for the health of the living.'

Plans for the complete rebuilding of Euston began c.1900 but lack of money and the First World War delayed any decision. In 1935 the Railways (Agreement) Act granted a government loan towards the rebuilding of the station, hotels and offices; and Percy Thomas, President of the RIBA, produced an ambitious design. The Great Hall would be demolished, the portico would be re-erected on the Euston Road and a vast new terminus would be built with accommodation on the roof for helicopters. Sir Josiah Stamp, Chairman of the LMSR, even threw a switch to set off charges at the Caldon Low Quarries and release 100,000 tons of limestone for the rebuilding. War again intervened.

Neither war nor protests stopped the rede-velopment plans of c.1960. The new terminus was designed by R. L. Moorcroft, architect of the London Midland Region, and opened by the Queen on 14 October 1968. Passengers pass through a 647-ft long colonnade of polished black granite and white mosaic horizontal facings which separates the piazza from the concourse. The concourse is 200 by 150 ft, clean, light, air conditioned, with a Travel Centre to the west, shops and lavatories to the east and ticket barriers to the north. From this characterless if airy and functional hall the pass-enger descends the sloping ramps to the gloomy platforms.

Leaving Euston Station For the first seven years (1837–44) the L&BR was open, trains were hauled by cable from Euston Station up to Camden Town. The power for the cables was supplied by two 60hp Maudslay and Field condensing engines which were below two large chimneys on either side of the line at Camden Town. Trains travelling towards Euston descended the bank from Camden unaided, after their engines were detached. The train still ascends the bank to Camden – though

without the cable – passing to the east of **Regents** *L:r.*
Park and through a cutting lined with black brick
walls. The high walls were built to keep back the
treacherous blue London clay but in the early years
of the railway they kept giving way under pressure.
Inverts were then built from wall to wall under the
railroad bed.

Approaching Euston (or leaving – back to the
engine) it is possible to see the **Post Office** *L:r.*
Tower, 620 feet high and now part of British
Telecom's empire.

2 **PARK STREET TUNNEL** The Park Street
Tunnel is 161 yards long. Before the railway was
built this was an area of market gardens. There was
also a small colony of firework-makers whose
leader, called Bunyan, led an ineffectual resistance
to the railway: 'you who clamber over folkses walls
with your ladders and your hammer, your levels
and your bevels and your devils'.

3 **REGENTS CANAL** The train crosses over the
Regents Canal with the imaginative **Pirate Castle**, *R:l*
a haven for children keen to learn canoeing and
sailing. The Regents Canal is the first part of the
Grand Union Canal system which can be seen on
the journey to the Midlands. It was built as an
extension from Paddington to the Thames at
Limehouse and opened on 1 August 1820.

4 **CAMDEN GOODS STATION AND THE
ROUNDHOUSE** Robert Stephenson sug-
gested the L&BR should buy 30 acres of land in
Camden Town to develop as a goods station. 'At
Camden we may see sheep from Perth, vegetables
from Covent Garden for Glasgow, fish for Birming-

ham. Coal in immense quantities is brought from the Midland Counties, Worcs and Lancashire. Underground are stables and warehouses of the most extensive character; and the gas consumed annually at the station exceeds 6 million cubic feet' (George Measom, 1859). The two tall chimneys above the engines which cable-hauled the trains from Euston were on either side of the line; there were 2,500 feet of double track for goods waggons and 12 miles of single track. In 1850, 500 to 2,000 cattle and 2,000 to 6,000 sheep arrived weekly at the station but now the area is a deserted wasteland with only the Roundhouse surviving.

The Roundhouse was built in 1847 as a *R:1* repair shed and designed by Robert Stephenson, Dockray and Normanville. It covers 2,234 square yards and has a diameter of 160 feet. The iron roof is supported by 24 cast-iron columns and beneath the central turntable is a honeycomb of tunnels which gave access to the inspection pits and allowed for the removal of clinker. In 1964 the Roundhouse was presented to Centre 42, the arts

The Roundhouse

centre founded by Arnold Wesker to bring
together the trade union movement and the arts;
and in 1986 it became an arts centre for the black
community.

5 **PRIMROSE HILL** (BR)   Primrose Hill was first   R:1
called Greenbury Hill after the names of the three
men executed for the murder of Sir Edmundsbury
Godfrey. They carried his body to the hill (which is
to the west of the line) after killing him near
Somerset House. The station is on the North
London line.

6 **PRIMROSE HILL TUNNEL**   The Primrose
Hill Tunnel is 1,182 yards long and has a handsome
southern entrance flanked by Italianate towers on
rusticated stone foundations. The materials beneath the black grime are cream stone and yellow
stock brick, but even in their filthy state the portals
are impressive. Stephenson and his secretary Budden were the designers. The contractors faced
enormous problems in the digging of the tunnel and
had to give up (see p. 390). Stephenson assumed
the tunnel could be built without an invert but the
pressure of the clay was so great that the thickness
of the brickwork had to be increased, an invert
constructed and Roman cement used for the
jointing instead of mortar.

7 **SOUTH HAMPSTEAD** (BR)

8 **KILBURN HIGH ROAD** (BR)   The Victorian
red-brick station buildings are difficult to see as
they are on the bridge across the line. But there is a
bright **mural** on the station wall. Kilburn was only   R:1
a small hamlet on Watling Street when the railway

was built: 'a place of residence by many genteel families ... with a number of country villas.' It even had its own spa called Kilburn Wells. A traveller leaving London by train in 1838 declared on reaching Kilburn that he was 'freed from the accumulated bricks and mortar of the metropolis' and began 'to breathe a fresher air'. Dick Turpin began his famous ride to York on the gallant Bess at Kilburn. The spire visible between the blocks of flats belongs to **St Augustine's Church**, designed L:r by John Loughborough Pearson in 1871–98. The spire is in a Normandy-Gothic style and rises to 254 feet. Nikolaus Pevsner describes the church as 'one of the best churches of its date in the whole of England, a proud, honest, upright achievement'. Inside is an *Annunciation* by Titian and a *Virgin and Child* by Filippino Lippi.

9 **QUEENS PARK** (BR) The large four- R:l platformed station is bypassed by the main line trains but has a particularly elegant train shed. Queens Park was laid out in about 1900 as an experiment in better quality working-class housing. The station is also served by the Bakerloo underground line.

10 **KENSAL GREEN** (BR)   R:l

11 **KENSAL GREEN TUNNEL** is 320 yards long and takes the train under the A404 to emerge next to Kensal Green Cemetery.

12 **KENSAL GREEN CEMETERY** The train is L:r below the cemetery in a cutting but there are glimpses of the tops of statues and gravestones. Kensal Green Cemetery was opened in 1832, the

first of the cemeteries which were built on a commercial scale and with new standards of mortuary hygiene. By the 1830s the graveyards of Inner London were in a ghastly state with drunken gravediggers replacing half-decomposed corpses with the bodies of the newly dead. A contemporary wrote with relief of the restoration of 'the good early Christian and even Pagan custom of interring the dead apart from the living'. The dead at Kensal Green include Brunel and his parents and the novelists Thackeray, Wilkie Collins and Trollope; also James Miranda Barry, Inspector General of the Army Medical Department who was discovered, on his death in 1865, to be a woman.

13 **WILLESDEN JUNCTION** (BR) Little can be *R:l* seen of this important railway junction as the main line trains bypass the station to the south. It began as a small roadside station, opened in 1841–2 as Acton Lane. This was replaced in 1866 by Willesden Junction which consisted of two groups of completely separate high-level platforms. There was no indication from which platform the next train would be leaving so the Junction was nicknamed 'Bewildering Junction' and 'The Wilderness'. Rebuilding took place in 1894 and the Junction became an important distribution point for parcels and goods, with marshalling yards, a freight locomotive depot and north carriage depot. The station forms the background to *Waiting for the Train*, a painting by James (Jacques-Joseph) Tissot (1836–1902) which depicts his mistress-model waiting on the platform surrounded by luggage.

14 **HARLESDEN** (BR) is distinguished by the *R:l* embattled **McVities factory** – 'McVities bake a *L:r*

better biscuit' – and the enormous red-brick **Heinz (57 Varieties) factory**.   *L:r*

15 STONEBRIDGE PARK (BR) In 1875 Stone-bridge Park was no more than a 'cluster of 60 or 80 smart new villas for city men' but suburban development soon changed this. In 1953 carriage servicing was transferred from the Willesden depot to a large new installation at Stonebridge Park which gave local employment a boost and thousands of new homes were built in the 1970s when the Stonebridge Comprehensive Develop-ment Area was formed.

Immediately north of Stonebridge Park is the **Brent Embankment and Viaduct**. The Embankment used up 372,000 cubic yards of earth which were brought from the cutting at Oxhey further up the line. The Viaduct once took the railway line over the River Brent; now it crosses over the A406 – the North Circular Road. It is built of stock bricks and was designed by Robert Stephenson.

16 WEMBLEY STADIUM Wembley Park was *R:l* first developed in the 1870s as a leisure centre and

Wembley Stadium

there were ambitious plans to build an English Eiffel Tower before it was discovered the land could not support the weight. In 1924 the British Empire Exhibition was held at Wembley and the stadium, designed by Sir John Simpson and Maxwell Ayrton, was built to hold 100,000. The stadium, track facilities and swimming pool were used for the 1948 Olympic Games: more recently the stadium has been the venue for the FA and Rugby League Finals, for hockey, greyhound and speedway racing, and for Bob Geldof's 'Live Aid' concert in July 1985.

17 **WEMBLEY CENTRAL** (BR)   In the 1840s the neighbourhood of Wembley was 'celebrated for stag hunting, on which occasions it is sometimes honoured by the presence of Her Majesty'. After the electrification of the railway line in 1920 the area changed dramatically with extensive residential and industrial building: the grounds of the 1924 British Empire Exhibition were intensively developed for the use of light industry.

18 **NORTH WEMBLEY** (BR)   Semi-detached housing of the 1930s and a variety of factories, including **British Oxygen**, surround the red-brick *R:l* station.

19 **SOUTH KENTON** (BR)

20 **HARROW ON THE HILL**   There is a good *L:r* view of Harrow on the Hill beyond the industrial estates which surround the railway line. **St Mary's Church spire** rises above the hill. The church is a *L:r* mixture of periods, dating from Norman times through to the 15th century. Inside is a memorial

by John Flaxman to John Lyon, farmer of the parish, who founded Harrow School. In the churchyard is an unusual tombstone to Thomas Port, engine driver, who was killed in 1838, the year the L&BR opened: 'Bright rose the morn and vig'rous rose poor Port/Gay on the train he used his wonted sport.' Harrow School began to expand in about 1800 and by the 1860s had become one of the most famous of the Victorian public schools. Trollope attended as a despised day pupil. Byron was also one of its pupils and wrote an early, not very good poem 'On the distant view of the village and school':

Again I revisit the hills where we sported,
The streams where we swam, and the fields where
   we fought;
The school where, loud warn'd by the bell, we
   resorted,
To pore o'er the precepts by pedagogues taught.

The name Harrow is derived from *hergae*, the Saxon word for temple or shrine. Once, the hill was thickly wooded and popular with royal hunters. The present King's Head public house is on the site of Henry VIII's hunting lodge.

21 KENTON (BR) *L:r*

22 HARROW AND WEALDSTONE (BR)
When the main line between Euston and Watford was widened for electrification in 1914–22, Gerard Horsley, a pupil of Norman Shaw, designed new stations. **Harrow and Wealdstone** is a Neo- *R:l*
Wren style building with a tower built of dark red brick with contrasting white terracotta string

courses. On the other side of the line are the older **yellow-brick platform buildings**.

L:r

23 **HEADSTONE LANE** (BR)   The red-brick sta- *L:r* tion is bypassed at high speed.

24 **HATCH END** (BR)   The imposing red-brick Victorian building just before the station adorned with 'Franco-Flemish' gables and dormers was opened in 1853 as the **Commercial Travellers School**. It was designed by Lane and Ordish; wings *R:l* were added in 1868 by Knightley; a chapel was added in 1904 by H. D. Creswell. The Commercial Travellers Benevolent Institution was founded to clothe, maintain and educate destitute orphans of deceased commercial travellers and the children of 'necessitous travellers'.

Hatch End Station is another of Gerard *L:r* Horsley's Neo-Wren stations (see Harrow and Wealdstone) in red brick and white stone and with two Queen Anne gables on the platform side, a cupola, clock and weathervane.

The train crosses the border between **Greater London** (formerly Middlesex) and **Hertford-shire**.

25 **CARPENDERS PARK** (BR)   Carpenders Park Station was rebuilt in 1952 for the extensive new housing – both council and speculative – in the area. The style of the station building is distinctly functional and severe, reflecting the character of the nearby LCC housing estate. The station first opened in 1914 but was no more than a wooden halt serving the local golf course.

26 BUSHEY (BR)   Immediately north of Bushey the line crosses the **River Colne** over the **Colne Viaduct**. The viaduct was once one of the main sights in the area with its five semi-circular brick arches, 30 feet high and with parapet walls 312 feet long. It cost the L&BR £10,000 and now passes through the industrial wasteland which has occupied the land between Bushey and Watford.

27 WATFORD JUNCTION (BR)   Before the railway arrived at Watford the town was declining. Silk-spinning had stagnated, tanning and candle-making were dying out. Even so there were objections from property owners to the railway coming any closer than half a mile from the town centre. However, the decline was reversed and now Watford is a large flourishing town with a population of over 77,000. The concrete high-rise block towering above the town belongs to the **YMCA** and is a particularly ugly result of the *L:r* expansion. Immediately east of the station is the **Department of Employment**, aptly housed in *R:l* the **London Orphan Asylum**. The Gothic style buildings were designed by H. Dawson in 1869–71 and are built in yellow stock brick with a clock tower.

   Watford Junction Station   has a mixture of buildings: single-storey yellow-brick **platform** *R:l* **buildings**, older **red-brick buildings** with white- *L:r* painted awnings and decorative valancing. The railway deliberately encouraged the expansion of Watford by offering free 21-year season tickets to purchasers of houses above a certain price. The ticket remained with the property. The Bakerloo and Metropolitan Underground lines arrived in 1917 and 1925.

MAP 2

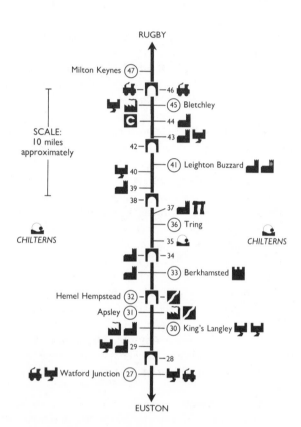

28 **WATFORD TUNNEL** The Earl of Essex and the Earl of Clarendon owned large estates at Watford – Cassiobury Park and The Grove – and Robert Stephenson was forced to build a tunnel 1 mile 57 yards long in order to get permission to cross their lands. Samuel Smiles commented 'this latter diversion ... inflicted on the public the inconvenience of the Watford tunnel ... and on the Company a largely increased outlay for its construction'. The Earls had been equally difficult when the Grand Junction Canal was being built across their land in 1794 and were able to obtain specially ornamental stretches of the canal for their parks as well as financial compensation. Stephenson and Budden gave the tunnel classical portals with semicircular arches 25 feet high and 24 feet wide surmounted by pediments. The tunnel was difficult to cut through the chalk and loose gravel, and ten men were buried under falling earth during the sinking of one of the shafts. 'One poor fellow was found, three weeks afterwards, standing perfectly upright with his trowel in his hand ... as employed at the moment of the dreadful occurrence' (Osborne's *London & Birmingham Railway Guide*, 1840).

29 **LANGLEYBURY CHURCH AND HOUSE** *L:r* The flint church of **St Paul's** (with a west tower and spire) was designed by H. Woodyer and built in 1865. Behind, in the trees, is the early Georgian **Langleybury House**.

30 **KING'S LANGLEY** (BR) Just south of the station is the **Booksellers' Provident Retreat**, *R:l* immediately next to the railway line. This was built by the firm of John Dickinson who established

several paper mills in the valley at the beginning of the 19th century (see p. 413).

King's Langley was named after the Royal Palace which was on the hill to the west behind the **parish church** (with its embattled tower). L:r Edmund Langley, the fifth son of Edward III, was born at the Palace and lived there most of his life. He was buried at the adjacent Dominican Friary until the Dissolution of the Monasteries, when his body was transferred to the parish church. Piers Gaveston, the unfortunate favourite of Edward II, was also buried in the Friary.

Ovaltine Factory

The large **factory** designed by Bowden and L:r Partners was begun in 1913 when **Ovaltine** (now **Wander Foods**) moved to King's Langley. Ovaltine was first manufactured in Switzerland: 1985 was the 75th anniversary of the first sales in Britain. In the late 1920s two farms were bought and the **thatched buildings and poultry farm** visible R:l from the train were built. In the 1930s Radio Luxembourg brought the bedtime drink into every home with its advertising jingle, 'We are the Ovaltinies, happy girls and boys'.

31 **APSLEY** (BR)   The paper manufacturing empire of John Dickinson has dominated the valley of the

River Gade from Watford to Hemel Hempstead
since the beginning of the 19th century. With the
financial help of his partner George Longman,
Dickinson bought **Apsley Mill** in 1809 (close to *R:1*
the station) and **Nash Mill** in 1811 (half a mile to *R:1*
the south). The mills were very old – both named
in Domesday Book as corn mills – and were
converted to paper mills at the end of the 18th
century. They are now owned by the Dickinson
Robinson Group. Apsley is the biggest manufactur-
er of envelopes in Europe and Nash produces
superior board for the printing industry.

The **Grand Union Canal** is now one of the *R:1*
features of the journey between London and the
Midlands. 'The way it seems to flirt with the railway
line' (Alan Crawford), offering glimpses of bridges,
locks and slow-moving narrow boats, is one of the
most attractive parts of the journey. It can be
followed almost all the way from Watford to
Rugby. Water from the canal is still used to cool
the turbines for the Dickinson mills: further
supplies of water come from artesian wells sunk
below the mills early in the 19th century.

32 HEMEL HEMPSTEAD (BR) Hemel Hempstead is to the north. The area immediately next to
the station is **Boxmoor**, famous for its watercress
beds growing along the **River Bulbourne**. Bob *R:1*
Snooks came to an untimely end in 1802 close to
the railway line. He was hanged from a chestnut
tree for robbing the mail and was buried immediately beneath it.

The railway line crosses over the River Bulbourne
and the Grand Union Canal just west of the station.
When the canal was dug at Boxmoor there was a

local outcry as it was planned to cross Boxmoor Commonland preserved for the benefit of the local people. The Company had to pay £900 for 25 acres of land and the money was used to build a new wharf on the canal and a workhouse.

33 **BERKHAMSTED** (BR)   There is a fine view of **Berkhamsted Castle** east of the line. The castle *R:l* was probably first erected in the late 11th century and in 1216 it was besieged by King Louis of France. Later it became an appendage of the Dukes of Cornwall and Chaucer lived there for a time when he was employed as clerk of the king's works and supervised the restoration of the buildings on the site. The main gateway and barbican were demolished by the L&BR to make way for the station. A mock Elizabethan structure was erected as compensation after the enraged inhabitants of Berkhamsted held a protest meeting in 1833, and was replaced when the line was widened in 1875. **St Peter's** is the large flint parish church. *L:r*

34 **NORTHCHURCH TUNNEL**   The tunnel is 342 yards long and has handsome stone portals. The tower of **St Mary's Northchurch** can be *L:r* seen just north of the tunnel. There is a gravestone in the churchyard to Peter the Wild Boy who died in 1785. He was found in the Forest of Hartswold near Hanover in 1725 and thought to be about 12 years old. Nothing could be discovered of his background and how he came to be living in the forest. He was brought to England where 'proving incapable of speaking or of receiving any instruction, a comfortable provision was made for him by Her Majesty at a farm house in this parish, where he continued to the end of his inoffensive life'.

35 Between Berkhamsted and Tring the railway line passes through the beautiful **CHILTERN HILLS**. *R:l* To the north-east the land on the high ground belonged to the ancient estate of **Ashridge**, much of which is now owned by the National Trust. Originally there was a monastery at Ashridge. This became a royal residence at the Dissolution of the Monasteries and then passed to the Dukes of Bridgewater and Earls Brownlow. In 1929 the mansion became the Bonar Law Memorial College for Unionist Workers; now it is a Management College.

36 **TRING** (BR)   Tring is about two miles away to the west. The townsfolk were so keen for the railway to come to their town that they built the road to the station. The station was first of all to be some 3½ miles away at the north end of Tring Cutting because the L&BR refused to pay the high price demanded by the profiteering landowner. The townsfolk intervened and paid the difference between the railway company's offer and the demand of the greedy landowner.

37 **ALDBURY CHURCH**   The tower of Aldbury *R:l* Church can just be seen about a mile from the station and beyond it, on top of the ridge, a **monument** to the 3rd Duke of Bridgewater. The *R:l* Greek Doric column has an urn on top and was erected in 1832 to commemorate the Duke's work for the promotion of canals (see p. 495).

38 **TRING CUTTING**   Samuel Smiles described the cutting as an 'immense chasm across the great chalk ridge'. 1½ million cubic yards of chalk were removed and some used to make the following

6-mile long embankment. The problems involved in cutting through the chalk and gravel defeated the contractor (see p. 390). When the railway navvies made the cutting they found the tusk and teeth of an elephant. At the point where the line crosses the **Icknield Way** at the northenmost end they unearthed Roman pottery and 16 human skeletons. The Icknield Way was the highway of ancient Britain and in use before the Romans arrived. The name comes from the tribe of Iceni whose queen at one time was Boudicca. Here it creates the boundary between **Hertfordshire** and **Buckinghamshire**.

39 CHEDDINGTON (BR)   The parish church of **St Giles's** is half a mile south of the station. The *L:r* small church contains fragments of the original Norman building: the tower was built in the 15th century.

40 MENTMORE   The rooftops, some outbuildings *L:r* and the church of the estate of Mentmore are just visible in the clump of trees on the hillside about a mile from the line. Mentmore became well known when the contents were sold at auction for several million pounds in 1978. The house became the 'seat of the World Government of the Age of Enlightenment' and the national centre of transcendental meditation. It was built in 1852–4 for Baron Meyer Amschel de Rothschild and designed by Joseph Paxton and his son in law G. H. Stoke. The mansion was sumptuously decorated and even had hot water heating and artificial ventilation. Paxton used the Jacobean style and there is much carved decoration outside and rich gilding inside the house.

The train crosses the boundary between **Buckinghamshire** and **Bedfordshire**.

41 LEIGHTON BUZZARD (BR) The tall octa- *R:1* gonal spire of **All Saints** dominates the town. The church was consecrated by Bishop Oliver of Lincoln in 1288 and contains interesting graffiti and carvings. These is a precise drawing by a mastermason working on the building of a four-light window and also an illustration of the ancient 'Simon and Nellie' story in which Nellie threatens Simon with a spoon while she is baking a cake.

The church close to the station is **St Barnabas** *R:1* which was designed by Benjamin Ferrey and built in

All Saints, Leighton Buzzard

1848. The **station** is built of yellow and red bricks with simple brackets supporting the platform awnings.

Leighton Buzzard is apparently named after 'the tun belonging to a family nicknamed Buzzard, who grew leeks'. The town grew steadily throughout the 19th century but received a boost to the local sand industry during the First World War. Sand was used as ships ballast, and when imported supplies were cut off Leighton's industry benefited. In 1919 a 2-foot gauge light railway was opened to maintain the sand traffic and in the 1930s and again in the early 1950s 100,000 tons of sand were carried annually. Now a local preservation society looks after the light railway.

42 LINSLADE TUNNEL The Linslade tunnel is 285 yards long. It is the only curved tunnel on the line and cuts through blue clay and iron sandstone. There are three tunnels with the original in the centre, its portals decorated with battlements and turrets.

The Great Train Robbery, in which the London to Glasgow mail train was robbed, took place just north of the tunnel on 8 August 1963.

43 LINSLADE CHURCH The ancient market town of Linslade is now part of Leighton Buzzard. **St Mary's Church Linslade** is over a mile to the *R:1* north. The church is built of yellow limestone and ironstone and has a 15th-century tower. Close beside it is the early 18th-century **manor farmhouse**. *R:1*

The train crosses the boundary between **Bedfordshire** and **Buckinghamshire**.

44 STOKE HAMMOND CHURCH St Luke's is *R:l*
built of ironstone with a Decorated central tower.
To the west are the masts of one of several
wireless transmitting stations in this area. *L:r*

45 BLETCHLEY (BR) The chimneys of the **Lon-** *L:r*
don Brick Company kilns reveal where the
materials for this brick-built Victorian railway town
were made. Bletchley was heavily dependent on
the brick industry until the 1960s. Four million
bricks were produced a week and one quarter of
the population was employed by the company.
Bletchley developed from a small market to a
flourishing industrial town with the arrival of the
L&BR, the Bedford Railway in 1846 and the
Buckinghamshire Railway in 1850 and the establishment of the brickworks. **St Mary's Church** was *L:r*
restored in the late 17th century by the antiquary
Brown Willis, who painted cherubs on the chancel
roof. He commemorated his parents with two plain
slabs on the church floor, unwilling to give them
'marble statues or fine Embellishments, whilst the
other part of God's house in which they lay wanted
a requisite Decency and Convenience'.

46 DENBIGH HALL BRIDGE Just over a mile
north of Bletchley Station the Denbigh Hall Bridge
carries the railway line over **Watling Street**,
(now the A5). Between April and September 1838
passengers on the L&BR had to leave the train at
Denbigh Hall and travel the next part of the
journey to Rugby by coach because the earthworks
in between were unfinished (see p. 392). There
was nothing more than an inn at Denbigh Hall. This
was on the site of a cottage where the Earl of
Denbigh had found refuge when caught in a
snowstorm.

47 MILTON KEYNES (BR)   Milton Keynes is British Rail's newest station, opened in May 1982. The five platforms are linked by a covered overbridge. The platform buildings are covered in glistening cream tiles with clear plastic awnings. There are facilities for disabled passengers and ample car parking and a city bus network to the surrounding residential and industrial estates.

Milton Keynes began to grow after 1967 when 22,000 acres was designated for the city. The population is expected to be 200,000 by the 1990s. The station is part of Central Milton Keynes which contains the Borough Council headquarters, one of the largest shopping areas in Europe, a library, cafés, bars and restaurants. Some of the buildings have trees and shrubs inside them, others are built around courtyards, lawns and fountains. Cyclists and pedestrians have been specially provided for with their own network of Redways – reddish asphalt tracks – which cover the city's residential areas, industrial estates and parkland. The housing is particularly imaginative and varied and some of the brick and timber developments with tile or slate roofs can be seen from the train. The houses are grouped in various ways, some around courtyards, in crescents or squares, others in small mews or winding lanes. Most have gardens but every 'village' has a safe open space for children to play in. The Development Corporation prides itself on creating a city with fresh air, greenery and open spaces 'where the trees grow taller than the buildings'.

48 ST LAURENCE'S BRADWELL   was built in   *R:1* about 1200 and has a west tower and a saddleback roof. On the other side of the line is a fragment of the 14th-century church belonging to **Bradwell**

MAP 3

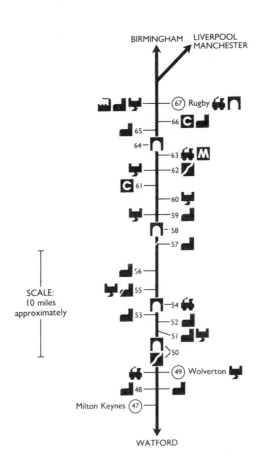

Abbey. It looks like a small chapel all on its own in   *L:r*
a field. A Benedictine Priory was founded at
Bradwell c.1155 and given to Cardinal Wolsey by
Henry VIII at the Dissolution of the Monasteries.

49 WOLVERTON (BR)   South of Wolverton are   *R:l*
fibreglass sculptures of alarmingly lifelike black-and-
white cows standing in a field close to the railway
line. When the L&BR decided to develop Wolverton for their locomotive works it was only a hamlet
of 417 inhabitants, but by the end of the 19th
century some 5,000 men were employed in the
works. The works extend to the north and south
of the station, and one long **red-brick shed** before   *L:r*
the station still has camouflage colours from the
Second World War painted on the walls (now
Dunlop and Ranken Steel Service Centre). Houses
were built at Wolverton by the railway company
together with a church, schools and supplies of gas
and water. From 1854 housing developed to the
east of Wolverton, at **Bradwell**, as the original   *R:l*
landowner refused to sell any more of his land to
the company.

Wolverton Station was rebuilt in 1881 and has
attractive red-brick platform buildings and an
immaculate white wooden footbridge. In the 1840s
Wolverton was famous for its refreshment rooms
which did good trade as every express train
stopped for ten minutes. Stout and Banbury cakes
were the favourites – 182,500 Banbury cakes were
consumed a year. Seven young ladies were employed as waitresses. 'As these youthful hand-
maidens stand in a row behind bright silver urns,
silver coffee pots, silver tea pots, cups, saucers,
cakes, sugar, milk, with other delicacies over which
they preside, the confused crowd of passengers,

simultaneously liberated from the train, hurry towards them with a velocity exactly proportionate to their appetite' (Sir Cusack P. Roney, *Rambles on Railways*, 1868).

50 WOLVERTON VIADUCT AND EMBANKMENT   The train crosses over the **River Great Ouse** on a viaduct 660 feet long, with six elliptical arches, each of 60 foot span. The viaduct is at the centre of an embankment 1½ miles long and 48 feet high. The canal company disputed the right of the L&BR to drive piles into the canal banks to build a temporary wooden bridge over the river while the embankment and viaduct were being constructed. Consequently Robert Stephenson and a team of navvies took advantage of Christmas Day festivities and erected a temporary bridge on 25 December 1834. On 30 December the canal company pulled it down and the case had to be settled in court with Chancery settling for the railway.

The embankment caused problems as well. It was composed partly of alum shale and this decomposed and then spontaneously combusted, to the amazement of the locals: 'Dang it, they can't make this here railway arter all, and they've set it o' fire to cheat their creditors' (L. T. C. Rolt, *George and Robert Stephenson*).

51 CASTLETHORPE   There was originally a station at Castlethorpe which is about 4 miles to the north of Wolverton. The parish church of **St Simon and St Jude** is close to the railway line. It *R:l* was built in the 13th–15th centuries but the tower had to be rebuilt after it collapsed in 1729. The **large stone farmhouse** between the church and *R:l* the line was built in the 17th century.

52 HANSLOPE CHURCH Nikolaus Pevsner described **Hanslope steeple** as the finest steeple in *R:l* Buckinghamshire. It rises to 180 feet and is a landmark for miles around. The original spire was built in the 15th century but was rebuilt after it was destroyed by lightning in 1804. The crockets decorating the ribs of the spire had a practical use. They provided a way for a brave volunteer to reach the weathercock in the event of its sticking.

Between Castlethorpe and Ashton the train crosses the boundary dividing **Buckinghamshire** from **Northamptonshire**.

53 ASHTON **St Michael's Church** close to the *L:r* line is basically medieval but the tower was built in 1848 to the design of R. C. Hussey. Inside is the earliest alabaster effigy in the county: of Sir John de Herteshull, who died c.1365. This is an area of rich pasture, dairy herds grazing on the gently undulating landscape, and fields of vivid yellow rape (in May and June) providing a startling contrast to the luxurious greens of the meadows.

54 ROADE OR BLISWORTH CUTTING This mighty earthwork stretches 1½ miles between Roade and Blisworth. The digging caused Robert Stephenson and his team of navvies enormous problems (see p. 390) as they cut their way through the tons of limestone and clay with only gunpowder to assist their progress. About a mile away to the west and parallel to the cutting is an earlier marvel of engineering – the tunnel which carries the Grand Union Canal (formerly Junction) under the same ridge of hills from the valley of the Great Ouse to the valley of the Nene. The tunnel is perfectly straight, 3,075 yards 2 feet long, and took 11 years to dig.

Roade Station was at the south end of the cutting. It was closed in 1964. Roade was one of the rare villages not to be affected by the arrival of the railway. Between 1850 and 1930 the population remained static at about 700.

The **line to Northampton** leaves to the north *R:l* east. The cutting was deepened in 1875 when this line was opened.

55 **BLISWORTH   St John the Baptist** has a *L:r* Perpendicular tower. The remains of the station at Blisworth can easily be spotted in front of the attractive yellow brick **Railway Hotel** which is *L:r* close to the line.

56 **GAYTON**   There is a monument in **St Mary's** *L:r* **Church** (tower crowned with 4 pinnacles) to Francis Tanfield who died in 1558. The Tanfields built the 16th century **manor house** nearby.

57 **BUGBROOKE   St Michael's** (decorated tow- *R:l* er with recessed spire) is a 13th-century church. Osborne, the Victorian author of popular railway guides, was disturbed by the name of the village which 'would, doubtless, be an object of romantic interest to the imaginative traveller if it were not for the associations which its name suggests, always unpleasing to persons going to or coming away from the World's Emporium'.

58 **STOWE HILL TUNNEL**   The tunnel is 492 yards long and takes the train under Watling Street. The north entrance is embattled – the favourite Victorian design for tunnels.

59 WEEDON The parish church of **St Peter's** has *R:l*
a Norman tower and is built of attractive yellow-
orange stone. It is tucked between the railway line
and the canal. In the churchyard there is a
gravestone to 'Alice Old, widow' who lived,
unbelievably, in the reigns of Elizabeth I, James I,
Charles I, Charles II, James II and William and Mary,
dying in 1691.

Weedon Barracks A large fortified depot *L:r*
was built at Weedon in 1803 as a precaution against
invasion by Napoleon. George III and his cabinet
would be able to retreat to a safe place in the
centre of England from where to direct operations.
A branch canal was opened in 1804 to serve the
depot and this entered the depot under two
portcullises. The yellow-brick building which was
part of George III's royal pavilion, the gatehouse
complete with cupola and behind it the long ranges
of red-brick and ironstone depot buildings have
remained to this day, though the canal has been
disused since c.1920.

60 BROCKHALL HALL The Elizabethan house *R:l*
can just be seen in the trees on the hillside to the
east. The owner, Thomas Reeve Thornton, gave
the house a Gothic revamp in the early 19th
century. He caused Robert Stephenson trouble
over the route of the L&BR and forced him to
deviate from his original line. Now the **M1**, the
Grand Union Canal, the railway and the A5 all
follow parallel routes in front of the hall.

61 DAVENTRY The **BBC Broadcasting Sta-** *L:r*
tion about three miles to the west is close to
Daventry. It is on Borough Hill, the site of an Iron
Age hill fort which was used by the Romans for a

villa. Excavations in 1972 revealed farm buildings and native huts from the first century AD. When the masts were erected relics were found of the camp of King Charles I's army, established in the last days of the Civil War. The Royalists received the news of Cromwell's arrival in the county at the camp on 12 June 1645 and two days later were defeated at the Battle of Naseby. The Empire Service was begun at the broadcasting station on 19 December 1932. During the Second World War the short-wave transmitters and aerials were increased at the station to broadcast the Voice of Britain to the world.

62 **WHILTON**   There are six locks on the Grand Union Canal at Whilton. Narrowboats can be seen in **Whilton Marina**. **Whilton Lodge**, the large *R:l* white house west of the line, is beside Watling *L:r* Street and on the site of a Roman settlement known as Bannaventa, a walled town of 30 acres.

63 **WATFORD GAP AND THE M1**   The **red-** *R:l* **and black-brick engine house** marks the site of the original station at Watford. The **M1** motorway *R:l* is parallel to the railway line. The first section was opened on 1 November 1959.

64 **KILSBY TUNNEL**   The Kilsby Tunnel is 2,423 yards long and was the most difficult work on the L&BR (see p. 390). Critics of the railway were horrified by the prospect of such a long deep tunnel and one proposed all locomotives should be fitted with a diaphragm, stiffened with whalebone, to promote ventilation in the depths. Stephenson consequently built two huge ventilation shafts 60 feet in diameter and over 100 feet deep, crowned

with castellated towers. On one occasion, in April 1837, the navvies rioted and the militia were called from Weedon Barracks to restore order.

65 KILSBY VILLAGE   Some 1,000 navvies camped *L:r* in and around the village of Kilsby while work proceeded underground. Their heavy drinking and enormous appetites caused much distress among the staid countryfolk. The parish church of **St Faith's** can be seen from the train. It has a *L:r* 13th-century tower with a small recessed spire.

The train crosses the boundary between **Northamptonshire** and **Warwickshire**.

66 HILLMORTON   Just   before   **Hillmorton** *R:l* **Church** is the 900-acre site of the **GPO Radio Station** which played a vital role during the *R:l* Second World War. The church of **St John the Baptist** is below the line, and has a red ashlar *R:l* tower c.1300. The embankment which the train runs along was made out of material excavated from the Kilsby Tunnel.

67 RUGBY (BR)   The disused **viaduct** (engineers *R:l* Charles Vignoles and Thomas Jackson Woodhouse) which can be seen crossing the Avon Valley to the north, used to carry the Midland Counties Railway to Leicester. The eleven 50 feet semi-elliptical arches are faced in blue engineering brick. The line is also crossed by a large cantilever bridge belonging to the Great Central Railway.

When the railway line was built passing close to **Rugby School** it was welcomed by the headmas- *L:r* ter Dr Thomas Arnold: 'I rejoice to see it and think that feudalism is gone for ever. It is so great a blessing to think that any one evil is really extinct.'

It was at Rugby School that the game of rugby was invented in 1823. William Webb Ellis 'with a fine disregard for the rules of football as played in his time, first took the ball in his arms and ran with it'. William Butterfield designed the principal school buildings including the chapel (1872) whose octagonal central tower with a pyramid roof can be seen over the roof tops. There is a medallion in the chapel to the poet Rupert Brooke who was educated at Rugby and died in 1915 on the way to the Dardanelles. The tall stone spire belongs to the parish church of Rugby, **St Andrew's**, which was *L:r* also designed by William Butterfield in 1877–85.

Rugby Station presented Robert Stephenson with problems in the winter of 1833: 'The works at this point are at present in rather a backward state, owing to the severe and continuous frost, which has almost entirely put a stop to the brickwork and permanent road.' The present station is actually the third to be built. Rugby was constantly expanding in the 19th century with the arrival of more railway lines. The huge island platform with outer faces long enough to handle two main line trains at the same time was constructed in 1886. A massive wrought iron train shed spans the central concourse and buildings. Red-brick walls in an Italianate style enclose the tracks to the north and south. Unfortunately the station is in a dilapidated state – only a reflection of its past grandeur.

Rugby is dominated by the **GEC Works** and **Portland Cement**. The GEC has large factories on both sides of the track. The **Victorian** *L:r* **building in red brick** is adorned with a flamboyant red-brick tower. There are dozens of trading companies within the General Electric Company. Products made at Rugby include

MAP 4

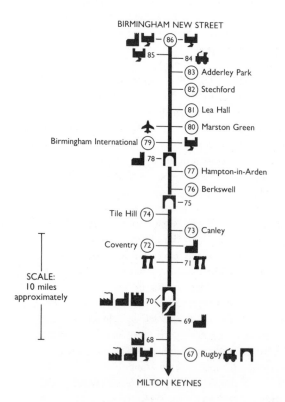

BIRMINGHAM NEW STREET

86
85
84
83 Adderley Park
82 Stechford
81 Lea Hall
80 Marston Green
Birmingham International 79
78
77 Hampton-in-Arden
76 Berkswell
75
Tile Hill 74
73 Canley
Coventry 72
71
70
69
68
67 Rugby

SCALE:
10 miles
approximately

MILTON KEYNES

'complete power stations', motors and generators for mills, mining, oil rigs and steelworks, turbines, generation systems and auxiliary drives for ships, submarines, floating cranes and docks.

68 RUGBY PORTLAND CEMENT CO LTD *L:s* The vast quarry below the railway line is an awesome sight as the train pulls out of Rugby (or approaches the town from the west).

69 CHURCH LAWFORD St Peter's is rock- *R:l* faced and was built in 1872 to the design of Slater and Carpenter. It is close to the **River Avon** which meanders to the north of the railway line. Church Lawford Cutting involved the removal of nearly ½ million cubic yards of earth which was used to make the Brandon Embankment to the west.

70 WOLSTON and BRANDON CASTLE Wolston Priory is a large medieval house below *L:r* the line built of a mixture of materials. It is mostly of red sandstone but one side is of lias and two of the gables are timber-framed: the windows are mullioned. **St Margaret's Church** tower was *L:r* built in 1760 by Job Collins. The church is visible as the train crosses the 15-arch **viaduct** over the **River Avon**. On the west bank are the ruins of **Brandon Castle** which was built early in the 13th *L:r* century and has an oblong keep.

East of Coventry the train crosses between **Warwickshire** and the **West Midlands**.

71 CHEYLESMORE CEMETERY The cemetery *L&R* on the outskirts of Coventry, (now among housing estates and allotments) was laid out by Sir Joseph Paxton and opened in 1847. Paxton (the designer of the Crystal Palace) was MP for Coventry and there is a monument to him at the north entry to the cemetery, designed by Joseph Goddard.

72 **COVENTRY** (BR) Coventry is famous for three things: the ride of Lady Godiva, the bombing raids of the Second World War and Sir Basil Spence's Cathedral.

Coventry Station was designed by W. R. Headley, architect to the Midland Region of British Rail and built in 1959–62. The original station – which was one of few 19th-century stations to have a Ladies with a female attendant – had survived the bombing which destroyed so much of the city, but was demolished by British Rail. However, the new glass and concrete station, though unremarkable from the train, is clean and well laid out with a patio garden beside the waiting room.

Lady Godiva made her famous ride through the streets of Coventry to remit the heavy taxes imposed on the citizens by her husband Leofric 5th Earl of Mercia. Tennyson composed his poem on Godiva on a visit to Coventry:

> I waited for the train at Coventry;
> I hung with grooms and porters on the bridge,
> To watch the three tall spires; and there I shaped
> The city's ancient legend . . .

The **Cathedral of St Michael** was almost totally destroyed in a bombing raid on 14 November 1940. The steeple, however, survived, and was

Coventry Cathedral

used by Sir Basil Spence as part of his new cathedral. This **blackened steeple** can be seen *R:I* from the train rising 295 feet above the city. It was built in 1371–1430: Ruskin described it reaching 'half-way to the sky'.

73 CANLEY (BR)   The old Standard Triumph production line was at Canley but it no longer produces cars now, concentrating on research and administration. The last car produced at Canley was the TR7.

74 TILE HILL (BR)   The old Standard Triumph paint shop at Tile Hill is now closed.

75 BEECHWOOD TUNNEL

76 BERKSWELL (BR)   The stations on this stretch between Coventry and Birmingham were opened for the local residents and are mostly very small, merely with platform shelters.

77 HAMPTON-IN-ARDEN (BR) Hampton-in-Arden is surrounded by rich farmland and is a popular place for wealthy Birmingham commuters to live. 'The village contains some cottages designed by W. E. Nesfield in the 1860s which are good early examples of the revival of interest in vernacular architecture in the late 19th century' (Alan Crawford).

78 BICKENHILL CHURCH The Perpendicular spire of **St Peter's** can be seen between the *L:r* bridges under the **M42** and under the A45(T).

79 BIRMINGHAM INTERNATIONAL (BR) Birmingham International Station was built to serve the National Exhibition Centre and is linked by a covered walkway and escalators. It is one of few major stations to be built since the war and has five platforms with platform buildings of yellow brick and brown tiles. The platform canopies are clad in purple-brown metal.

   The National Exhibition Centre was *R* opened by the Queen in February 1976. The interconnected halls cover 11,840 square feet. The Metropole Hotel on the other side of Pendigo Lake from the railway line contains 18 banqueting and conference suites with air conditioning and equipment for multi-lingual translation in the meeting rooms. The International Arena, with bright orange girders rising from the roof, can seat up to 12,000. Delegates attending a convention in the arena can be provided with 'executive lunch trays' without even leaving their seats. All this is intended to create a vast money-making complex – Europe's most modern exhibition centre – attracting visitors from all over the world to exhibitions and conferences as well as giving the residents of Birmingham a new supply of entertainment with concerts, cabarets and restaurants.

The first British Telecom shareholders meeting was held in the exhibition centre in 1985.

80 MARSTON GREEN (BR)   This small local station with white wooden platform buildings decorated with curly brackets is at the north end of the runway of **Birmingham Airport**. The airport *L:r* was opened in July 1939 by the Duchess of Kent. Spring 1984 saw the opening of a new £50 million terminal building and apron. Plans to expand the airport were greeted with protests over the increase in noise from the local residents of Sheldon and Marston Green, and two vast landscaped noise barriers were built to screen neighbouring estates from the runways. An unusual method of communication between the airport and Birmingham International Station is the Maglev transit link. Cars, supported on a magnetic field, 'fly' about half an inch above an elevated track connecting rail and air services.

81 LEA HALL (BR)

82 STECHFORD (BR)   The station was opened in 1844 and within forty years an industrial estate had been established in the area. Houses began to be built in large numbers at the turn of the century and by 1930 all the once-agricultural land was covered to create a suburb of Birmingham.

83 ADDERLEY PARK (BR)

84 CURZON STREET The L&BR terminated at Curzon Street until the growth in the volume of traffic necessitated the building of a bigger and much more central station at New Street (see below). Philip Hardwick designed the **grand entrance** for Curzon Street, a three-storey stone *R:l* block with four massive Greek Ionic columns designed as the answering monument to the Doric Arch at Euston. Unlike the Euston arch, the Curzon Street entrance has managed to survive and was sold a few years ago by BR to the City of Birmingham who are refurbishing it. Behind, though now unconnected with the entrance, is an enormous goods depot.

85 GUN BARREL PROOF HOUSE Below the *L:r* line at the junction known as Proof House Junction is the Gun Barrel Proof House where guns made in Birmingham are still tested. The small brick building was designed in 1813 by John Horton and the handsome trophies above the central door were designed by William Hollins.

86 BIRMINGHAM (BR) The **Rotunda**, a 24- *L:r* storey cylindrical building containing shops and offices, was designed by James A. Roberts and built in 1964–5. The tower is clad in fine white glass mosaic with aluminium sash windows and dominates the 3-acre Bull Ring Centre. The Bull Ring is the name of the market which has been held in Birmingham since the 12th century. The blackened spire belongs to **St Martin's in the Bull Ring**. *L:r* The sandstone church was originally built in the 13th century but – except for the tower and spire – it was rebuilt in 1873–5 by J. A. Chatwin in the style of the early 14th century. Bombing during the

Second World War destroyed much of Chatwin's work and the church was restored in 1957. Some of the stained glass is by Edward Burne-Jones and William Morris.

Birmingham's **Post Office Tower** is 500 feet *R:1* high and is a main link in the 'post office ultra high frequency micro wave television and telephone network'. Dish- and horn-type aerials are carried on the four circular concrete platforms.

Post Office Tower, Birmingham

Birmingham New Street The first station at New Street had a massive crescent-shaped train shed with a span of 211 feet supported by decorated brick walls and designed by E. A. Cowper. When George Borrow passed through on a holiday he commented, 'that station is enough to make one proud of being a modern Englishman'. Traffic grew, however, and the station became increasingly inadequate. In 1923 a dissatisfied traveller passed judgement: 'it is on a cold, wet night that the station reaches its most repulsive. It is ill-lit by a faulty gas system, devoid of adequate seating, the roof leaks in countless places, the lavatories proclaim their presence.' And in 1964 the former President of Birmingham's Chamber of Commerce declared 'I know of no other station in this country, Europe or the United States, which for filth, muck and severe dishevelment compares to New Street.' The result of decades of criticism was the demolition of the Victorian station and the erection of a vast and coldly efficient airport-like terminal which cost some £4½ million. Escalators take passengers up from the windy platforms to the concourse. Above the concourse is a large shopping centre. The main entrance to the station offers a glimpse of the concrete jungle which has engulfed a large part of the centre of Birmingham.

The **Stephenson Tower** is part of the complex, a tower-block of flats built around the chimney which serves the New Street boiler rooms. Although they were originally intended as council housing, British Rail found it more profitable to sell the flats to private individuals. However, these unfortunate residents have discovered the chimney has a disastrous effect on washing hanging from their balconies.

A Victorian traveller found Birmingham unattractive in 1851: 'There are few towns more uninviting than Birmingham; for the houses are built of brick toned down to a grimy red by smoke, in long streets crossing each other at right angles –

and the few modern stone buildings and blocks of houses seem as pert and as much out of place as the few idle dandies who are occasionally met among the crowds of busy mechanics and anxious manufacturers.' The smoke has cleared and it is now the 'few modern stone buildings' of the mid-19th century together with examples of later 19th-century city architecture which prevent Birmingham from succumbing totally to the concrete sterility of its station, shopping centre and car parks.

EUSTON
TO
LIVERPOOL

Introduction

Passengers travelling to Liverpool follow the original London and Birmingham Railway as far as Rugby (see p. 428). They then continue on the Trent Valley Railway which bypasses Birmingham, joining the original Grand Junction Railway line at Stafford. The Grand Junction Railway used to connect with the Liverpool and Manchester Railway at Earlestown to the west of Liverpool, but a new line was laid via Runcorn which takes the train across the River Mersey on William Baker's girder bridge.

The Trent Valley Railway Company was founded in 1843 with Edward Watkins as Secretary: its aim to expand the industries already established in the Trent Valley. The first sod was cut in November 1845 by Sir Robert Peel, Prime Minister and MP for Tamworth (1830–50). He praised the self-sacrifice of the landowners: 'I assure them that there are many persons in this neighbourhood who have not scrupled to sacrifice private feeling and comfort, by consenting to their land being appropriated to the Trent Valley Railway. They have given consent from a conviction that this undertaking was one conducive to the public benefit, and that considerations of private interest should not obstruct the great one of the public good.' Nevertheless the owner of Shugborough Park was able to demand ornate entrances to the tunnel which the railway company dug under his estate.

The engineers for the line were Robert Stephenson and George Bidder and the contractor was Thomas Brassey. The line was opened in December 1847. The stations were designed by John William Livock, but many have been demolished. Tamworth and Lichfield have gone, also Stafford. The imaginative Jacobean-style building at Stafford was replaced by a 1960s functional design.

The Grand Junction Railway was opened on 4 July 1837 from Lime Street Station in Liverpool to a temporary terminus at Birmingham (Vauxhall). A scheme to link Birmingham with Birkenhead (the Mersey ferry-head to Liverpool) was discussed in Parliament as early as 1824 but opposed by landowners and canal-owners in Cheshire, the latter fearing – quite rightly – they would lose money. One canal agent from Nantwich was overheard by George Stephenson warning local farmers that the locomotive gave off breath as poisonous as a dragon's.

Joseph Locke surveyed the line which joined George Stephenson's Liverpool and Manchester Railway at Earlestown and from there had access to Liverpool or Manchester. It was not too expensive to build – £18,846 a mile as compared with Robert Stephenson's London and Birmingham Railway's £53,000. The opening was celebrated at Stafford by the Mayor firing a 21-gun salute with ancient cannon at the approach of 'Wildfire' pulling eight 1st class coaches – the first train to Birmingham.

With the threat of competition the Liverpool and Manchester Railway and the Grand Junction amalgamated to become the London and North Western Railway in 1846. Their headquarters were established at Crewe which was turned from a village into a thriving railway town in only a few years (see p. 464). Francis Webb, locomotive superintendant of the LNWR for 32 years, was largely responsible for building up Crewe. John Ramsbottom, famous for making the celebrated 'Lady of the Lake' class 2–2–2 express locomotive was also working at Crewe. Sir Cusack P. Roney honoured Ramsbottom in his *Rambles on Railways* (1868): 'one man who, if he had been in Egypt, with works not a quarter the size and not half so ably carried out, would have been at least a Bey, more probably a Pacha, in Austria a Count of the Holy Empire; in any other country in the world, except England, with crosses and decorations, the ribbons of which would easily make a charming bonnet of existing dimensions. But in England the earnest, persevering, never tiring JOHN RAMSBOTTOM is John Ramsbottom – no more.'

MAP 5

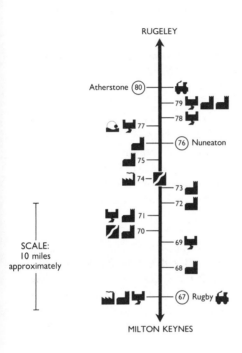

RUGELEY

Atherstone (80)

79

78

77

(76) Nuneaton

75

74

73

72

71

70

69

68

(67) Rugby

SCALE:
10 miles
approximately

MILTON KEYNES

68 NEWBOLD ON AVON The red sandstone church of **St Botolph's** (Perpendicular tower) is in *R:l* the trees about half a mile from the line. The countryside around Newbold was fashionable in the 18th century because there was a spa at Newnham Regis nearby: 'The Air of this Country is exceeding Pleasant and Wholesome, the Sea being so remote that it is not infected with its noisome fumes' (*The Track of the Royal Scot*, LMS Route Book No 3).

69 NEWBOLD REVEL Newbold Revel (now St *R:l* Paul's College) at Stretton-under-Fosse is a red-brick mansion built for Sir Fulwar Skipwith in 1716. The architect was probably Francis Smith of Warwick and additions were made c.1900 by Edgar Wood. It is set in a park about a mile to the north of the line.

70 BRINKLOW is opposite Stretton-under-Fosse. There was a station for Brinklow beside the bridge which now carries the Fosse Way (A427) over the railway line. The parish church of **St John Baptist** *L:r* (Perpendicular tower) is about a mile from the line. A motte and bailey castle east of the church helped to guard the Fosse Way. There is a view of **Coventry** beyond the church (see p. 56). The *L:r* **Oxford Canal** flows beside the railway line *L:r* between Brinklow and Ansty. Both railway and canal pass under the **M6** to the north of Brinklow.

George Eliot described a journey through this countryside, 'watered at one extremity by the Avon, at the other by the Trent' in *Felix Holt*: 'As the morning silvered the meadows with their long lines of bushy willows marking the watercourses, or burnished the golden corn-ricks clustered near

the long roofs of some midland home-stead, [one]
saw the full-uddered cows driven from their
pasture to the early milking.'

71 **ANSTY St James's** was mostly designed by *L:r*
George Gilbert Scott in 1856 and has a small west
tower with an octagonal bell-stage and spire.
Ansty Hall is immediately next to the church. It is *L:r*
built of red brick and has the date 1678 over the
doorway. The top storey was added in 1800.
Church and Hall are about half a mile from the line,
situated beside the Oxford canal. But the **M69** (due
to open Spring 1987) cuts through the pastoral
landscape.

72 **SHILTON St Andrew's** with its Perpendicular *R:l*
tower is next to the railway line close to where the
station was originally sited and just before the line
passes over the **M69**.

73 **BULKINGTON CHURCH St James's** has a *R:l*
high 14th-century ashlar tower. Inside is a font
made out of an antique Roman column. It was
brought back by Richard Hayward of nearby
Weston Hall (now a public house) as one of the
spoils of his Grand Tour. Hayward was a talented
sculptor and carved the bowl of the font. After his
death the font was given to the church.

74 **BEDWORTH** is an industrial village with a *L:r*
colliery and granite quarry and large crushing plant.
The granite forms an unusual interruption in the
red marl and sandstone scenery. It covers 7 square
miles and has been extensively used for building.
The colliery is at the north-eastern edge of the
Warwickshire coalfield which extends over the

West Midlands plain. The line passes over the **Ashby de la Zouch Canal**, part of the network of canals which criss-crosses the Midlands and which helped to bring about the dramatic industrialisation of this part of Britain. George Eliot found the contrast between the industrial and rural pursuits of the region particularly striking: 'in these midland districts the traveller passed rapidly from one phase of English life to another: after looking down on a village dingy with coal-dust, noisy with the shaking of looms, he might skirt a parish all of fields, high hedges, and deep-rutted lanes.'

75 **ATTLEBOROUGH**   The spire of **Holy Trin-** *L:r*
ity can be seen across the top of the houses. Attleborough is now a suburb of Nuneaton. The population was expanding so rapidly at the beginning of the 19th century that the Earl of Harrowby gave the land on which to build Holy Trinity (designed by T. L. Walker and built in 1841–2 at a cost of £2,629).

76 **NUNEATON** (BR)   Nuneaton was named after the Benedictine Nunnery founded in c.1155–60. From Norman times until the 1930s a curfew bell was rung nightly in the town. Nuneaton expanded rapidly in the late 18th and early 19th centuries with the coming of canals and then the railway. A variety of industries brought the town wealth and prosperity: the manufacture of bricks and tiles, hatting, clothing and spinning. George Eliot was born in 1819 at Arbury Farm, two miles to the south-west of Nuneaton; Arbury Mill became the setting for *The Mill on the Floss*.

  St Nicholas has a large dark-grey stone *L:r*
Perpendicular tower. There is a gruesome monu-

ment inside to Antony Trotman who died in 1703. A full-length skeleton lies in a winding sheet which is tied to the framework of the monument. It looks rather like the skeleton of Antony Trotman swaying in a hammock.

Nuneaton Station was rebuilt in 1909 and has a Neo-Georgian facade with circular windows and a clock tower. The red- and yellow-brick platform buildings and elaborate brackets supporting the awnings belong to the older Victorian station.

77 **TUTHILL WINDMILL** The base of Tuthill *L:r*
Windmill can be seen on top of the **Hartshill Ridge** which overlooks Nuneaton. The ridge is made of ancient rocks – red and purple Cambrian shales and quartzites 5–6 million years old with diorite (an igneous rock) injected into them – on the edge of the Warwickshire coalfield. The quartzite and diorite are quarried for road-metal. Michael Drayton, the poet who composed 'Fair stood the wind for France' was born at Hartshill. He is thought to have become a page to Sir Henry Goodere of Polesworth. Goodere was a cousin of Sir Philip Sidney and friend of John Donne, who wrote his poem 'Good Friday' on leaving Polesworth in 1613.

78 **CALDECOTE HALL** was designed in 1879–80 *R:l*
by R. J. and J. Goddard in red brick in a Jacobean style and cost over £21,000.

79 **WITHERLEY AND MANCETTER** St *R:l*
Peter's, Witherley is over a mile from the line beside the **River Anker** and just into **Leicestershire**. In 1924 the spire was struck by lightning and

449

crashed through the nave. It cost £5,500 to restore
in 1926. **St Peter's**, Mancetter, is closer to the line   R:l
and has a Perpendicular tower. The **Manor House**
(timber framed c.1330) is between the church and
the railway line. There was a Roman settlement at
Mancetter called Manduessedum.

80 **ATHERSTONE** (BR)   is an ancient stronghold
of the hatting industry. The local firm of Messrs
Wilson and Stafford became well known during the
Second World War for making most of the bush
hats used by the troops in Burma and the Far East.

    Atherstone Station has a particularly attrac-   R:l
tive Tudor-style station house of diapered red
brick. It was designed by J. W. Livock but is no
longer used by BR. A **large sign** just south of the   R:l
station declares '102 miles to London': it is
attached to a red brick building.

81 **MEREVALE HALL**   looks like a castle with its   L:r
embattled towers and walls, magnificently sited on
the hill side west of Atherstone. It is actually a
Victorian   house,   designed   in   the   Gothic–
Elizabethan style by Edward Blore in 1838–44.
Merevale is the home of the Dugdales, descendants
of Sir William Dugdale (1605–86), the compiler of
the *Monasticon*, an account of English monastic
houses. The fragments of Merevale Abbey, a
Cistercian house founded in 1148 by Robert Earl
Ferrers, are in the park. Blore's employer was
William Stratford Dugdale MP, a Tory landowner
with very decided ideas about his workers. The
first workers he hired were members of the union
and went on strike. They were instantly sacked by
Dugdale: 'by September I collected another set of
workmen who conformed to my rules and not to

MAP 6

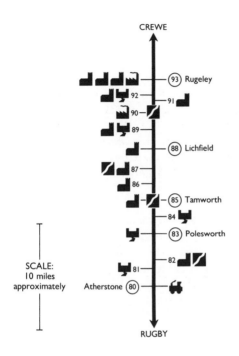

CREWE

93 Rugeley

92

91

90

89

88 Lichfield

87

86

85 Tamworth

84

83 Polesworth

82

81

SCALE:
10 miles
approximately

Atherstone 80

RUGBY

those of the Union – we had no more trouble with them during all the time the house was building.' There was no central heating and only one bathroom at Merevale. Blore's ex-pupil Henry Clutton designed the lodge gateway in 1848–9.

82 **GRENDON CHURCH**   The stately tower of *R:l* Grendon Parish Church was added in 1845 by R. C. Hussey to the much older medieval church. Inside are monuments to the Chetwynds, an important landowning family in the area who lived at Grendon Hall and Pooley Hall. The **Coventry Canal** and the **River Anker** flow between the railway line *R:l* and the church.

83 **POLESWORTH** (BR)   Immediately after Poles- worth Station is **Pooley Hall**, a large brick *L:r* mansion said to have been built in 1509 by Sir Thomas Cokayne. Pooley Hall gave its name to the nearby colliery which was one of the first to adopt the principle of direct conversion of coal into electricity. At one time the colliery lighted all the houses within a radius of 5 miles.

West of Polesworth the train crosses the boundary between **Warwickshire** and **Staffordshire**.

84 **AMINGTON HALL**   is the large Georgian *R:l* ashlar-faced mansion about a mile to the north.

85 **TAMWORTH** (BR)   Tamworth is famous for its pigs, pork pies and pasties, as well as being the birthplace of Sir Robert Peel, Prime Minister under both William IV and Queen Victoria. The town centre is to the south of the station with the earthworks of a Norman castle, the medieval parish

church of **St Editha** and the Town Hall built by *L:r*
Thomas Guy, founder of Guys' Hospital in London.

Tamworth Station was one of J. W. Livock's finest achievements but it was rebuilt to serve one of Britain's busiest mail exchange points. The train crosses the **River Anker** just to the east of the station.

86 HOPWAS Hopwas Hays Wood (now partly *L:r*
taken over by the Ministry of Defence for firing ranges) is on the other side of the **River Tame**. **St Chad's**, Hopwas, is a very small church on the south side of the wood over a mile from the railway line. It was built in 1881 by John Douglas and has a shingled spirelet on top of the tower. The base is of brick but the upper parts are timber framed.

87 WHITTINGTON CHURCH **St Giles's** has a *L:r*
medieval tower with a later spire.

The **Coventry Canal** can be seen at Whittington. It is to the west of the line; then the line crosses over the canal, just before going under the A38 and into Lichfield.

88 LICHFIELD (BR) The railway-guide writer George Measom was hardly fair to Lichfield when he wrote in the mid-19th century: 'though Lichfield will repay the traveller for spending a few hours in examining the buildings and monuments . . . yet the city will appear intolerably dull, and he will be glad to return to the station and good-looking red brick building.' Livock's station has recently been demolished but at least some of the fine Georgian houses of Lichfield have survived. Dr Johnson was born in the city in 1709. His father was a bookseller and his house is now a museum. Johnson was immortalised in his biography written by James Boswell. His most famous work was his *Dictionary of the English Language*, first published in 1755. Erasmus Darwin was also born in Lichfield and his 18th-century house is still standing. Darwin was a physician and scientist and the grandfather of Charles Darwin. He wrote the prophetic poem 'The Botanic Garden':

> Soon shall thy arm, Unconquered Steam, afar
>   drag the slow barge, or drive the rapid car;
> Or on wide waving wings expanded bear the
>   flying chariot through the fields of air.

The Lichfield Heritage Centre, opposite Samuel Johnson's house, gives an insight into the town's history.

Lichfield Cathedral is easily distinguished by its *L:r* three spires known as 'the ladies of the Vale'. It was badly damaged by the Roundheads during the Civil War after the Royalists fortified it. The central spire was destroyed and lead was torn from the roof. Since then the cathedral has been extensively restored by James Wyatt (1788–95), Sydney Smirke (1842–6), George Gilbert Scott (1857) and John Oldrid Scott. Inside the cathedral is St Chad's Gospel (St Chad was the first bishop), an illuminated manuscript codex.

89 HANCH HALL is close to the railway line and *L:r* surrounded by trees. It is easily distinguished by the blue-painted woodwork and small bell tower. One of the rooms in the house has early 16th-century timbers and another was a Victorian ball room.

Lichfield Cathedral

In the distance is the tower of **St James's,** *L:r* **Longdon**. George Eliot described the hedgerows which still surround the fields and border the railway line: 'liberal homes of unmarketable beauty – of the purple-blossomed ruby-berried nightshade, of the vivid convulvulus climbing and spreading in tendrilled strength till it made a great curtain of pale-green hearts and white trumpets.'

90 ARMITAGE The railway line passes between *L:r*
the **Trent and Mersey Canal** and the **River
Trent**. The enormous factory close to the line is
owned by Armitage Shanks 'better bathrooms'.
The building of canals in the Midlands in the second
half of the 18th century did more than boost
industry and commerce. Agriculture also benefited
and the standard of living of ordinary people was
improved: 'the cottage, instead of being half
covered with miserable thatch, is now covered
with a substantial covering of tiles or slates,
brought from the distant hills of Wales or Cumber-
land. The fields, which before were barren, are
now drained and by the assistance of manure,
conveyed on the canal toll-free, are clothed with a
beautiful verdure. Places which rarely knew the use
of coal are plentifully supplied with that essential
article upon reasonable terms' (Thomas Pennant,
1782).

91 MAVESYN RIDWARE CHURCH St Nich- *R:l*
olas has a Perpendicular tower. Inside is the
Mavesyn Chapel containing a monument to Sir
Robert Mavesyn who died fighting for Henry IV at
the Battle of Shrewsbury in 1403.

92 ARMITAGE PARK (HAWKESYARD PRIORY) *L:r*
AND ST JOHN'S CHURCH Armitage Park is
a pinnacled and battlemented Gothic stuccoed
house built in 1760 by Nathaniel Lister. It was
bought by Mrs Josiah Spode (widow of the famous
potter who died in 1827 leaving a fortune) in 1839
and renamed Hawkesyard by her son Josiah Spode
IV. He left the house to Dominican monks on his
death in 1893. They employed E. Goldie to design
their priory (1896–1914) behind the house, but still

use the 18th-century house for retreats and conferences. **St John's Church** is situated on a *L:r* rock above the **River Trent** some distance behind the priory. The short tower was built in 1632 and the rest of the church is in the Norman style, built in 1844–7 to the design of a Stafford architect called Henry Ward.

93 **RUGELEY** (BR) The **power station** before *L:r* Rugeley Station was opened in 1963. Three churches can be seen from the line. The spire belongs to the Roman Catholic church of **St Joseph and St Ethelreda** and was designed by Charles Hansom in 1849–50. The towers belong to *L:r* the old medieval **St Augustine** and the 19th- and 20th-century **St Augustine** (with the larger tower).

Rugeley was given unwelcome publicity in the mid-19th century over the gruesome practices of Dr Palmer who murdered his wealthy patients with strychnine. The townsfolk were so upset by their notoriety that a deputation was sent to Palmerston asking him to change the name of the town – to no avail.

Rugeley Power Station

MAP 7

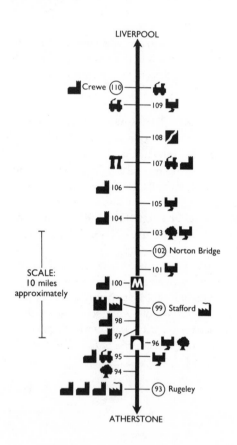

LIVERPOOL

Crewe (110)

109

108

107

106

105

104

103

(102) Norton Bridge

101

M 100

(99) Stafford

98

97

96

95

94

(93) Rugeley

SCALE:
10 miles
approximately

ATHERSTONE

94 CANNOCK CHASE is practically all that re- *L:r* mains of the great forest which once covered Staffordshire. The heath and woodland grows on the dry sandy soils of the Bunter Sandstone which crosses the Midland plain. The area has remained uncultivated because of its impractical nature and is now preserved as a place of recreation.

95 COLWICH The attractive limestone **station-** *L:r* **house** of Colwich survives beside the line. It is one of the few remaining stations designed by John William Livock in 1847 for the Trent Valley Railway and has his distinctive gables and diamond tiles.

St Michael's Church has a high west tower *L:r* built in 1640. Inside the church are monuments to the Anson, Sparrow and Wolesley families. Lord George Anson was a celebrated admiral and circumnavigator and his fortune – made capturing Spanish treasure galleons – was used by his brother Thomas to improve Shugborough House and Park (see below). Sir William Wolesley drowned in his carriage when the mill dam suddenly burst in a thunderstorm in 1728. The four horses were also drowned but the coachman was carried to an orchard and hung on to an apple tree until the waters fell.

St Mary's Abbey was built c.1825 as Mount *R:l* Pavilion by Viscount Tamworth, son of the 7th Earl Ferrers. It is in the Tudor Gothic style with a castellated front. A Benedictine order of contemplative nuns moved into the mansion in 1834.

The line divides immediately after Colwich: to the west is the line to Stafford, Crewe and Liverpool, to the north the line to Macclesfield, Stockport and Manchester.

96 SHUGBOROUGH TUNNEL Shugborough Tunnel is 776 yards long and has distinctive ornamental portals designed by J. W. Livock to the satisfaction of the owner of Shugborough. The tunnel was the largest engineering work on the Trent Valley Railway and its flamboyant entrances earned it the nickname the 'Gates of Jerusalem'. Livock also had to decorate the Lichfield Drive Bridge (with sea horses and lions) so that the railway could cross the park.

There is a brief glimpse of **Shugborough Park** *R:l* **and House**. Shugborough Hall was built in 1693 for William Anson and enlarged in the 18th century by his grandson Thomas, who also filled the park with the buildings designed by James 'Athenian' Stuart. Thomas Anson was a founder member of the Society of Dilettanti which sent Stuart to Athens to draw the principal buildings. These provided the inspiration for the Arch of Hadrian, the Tower of the Winds, the Doric Temple and the Lantern of Demosthenes. The 2nd Lord Lichfield inherited the property in 1854. The present Lord Lichfield occupies a flat in the house which is now owned by the National Trust and open to the public. The Staffordshire County Museum is housed in a stable block and Shugborough Park Farm, the old home farm of the estate, is now a working museum of farming.

97 WALTON ON THE HILL CHURCH St *L:r* **Thomas's** was designed by Thomas Trubshaw and built in 1842. The tower has a recessed spire.

98 BASWICH CHURCH Holy Trinity has a *L:r* medieval tower with an 18th-century top.

99 STAFFORD (BR) is approached from the east along the **Queensville Curve** which gives a fine view of the town. The expansion of Stafford in recent years is clearly revealed by the extensive new housing on both sides of the line. Stafford has been a prosperous town since the Middle Ages when wool and cloth were the chief industries. In the late-18th century shoemaking became important (the Lotus Boot Factory was established close to the station) followed by the production of table salt. Brine was discovered by accident when the corporation was sinking a bore-hole to provide a fresh water supply for the town. Engineering then became important with the Castle Locomotive Works of W. G. Bagnall Ltd and a large **GEC** *R:I* **factory** where diesel engines, earthquake testing equipment and transformers are some of the products. Research and development of new engineering materials is also carried out; microchemical, spectrographic, X-ray and electron microscopy techniques are used in the laboratories. Opposite the GEC factory are the works of BRC – **British Reinforced Concrete.** *L:r*

Stafford Station used to be Livock's Jacobean-style building, built in 1843–62, but this was demolished and replaced with a functional, far less characterful station in 1961–2, designed by W. R. Headley, architect to the Midland Region of BR. Dickens commented on the decline of the coaching inn in Stafford after the arrival of the railway: 'The extinct town inn, the Dodo . . . possesses interminable stables at the back . . . horseless.'

Stafford Castle can be seen on top of the hill *L:r* to the west of the town, almost engulfed by trees. The Normans erected a motte and bailey castle on the site and this was used by Ralph de Stafford in

1348 to build a new fortification. The Roundheads besieged the castle during the Civil Wars and it was eventually demolished in 1643 though Lady Stafford put up a valiant defence. Sir George Jerningham, later Lord Stafford, reconstructed the castle in c.1817 but little now remains.

100 SEIGHFORD CHURCH The 17th-century *L:r* brick tower of **St Chad's** decorated with Gothic pinnacles (1748) can be seen just after the train passes under the **M6**.

101 SHALLOWFIELD AND IZAAK WALTON'S *R:l* **COTTAGE** The small timber-framed and whitewashed cottage (open to the public) is easily missed. It is below the line, only a short distance away and on its own close to a road bridge over the railway. The cottage was built in about 1600. Izaak Walton did not live in it, but gave the cottage and the rest of his Halfhead Farm Estate to the town of Stafford to be used for charitable purposes. The cottage was opened as a museum in 1924 and the original thatched roof replaced by tiles after a fire in 1939.

102 NORTON BRIDGE (BR)

103 MEECE BROOK is where Piscator drew in- *R:l* spiration and fished in Izaak Walton's *The Compleat Angler*. It meanders close to the railway line for some miles north of Norton Bridge. Beyond the river to the east are the trees of **Swynnerton Park**, the estate of Lord Stafford.

On the hillside about 1½ miles east of the line is a magnificent **water tower**. The yellow- and red- *R:l*

brick square tower has giant arches supporting the
water tank. It is part of the system providing water
for the Five Towns over the hills to the east.

104 **STANDON CHURCH** **All Saints** is opposite *L:r*
Swynnerton Park on the west side of the line. The
tower dates from the 14th century and the church
was restored by George Gilbert Scott in 1846–7.

105 **HATTON PUMPING STATION** This is a *R:l*
splendid example of Victorian industrial architecture. The yellow- and red-brick buildings were
erected in 1890–98 and include a tall chimney and a
central building with an Italianate tower. Inside are
Corinthian columns. The water-bearing stratum
beneath the surface is known as the Bunter Bed.

106 **CHAPEL CHORLTON** The medieval tower *L:r*
of **St Laurence's Church** was remodelled by
James Trubshaw Junior in 1826–7.

107 **MADELEY** There used to be a station for *R:l*
Madeley village which is to the east of the line. The
church of **All Saints** has a Perpendicular tower *R:l*
and some of the stained glass is by William Morris,
Edward Burne-Jones and Ford Madox Brown. With
sharp eyes you may spot the **monument** marking *L:r*
the 12 allotments and fountain erected by Lady
Houghton, sister of the 3rd Baron Crewe (see
Crewe Hall p. 464) in 1850, in memory of her aunt
and as a gift to the poor.

108 **BETLEY MERE** There are meres – small lakes *R:l*
– dotted throughout this part of the country. The
largest is 156 acres. They were formed as a result
of the extensive salt working in the red marl of the

Cheshire Plain. The salt occurs in the red marl in beds with an average thickness of 100 feet. Extraction has caused the surface to subside thus creating the meres which are usually surrounded by reeds and birch trees.

The train crosses between **Staffordshire** and **Cheshire**.

109 CREWE HALL About a mile south of Crewe Station, the train passes **Basford Hall Sidings**. *L:r* Across the fields to the east and almost hidden by a large clump of trees is **Crewe Hall**. It is just *R:l* possible to see the tower appearing above the treetops. The original Crewe Hall was built by Sir Randolph Crewe in 1615–36. The 3rd Baron Crewe employed Edward Blore to restore the house in 1830–40. Blore spent £30,000 but his work was destroyed by fire in 1866. E. M. Barry rebuilt the hall giving it the ornate tower with four chimneys disguised as pinnacles.

110 CREWE (BR) When the Grand Junction Railway arrived at Crewe in 1837 the population was about 200, living in small farms and cottages. By 1842, however, the station was the focus of four railway lines and the locomotive works which had been moved from Edge Hill were about to begin production. The railway company built houses, churches and schools and by 1851 the population had risen to 4,571. The salary of the curate and the schoolmaster were paid by the company which also provided a doctor and two policemen, organised the supply of mains water, the emptying of ash pits, cess pools and privies, and even set up a savings bank for their employees. Four classes of houses

MAP 8

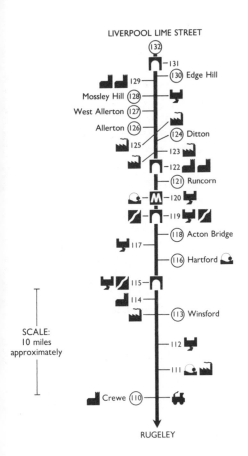

LIVERPOOL LIME STREET

(132)

—131

(130) Edge Hill

129

Mossley Hill (128)

West Allerton (127)

Allerton (126)

(124) Ditton

125

123

—122

(121) Runcorn

—120

—119

(118) Acton Bridge

117

(116) Hartford

115—

114

(113) Winsford

112

111

SCALE:
10 miles
approximately

Crewe (110)

RUGELEY

were built: 'first, the villa-style lodges of the superior officer; next a kind of ornamental Gothic constitutes the house of the next in authority; the engineers domiciled in detached mansions, which accomodate four families, with gardens and separate entrances; and last the labourer delights in neat cottages of four apartments, the entrances within ancient porches.' (1846).

Crewe Station consists of three broad island platforms each with creamy-yellow brick buildings decorated with red and dark blue brick dressings, all under a lateral train shed. The bay windows have Greek heads on the keystones. Immediately next to the station is the **Crewe Arms**, built in the *R:l* Jacobean style and opened in 1837. It was taken over by the LNWR as their railway hotel in 1864. Rather less decorative is the 13-storey block by the station which is **Rail House**, designed by F. S. Curtis and R. C. Moorcroft, British Rail architects, and erected in 1967–8.

The parish church of **Christ Church** is close to *L:r* the line, north of the station. It was paid for by the Grand Junction Railway and begun in 1843. The architect was probably John Cunningham of Liverpool who also designed the first railway cottages at Crewe. The tower was designed by J. W. Stansby, engineer on the railway company staff and added in 1877. It was originally finished with an iron crown made at the railway workshops.

III The countryside to the north of Crewe is flat – mostly dairy pastures on top of the vast **CHESHIRE SALTFIELD**. The saltfield has been worked by the Ancient Britons, the Romans and up to the present day. The chief towns on the field – Nantwich, Northwich, Middlewich – share the same last syllable which means white. The saying 'worth your salt' was from Roman soldiers being paid with salt instead of money. In Saxon times salt was taxable and Domesday Book records the unusual laws of the area: 'whoever committed an offence within these bounds could atone for it by paying 2s. or 30 boilings of salt, except for homicide or theft, for which the offender was adjudged to death.' Sources of salt are the brine springs and mines of rock salt. Now the salt is made into the chief alkalis of commerce including soda and bleaching powder. ICI Alkali is at Northwich (one of the birthplaces of the chemicals industry in Britain) and United Alkali (now ICI) at Widnes. The wealth of the area is revealed by the fine farm-houses and manor houses to be seen from the line.

112 **LEA HALL** at Wimboldsley is an attractive *R:l* 18th-century red-brick house with a half-timbered barn.

113 **WINSFORD** (BR) Winsford is the headquarters of **ICI Salt Ltd**. The country's largest rock salt *L:r* mine is here. In the mid-19th century there were '25 salt works here, some of them being like little towns in extent'. The chimneys belonged to the open fires over which the brine was evaporated in large pans. Almost all the working population of the town were employed in the salt industry which was given an important boost with the arrival of the railway. Winsford Station was rebuilt in the 1960s for the electrification of the line and the platform buildings are in the mustard yellow colour which is common to all contemporary stations on this route to Liverpool.

114 OVER CHURCH St John the Evangelist *L:r*
(thin broach spire) was built in 1860–3 by John
Douglas for his early patron Lord Delamere.

Over, Winsford, Swanlow and Wharton are all
involved in the salt and chemicals industries. Over is
also the birthplace of Robert Nixon, the 'Cheshire
Prophet'. The predictions of this illiterate plough-
boy are part of local folklore.

115 VALE ROYAL AND THE WEAVER *L:r*
VIADUCT The **River Weaver** is close to the
railway line, though often hidden by the sides of the
cuttings. It flows through the ancient estate of Vale
Royal Abbey. The Abbey was founded by Edward I
and consecrated by the Bishop of St Asaph in 1277.
The King, Queen Eleanor and their son Alphonso
laid the first stones. When only a Prince, Edward
had been caught in a storm returning from the
Crusades and vowed that if he was saved he would
raise an Abbey. The remains are now covered up
but a house was built on the site by Sir Thomas
Holcroft after the Dissolution of the Monasteries.
The house passed to the Cholmondeleys – Lords of
Delamere – until 1947 and then became the
headquarters of the Cheshire Constabulary. The
inside of the house was fashionably gothicised in
c.1800 and Edward Blore added a clock turret and
gables.

The gothic gables of **Vale Royal** can just be *L:r*
seen in the trees as the train crosses over the
Weaver Viaduct. One of the first railway writers.
E. C. Osborne, described the magnificent view
from the centre of Joseph Locke's viaduct soon
after it was opened in 1837: '70 feet above the
water, high in air, and midway between the two
arms of the valley. The hall or abbey, nearly hid

amongst the luxuriant foliage around, gleams through the vista in the distance – the river moves slowly on, bearing on its surface the stately barge, or still larger and loftier vessel; – the solitary traveller through the Vale winds his way along the devious path, and the glorious hills and woods bound the scene, as an everlasting barrier against all encroachment.'

116 **HARTFORD** (BR) Just north of the station, the train passes under the railway line between Chester and Manchester which marks the edge of the Vale Royal Abbey lands. A field just beside the line is called **Gibbet Hill** after the local gibbet erected *R:l* to deal with unfortunate offenders.

117 **WEAVERHAM HOSPITAL** Part of Grange Hospital, Weaverham, is **Hefferstone Grange**, a *L:r* fine brick manor house, built in 1741, with a stable block adorned with a cupola. In front are the green huts, part of the hospital complex.

118 **ACTON BRIDGE** (BR)

119 **DUTTON VIADUCT** Immediately north of the viaduct is the attractive half-timbered and red-brick **Dutton Lodge Farm**. The Dutton *R:l* Viaduct is ¼ mile long, 65 feet above the water, 25 feet wide and has 20 arches each with a span of 65 feet. The views to the east and west are magnificent with the **Weaver Navigation** and the old course of the **River Weaver** passing underneath.

120 **NORTON WATER TOWER** After passing *R:l* over the **M56** there is a good view of Norton Water Tower. This ornate tower with a pierced

base was built c.1890–2 for Liverpool Corporation and designed by the municipal water engineer G. F. Deacon. To the south west are the **Frodsham and Helsby Hills** which form a dramatic 'edge' to *L:r* the flat valley of the **River Mersey**.

121 RUNCORN (BR) The station is approached from the south through a rocky cutting. It is in the same mustard-yellow painted metal and concrete as the other 1960s post-electrification stations on this line.

In the 16th century Runcorn was no more than 'a poor townlet by a salt creke'. It only began to expand when the Bridgewater Canal was extended to the town in 1773. The opening of the railway bridge across the Mersey in 1869 dramatically improved the town's communications and consequent residential and industrial development. In 1964 Runcorn was given a further boost with the establishment of the Runcorn Development Corporation. Its aim was to provide additional employment and housing for people in the North Merseyside area. The chief architect was F. Lloyd Roche who has planned for an eventual population of 90,000.

122 CROSSING THE RIVER MERSEY The road and rail bridges dominate Runcorn to the south and Widnes to the north. The **railway bridge** was designed by William Baker and consists of three lattice girder spans of 305 feet, built up piece by piece on the spot. It is approached from Ditton Junction to the north on a viaduct of 59 arches rising to a height of 75 feet. Work began on the bridge in April 1864 and the first passenger train crossed on 1 April 1869. The bridge was given a flamboyant Gothic look but the embattled towers are now sadly soot-blackened. It shortened the distance between Crewe and Liverpool by over 8 miles.

Immediately next to Baker's bridge is the eau de nil **road bridge** designed by Mott, Hay and Anderson and built in 1956–61. The roadway hangs from a single steel arch with a span of 1,082 feet – the third largest steel arch in the world when the bridge was built.

All Saints, Runcorn   Below the bridges on *R:l* the south bank is All Saints, a red-stone church built in the Early English style with a high steeple. It was designed by Salvin and erected in 1847–9.

St Mary's, Widnes   On the north bank is St *R:l* Mary's, a large red-stone church with a substantial tower, built in 1908–10 and designed by Austin and Paley.

123 **WIDNES WEST BANK**   Since John Hutchinson *L&R* established his soda factory in Widnes in 1847 the town has become a centre for the chemical industries (ICI). Widnes West Bank was planned with a grid layout in the 1860s and 1870s. The Hutchinson's Estate of 1862 provided housing for workers on one of the first industrial estates in the country. A promenade was provided along the riverside for recreation.

124 **DITTON** (BR)   Travelling away from Liverpool there is a fine view of the bridges over the Mersey as the line curves from Ditton Junction down to Widnes. Before the railway bridge was built across the Mersey, the main line from London to Liverpool continued north from Acton Bridge to Earlestown and then turned westwards along the

original Liverpool and Manchester Railway. The line from Ditton to Halewood and Speke was part of the St Helens Railway, absorbed by the LNWR in 1864.

125 The **FORD MOTOR WORKS** at **HALE-** *L&F* **WOOD** began production in 1963. The works cover 365 acres and are the second largest complex in Britain (the largest is at Dagenham) producing Escort cars, vans and estates.

126 **ALLERTON** (BR)   The railway line from Speke via Allerton to Edge Hill was opened by the LNWR on 15 February 1864. In the 19th century Allerton was not a suburb of Liverpool but a popular country retreat for some of the richest merchants of the city where they built mansions designed by leading architects of the day. Some of the houses have survived though they are not visible from the train. The plantation-owner William Shand and the colliery-owner J. Grant Morris employed Alfred Waterhouse. The cotton merchant Joseph Leather employed George Gilbert Scott and Tate the sugar refiner built two houses designed by Norman Shaw.

127 **WEST ALLERTON** (BR; 1939)

128 **MOSSLEY HILL** (BR)   About a mile north of Mossley Hill Station is **Wavertree School**, a fine *R:l* red- and black-brick Victorian school with central tower, clearly visible across the playing fields.

129 **THE CATHEDRALS OF LIVERPOOL**   As *L:r* the train crosses **Wavertree Junction** there is a good view across the slate roofs of Liverpool of the two cathedrals. The more conventional Gothic-

style building in red sandstone is Anglican; the circular building with its unusual lantern is Roman Catholic.

Sir Giles G. Scott won the competition for the Anglican Cathedral in 1903 but redesigned it in 1910–11. It was still not finished when he died in 1960 but was consecrated by the Queen on 25 October 1978. The tower rises 331 feet above the city and is particularly impressive from the graveyard below. Scott developed the Gothic style 'to something original and modern, monumental and sublime, yet delicate and romantic' (Gavin Stamp, *Britain in the Thirties*).

The Catholic Cathedral was originally to be designed by Lutyens but only the crypt was built when work was abandoned in 1940. Frederick Gibberd won the competition to complete the cathedral in 1960 and built on top of Lutyens's

Roman Catholic Cathedral, Liverpool

crypt. The cathedral is 194 feet in diameter and on top is a fully glazed lantern weighing 2,000 tons crowned with pinnacles rising to 290 feet. The stained glass in the lantern is by John Piper and Patrick Reyntiens. The whole building cost £1½ million.

130 EDGE HILL (BR)   The main line to London joins the Liverpool to Manchester line just east of Edge Hill Station in a maze of junctions, sidings, signals, cables and soot-blackened walls. Olive Mount Cutting is east of Edge Hill but the dramatic steep-sided cutting has been widened to take additional tracks. The *Liverpool Mercury* for 10 August 1827 described the first recorded death of a railway navvy at Edge Hill: 'the poor fellow was in the act of undermining a heavy head of clay, 14 or 15 feet high, when the mass fell upon him, and literally crushed his bowels out of his body.'

Edge Hill Station was opened in 1836 in time for the inaugural service to Birmingham on the Grand Junction Railway. The station expanded over the years to include a goods depot, the Grand Junction Railway's locomotive works and the associated sidings, yards and marshalling yards. The original red sandstone buildings designed by John Cunningham were restored for the 150th anniversary of the Liverpool and Manchester Railway.

131 TUNNELS INTO LIVERPOOL LIME STREET   The train approaches Lime Street Station through a series of tunnels – Overbury Street, Mount Pleasant and Russell Street – and under several bridges. There are glimpses of high rocky walls covered with wet lichen and ferns above the track.

The tunnel under Liverpool was the first of the great Victorian railway tunnels and dug for the Liverpool and Manchester Railway. It is 1 1/4 miles long and gave employment to 300 miners. Four men were killed during the excavations which proved harder than expected. The pilot tunnel ran 13 feet out of true in places. 'Unexpected veins of soft blue shale and quicksand threatened to drown the workings and water made it difficult to build masonry lining.' The more daring Liverpool citizens descended one of the 60 feet shafts in a bucket to watch the work in progress: 'some infernal operation in the region of Pluto'.

132 **LIVERPOOL** (BR)   Liverpool began to expand at the end of the 17th century with the trade in sugar, tobacco and cotton from the West Indies and Virginia. It was the slave trade, however, which brought greater wealth from the beginning of the 18th to the beginning of the 19th centuries. Daniel Defoe, visiting the town in 1724–7, wrote 'no town in England, except London, ... can equal Liverpoole for the Fineness of the Streets and Beauty of the Buildings.' Slaves laid the foundations for Liverpool's golden age as England's prime Atlantic port, picking the cotton that was brought to the factories of Lancashire and turning some of the citizens into millionaires. The extraordinary Royal Liver Building, designed by W. Aubrey Thomas (1908–10) and the Dock Office Building by Arnold Thornely reflect the pomp and circumstance of the port – now sadly lost.

Lime Street Station   The present station is not the earliest. The first was built in 1836, designed by John Cunningham with an entrance screen by Foster the Younger. This was replaced in

1846–51 with a train shed by Richard Turner and Joseph Locke assisted by Sir William Fairbairn and buildings by Sir William Tite. The train shed, 135 feet across, was the first iron roof to cover a terminus in a single span. The girders were made in Turner's Dublin works. (Turner was a contractor for the Palm House at Kew Gardens at the same time.) Rebuilding took place again in 1867 when William Baker built the iron train shed which now covers the northern half of the station. When completed it had a span of 219 feet, the largest in the world until one was built at St Pancras of 240 feet. A further extension was made in 1874–9 when an almost identical train shed (spanning 186 feet) was built over the southern half of the station. The train sheds are not as impressive as those at London termini such as St Pancras and Kings Cross because they are much lower. However, the departure from under the train sheds into the steep-sided cutting and through the rock glistening black, red, yellow and green has its own particular atmosphere. Tite's buildings survive in the yellow-golden sandstone back wall of the station across the concourse from the ticket barriers and containing ticket offices, barber's shop, various stalls etc. Major reconstruction and redevelopment has been completed at Lime Street Station (1985): part of the old wall has been replaced by plate glass decorated with engravings; hanging baskets are already up; a fresh and airy atmosphere is being created.

Alfred Waterhouse designed the LNWR's railway hotel which still stands outside the station – once adjoining the northern train shed at its western end. The flamboyant block is now offices and has recently been cleaned. It was built in

1868–71 and consists of five storeys with rows of dormers on top, chimneys and eruptions of towers and spires. The hotel had lavish plumbing for its time with 37 water closets and 8 baths serving the 200 rooms.

EUSTON
TO
MANCHESTER

Introduction

Passengers travelling to Manchester follow the original London and Birmingham Railway as far as Rugby. They then continue on the Trent Valley Railway which bypasses Birmingham. Those travelling via Stoke on Trent leave the Trent Valley Railway after Rugeley and continue northwards to Macclesfield on the North Staffordshire Railway. From Macclesfield to Manchester they follow the Manchester and Birmingham Railway. Passengers travelling via Crewe use the original Grand Junction Railway between Stafford and Crewe and then join the Manchester and Birmingham Railway to reach Manchester via Wilmslow.

The Trent Valley Railway Company was founded in 1843 with Edward Watkins as Secretary. Its aim to expand the industries already established in the Trent Valley. The first sod was cut in November 1845 by Sir Robert Peel, Prime Minister and MP for Tamworth (1830–50). He praised the self-sacrifice of the landowners: 'I assure them that there are many persons in this neighbourhood who have not scrupled to sacrifice private feeling and comfort, by consenting to their land being appropriated to the Trent Valley Railway. They have given consent from a conviction that this undertaking was one conducive to the public benefit, and that considerations of private interest should not obstruct the great one of the public good.' Nevertheless the owner of Shugborough Park was able to demand ornate entrances to the tunnel which the railway company dug under his estate.

The engineers for the line were Robert Stephenson and George Bidder and the contractor was Thomas Brassey. The line was opened in December 1847. The stations were designed by John William Livock, but many have been demolished. Tamworth and Lichfield have gone, also Stafford. The imaginative Jacobean style building at Stafford was replaced by a 1960s functional design.

The North Staffordshire Railway was centred on Stoke on Trent and it was of vital importance to the Potteries. The completion of the Trent and Mersey Canal in 1777 had made a dramatic difference to the wealth and prosperity of the area but the railway was to provide much faster, more efficient and cheaper transport. H. A. Hunt designed the stations for the North Staffordshire Railway. His favourite style was Jacobean and his masterpiece was the group of buildings at Stoke on Trent.

The Grand Junction Railway was opened on 4 July 1837 from Lime Street Station in Liverpool to a temporary terminus at Birmingham (Vauxhall). A scheme to link Birmingham with Birkenhead (the Mersey ferry-head to Liverpool) was discussed in Parliament as early as 1824 but opposed by landowners and canal owners in Cheshire, the latter fearing – quite rightly – they would lose money. One canal agent from Nantwich was overheard by George Stephenson warning local farmers that the locomotive gave off breath as poisonous as a dragon's.

Joseph Locke surveyed the line which joined George Stephenson's Liverpool and Manchester Railway at Earlestown and from there had access to Liverpool or Manchester. It was not too expensive to build – £18,846 a mile as compared with Robert Stephenson's London and Birmingham Railway's £53,000. The opening was celebrated at Stafford by the Mayor firing a 21-gun salute with ancient cannon at the approach of 'Wildfire' pulling eight 1st class coaches – the first train to Birmingham.

With the threat of competition the Liverpool and Manchester Railway and the Grand Junction amalgamated to become the London and North

Western Railway in 1846. Their headquarters were established at Crewe which was turned from a village into a thriving railway town in only a few years (see p. 464). Francis Webb, locomotive superintendant of the LNWR for 32 years, was largely responsible for building up Crewe. John Ramsbottom, famous for making the celebrated 'Lady of the Lake' class 2–2–2 express locomotive was also working at Crewe.

Though the combination of the Liverpool and Manchester Railway and the Grand Junction Railway provided Manchester with access to London, merchants and businessmen of the city wanted their own independent, direct line to the south and the Manchester and Birmingham Railway was incorporated in 1837. The first part of the line reached Stockport in 1840 and on 21 December the laying of the last stone of the 600 yard long viaduct over the Mersey was celebrated. The Manchester and Birmingham Railway built two lines (the alternative routes used by BR), the first to join the Grand Junction Railway at Crewe, the second to join up with the North Staffordshire Railway at Macclesfield. Crewe was reached in 1842. The line was first opened only as far as Sandbach (May 1842) as the Grand Junction Railway refused to allow Manchester and Birmingham trains to run on their tracks. After three months of talks, the line was finally opened all the way through to Crewe. The second line reached Macclesfield on 24 November 1845. A short tunnel into the town brought the line to the end of the North Staffordshire Railway on 18 June 1849.

There are two routes to Manchester from Euston: half of InterCity trains travel via Stafford, Stoke on Trent and Macclesfield; half travel via Stafford, Crewe and Wilmslow.

EUSTON
TO
MANCHESTER

VIA
STOKE ON TRENT

Euston to Watford (see pages 396-409)
Watford to Milton Keynes (see pages 410–420)
Milton Keynes to Rugby (see pages 421-429)
Rugby to Atherstone (see pages 445-450)
Atherstone to Rugeley (see pages 451-457)

MAP 9

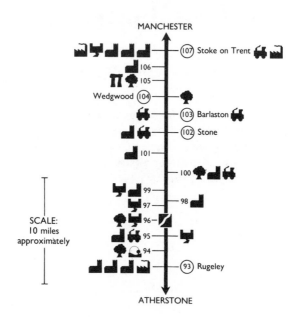

MANCHESTER

107 Stoke on Trent

106
105

Wedgwood 104

103 Barlaston

102 Stone

101

100

99
97
98

96

95

94

93 Rugeley

SCALE:
10 miles
approximately

ATHERSTONE

94 CANNOCK CHASE is practically all that re- *L:r*
mains of the great forest which once covered
Staffordshire. The heath and woodland grows on
the dry sandy soils of the Bunter Sandstone which
crosses the Midland plain. The area has remained
uncultivated because of its impractical nature and is
now preserved as a place of recreation.

95 COLWICH The attractive limestone **station-** *L:r*
house of Colwich survives beside the line. It is one
of the few remaining stations designed by Livock in
1847 for the Trent Valley Railway (see p. 480) and
has his distinctive gables and diamond tiles.

St Michael's Church, Colwich has a high west *L:r*
tower built in 1640. Inside the church are monuments to the Anson, Sparrow and Wolesley
families. Lord George Anson was a celebrated
admiral and circumnavigator and his fortune – made
capturing Spanish treasure galleons – was used by
his brother Thomas to improve Shugborough
House and Park (see p. 486). Sir William Wolesley
drowned in his carriage when the mill dam
suddenly burst in a thunderstorm in 1728. The four
horses were also drowned but the coachman was
carried to an orchard and hung on to an apple tree
until the waters fell.

St Mary's Abbey was built c.1825 as Mount *R:l*
Pavilion by Viscount Tamworth, son of the 7th Earl
Ferrers. It is in the Tudor Gothic style with a
castellated front. A Benedictine order of contemplative nuns moved into the mansion in 1834.

The line divides immediately after Colwich: to
the west is the line to Stafford, Crewe and
Liverpool, to the north the line to Macclesfield,
Stockport and Manchester.

96 SHUGBOROUGH PARK The **Trent and** *L:r*
Mersey Canal and the **River Trent** (which
follow the railway line all the way to Stoke on
Trent) flow between the railway line and Shugborough Park but it is just possible to see the house
and several of the unusual buildings in the park.
Shugborough House, now owned by the National
Trust and open to the public, was built in 1693 for
William Anson and enlarged in the 18th century by
his grandson Thomas who also filled the park with
the buildings designed by James 'Athenian' Stuart.
Thomas Anson was a founder member of the
Society of Dilettanti which sent Stuart to Athens
to draw the principal buildings. These provided the
inspiration for the Arch of Hadrian, the Tower of
the Winds, the Doric Temple and the Lantern of
Demosthenes. The 2nd Lord Lichfield inherited the
property in 1854. The present Lord Lichfield
occupies a flat in the house.

Shugborough House

97 INGESTRE HALL with its distinctive green *L:r*
cupola is about a mile from the line and set in a park
landscaped by Capability Brown in 1756. Sir Walter
Chetwynd built the house early in the 17th
century. The Talbots took over the estate in 1767,

becoming the Earls Talbot in 1784 and the Earls of Shrewsbury in 1856. After a fire in 1882, John Birch reconstructed Jacobean-style rooms behind the original front. He also 're-Jacobeanised' parts of the house which had been altered by Nash for the 2nd Earl Talbot in 1808–10 when the Georgian style was fashionable. The Shrewsburys sold the hall in 1960. It is now used by West Bromwich Borough Council for residential courses in the arts.

98 **HIXON CHURCH** **St Peter's** was designed *R:l* by George Gilbert Scott and consecrated in 1848. It has a north tower with a broach spire.

99 **WESTON** **St Andrew's Church** has an early *L:r* English tower but the rest is Victorian and was designed by George Gilbert Scott and William Butterfield. **Abbeylands**, the Jacobean-style house close to the church, was also designed by Scott in 1858. They can be seen just as the train passes under the A51. **Weston Hall** is the Jacobean stone *L:r* house to the west of the church.

100 **SANDON PARK** The neo-Jacobean **entrance** *R:l* **lodge** to Sandon is close to the railway line at the south end of the park. The house is not visible. It was designed by William Burn in 1852 for the 2nd Earl of Harrowby, Dudley Rider. The 2nd Earl was a politician, a fellow of the Royal Society and a promoter of reform in the treatment of tenants. He also established Staffordshire's county agricultural society. **All Saints Church** can be seen in the *R:l* park. It dates from the 13th to 14th centuries and has a Perpendicular tower.

    Sandon had its own station, opened in 1849, and the attractive red-brick **station building** is *R:l* still beside the line at the north end of the park

(now a private house). A special porte-cochère was
built for the Earl's carriage. **Sandon village** R:l
contains several buildings designed by Sir E. Guy
Dawber in c.1905 for the Sandon Estate including
the Dog and Doublet Inn and the Village Club.
They are in the same neo-Jacobean style as the
entrance lodge.

101 **ASTON BY STONE** The church of **St** L:r
Saviour was built in 1846 to the design of James
Trubshaw. The steeple was added in 1876 and is by
J. R. Botham. Aston is an attractive village, sepa-
rated from the railway line by the **Trent and
Mersey Canal** and the **River Trent**, both of
which follow the line to Stoke.

102 **STONE** (BR)   Stone had an Augustinian Priory in
the Middle Ages. The church of **St Michael** L:r
(tower with pinnacles) was built in 1753–8 in the
Gothic revival style. Peter de Wint, the 19th-
century watercolourist, was born at Stone; also
Richard Barnfield, the 16th-century poet of the
Staffordshire countryside.

   Stone Station is particularly attractive. The L:r
patterned brick building with stone dressings and
three Dutch gables was designed by H. A. Hunt for
the North Staffordshire Railway (see p. 481) and
built in 1848. There are also two pretty **cottages** L:r
beside the level crossings to the south and north of
the station, both in the Jacobean style.

103 **BARLASTON** (BR)   After the elegant parklands
of Shugborough, Ingestre and Sandon, the train
now enters the industrial region of the Potteries.
Barlaston was created as a model village by the
architect Keith Murray. The Wedgwoods decided

to move south of Etruria in 1936 (see p. 493) to establish a new factory and village in a park setting. This has since spread to cover the area around the railway line between Barlaston and Wedgwood Stations.

Barlaston Station has fine **red-brick build-** *R&L*
ings on both sides of the line in H. A. Hunt's favourite Jacobean style.

104 **WEDGWOOD** (BR)   Wedgwood Station serves the factory established to the east of the line by the Wedgwoods in 1936. The Wedgwoods – Josiah in particular – were responsible for the dramatic increase in industrial output and prosperity which overtook the Trent Valley and neighbouring towns at the end of the 18th century (see p. 493). South of the station and to the east of the line is the **park** *R:l* containing Wedgwood Hall and the village church; north of the station and to the east is the **Wedgwood Visitor Centre** which consists of the pottery and museum where one can see all stages of pottery creation; and paintings, exhibitions and films.

105 **TRENTHAM PARK**   The estate of Trentham *L:r* covers the hillside to the west of the line. The **monument** to the 1st Duke of Sutherland is visible in the trees. It was erected in 1836 and consists of a large bronze statue of the Duke by Chantrey on top of a plain column which overlooks an enormous lake designed by Capability Brown. Trentham Park was designed by Charles Barry and built in 1833–42 for the 2nd Duke, George Granville Leveson-Gower. Trentham and Stafford House in London became important social centres in the 19th century. The Duchess was Mistress of

the Queen's Robes and kept Victoria company after the death of Prince Albert. Not only royalty but the celebrated Italian hero Garibaldi were visitors to Trentham. Disraeli renamed it Brentham in his novel *Lothair*. The house was on the grand scale but unfortunately it was demolished in 1910–12. The grounds, Trentham Gardens, are open to the public.

106 BOOTHERN CHURCH The Victorian church of **All Saints** is on the hillside, its blackened spire *L:r* evidence of the industrial pollution which once characterised this area, the product of the coal mines of the Staffordshire coalfield and the coke ovens of the potteries.

107 STOKE ON TRENT (BR) The embattled **church tower** south of the station with four *L:r* pinnacles belongs to **St Peter ad Vincula**. The church was built in 1826–9 and is a Commissioner's type of church, designed by Trubshaw and Johnson and built to cope with the rapidly expanding population of Stoke. Inside are monuments to the great pottery families, Josiah Wedgwood, Josiah Spode and John Bourne. Josiah Wedgwood's monument by Flaxman has the inscription, he 'converted a rude and inconsiderable manufactory into an elegant art and an important part of national commerce'.

Stoke on Trent Station, together with the *R:l* North Stafford Hotel and housing for railway employees, were all built around Winton Square in 1847–50 to form one of the most impressive examples of railway architecture in the country. Stoke was originally at the centre of the North

Staffordshire Railway and H. A. Hunt used his
Jacobean style for the buildings which are in dark
red brick with black brick diapers and stone
dressings. The hotel is a replica of an early Jacobean
manor house. The station has a facade with three
gables and a central bay with a huge oriel window
lighting up the company's boardroom. In 1893 the
station was reconstructed behind Hunt's facade and
given an overall roof in the ridge and furrow style
supported on close spaced steel girders.

Stoke is one of the Potteries, the five towns
which became the centre of the pottery industry at
the end of the 18th century: Tunstall, Burslem,
Hanley, Stoke and Longton. Arnold Bennett, novelist of the Five Towns, renamed them Turnhill,
Bursley, Hanbridge, Knype and Longshaw. In 1925
the city of Stoke was formed as a conurbation
made up of the Potteries. The distinctive **kilns** can *L&R*
still be seen amongst the buildings close to the
railway line – bottle-shaped or conical or like
chimneys with swollen bases. They are fast disappearing, however, along with many of the
factories, their work and their markets. In 1971 the
city of Stoke had more derelict land than any other
county borough in England. The prosperity which
came with the Industrial Revolution was achieved
at appalling cost, particularly in its use of child
labour. A report on the Staffordshire potteries in
1843 described the use of the children: 'with
perspiration standing on their foreheads, after
labouring like little slaves, with the mercury 20
degrees below freezing ... many die of consumption, asthma and acute inflammation.' The magnifi-
cence of Stoke on Trent's **Town Hall** reflects only *L:r*
one side of life in the Potteries. It was designed by
Henry Ward and built in 1834–50. The centre has a

491

MAP 10

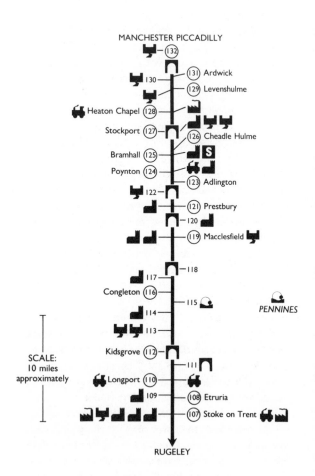

MANCHESTER PICCADILLY

132

131 Ardwick

130

129 Levenshulme

Heaton Chapel 128

Stockport 127

126 Cheadle Hulme

Bramhall 125

S

Poynton 124

123 Adlington

122

121 Prestbury

120

Macclesfield 119

118

117

Congleton 116

115

PENNINES

114

113

Kidsgrove 112

111

Longport 110

109

108 Etruria

107 Stoke on Trent

RUGELEY

SCALE:
10 miles
approximately

Stoke on Trent Potteries

giant upper portico of unfluted Ionic columns and can be seen from the train.

Our Lady of the Angels is the large yellow *L:r* and red brick Gothic style building north of the station. The Roman Catholic convent was designed by Charles Hansom in 1857 and enlarged by A. E. Purdie in 1884–5.

Holy Trinity, Hartshill Road, is on the hillside *L:r* above the railway line and just beyond Stoke Infirmary. It was designed by George Gilbert Scott in 1842. It was paid for by Herbert Minton and is lavishly adorned inside with Minton tiles.

108 **ETRURIA** (BR) Etruria was the centre of the Wedgwood empire. Josiah Wedgwood (1730–95) came from a family of potters in Burslem and after rising to become a master-potter in 1759 and Queen's potter in 1762, he bought a site between Burslem and Stoke in 1766 for £300, called it Etruria and built a factory, village and mansion. The warehouses and kilns along the canal were demolished in the 1960s but the canal itself is a result

of Wedgwood's energy. He was ardent in his campaign to have the canal built: it would make a dramatic difference to his own problems of transport. The Trent and Mersey Canal was finally opened in 1777 (see p. 456). Etruria was the site for the 1986 National Garden Festival and has remained a featured garden since the Festival.

109 WOLSTANTON CHURCH The spire of the *L:r* high Victorian **St Margaret's** can just be seen to the west.

110 LONGPORT (BR) The station has the familiar pretty North Staffordshire buildings: **red brick and Jacobean style** to the west, single storey *L:r* **red brick with limestone trims** to the windows to the east. *R:l*

There is considerable industry along this part of the Trent Valley with steel works and collieries and the living and dead pottery works jostling for space close to the canal and railway. Beyond Westport Lake is the pottery town of **Tunstall**. George *R:l* Moore described the landscape of the Potteries in *A Mummer's Wife*: 'It was one of those terrible cauldrons in which man melts and moulds this huge age of iron ... wide widths of walls, bald rotundities of pottery ovens, reigned supreme; before them nature had disappeared, and the shrill scream of the steam train as it rolled solemnly up the incline seemed man's cry of triumph over vanquished nature.'

111 HARECASTLE TUNNELS The mile-long *R:l* railway tunnel which was dug in 1848 is now by-passed. Parallel to the railway tunnel but considerably older are the **Harecastle Canal**

Tunnels for the Trent and Mersey Canal. The first tunnel was dug in 1766–77 by James Brindley and is 2,880 yards long. The second, by Telford, is 2,926 yards long and was dug in 1824–7. Brindley (1716–72), under the patronage of the Duke of Bridgewater (see p. 504), was responsible for designing and building 360 miles of canals in the North of England and Midlands.

112 **KIDSGROVE** (BR)   The train passes through a short tunnel to reach Kidsgrove Station.

113 **RAMSDELL HALL**   The impressive baronial *L:r* gates just across the canal are the entrance to Ramsdell Hall, a fine red brick mansion built c.1720–60. Slightly further north is the **Old** *L:r* **Parsonage**, a handsome white house with Corinthian columns supporting the porch.

114 **ASTBURY CHURCH**   The Decorated tower *L:r* and recessed spire of Astbury church can be seen about a mile from the line. Astbury has another tower at the western end, a three-storeyed porch added in the late 15th century, making the church one of the 'most exciting' in Cheshire (N. Pevsner). The countryside here is rich pastureland, a contrast to the industrial valley to the south.

115 The hills to the east are the western edge of the **Pennines**. The moorlands of the Pennines are *L:r* formed of Millstone and Moorstone Grit and, at this point, Yoredale Rock. There are two outcrops of the dark Yoredale Rock above the railway line: the **Old Man of Mow**, 1100 feet high, opposite *R:l* Ramsdell Hall, and **The Cloud**, 1125 feet high, just

past Congleton. The Old Man of Mow or Mow Cop once had flourishing gritstone quarries.

116 **CONGLETON** (BR)   The North Staffordshire Railway Company's familiar Tudor-Jacobean-style building at Congleton has been replaced by a new red-brick station. Congleton became an important centre for silk-weaving in the 18th century. John Clayton of Stockport and Nathaniel Pattison of London established Clayton's Mill in c.1752. By 1817 the town had 17 silk mills and 5 cotton mills.

117 **BUGLAWTON CHURCH St John the** *L:r* **Evangelist** was designed in 1840 by R. B. Rampling and has a recessed spire.

118 **THE   CONGLETON   AND   DANE VIADUCTS**   carry the railway line over the Biddulph branch of the North Staffordshire Railway, the **Trent and Mersey Canal** and the **River Dane**, and offer fine views of the country-side to the west and east with the rocky outcrop 'The Cloud' rising above the **Dane Valley**. The viaducts were designed by J. C. Forsyth, engineer for the North Staffordshire Railway, and were completed in 1849. The Congleton, to the south, has 16 arches 130 feet high; the Dane is built of blue brick and has 20 arches. They mark the boundary between **Staffordshire** and **Cheshire**.

119 **MACCLESFIELD** (BR)   The steeple of **St Paul's** church dominates the town from its *L:r* elevated position just south of the station. It is a Commissioners' church and was designed by W. Hayley and built in 1843–4.

The parish church of **St Michael** (founded by *L:r*

Queen Eleanor at the end of the 13th century) is on top of the steep escarpment just north of the station. The tower is Perpendicular but most of the church was rebuilt in 1898–1901 by Sir Arthur Blomfield. The unusual Pardon Brass is inside. It is to Roger Legh who died in 1506 and gives him the confident assurance that the pardon for offering 5 Paternosters, 5 Aves and one Creed is 26,000 years and 26 days.

Macclesfield was built up on the manufacture of silk and cotton. The first silk mill was established in 1743 by Charles Roe who also started copper works 15 years later. By 1900 there were 30 silk mills in the town and many cotton factories.

Messrs Arighi, Bianchi

Messrs Arighi, Bianchi survives from the late *R:l* 19th century, a fine example and immaculately maintained, with a front of arched cast iron and glass.

120 **HURDSFIELD CHURCH Holy Trinity** is *R:l* another Commissioners' church, built with the intention of Christianising the expanding work-force. It was designed by William Hayley and built in 1837–9. Its limestone tower (recently cleaned) overlooks the industrial estate of Hurdsfield in which a diversity of industries are being developed including the making of pharmaceutical products.

The **tunnel** through which the train passes below Hurdsfield was dug in 1849.

121 **PRESTBURY** (BR)   With a local railway service (the line between Cheadle and Macclesfield was opened in 1845) and the close proximity of Macclesfield and Stockport, Prestbury has been developed as a commuter village for the most prosperous workers of the area. **St Peter's** has a *L:r* medieval tower but was rebuilt in the late 19th century. It is in one of the prettiest and most visited villages in Cheshire, rich in timbered cottages and well-tended gardens.

122 **MILL HOUSE, ADLINGTON**   After a short *L:r* tunnel the train passes the fine timber-framed E-shaped Mill House Farm which is close to the line. It was built in 1603 by the Legh family as a Dower House. The Leghs inherited the Adlington estates in 1315. Colonel Thomas Legh was an active Royalist during the Civil Wars and his widow Ann lived in the Dower House for many years. The

house has stone slated roofs and stone stacks, wood mullioned windows and casements with leaded lights.

123 ADLINGTON (BR)   The trustees of the Adling-ton estates (the landowner Charles Richard Bon-astre Legh was a minor) were paid £12,712 3s 9d by the LNWR as purchase money for land taken by the railway and in compensation for damage caused. Just over 56 acres of Legh land were used through Adlington, Butley and Prestbury.

124 POYNTON (BR)   The first station was some distance from the village to the south and closed when the present one was opened on 1 August 1887. This consists of a smart **red-brick house** *R:1* with ornate brackets painted mustard yellow. **St** *R:1* **George's** is a Victorian church, its steeple de-signed by J. Medland and Henry Taylor.

Just north of Poynton the train crosses the boundary between **Cheshire** and **Greater Man-chester**.

125 BRAMHALL (BR)   Bramhall has been intensively developed since the 1930s with housing estates surrounding the **golf course** and the grounds of *R:1* Bramhall Hall (which is one of the finest timber-framed houses in the country and open to the public). **St Michael's** is an Edwardian church; the *R:1* brick tower, by G. G. Pace, was added in 1960–3.

126 CHEADLE HULME (BR)   The first station at Cheadle Hulme was opened in 1842, a quarter of a mile away on the Manchester to Crewe line. The present station was opened in 1866 at the junction with the line to Macclesfield (though the buildings are 20th-century). The railway line has moved away from the ridge of hills to the east and the view to the north is of the enormous industrial conurbation which surrounds Manchester – chimneys and spires, patches of wasteland, occasional trees, old and new factories and housing estates.

127 **STOCKPORT** (BR)   The most spectacular feature of Stockport is the railway **viaduct** which carries the line high over the **River Mersey**.

Stockport Station has red-brick platform buildings patterned with black brick and yellow brick window trims. The awnings and valancing are painted a sandy colour and supported by elegant brackets. The signal boxes at either end of the station are in the same red and black brick with sandy coloured wooden tops.

Like Macclesfield (see p. 496) **Stockport** began to expand with the silk industry followed by the cotton industry. One of the first cotton mills was built by Sir George Warren on the site of the medieval castle. It was specially designed as a circular building with battlements. The old town was close to the River Mersey in the valley rising steeply up to the market place and parish church. **St Mary's** was mostly rebuilt in 1813–17 to the *R:l* design of Lewis Wyatt and is in a Perpendicular Gothic style with a west tower. John Wainwright, composer of the tune to the well-known hymn 'Christians Awake', was organist of St Mary's and was buried in the church in 1768. The **Market** *R:l* **Hall** has an iron and glass cover erected in 1861. Throughout the 19th century houses and factories began to spread over the higher ground on both sides of the river. Hat-making became an important local industry, followed by engineering. From the viaduct there is a good view of the mills, warehouses and factories below and also of **Mersey-way**, a pedestrian way made by covering up part of the river and now part of the new shopping precinct. George Watson Buck designed the viaduct which is 600 yards long, has 27 arches and is 111 feet above the bed of the Mersey. It was built for the Manchester and Birmingham Railway and before it was completed (1840) there was a temporary station at the north end – where the LNWR goods warehouse is now sited – which lasted until 1959 as Heaton Norris.

The Wren-style tower of the **Town Hall** is *R:l* visible to the east of the station. The Town Hall was designed by Sir Alfred Brumwell Thomas and built in 1904–8 of white stone.

128 HEATON CHAPEL (BR) The station was opened in January 1852. The red-brick **ticket** *L:r* **office** above the cutting is patterned with black brick. The Edwardian factory of **McVities & Price** *R:l* **Biscuits** is beside the line.

129 LEVENSHULME (BR) The station was opened in August 1842. The half-timbered two-storey house just by the line is **Slade Hall**. It was built in *L:r* 1585 and the timbering is mostly in a herring-bone pattern. The back of the house is of early 19th-century brick. Inside, there is a frieze in one of the rooms of naive plasterwork depicting hunting scenes.

130 MANCHESTER UNIVERSITY The **high** *L:r* **tower** with a steep pyramid roof belongs to the east range of Manchester University and was built in 1883–7. The university began as Owens College (1851) and moved to its present site in 1873. Alfred Waterhouse began work as architect of the new buildings in 1870. The University, together with the Institution of Science and Technology, the Municipal College of Technology and the College of Art, have recently been brought together on a vast campus more familiar in American universities, under the plan of Sir Hugh Wilson and Lewis Wormesley.

Manchester University

131 ARDWICK STATION (BR) is on the line to *R:l* Huddersfield and Leeds. In 1830, just before the railway was built, Ardwick was 'a fashionable residential quarter for Manchester merchants'.

132 MANCHESTER (BR) Manchester Piccadilly Station is approached on a **viaduct** of 16 arches from which the flamboyant clock tower of the old **Magistrates' Court** in Minshull Street can be *L:r* seen. This Italian Gothic-style building adorned with gables and turrets was built in 1871 and designed by Thomas Worthington.

Manchester Piccadilly was opened as London Road in 1862 and enlarged in 1881 when the iron- and glass-roofed train sheds were erected. The train sheds are supported by iron pillars painted white and blue and decorated with leafy capitals and ornate brackets. The front of London Road was 'a beautiful stone building in the Italian style': now it is dull glass and steel. The station was rebuilt in 1960 as part of the plan to adopt the 25kV system of electric traction and was renamed Piccadilly on the opening on 12 September. R. L. Moorcroft, Midland Region's architect, was the designer.

A visitor to Manchester in 1851 wrote to warn fellow travellers: 'dreadful fires occur occasionally in Manchester. If such a catastrophe should take place during the stay of a visitor, he should immediately pull on an overcoat, even though it be midnight, and join in the crowd. An excellent police of 300 officers and men renders the streets quite safe at all hours; and a fire of an old cotton factory, where the floors are saturated with oil and grease, is indeed a fearfully imposing sight. It also affords an opportunity of some familiar conversation with the factory hands.' Even in 1926 there were plenty of factories to catch fire, as a continental visitor observed: 'At Manchester since the war 400 large new factories for cotton spinning have been built, several of them of the size of the Royal Palace in Berlin, and thousands of smoking obelisks of the steam engines 80 to 180 feet high destroy all impression of church steeples.'

The prosperity of Manchester was made out of cotton and cheap factory labour. Weaving flourished in the Middle Ages after Edward III settled a colony of Flemish weavers in the town but it was not until the 18th century that expansion began. The River Irwell was made navigable in 1721. Then the Duke of Bridgewater employed James Brindley to cut a canal from his coal mine at Worsley to Manchester. This was extended to Runcorn in 1776 and the means was created by which raw cotton could be transported direct to the centre of Manchester. St Peter's Square, the site of Alfred Waterhouse's extraordinary gothic Town Hall and Charles Barry's Grecian Royal Institution, is also a grim reminder of St Peter's Fields where the Peterloo Massacre took place in 1819. Many of the rich merchants of Manchester who paid for the city's monumental public buildings forced their workers to endure appalling conditions in their factories. Friedrich Engels's *Condition of the Working Class in England* (1844) gives a moving account of the deprivation experienced by Manchester workers while their employers grew rich. De Tocqueville remarked on the 'pure gold' made in Manchester flowing from the 'filthy sewer'; the novelist Mrs Gaskell revealed the inequalities in *Mary Barton, A Tale of Manchester Life* (1848).

EUSTON
TO
MANCHESTER

VIA
CREWE

MAP 11

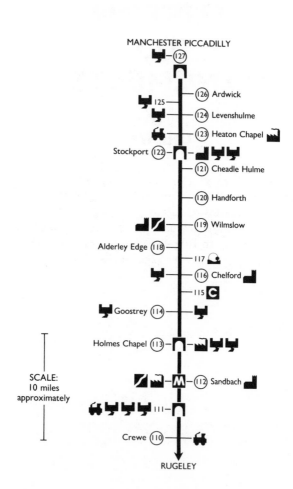

MANCHESTER PICCADILLY

127

126 Ardwick

125

124 Levenshulme

123 Heaton Chapel

Stockport 122

121 Cheadle Hulme

120 Handforth

119 Wilmslow

Alderley Edge 118

117

116 Chelford

115 C

Goostrey 114

Holmes Chapel 113

SCALE:
10 miles
approximately

112 Sandbach

111

Crewe 110

RUGELEY

110 CREWE When the Grand Junction railway arrived at Crewe in 1837 the population of about 200 lived in small farms and cottages. By 1842, the station was the focus of four railway lines and the locomotive works which had been moved from Edge Hill was about to begin production. The railway company built houses, churches and schools, and by 1851 the population had risen to 4,571. The salaries of the curate and the schoolmaster were paid by the company which also provided a doctor and two policemen, organised the supply of mains water, the emptying of ash pits, cess pools and privies and even set up a savings bank for its employees. Four classes of house were built: 'first, the villa-style lodges of the superior officer; next a kind of ornamental Gothic constitutes the house of the next in authority; the engineers domiciled in detached mansions, which accommodate four families, with gardens and separate entrances; and last the labourer delights in neat cottages of four apartments, the entrances within ancient porches'.

Crewe Station consists of three broad island platforms each with creamy yellow brick buildings decorated with red and dark blue brick dressings, all under a lateral train shed. The bay windows have Greek heads on the keystones. Immediately next to the station is the **Crewe Arms** built in the R:1 Jacobean style and opened in 1837. It was taken over by the LNWR as their railway hotel in 1864. Rather less decorative is the 13-storey block by the station which is **Rail House**, designed by F. S. Curtis and R. C. Moorcroft, British Rail architects, and erected in 1967–8.

North of Crewe Station (at North Crewe Junction) the **line divides**: the old Grand Junction

Railway continues northwards to Liverpool; the old Manchester and Birmingham Railway takes passengers north-east towards Manchester.

111 THE CHESHIRE COUNTRYSIDE Once the suburbs of Crewe have been left behind, the train enters the rolling countryside of the Central Cheshire Plain. Cheshire is one of the least known of English counties, but the countryside is not unattractive. Dotted with small lakes or meres, it is typically English: lush, gentle, pastoral, with prosperous farms, large estates and many half-timbered cottages.

About three miles to the north-east of Crewe the line passes close by **Railway Farm**, two *L:r* storeys, red brick with a barn beside it; then **Brook Farm** and, further away among the trees, *L:r* **Elton Hall**. This is just before the **Elton Embankment** – a cellular embankment built with adjustable rugby-style goal posts to prevent the overhead wires (the line was electrified in 1960) from sagging in an area where subsidence occurs (Rex Christiansen, *The West Midlands*, Newton Abbot, 1973).

112 SANDBACH (BR) Sandbach is about two miles to the east. The town is famous for its two Saxon crosses in the cobbled marketplace. The crosses are believed to have been erected to commemorate the conversion of Penda King of Mercia and his marriage to a Christian princess. Sandbach is one of the Cheshire salt towns: it is also the home of the Fodens Motor Works, famous for their prize-winning brass band.

Sandbach Station is really in the village of

Elworth. **St Peter's** is the parish church, rock- *R:l*
faced with a bellcote, designed by John Matthews.
It is a Commissioner's church, erected in 1845–6
with the intention of bringing religion to the
population which was rapidly expanding with the
development of local industries (notice the red-
brick **Elworth Wire Mills**). *R:l*

Just north of the station the line to Middlewich
branches to the north-west. Middlewich is the
second oldest salt town in Cheshire, connected to
Elworth and Sandbach by not only the railway but
the A533 and the **Trent and Mersey Canal**. *L:r*
Industry is intensive along these lines of communication (chemicals works and beyond, a salt
factory).

The railway line crosses the **M6** halfway between
Sandbach and Holmes Chapel.

113 HOLMES CHAPEL (BR) **Fisons** is just south *R:l*
of the station. The impressive building is one of
their pharmaceutical production sites. To the north
of the station the train passes over the **Dane
Viaduct**, designed by G. W. Buck and built for the
Manchester and Birmingham Railway in 1840–1. It
has 23 arches 63 feet wide and is 105 feet high.
There are good views from the viaduct of the
Cheshire countryside. **Saltersford Hall** (half- *R:l*
timbered) is on the hillside and then **Saltersford** *R:l*
Farm down in the valley, their names reflecting
the most important local industry.

114 GOOSTREY (BR) is to the east of the station.
Just to the north is **Blackden Manor** and on the *R:l*
other side of the line, as the train crosses a long
embankment, **Blackden Hall**. The Hall is close to *L:r*

the line, a very attractive timber-framed house.

115 JODRELL BANK Although the train passes
Jodrell Bank in a cutting a mile long, there is a clear
view of the **observatory**. Sir Bernard Lovell was *R:l*
the first director of the radio astronomy laboratory
of Manchester University (now the Nuffield Radio
Astronomy Laboratories). The first instrument –
Mark I – was erected in 1952–7 and was able, just
before completion, to track the first Sputnik. The
circular bowl of Mark I is 250 feet in diameter; the
telescope is one of the largest fully steerable radio
telescopes in the world.

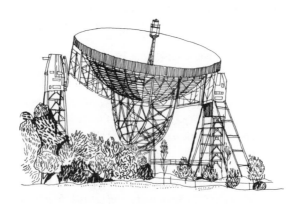

Observatory, Jodrell Bank

116 CHELFORD (BR)   The new houses close to the
line are on an estate called **Mere Court**. The **old** *L:r*
village is a mile to the south east. Its Georgian
parish church has a Victorian spire.   *R:l*

117 ALDERLEY EDGE   The ridge thickly covered *R:l*
with trees which can be seen to the east of the line
is Alderley Edge. 650 feet high and 2 miles long, the

ridge provides a fine viewing-point for the surrounding countryside of Cheshire and Lancashire. It is associated with many local myths and legends and features in the writings of Alan Garner. One spot on the ridge is supposed to be where a countryman was led by a wizard and shown the iron gates of a cave in which warriors were sleeping. A stone on top of Alderley Edge marks where a beacon flared to warn of the approach of the Spanish Armada to the shores of England.

118 ALDERLEY EDGE (BR) When the railway arrived at Alderley Edge in 1842 the village was transformed into a commuter town for affluent Mancunians, full of fine early Victorian houses. The bright station, recently painted, shows that Alderley (like Wilmslow to the north) is still heavily used by railway commuters. It offers the combination of easy and quick access both to the centre of Manchester and to the pastoral delights of Cheshire. A considerably long time before the railway came to Alderley it was a camp site for mesolithic hunters. Their flint caves, flakes and microliths have been found in the area.

119 WILMSLOW (BR) Just like Alderley Edge, Wilmslow developed as a commuter town for Manchester and still has a well-kept, heavily used railway station (red-brick, cream-painted pillars, sandy painted decorative valances). The parish church of **St Bartholomew's** is on the banks of *L:r* the **River Bollin** (the River Bollin meets the **River Dean** at Twinnies Bridge in Wilmslow). It is mostly 16th century, including the tower, and inside has several fine 16th-century monuments, and a 15th-century brass to Robert Booth and his

St Bartholomew's, Wilmslow

wife, Booth's right foot resting on a dog representing faithfulness. Some of the glass in the church is by Morris and Co.

Wilmslow was the home of Samuel Finney, portrait painter, favourite of Queen Caroline and ruthless magistrate. He was so successful in controlling drunkenness and disorder in the town in the 18th century that Wilmslow has had a reputation for respectability ever since.

120 HANDFORTH (BR)   New houses now join up Wilmslow and Handforth. Manchester's suburbs are spreading as the population within a mere 2½ miles of the city has passed 10 million.

121 CHEADLE HULME (BR)   The first station at Cheadle Hulme was opened in 1842 a quarter mile south. The present station was opened in 1866 at the junction with the line to Macclesfield (though the buildings are 20th-century) and serves the lines to Manchester from Crewe and Stoke on Trent. The view to the north is of the enormous industrial conurbation which surrounds Manchester – chimneys and spires, patches of wasteland, occasional trees, old and new factories and housing estates.

122 **STOCKPORT** (BR)   The most spectacular feature of Stockport is the railway **viaduct** which carries the line high over the **River Mersey**.

Stockport Station   has red-brick platform buildings patterned with black brick and yellow brick window trims. The awnings and valancing are painted a sandy colour and supported by elegant brackets. The signal boxes at either end of the station are in the same red and black brick with sandy-coloured wooden tops.

Like Macclesfield (see p. 496) **Stockport** began to expand with the silk industry followed by the cotton industry. One of the first cotton mills was built by Sir George Warren on the site of the medieval castle. It was specially designed as a circular building with battlements. The old town was close to the River Mersey in the valley rising steeply up to the market place and parish church. **St Mary's** was mostly rebuilt in 1813–17 to the R:1 design of Lewis Wyatt and is in a Perpendicular Gothic style with a west tower. John Wainwright, organist of St Mary's, was buried in the church in 1768. He composed the tune of the well-known hymn 'Christians Awake'. The **Market Hall** has an R:1 iron and glass cover erected in 1861. Throughout the 19th century houses and factories began to spread over the higher ground on both sides of the river. Hat-making became an important local industry, followed by engineering. From the viaduct there is a good view of the mills, warehouses and factories below and also of **Merseyway**, a pedestrian way made by covering up part of the river and now part of the new shopping precinct. George Watson Buck designed the viaduct which is 600 yards long, has 27 arches and is 111 feet above the bed of the Mersey. It was built for the Manchester and Birmingham Railway and before it was completed (1840) there was a temporary station at the north end – where the LNWR goods warehouse is now sited – which lasted until 1959 as Heaton Norris.

The Wren-style tower of the **Town Hall** is *R:l* visible to the east of the station. It was designed by Sir Alfred Brumwell Thomas and built in 1904–8 of white stone.

123 **HEATON CHAPEL** (BR) The station was opened in January 1852. The red-brick **ticket** *L:r* **office** above the cutting is patterned with black brick. The Edwardian factory of **McVities & Price** *R:l* **Biscuits** is beside the line.

124 **LEVENSHULME** (BR) The station was opened in August 1842. The half-timbered two-storey house just by the line is **Slade Hall**. It was built in *L:r* 1585 and the timbering is mostly in a herring-bone pattern. The back of the house is of early 19th-century brick. In one of the rooms inside there is a frieze of naive plasterwork depicting hunting scenes.

125 **MANCHESTER UNIVERSITY** The **high** *L:r* **tower** with a steep pyramid roof belongs to the east range of Manchester University and was built

in 1883–7. The university began as Owens College (1851) and moved to its present site in 1873. Alfred Waterhouse began work as architect of the new buildings in 1870. The University, together with the Institution of Science and Technology, the Municipal College of Technology and the College of Art, have recently been brought together on a vast campus more familiar in American universities, under the plan of Sir Hugh Wilson and Lewis Wormesley.

126 ARDWICK STATION is on the line to Hud- R:l dersfield and Leeds. In 1830 just before the railway was built, Ardwick was 'a fashionable residential quarter for Manchester merchants'.

127 MANCHESTER (BR) Manchester Piccadilly Station is approached on a **viaduct** of 16 arches from which the flamboyant clock tower of the old **Magistrates' Court** in Minshull Street can be L:r seen. This Italian Gothic style building adorned with gables and turrets was built in 1871 and designed by Thomas Worthington.

   Manchester Piccadilly was opened as London Road in 1862 and enlarged in 1881 when the iron- and glass-roofed train sheds were erected. The train sheds are supported by iron pillars painted white and blue and decorated with leafy capitals and ornate brackets. The front of London Road was 'a beautiful stone building in the Italian style': now it is dull glass and steel. The station was rebuilt in 1960 as part of the plan to adopt the 25kV system of electric traction and was renamed Piccadilly on the opening on 12 September. R. L. Moorcroft, Midland Region's architect, was the designer.

   A visitor to Manchester in 1851 wrote to warn

fellow travellers: 'dreadful fires occur occasionally in Manchester. If such a catastrophe should take place during the stay of a visitor, he should immediately pull on an overcoat, even though it be midnight, and join in the crowd. An excellent police of 300 officers and men renders the streets quite safe at all hours; and a fire of an old cotton factory, where the floors are saturated with oil and grease, is indeed a fearfully imposing sight. It also affords an opportunity of some familiar conversation with the factory hands.' Even in 1926 there were plenty of factories to catch fire, as a continental visitor observed: 'At Manchester since the war 400 large new factories for cotton spinning have been built, several of them of the size of the Royal Palace in Berlin, and thousands of smoking obelisks of the steam engines 80 to 180 feet high destroy all impression of church steeples.'

The prosperity of Manchester was made out of cotton and cheap factory labour. Weaving flourished in the Middle Ages after Edward III settled a colony of Flemish weavers in the town but it was not until the 18th century that expansion began. The River Irwell was made navigable in 1721. Then the Duke of Bridgewater employed James Brindley to cut a canal from his coal mine at Worsley to Manchester. This was extended to Runcorn in 1776 and the means was created by which raw cotton could be transported direct to the centre of Manchester. St Peter's Square, the site of Alfred Waterhouse's extraordinary gothic Town Hall and Charles Barry's Grecian Royal Institution, is also a grim reminder of St Peter's Fields where the Peterloo Massacre took place in 1819. Many of the rich merchants of Manchester who paid for the city's monumental public buildings forced their workers to endure appalling conditions in their factories. Friedrich Engels's *Condition of the Working Class in England* (1844) gives a moving account of the deprivation experienced by Manchester workers while their employers grew rich. De Tocqueville remarked on the 'pure gold' made in Manchester flowing from the 'filthy sewer'; the novelist Mrs Gaskell revealed the inequalities in *Mary Barton, A Tale of Manchester Life* (1848).

Index